JAN   2016

Arendt and America

ARENDT AND AMERICA

Richard H. King

The University of Chicago Press

Chicago and London

Richard H. King is professor emeritus of U.S. intellectual history at the University of Nottingham, UK. He is the editor of *Obama and Race: History, Culture, Politics,* coeditor of *Hannah Arendt and the Uses of History: Imperialism, Race, Nation, Genocide,* and the author of *Race, Culture, and the Intellectuals, 1940–1970,* among other books.

The University of Chicago Press, Chicago 60637
The University of Chicago Press, Ltd., London
© 2015 by The University of Chicago
All rights reserved. Published 2015.
Printed in the United States of America

24 23 22 21 20 19 18 17 16 15   1 2 3 4 5

ISBN-13: 978-0-226-31149-4   (cloth)
ISBN-13: 978-0-226-31152-4   (e-book)
DOI: 10.7208/chicago/9780226311524.001.0001

Library of Congress Cataloging-in-Publication Data

King, Richard H., author.
    Arendt and America / Richard H. King.
        pages cm
    Includes bibliographical references and index.
    ISBN 978-0-226-31149-4 (cloth : alk. paper) — ISBN 978-0-226-31152-4 (e-book)
1. Arendt, Hannah, 1906–1975. 2. United States—History—20th century. 3. Political scientists—Unites States—Biography. I. Title.
    JC251.A74K56 2015
    320.5—dc22

                                                2015011456

♾ This paper meets the requirements of ANSI/NISO Z39.48-1992 (Permanence of Paper).

To Steve and Larry

CONTENTS

Introduction

Hannah Arendt's World

At Hannah Arendt's funeral, December 8, 1975, her friend of a half-century, philosopher Hans Jonas, reflected on the difference it made that Arendt had come to the United States. After suggesting that she had first become politicized in her Parisian exile in the 1930s, Jonas observed: "Still, what would have become of that, had she not come to these shores—who knows? It was the experience of the Republic here which decisively shaped her political thinking, tempered as it was in the fires of European tyranny and catastrophe, and forever supported by her grounding in classical thought. America taught her a way beyond the hardened alternatives of left and right from which she had escaped; and the idea of the Republic, as the realistic chance for freedom, remained dear to her even in its darkening days."[1] Certainly Arendt herself believed that there was something different—and politically liberating—about the American political culture, particularly the achievement of the Framers. Jonas aptly captured it with the phrase "the idea of the Republic."

If the Republic was the great American experience that Arendt responded to, then the first of the two major themes of Arendt's work is "beginning anew." In the last paragraph of "Ideology and Terror," an essay added to the second edition of *The Origins of Totalitarianism* (1958), she connected new beginnings with what she called "natality": "Beginning, before it becomes a historical event is the supreme capacity of man; politically, it is identical with man's freedom. *Initium ut esset homo creatus est*—'that a beginning be made man was created' said Augustine. This beginning is guaranteed by each new birth; it is indeed every man."[2] Of course, beginning anew also describes what America had meant to other immigrants before and after Arendt's generation of refugees and survivors escaped Nazi-controlled Europe in the 1930s and early 1940s. Indeed, it characterizes the "promise" of American life in general and is hardly confined to immigrants and newcomers.

As a place of new beginnings, America was also a symbol of modernity. Arendt's friend, the art critic Harold Rosenberg, named a group of postwar American artists "action painters" and saw them as representatives of "the tradition of the new." The parallels with Arendt's concerns are striking. But the phrase "tradition of the new" is also interesting because it refers to a self-undermining quality to tradition in America. The seminal American political tradition that Arendt identified in *On Revolution* (1963) was, as Jonas suggests, a republican not a liberal one. And as J. G. A. Pocock was to emphasize in *The Machiavellian Moment* (1975), the republican (civic humanist) political tradition emphasized the need to overturn corrupt political regimes and to start over again, *corso-ricorso*. What this suggests is that America has always been divided between the desire to *begin things anew* and the impulse to *start things over again*, the tendency to make a radical break or to revitalize earlier forms, to escape history or to repeat it.[3]

Indeed, as the Vietnam and Watergate crises erupted in the first half of the 1970s, Arendt wrote of the need to start over again, before corruption triumphed completely. For a long time, she had thought that America's status as a republic was threatened by the culture of consumption and the politics of self-interest. These two traits of mass society were threats to a republican political culture of political participation and concern for the public realm. In fact, mass society, much more than mass culture, was a leitmotif in her work from the late 1940s on, but it has been strangely neglected, except by Peter Baehr, in the analysis of her conceptual arsenal. All the more reason, then, to see Arendt's view of America as divided between the promise of new political beginnings as a republic of citizens *and* the threat of decline into a nation of consumers, indifferent to the public realm and under "the rule of nobody," that is, bureaucracy.[4]

Thinking in, Thinking about America

In this introduction, I want to sketch in how Arendt came to America in 1941, halfway through her life, and what she brought with her by way of intellectual and cultural equipment. This will also involve a look at her early thinking about the nature of her adopted country, as compared with predecessors such as Max Weber and Alexis de Tocqueville. After discussing her position among the New York intellectuals in the postwar/Cold War world, I will conclude by offering some generalizations about her style of thought and then provide a chapter-by-chapter outline.

I begin with the assumption that Arendt's life and thought were changed by coming to America, contrary to Marshall Berman's contention about Arendt, philosopher Herbert Marcuse, and psychoanalyst Heinz Hartmann that "America had taken them in but played no essential role in the growth of their minds and ideas."[5] Arendt herself thought otherwise, at least in specific cases. As she wrote to her former mentor, philosopher Karl Jaspers, in 1960, her thinking about the importance of judicial proceedings, such as the Eichmann trial, had been "infected by the Anglo-Saxon spirit."[6] More generally, the question must be asked as to whether Arendt ever *became* an American rather than German thinker. In some ways, this whole book is a meditation on that issue, but certainly she retained a fascination with American concerns over the years. To anticipate, her chief contribution to American intellectual history and political thought was an American version of republicanism; her great worry was that this republic would be lost.

Perhaps this is why Arendt's engagement with America does not fit very comfortably with somewhat similar examples in trans-Atlantic intellectual history. Unlike Friedrich Nietzsche or Martin Heidegger, she actually came to America in 1941, and unlike Max Weber or Alexis de Tocqueville, her choice to come to America was not a free one. Yet she remained there for the rest of her life; and, unlike some of her émigré compatriots (Bertolt Brecht, Theodor Adorno, and Thomas Mann), who returned to Europe after the war, she never seriously considered returning to Europe to live, though she, like them, was frightened by the rise of Senator Joe McCarthy, and in the late 1960s, she found New York City an increasingly dangerous place to live. Overall, then, except for her doctoral thesis in Germany—which dealt with the concept of love in Saint Augustine and her *Habilitationschrift* on the German-Jewish cultural figure, Rahel Varnhagen (of which she had finished eleven chapters in 1933 and then completed the last two in 1938 in Paris, where she had fled after the Nazis came to power in 1933)—the vast majority of Arendt's published work was completed in America, not in Europe. All of this meant that Arendt could, and did, make changes in her original assessment of America over the years and she also tried to influence the reception of her own work in the United States.[7]

Let me be clear. Arendt's complex relationship to America isn't the only important thing about her thought. But that body of thought only makes full sense when her relationship to America, in her life *and* thought, is taken into account. Put most strongly, the United States was not just where she lived and where her thought was first published. It was a crucial theme and concern *of* her thought. This means that I have stressed Arendt's interaction with American intellectuals, with American thought and culture, and with America as a place and set of institutions rather than treat her life and thought as detached from where she actually lived, as though the life of the mind was lived no place particularly. She taught her American contemporaries, friend and foe, a good deal but she also learned from them. She was concerned, as a political thinker, with the origins of American political thought and institutions. Above all, as a citizen, she was concerned about the survival of the American republic.

Arendt as Refugee

All that said, the interaction between Hannah Arendt's own sense of self and where she lived was a complex one. In coming to America, she had lost her home and country—as had millions of other Europeans. But as a person of the word, as a literary intellectual and thinker, she had lost her culture and, potentially, her language. Educated at Marburg with Martin Heidegger and at Heidelberg with Karl Jaspers between 1924 and 1929, she had the best philosophical education of her time. Intellectually she was thoroughly integrated into a German philosophical culture that then proceeded to betray its Jewish students and colleagues. Her mentor and one-time lover, Martin Heidegger, became *Rektor* at Marburg and delivered an infamous inaugural address in 1933 that committed the university to work toward a Nazi-inspired national rejuvenation. No wonder she ended the essay "Ideology and Terror" by offering a phenomenology of isolation, solitude, and loneliness (or abandonment). That was her way of describing what it had meant to lose a world.[8]

The semantics of the émigré experience are tricky. Clearly Arendt was in "exile" in America, but hers was "the voice of a refugee and not a survivor," claims Gabriel Motzkin. Having fled Germany in 1933—she was jailed eight days by the Gestapo for illegal research work and also aiding fleeing radicals—Arendt fled to Paris (via Prague and Geneva), where she lived throughout the rest of the 1930s. There she worked for a Zionist children's organization, got to know various other émigré intellectuals, including Bert Brecht and Walter Benjamin, and also met Heinrich Blücher, a former member of the Kommunistische Partei Deutschlands (KPD) and a gentile, whom she married in 1940. The same year she was interned in Gurs in southern France for a time. She had been separated from Heinrich, but fortuitously ran into him in Marseille. Having been cleared for visas, they escaped in January 1941, crossing into Spain, then into Portugal. From Lisbon, the two came to New York, arriving in May 1941, with her mother following only a few days afterward on a separate ship.[9]

With all this, it is hardly surprising that "statelessness" as a legal status and as a personal experience was so crucial in her thought. Intellectually and culturally, the question-answer she gave to Günter Gaus in an interview in 1963—"What Remains? The Language Remains"—underscored her enduring commitment to German thought and culture but not to the German nation or state.[10] Arendt was grateful to America for having given refuge to herself, her husband, and her mother, Martha Arendt, and she was more deeply involved than most émigré intellectuals in the political, intellectual, and cultural life of America in her time. But hers was not exactly an *American* life. How could it have been otherwise?

Once in New York, she set about learning English (she and Walter Benjamin had begun studying it together in Paris). She gradually made contacts and became part of intellectual networks. Her name began appearing in Jewish magazines and general interest intellectual journals such as *Partisan Review* and the new *Commentary*. She was impressed by the American intellectuals she met after having escaped the poisonous intellectual atmosphere in Germany and the uncertain mood in Paris as an unsettled exile. She found her American friends "without fanaticism" and willing to work from an oppositional position rather than striving for influence and success.[11] Though living in New York City did shape her thought in important ways, Arendt was not influenced by any other American thinkers to the degree she was by the Framers, such as John Adams, Thomas Jefferson, and James Madison. She did not really interest herself in pragmatism, America's one claim to philosophical fame. But she was much more enthusiastic about American literature and might have agreed with philosopher Stanley Cavell's penetrating question from the early 1970s: "Why has America never expressed itself philosophically? Or has it—in the metaphysical riot of its greatest literature?"[12] Certainly, she drew on the work of both Herman Melville and William Faulkner in particular to help develop her political thought.

Not surprisingly, Arendt missed the philosophical culture of pre-Nazi Germany. As she explained, with a note of exasperation, to Karl Jaspers: "Sometimes I wonder which is more difficult—to impart to Germans some sense of politics or to give America a light dusting of philosophy."[13] It is easy to bristle at such a glib judgment about both cultures. But Arendt later explained, as it were, that it was "incomparably easier" to think philosophically in German but "incomparably better" to think politically in English and, to a degree, in French. The more complex traditions of political experience, she assumed, had shaped the very grammar and semantics of the language.[14] Besides this specific criticism of America, she also was known to object to a general American anti-intellectualism, even though she admired, as noted, the American intellectuals she had met.

Arendt also seemed less interested in America the place and the experience than was either Alexis de Tocqueville or Max Weber, both of whom traveled extensively and enthusiastically around the United States in the time they spent there. From when they arrived in 1941, Arendt and her husband Heinrich Blücher lived in New York City and often vacationed in Palenville, NY, up the Hudson River and near to Bard College, where he taught from the early 1950s on. Occasionally, they went to Cape Cod, in Massachusetts, where many other New York intellectuals spent part of the summer. She taught at the University of California at Berkeley in the spring 1955, and the train trip across the continent caused her to marvel at the vastness and beauty of her new homeland. But otherwise the American landscape or the less well-known byways of the country seemed to make little impact. She spoke at Emory University in suburban Atlanta in late 1964, but beyond that, she never spent any time in the South because she found segregation and racism so distasteful. I never ran across evidence that she considered traveling around the country by herself, though Simone de Beauvoir spent four months in 1947 touring America by train and bus.[15]

Nor did she ever really propose a comprehensive overview of the American experience to match Alexis de Tocqueville's *Democracy in America*. Max Weber was most interested in social and the economic matters, as shaped by religious ideas and institutions, precisely the areas of thought and activity that Arendt was least drawn to. But he was also fascinated by American politics, from the messy realities of urban political machines to the democratic ethos of the country generally, while she was concerned mainly with the founding of the American political system. Along with Arendt, Weber stressed America's pluralistic nature, except he saw it in terms of congeries of regional, economic, religious, ethnic, racial, and political groupings, while Arendt's idea of pluralism was more abstractly formulated in terms of the ontology of human difference and the separation of state from religion, race, and/or ethnicity.[16]

Seyla Benhabib's description of her as a "reluctant modernist" captures something essential about her position.[17] But as conflicted as she was about modernity in general and America in particular, she was never caught in the self-contradictory positions that marked the thought of another émigré philosopher, the conservative Leo Strauss (and many of his disciples). Catherine and Michael Zuckert have characterized the Straussian stance as organized around three tenets, each of which is incompatible with one of the other two: "American is modern," "Modernity is bad," and "America is good."[18] Arendt was at times tempted by views of historical decline, but she never succumbed to any doctrinaire kind of *Kulturpessimismus*. In fact, her celebration of America's ethnic pluralism, a new kind of modern society, was hard to square with her commitment to the republican tradition, which entails some notion of a unitary citizen body and public good.

Never a defender of capitalism, Arendt was more concerned with the political realm than with either the social or the cultural realms. The neo-Marxist Frankfurt School saw America as the homeland of advanced capitalism and the culture it had spawned. The Frankfurters did not object to American modernity, though their critique of the Enlightenment surely encompassed the founding ideas and institutions, bourgeois to the core, of the United States. Rather, it was capitalist modernity that bore the brunt of their critical attacks, especially the ways it had debased the high culture that most Central European émigrés considered the most salient difference between the Old and New World. Arendt never really developed a full-blown critique of mass culture and saw it, mainly, as an adjunct of the social sphere where consumption and the transitory were so important. In her eyes, mass culture hardly merited the theoretical thrashings to which the Frankfurt School or her friend, Dwight Macdonald, subjected it.[19]

Overall, Arendt lacked what Germans call *Fingerspitzengefühl* (or an intuitive feeling) for America's deceptively complex culture, though she occasionally alluded to that complexity. She had no particular ties to the American Jewish community; the second great wave of immigration, roughly 1870–1914, brought mainly *Ostjuden* not German (or Sephardic) Jews to the United States. Significantly, the only American revolution she took up in *On Revolution* (1963) was the War of Independence not the Civil War of 1861–65, which historian Charles Beard called "the Second American Revolution." Part of the problem with her controversial essay, "Reflections on Little Rock" (1959), was its lack of grounding in the history of the "American dilemma" in the South or the North. Yet Arendt, unlike other European émigrés, including many radical ones, did understand the seriousness of America's racial struggles (and their origins in slavery) and engaged with the issue of race in the 1960s, even after her controversial Little Rock piece might have taught her to stay away from the issue.[20] Neither Leo Strauss (or most of his followers) nor the Frankfurter theorists ever grappled with the American race question in the way that Arendt did.

Nor, having arrived in America after the Depression, did Arendt ever have much sense of the flowering of American regional and ethnic-racial cultures during the 1930s. Her good friend Alfred Kazin's classic, *On Native Grounds* (1942), should have helped her make the connections between American modernism and its regional roots, particularly in the Midwest and the South, but I see no evidence that it did. She had little appreciation of the religious dimension and culture of the Civil Rights Movement in the South and certainly had little sympathy with its union of politics and religious. But she was not entirely oblivious to the literary culture of the United States and what it revealed about the country. For instance, while in Berkeley in the spring of 1955, she spent the day with longshoreman-intellectual, Eric Hoffer, whose book *The True Believer* was a popular analysis of the totalitarian mentality in the 1950s. Arendt was charmed and told him in a thank you note: "I think I never understood the Walt Whitman side of this country so clearly before I met you and you told me how you used to wander and live with the elements, where every man is your brother and nobody is your friend."[21]

Of those who have written about Arendt, only George Kateb has tried to go below the surface of her dislike of America as a mass society—its anti-intellectualism, its tendency toward conformism, and its obsession with consumption—and figure out if there was something more basic that bothered Arendt about America. His answer is what he calls "American wild-ness."[22] His definition of wildness covers a multitude of sins (and virtues), ranging from folksiness and a certain rough-hewn manner to a disdain for institutions, including the law itself, and a certain attraction to "excess and extremism."[23] For instance, both Ralph Waldo Emerson and Henry David Thoreau were deeply suspicious of the claims of tradition, while looking to Nature (with a capital N) and to the experience of the not-human as a source of ethical values. Their deep-seated anti-institutionalism sometimes expressed itself in a rejection of politics altogether.

It is undeniable that Arendt was put off by some of what Kateb identified. Philosophically, nature was far from being a standard of value or worth, since her commitment was to "the world" of meaning, the human artifice. Her read-ing of Herman Melville's *Billy Budd* assumed that Budd, a child of nature, was destined to act in ways destructive of the human law and institutions, even though, or perhaps because, he is an innocent. Conversely, Kateb has also warned, quite perceptively, that American intellectuals can be seduced by Eu-ropean ideas that do not actually translate well into American realities: "The trouble is," he suggests, that European thought "may be too interesting."[24]

But if wildness is associated with a democratic ethos, Arendt's champi-oning of participatory politics would make her more democratically inclined than Kateb, who champions the tamer representative democracy *against*

Arendt. As we shall see, she feared the strong state and her attitude toward obedience as a political virtue was problematic. She once asserted that "no one has the right to obey" (*Keiner hat das Recht zu gehorchen*), and one of her last essays offered a fresh analysis of civil disobedience as a uniquely American way of enhancing the political realm.[25] It is hard to square much of Arendt's political thought with a "tender concern for political authority" (Kateb's words), unless we understand political authority in her sense as popular support for the political institutions of a country.[26] In fact, her preferences for Faulkner and Melville would suggest an attraction to the radical, even nihilistic, streak in American literature. From this point of view, it may have been pragmatism's failure to grapple with the modern problem of nihilism that explains her indifference toward it. Or perhaps she had had more than her fill of the intellectualized violence that totalitarian intellectuals in Europe were fond of apotheosizing.

What about America's much condemned individualism and conformity? Almost everyone talked of their relationship to each other in the post–World War II effort to define and explain American national character.[27] Arendt had no love for economic individualism as such and certainly not for pursuit of pleasure through consumption or "doing one's own thing." Nor, as we have seen, did she care for the cultivation of subjectivity. On the contrary, she always stressed the intersubjective nature of political speech and action. Her prototheoretical thoughts on identity formation provided an underpinning for her notion of the political self: "My identity is bound up with my appearance and thus with others. I receive my 'self' qua identity from others."[28] But Arendt was not always averse to the exploration of the self. Particularly in her later thought, she explored thinking and judgment as essentially private activities that went on, first of all, within an individual. *Einsamkeit* (solitude), being by oneself, was necessary in order for the individual to hear him- or herself think. Finally, it was the privacy needed for both thought and moral rumination that led her to the title of the essay "Thinking and Moral Considerations," which suggested an elective affinity between thinking and conscience.[29]

Arendt only ever addressed the thought of the emblematic American proponent of individualism, Ralph Waldo Emerson, once and that was in one short acceptance speech when she received the Emerson-Thoreau medal, bestowed by the American Academy of Arts and Sciences in 1969. On that occasion, Arendt mentioned neither man's individualism; indeed, she did not speak of Thoreau at all. Rather, her praise for Emerson focused on the fact that he was one of the only American figures with whom European thinkers were "intimately acquainted" and suggested that he was an "American Montaigne," a "humanist," not a professional "philosopher," and a seeker after "wisdom" and "serenity," not a philosopher in search of the truth. This explained, she thought, why Nietzsche "liked Emerson so much." But, Arendt also noted Emerson's "innocent cheerfulness" and the fact that he seemed "untroubled." Her appreciation of Emerson thus called attention, indirectly, to the fragility of humanism in the modern world. On the matter of individualism as an American trait, Arendt was surprisingly silent.[30]

Forging an American Reputation

Arendt did not learn English all at once. For several years, she worked with a translator—for *Partisan Review* it was William Barrett—to turn her pieces into English. But by 1944, she had already published essays in *The Review of Politics, Jewish Social Studies, Menorah Journal, Contemporary Jewish Record*, and her first piece (on Franz Kafka) in *Partisan Review*.[31] But freelance writing did not bring in much money to support herself, her husband, and her mother. She became director of the Commission on European Jewish Cultural Reconstruction in 1944, and between 1948 and 1952, she was executive director of Jewish Cultural Reconstruction. This latter position took her to Europe in 1949–50 for the first time since 1941 for six months. She was also named to a "senior editorial post" at Schocken Books in the mid-1940s. There she helped edit Gershom Scholem's second edition of *Major Trends in Jewish Mysticism* and prepared Kafka's diaries for publication in English. She also enjoyed a long conversation with T. S. Eliot after he had been received brusquely by the Schockens.[32] What this indicates, aside from Arendt's ability to work the levers of cultural power and skillfully negotiate cultural networks, were the greater opportunities in the United States than, say, Great Britain, for Jewish immigrants to find jobs and to publish their work. Publications were more open and publishing outlets were better developed. The American Jewish community was larger, wealthier, and better organized than Britain's. Overall, German intellectual émigrés were influential far out of proportion to their numbers in the United States. Besides that, there was a general decline in anti-Semitism after the war on both sides of the Atlantic.[33]

By the end of the 1940s Arendt and her husband were part of several circles in *her* New York (and Chicago). They included German-Jewish refugee academics and intellectuals (Hans Baron and Hans Morgenthau); New York Jewish intellectuals who were *Ostjuden* (Alfred Kazin, Irving Howe); and, gradually, gentile intellectuals and academics (Dwight Macdonald, Mary McCarthy, William Barrett, and J. Glenn Gray). Though overlapping significantly, these circles also offered her different things. Not surprisingly, Arendt's reputation in all circles was sky-high after the publication of *The Origins of Totalitarianism* (1951).

In fact, until the Eichmann controversy of 1963–65, Arendt's intellectual brilliance and passionate, often ferocious, engagement with ideas went largely unquestioned. Her immediate intellectual reference point was the New York group, whom Howe once described as "latecomers" to Marx, Freud, and modernism generally. They exuded what he described, self-servingly, as a "style of brilliance" and cultivated a "position taking writing" (Harold Rosenberg).[34] Howe claims Arendt was "discovered" by *Partisan Review* coeditor Philip Rahv around 1944. Aside from Barrett, her early translator, and Sidney Hook, a disciple of John Dewey who spent time in Germany around 1930 and had read widely in German philosophy, Arendt was the only trained philosopher in the group. She never had much time for Freud and only began reading Marx seriously in the 1950s.

Almost everyone who has sought to capture the temper of those times has written about the particular way Arendt combined intellectual power and erotic appeal. She was not conventionally attractive but, as Barrett says, "she was very handsome indeed" or as Howe observed "a remarkably attractive person." Always the quipster, poet Delmore Schwartz called her "The Weimar Flapper," while Kazin remembered her appeal when he first met her in 1946, though he later wrote that "I was never quite sure what she looked like."[35] Part of her allure was a certain strangeness underlined by her strong, almost parodic, German accent when she spoke English, though she had refused to learn English in Germany.[36] Underpinning her personal qualities of fearlessness, contentiousness, self-confidence (and arrogance) was the power and prestige of German philosophy and *Bildung* in general. One measure of the attention paid to *Origins* was Arendt's appearance on the cover of *The Saturday Review* (March 24, 1951). She was a big-league "explainer" of a richly intellectual, cosmopolitan world of thought and the traumatic devastation it had suffered under over a twelve-year nightmare. Indeed, as David Laskin has written, she "made the war exist" for American intellectuals and approached what had happened "with a moral complexity," for which "she paid a terrible price."[37] *Origins* was a kind of secular theodicy—that is, it was an attempt to explain the suffering and evil of the Holocaust. Indeed, part of her did not want to convince her readers that the mass murder of the Jews made any sense or had any historical purpose.

She was at the moral and intellectual center of the New York group and assumed roles ranging from queen mother to den mother to obscure object of desire. In his journals, Alfred Kazin returns repeatedly, even compulsively, to her role as educator, a moral exemplar and a true "original." However, as the two grew further apart, Kazin was more willing to see the negative side of the stature imputed to her. He saw her "imperiousness of outlook . . . behind all these quarrels of her American friends" and later spoke of the way she "[held] court" and "does believe herself to be the Chosen One."[38] Much of the resentment derived from Arendt's know-it-all attitude (*Besserwisserei*) about America—and everything else. Kazin remembers how "Saul Bellow found it outrageous to be lectured on Faulkner—another novelist!—by someone from Königsberg." Indeed, what Bellow wrote in 1978 to Leon Wieseltier about Arendt captured this resentment well. Of Russian origins, Bellow referred to Arendt as "that superior Krautess."[39] With a similar mix of *ressentiment* and insight, he expanded on this thought a few years later: "Her standards were those of a 'noble' German intelligentsia trained in the classics and in European philosophy. . . . Hannah not only loved it, she actively disliked those who didn't share it, and she couldn't acknowledge this dislike. . . . What got her gets us all: attachment to the high cultures of the 'diaspora.' The Eros of these cultures is irresistible. At the same time assimilation is simply impossible—out of the question to reject one's history."[40] Kazin was disarmingly candid when he admitted: "I am a sucker for this kind of advanced European mind." [41] Still, Arendt's commitment to German thought and culture had its limits. In her interview with Gaus, she insisted: "The Europe of the pre-Hitler period? I do not long for that I can tell you." [42]

It is hard to assess the degree to which her gender helped or hindered her. Many male intellectuals were unaccustomed to dealing with as formidable a mind as Arendt's. Despite their desire to shed religious, racial, and ethnic biases, at least up to the end of the war, most of the New York intellectuals, of both sexes, held pretty conventional attitudes toward women, marriage, and the family. In fact Arendt and friends such as Mary McCarthy, Elizabeth Hardwick, Diana Trilling, Caroline Gordon, and Jean Stafford were, as Laskin has noted, "the last generation before feminism."[43] They believed they could do their own work, be good wives, *and* preserve their womanliness. That is, they assumed they could do it all. For her part, Arendt loathed the idea of the "exceptional Jew" (*Ausnahmsjude*) in whatever context; and, by extension, she wanted to live a gender-free intellectual life as far as intellectual recognition was concerned. Neither the Frankfurt School nor the Straussians included anywhere near the number of active woman that the New York intellectuals did.

Her biographer and former student, Elisabeth Young-Bruehl, has testified to Arendt's gift for friendship, and there is no sense in disputing that judgment. But she could certainly be catty in private letters and insensitive in her treatment of others. She could act as though the attraction she held for the younger men like Kazin gave her the right to imperiously claim them from their wives on certain occasions.[44] She lost several friends over the Eichmann affair, most notably her early mentor, Kurt Blumenfeld, and Gershom Scholem. Yet she also made a point of not persisting in the arguments about her book with Harold Rosenberg so as to not ruin their friendship.[45] She could certainly be generous, too. Along with Dwight Macdonald, she was among those who regularly sent packages of food and clothing to Germany (especially to Karl and Gertrud Jaspers) just after the war. Later, she belonged to groups that helped aid political refugees from Spain and France and was involved with PEN, an international organization of writers concerned with freedom of speech, and Amnesty International. That she wrote enough letters to make up at least five sizable published volumes (and counting) speaks volumes, quite literally, of the responsibility she felt for preserving a rich private life. Loyalty to friends was at, or near, its center.

Arendt herself felt under siege from many quarters and directions during the 1960s, but she never came close to joining the first-generation neoconservatives, in part because it was the neoconservatives in waiting who led the attack on her in the Eichmann case and on other issues. In his 1975 *Commentary* article, "Hannah Arendt's America," Nathan Glazer, one of the original neocons, began by praising Arendt as "our teacher" and agreed with her that a growing retreat from public life on the part of many Americans was a bad thing. However, he then proceeded to criticize her alarmism concerning Nixon and Watergate; thought she underestimated the threat of the Soviet Union; and also rejected her claim that the U.S. government's foreign policy was primarily concerned to salvage its own image.[46] Clearly, she remained too willing to criticize America and its disastrous intervention to join the nationalistically oriented neoconservatives based in *Commentary* and also *Public Interest*.

Aside from a certain amount of ritual grumbling about teaching, she seems to have enjoyed it and was popular with students. Stephen Salkever, a teacher of political philosophy at Bryn Mawr, remembers showing Arendt around the campus on a visit in the early 1970s: "She had more energy and intellectual vivacity than anyone I've ever seen before or since, zipping around the room throwing off these remarkable things." Michael Hereth, a student of political philosopher Eric Voegelin, admired Arendt's desire "to convince . . . by saying, 'You must understand,'" while Voegelin would respond to student questions with: "You have to read that and when you read that, you won't pose any silly questions." That is, Arendt cared enough about students to try to make sure they "understood."[47] She also, as we shall see, generally sympathized with the student protests in the 1960s and early 1970s. Overall, it was not just that Arendt was open to students. She somehow seemed to identify with them, if not always on a personal level, at least with their passion to know and their openness to the world.

Personal Style and Modes of Thought

On a personal level, there was a "deep but nonspecific melancholy" about Arendt. Her stormy adolescence in Königsberg was marked by "independence" and "willfulness," traits that did not entirely disappear from her adult personality. Left fatherless at an early age, it is hardly surprising that, as a very bright student, she was drawn to several older men—Karl Jaspers and Kurt Blumenfeld as mentors and Martin Heidegger as a lover. She was significantly scarred by the affair with Heidegger, which began when she was his eighteen, but she extricated herself from it and handled the turmoil of the loss and personal hurt without being permanently incapacitated. She was also deeply relieved when she found that she could fall in love with Heinrich Blücher in the mid-1930s in Paris after her first marriage to Guenther Stern had failed.

In *New York Jew*, Kazin wrote movingly of her "intellectual loneliness that came out as arrogance" but also of her "intellectual courage" that was linked to the fact that she "never stopped thinking."[48] Another manifestation of the complex relationship between loneliness and the life of the mind was a tendency to take exception to contemporaries who worked the same intellectual territory as she did. Intellectuals, particularly those whose world has been destroyed by history, can be notoriously contentious and prickly. Outside the immediate New York circle, Arendt and fellow émigrés such as Theodor Adorno and Leo Strauss never had a good word to say about the other. In both cases, Arendt brought a previous history of enmity to the New World, which only deepened over the years. Only with another émigré, Eric Voegelin, did Arendt carry on a normal intellectual and personal acquaintance bordering on friendship, and she later helped organize a Festschrift in his honor.[49]

Self-assurance and sense of independence, even fearlessness, were qualities that everyone noted in Arendt and which Margarethe von Trotta has captured well in her 2012 film *Hannah Arendt*. As Kazin was moved to observe: "With Arendt you *always* know where you are . . . the slightest criticism dumbfounds her"; and he also spoke euphemistically of her "sometimes too commanding mind."[50] When under attack, she could resort to dismissive sarcasm and was known to harbor grudges for quite a long time. She simply refused, for instance, to respond to one of the two critics of her Little Rock article in *Dissent*, once she decided that he (Melvin Tumin) had gone beyond the bounds of propriety in his criticisms of her piece. This self-assurance is related to the charge that Arendt was tone-deaf to personal feelings, including those of her fellow Jews. A former student, the sociologist Richard Sennett, has suggested that by focusing so exclusively on the public world, the importance of political action, and the danger of particularistic identities (race, religion, nation), Arendt made of "impersonality" a "positive value."[51] Though easily misunderstood and perhaps overstated by Sennett, there is something to his criticism.

Arendt's thought is interesting not only because of what she wrote about but also because of the way she approached the problems that concerned her. She disliked methodological debates, but she was, in colloquial terms, a "splitter" rather than a "lumper," a tendency of which she was quite aware. As she wrote in her *Denktagebuch* in 1970: "The process of clarification that occurs in the thinking process comes about through distinctions. The opposite of thinking by distinctions is thinking by association—as practiced by psychoanalytic therapists." Besides the obligatory putdown of psychoanalysis, she also granted that thinking in terms of distinctions "led into the construction of models, of 'ideal types.'"[52] Put another way, her tendency to think in terms of binary oppositions was accompanied by a tendency to essentialize the entities (ideas, theories, traditions) in question, to freeze them into permanent difference.[53]

Specifically, her style was not so much to render a matter more complex by adding to or expanding on it; rather she sought to reverse conventional opinion, to show how it was different from, rather than similar to, what had previously been thought. The following are some of the contrary positions and intellectual surprise packages she sprung on her readers. Modern anti-Semitism has little to do with religious beliefs; evil appears not just in ideologues and pathological killers but in the banal doings and sayings of middle-level managers and bureaucrats; America's political culture was not liberal but republican in origins; political power is not dependent on the means of violence; politics and morality stand in a problematic relationship; and morality is primarily about one's relationship to oneself. This meant that her judgments could lack nuance, at least on first hearing, and were often delivered without preparing the reader for them. Though the idea of "banality of evil" was, and is, a difficult one, it is not impossible to understand what she was getting at when she used it. Yet Arendt never really took the time in *Eichmann in Jerusalem* (1963) to develop it fully, something that surely must have made a difference to its reception.

Clearly, Arendt was a great original. But her thought rarely settled issues. Indeed, it was designed to unsettle. She didn't shut issues down but opened them up for reassessment. Her thinking was restless and always underway. Although she ranged widely over a considerable number of pressing contemporary issues, a deeper exploration of her thought reveals some constants: the idea of living in "dark" and unprecedented times; the primacy of the political sphere over the social or the private sphere of human existence; a concern with the tension between action and thought, politics and morality; and, in relationship to America, the need to preserve the republic and to ward off the threat of mass society and its political effects. Overall, the prime quality she cultivated in her life and thought was "worldliness." Personally, the obligation to protect, and cultivate, ties of friendship and intimacy with others was matched by a political worldliness that entailed the obligation to care for the shared public world, not for a world to come after death. It was worldliness in these matters, rather than an obsession with the state of her soul or excessive preoccupation with motives and intentions, that she sought to explore in her thought.

One difficulty with Arendt's thought has been knowing what to name what she was doing. In a general way, Arendt's work can be understood in terms of three different registers. First, she was concerned to develop something like a philosophical anthropology, a conception of human beings (not nature) and what they were "about." In this category, belong her categorizations of human activity (the *vita activa* of labor, work, and action) and her commitment to the primacy of the political sphere. The publication of her *Denktagebuch* has helped us understand more about the underpinnings of her thought. Second, she developed a kind of grand narrative (but not a philosophy of history) of the fate of politics and the political realm in Western thought. She began, of course, with the Greeks and Romans, then moved swiftly to Machiavelli and the early modern political philosophers such as Thomas Hobbes, John Locke, and Jean-Jacques Rousseau and located the emergence of political modernity with the two great revolutions of the late eighteenth century. Thereafter, Arendt's history of the political drew a firm distinction between, on the one hand, the republican ideal of politics and the council system of political democracy and, on the other, the Jacobin-Bolshevik conception of social revolution. Third, as an engaged public intellectual, Arendt brought her theoretical work and historical concepts to bear on contemporary political life (and, earlier, on the horrible years between the wars and down to the end of World War II). Overall she thought she and the world she inhabited were characterized most saliently by the experience of crisis.

Arendt herself worked in and around three academic disciplines. First, her training in philosophy (and theology) was tremendously important to her but she also denied that she was doing philosophy until very late in her life. To say she was ambivalent about it is an understatement. Second, Arendt preferred to call what she was doing political theory or political thinking (and *not* political philosophy). Over time, this also led to her exploration of the differences between ethical and political thinking. She objected to the tradition of political philosophy in the West due to its antipolitical, that is, unworldly, bias. Referring to "thinking" rather than "philosophy" gave a less formal and more provisional connotation to what she was doing. Third, though not trained as a historian, Arendt firmly believed in the value of historical research and tried to get facts, dates, and events correct. They were not just a trivial bother to her. She was no epistemological skeptic and had a sense that there was historically something like a "fact of the matter" that totalitarian regimes had tried to undermine or abolish. Arendt's first large and, perhaps, most powerful book, *The Origins of Totalitarianism*, was a strange hybrid of history, intellectual history, and political theory. But if her political thought was normatively inclined, if it proposed how things ought to be, she was also deeply concerned with understanding the historical origins of totalitarianism.

Arendt and America

Overall, *Arendt and America* should not be read as just one more run-through of Arendt's thought. Since the early 1990s in particular, several particularly important studies have done that with great skill. I am thinking, for instance, of Margaret Canovan's *Hannah Arendt: A Reinterpretation of Her Political Thought* (1992), Seyla Benhabib's *The Reluctant Modernism of Hannah Arendt* (1996), and numerous essays plus a single book on Arendt by George Kateb. Classic intellectual histories of Arendt's world — Erich Heller's *The

Disinherited Mind (1959), Karl Löwith's *From Hegel to Nietzsche* (1941), Martin Jay's *The Dialectical Imagination* (1973), Anson Rabinbach's *In the Shadow of Catastrophe* (1997), and even Richard Wolin's hostile *Heidegger's Children* (2001), along with Wolf Lepennies's *The Seduction of Culture in German History* (2006)—provide a rich contextualization of the European and German traditions Arendt was part of. But it is the lack of understanding of the impact of Arendt's thought on American thought and culture and of the impact of the New World on her thought that I hope to remedy, even though here Kateb and, of course, Elisabeth Young-Bruehl's indestructible *Hannah Arendt: For Love of the World* (1982) have laid strong foundations. Two books have recently appeared that overlap some with mine. They are Kathryn T. Gines, *Hannah Arendt and the Negro Question* (2014) and Frank Mehring, *The Democratic Gap: Transcultural Confrontations of German Immigrants and the Promise of American Democracy* (2014). With *Arendt and America* I hope to have provided a genuinely transnational/transatlantic treatment of one of the most important political thinkers of the twentieth century and of the twenty-first, too.

Introduction: Hannah Arendt's World

In this introduction, I focus on the basic purposes and themes of Hannah Arendt's writings about America and the way living in America influenced her work and her life in general. I attempt, then, to present Arendt as being of her time as well as place. Beyond that, I try to suggest some essential traits of Arendt's style and method as a thinker.

Origins in America

This first section of the book focuses on Arendt's work between the mid-1940s to the late 1950s as she was getting used to her new home and coming to grips with the Holocaust. Chapter 1 explores Arendt's distinction between guilt and responsibility as she—and Dwight Macdonald—sought to develop a morality adequate to the unprecedented destructiveness of the war just ended. The issues raised in this context powerfully influenced some of the intellectual leaders of the early New Left, in particular, some two decades later. Chapter 2 explores the widespread impact of *The Origins of Totalitarianism* on America intellectual and academic life, along with her introduction of the problem of evil into contemporary historical and political discourse. Chapter 3 follows her attempt to "work through," in more personal terms, the historical enormity of the Holocaust. This led her eventually to shift her focus from Europe to America, from the "dark times" of totalitarianism to the discovery of an American version of republicanism and the survival of authentic politics in the Hungarian uprising of 1956.

Arendt on American Culture and Thought

Between the end of the war and the beginning of the 1960s, Arendt was also busy trying to understand what made America society and culture tick. Chapter 4 explores her reading and thinking about American social character in the Cold War years, as it reflected some of the themes of Alexis de Tocqueville's work, and concludes with a look at the way Arendt warned against the dangers of formulating an explicit American ideology. She also assumed a kind of Tocquevillean stance in explaining (and defending) aspects of American politics and culture to European and (some) American intellectuals. Chapter 5 is organized around an epistolary dialogue with David Riesman, who was just finishing his *The Lonely Crowd* as Arendt was finishing *The Origins of Totalitarianism*. The correspondence with Riesman, who was also heavily influenced by Tocqueville, helped her formulate the concept of mass society (politics and culture) that remained part of her thought until the end of her life. Indeed, it was Arendt's engagement with Tocqueville and then Riesman that helped her develop the distinction—and tension—between the social and the political spheres, mass society and republican politics

Chapter 6 concludes this section of *Arendt and America* and deals with Arendt's emerging intellectual prominence in 1950s America just as pragmatism and progressive-liberal thought were fading from the scene. What took the latter's place was postwar conservative orientation represented, according to Morton White, by Reinhold Niebuhr and Walter Lippmann. Specifically, in relationship to these developments, I explore the ways in which Arendt, finally, was not a conservative and then focus on the largely nonexistent relationship between Arendt and American pragmatism.

Arendt on Race

Arendt's discussions of race in America were acute and extremely timely but also often controversial. Chapter 7 deals with her experience of anti-Semitism and racism in America and examines what she meant by race and its relevance to American realities in comparison with its history elsewhere. I conclude with a close examination of Arendt's dealings with two African students in her class at Berkeley, where she taught in the spring of 1955. This episode raises the question of the public versus private discourses of race in her life and thought. Chapter 8 establishes a set of contexts for understanding, then analyzing, her short essay "Reflections on Little Rock" (1959), which aroused such resistance in liberal circles in the North. I also suggest that Arendt's skepticism about the wisdom of the *Brown v. Board of Education* decision of 1954 was not quite so rare among Northern liberals as we tend to think. The second half of the chapter focuses on the crucial role that the distinction between the social versus the political played in her analysis of school desegregation. I conclude with another look at "invisibility" as proposed by Ralph Ellison, one of her critics, and as implicitly challenged by Arendt.

The Eichmann Controversy

Arendt's *Eichmann in Jerusalem* (1963) was, of course, hugely controversial. In Chapter 9 I approach the book in terms of, first, the intellectual context in which the book was received and, second, the close attention she pays to Eichmann's use of language. My hope is that this will enrich the somewhat arid intellectual and institutional context that often surrounds the book. America circa the first half of the 1960s was primed for a book to set off a controversy on this topic. Beyond that, I also explore the sociology of the reception of the book in political, ethnic-national, religious, and gender terms. Whatever else, Arendt's reputation in America was never quite the same after this controversy.

Arendt on Revolution(s)

In chapter 10, I explore Arendt's major historiographical claim in *On Revolution* (1963) that the origins of the American system were republican (civic humanist) rather than liberal. This interpretation of the Framers' work anticipated by a year or so the republican "turn" that emerged among American historians such as Gordon Wood and Bernard Bailyn. In chapter 10, I also examine the treatment that liberals and conservatives (such as the Straussians) gave to the liberal and republican traditions, including Arendt's version. The chapter concludes with an analysis of Arendt's own failure to deal with the place of the rights tradition in American republicanism.

Chapter 11 takes a trans-Atlantic turn in assessing the implications of Arendt's thesis that the French Revolution was led astray (and into the Terror) by its attempt to solve the social problem, that is, the problem of want and poverty, by political means. But the American Revolution, she asserted, avoided this temptation and thereby avoided the Terror. Arendt's own evidence, however, suggests a variety of overlapping causes for the Terror, not just a socioeconomic one. In fact, *On Revolution* shows more awareness of slavery and race than Arendt is usually credited with. In general, America did undergo a social revolution—in the Civil War and Reconstruction—and thus the differences between the revolutionary experiences of France and in the United States were not quite as great as she proposed.

Arendt's last decade is explored in chapter 12. It was a time of frustration and divided loyalties. She was in sympathy with much of the political protest of the 1960s and wrote one of her best pieces on American political thinking—"Civil Disobedience"—during these years. Yet the rise of black power, militant student activism (at Columbia and in New York City, particularly), and the rhetoric of violence led her to spend much time working out the relationship of politics to violence, which seemed to move her in more conservative directions. Finally, she was pessimistic—though not totally—about the prospects for America in light of what was revealed by the Pentagon Papers and the Watergate scandal. She died unexpectedly in late 1975, still working on her *The Life of the Mind* and still addressing the complexities of contemporary affairs.

Conclusion: Again, Eichmann

In the conclusion, I return after five decades to look at the present-day American reactions to Arendt's *Eichmann in Jerusalem* triggered by the release of the feature-length biopic *Hannah Arendt* directed by Margarethe von Trotta in 2012. There has been something repetitiously familiar about the recent public debate about Arendt and the film. Same old arguments; same old lineups. Yet there are also signs that the nature and content of the debate, partly driven by historical work in Germany, is beginning to shift for the first time in a long time. The overall point of the conclusion is to examine and to affirm the ongoing importance of Hannah Arendt's thought in America—and elsewhere.

CHAPTER 1

Guilt and Responsibility

Near the end of Dwight Macdonald's 1945 essay "The Responsibility of Peoples," he cites a passage from an essay titled "Organized Guilt and Universal Responsibility," which had appeared in *The Jewish Record* earlier in 1945.[1] It was by a largely unknown writer, Hannah Arendt. What linked the two essays, above all, was an attempt to work out the relationship of guilt and responsibility in light of the moral and political problem of obedience to authority.[2] As an example of the kind of insight Macdonald brought to the discussion, he wrote later in his essay: "It is not the law-breaker we must fear today so much as he who obeys the laws."[3] And the Arendt essay that Macdonald mentioned, along with another piece that same year, "Approaches to the 'German Problem,'" foreshadows what was to come in *The Origins of Totalitarianism* (1951).

At first glance, very few of her New York intellectual colleagues were less like her than Macdonald (1906–82). Born into a well-off Protestant family, Macdonald attended Yale and then became an active participant in the complex (and sometimes comical) ideological battles of the 1930s in New York. Never an academic (with the exception of visiting positions later in his life), he wrote literary and especially film criticism for *Partisan Review* and later *Esquire*, while also dominating the postwar mass culture debate among American intellectuals. After serving on the editorial board of *Partisan Review* from 1937 to 1943, he and his wife Nancy founded the journal *Politics*, which appeared monthly for several years but eventually ran out of gas in 1949. While Arendt's style reflected the high seriousness of the European intellectual, Macdonald's prose was marked by considerable wit, as well as clarity and lucidity. Like Mark Twain and H. L. Mencken, he combined a finely honed moral sense with a sense of humor and even humility.[4] The last term hardly fits Arendt, but both she and Macdonald had an uncanny ability to identify the crucial moral and political issues of the time, while remaining fiercely independent.

Exploring the relationship between politics and ethics has been a strong tradition in American thought, with Henry David Thoreau standing as its founder. Another contributor to this tradition, Randolph Bourne, condemned John Dewey's instrumentalist philosophy for failing to explore the dubious morality of supporting the American participation in World War I as a way of creating a more progressive society. Then in light of the Moscow Trials of the 1930s and Soviet charges against Leon Trotsky, Marxism itself was attacked for justifying the use of any means necessary to achieve its revolutionary ends. The related matter of ethical relativism was also much debated, since the Marxian teaching was that all morality was class morality, that is, it was socially and historically shaped by class interests. Orthodox Marxists gave as well as they got in these debates of the 1930s, but they were hard put to match the debating skills of philosopher Sidney Hook, a disciple of Dewey, who led the attacks on Stalinist orthodoxy. On the eve of World War II, Reinhold Niebuhr urged Christians and other "children of light" to recognize the necessity of adopting violent means, that is, going to war, to defeat the "children of darkness." The American people, inclined to object to organized violence and suspicious of the war aims of imperialist powers, had to shed their pacifist inclinations in the international arena. Finally, the 1930s also saw the emergence of a new ethical conservatism that—in opposition to the alleged relativism of Deweyan pragmatism and the realism of Marxists and Niebuhrians—emphasized the need to ground morality in natural law or theological claims.[5]

For his part, Macdonald maintained a resolute antiwar position throughout World War II. He had been influenced by Randolph Bourne's earlier attacks on Dewey, but also belonged to the Trotskyist faction that no longer considered the Soviet Union to be even a "degenerated workers state." Thus he largely escaped the war fervor and triumphalism that swept others away.[6] In contrast, Arendt supported the war and even called for the organizing of a Jewish army to fight against the Nazis in Europe.[7] But what they shared was a concern with the moral and political dilemmas faced by the average citizen or soldier in Germany—and in an interesting twist—in America and Britain. This focus was part of their concern with the question of whether a whole population could be considered guilty of war crimes, that is, what was the status of the concept of collective guilt, a controversial political issue in the United States near the end of the war?

It is difficult to pinpoint the intellectual sources of Arendt's mid-1940s exploration of political guilt and responsibility. Writing as she often did in response to specific events of high moral and political urgency, she rarely grounded her positions philosophically or contextualized them in an academic manner. Her two main terms of reference—"guilt" and "responsibility"— echoed the dichotomy Max Weber proposed between an "ethic of conscience" (*Gesinnungsethik*) and an "ethic of responsibility" (*Verantwortungsethik*) in his influential essay of 1919, "Politics as a Vocation" ("Politik als Beruf").[8] Iron- ically, Arendt had always resisted the attempts of her mentor, Karl Jaspers, to convince her of the superior quality of Weber's character, politics, and thought. Indeed, as Peter Baehr has noted, Arendt and Weber were at odds intellectually and politically, particularly on the issue of German nationalism.[9] Still, the opposition between those leaders who acted on the promptings of conscience and those who took into account the implications and impact of their decisions bore a certain resemblance to Arendt's distinction between guilt and responsibility (and, later, "morality" and "politics").

Because she thought what had happened during the war was a culmina- tion of a decisive break, or rupture, with the traditions of the West, Arendt also assumed that she had to learn to "think without bannisters" (*Denken ohne Geländer*) in the area of ethics, too. Closer to home, her thinking about ethical dilemmas was undoubtedly shaped by Jaspers's idea of a "boundary situation," those situations where "the chips are down," where it was a matter of life or death. Strikingly, Arendt never developed an ethics of the ordinary or the everyday. While the most important political and moral virtue for her seemed to be courage, she never developed a systematic virtue ethics either; nor was she a stickler for adherence to hard-and-fast rules of behavior. Those who adhered unbendingly to principles all too often swapped them for another set of quite different firm principles. The point was to maintain the flexibility to think in reference to the situation at hand. Clearly, as we will see with Adolf Eichmann, Arendt placed great stock in the capacity of moral agents to think themselves into the place of someone else and also to think what it is that we are doing when we act or fail to act. Thus, the title of one of her last great essays, "Thinking and Moral Considerations," showed the close link she posited between the capacity for thinking and making of moral judgments.[10]

Overall, then, her essays of early 1945 make clear that she was working with an ethics of judgment rather than one of rule following.[11] As Elisabeth Young-Bruehl once noted, for Arendt: "Moral judging, like aesthetic judging, is guided not by laws but by examples."[12] It depended more on constructing stories than developing theories of moral choice. No wonder Arendt assigned novels rather than works of philosophy or ethics to her students when they explored "the political experience in the twentieth century," the title of a course she offered several times in the 1960s.[13] Indeed "Organized Guilt and Universal Responsibility" was built primarily on examples and incidents rather than systematically developed principles or rules. Finally, her emphasis on judgment meant that Arendt was less concerned with the intentions of moral and political actors than with the impact of their decisions. In this respect, there was a strongly consequentialist cast to her moral thought, despite her debts to Kant.[14]

Thinking without Bannisters

Macdonald's long essay was not merely an American version of Arendt's wider-ranging one. For one thing, Macdonald was interested in "victims" and "bystanders," while Arendt spent most of her time in her mid-1940s essays (and later in *Origins*) on the "perpetrators," whether members of the Nazi elite, middle-level bureaucrats, or ordinary foot soldiers and camp personnel.[15] Later, she thought the survivor testimony in the Eichmann case was largely irrelevant to the case against him. Finally, where early postwar accounts of the camps drew on what Allied soldiers and journalists had witnessed and heard about Belsen and perhaps Buchenwald, Macdonald quite presciently homed in on the importance of the extermination centers of Auschwitz-Birkenau and Maidenek farther east.[16]

Both took Germany as their main target. But, more than Arendt, Macdonald drew brief comparisons between Germany and the Soviet Union and occasionally used the term "totalitarian" to link the two regimes as in "the totalitarian Stalin" and "the Nazis' fellow totalitarian regime in Russia."[17] As a confirmed anti-Stalinist radical and a recovering Marxist, he was not at all shy about making such connections, though they later proved to be controversial with the intellectuals, academics, and polemicists who interested themselves in Cold War politics. Arendt's analysis in the two 1945 articles, along with others she wrote in the second half of the 1940s, focused almost exclusively on the German situation and the global implications of the Holocaust. Neither Arendt nor Macdonald wrote much, if anything, about the Nuremberg Trials, which began on November 20, 1945, and continued until October 1, 1946. Macdonald later commented sardonically about the Soviet invasion of Finland in light of the Nuremberg principles, while Arendt's neglect of the war crimes trials derived from her conviction that what had happened in the camps was particularly beyond anyone's capacity to punish or to forgive. Only late did she come to see that the trials had a vital role to play in coming to terms with the past.[18]

Before turning directly to Arendt's "Organized Guilt" and Macdonald's "Responsibility of Peoples," a look at her *Partisan Review* essay of early 1945 "Approaches to the 'German Problem'" is in order. Combining broad historical reportage with sharp political analysis, it was the first of several Arendt essays in which she assumed the quasi-Tocquevillean role as bridge between America and Europe. In line with her opposition to the idea of collective guilt, she argued firmly against identifying "fascism with Germany's national character" and seeing Nazism as a direct product of the German, much less the Western, tradition. It was worse than that: Nazism represented the "breakdown of all German and European traditions," though she did grant that it may have been somewhat easier to "dream the stupid dream of producing the void" in Germany.[19] Skillfully shifting from a philosophical to a historical generalization, she contended that "The Nothing . . . could be defined in less mystical terms as the vacuum resulting from an almost simultaneous breakdown of Europe's social and political structures." She also described Nazism as a way of *"lying* the truth." That is, the morally nihilistic project of the Nazis represented a deeply twisted but accurate response to what had been, she thought, the spiritual sickness of contemporary Europe.[20]

Arendt spent the second half of the essay exploring the prospects for a republican and federal Europe. Specifically, she thought it should involve "nationalizing German heavy industry" and coordinating production in the industrial heartland of western Germany, eastern France, and Belgium. Anything like the Morgenthau Plan to dismantle German's industrial capability, she thought, could lead to the extermination of millions of Germans. She also prophetically noted the "sinister" implications of the proposed "population transfers" in eastern and central Europe. Overall, she thought that a European reconstruction based on the Resistance experience was much more promising than the "restoration" of the politics of "collective security, spheres of interests and alliance." In fact only Charles De Gaulle was "sincere" about such a return to status quo ante on Europe's part and he was considered out of touch.[21]

Arendt's "Organized Guilt" essay explored a series of issues having to do with: the difficulty in detecting the difference between Germans and Nazis; the Nazi attempt to establish the idea of shared collective German war guilt; the nature of Nazism beyond the clichés about thugs and perverts; and the fear of the racialization of international politics. Macdonald's "Responsibility of Peoples" was, as Stephen J. Whitfield once suggested, "a meditation on her argument" in "Organized Guilt," but with a much stronger American focus.[22] As a piece of high-level journalism, the text of "Responsibility" was replete with examples from newspapers and magazines and punctuated by Macdonald's broader effort to conceptualize the horrors his research had confronted him with. But it is also important to note here that Arendt's "Organized Guilt" essay was by no means a heavily scholarly or theoretical piece. Rather, it took the form of a set of reflections on contemporary events, with evidence and examples drawn from the contemporary media rather than historical archives or philosophical treatises.

That said, three issues in particular were central to both thinkers: (1) the uniqueness and/or the (ir)rationality of the German system; (2) the complicity, guilt, and responsibility of the German people; and (3) the possible relevance of all this to America.

Uniqueness and Irrationality

Macdonald began by discussing the uniqueness of the Nazi camp system. In this, he clearly anticipated Arendt's later analysis (in *Origins*), which stressed the centrality of the camp system to totalitarian systems of rule. He also shared her belief in the special nature of the Nazi system and the mentality informing it. He mentions the "gratuitous" nature of Nazi cruelty, some of which arose from individual pathology. The important point, as he saw it, was that violence was systematic and an "end in itself" not a "by-product" of larger plans or projects such as industrial development or the exigencies of war. Cruelty was "in conformance with the avowed Nazi moral code" rather than carried out, for instance, by rogue elements among the SS.[23] He also contrasted the German system with the Soviet Gulag. Despite the fact that, "in the last fifteen years, millions of peasants and political prisoners have been starved to death in State-created famines or worked to death of forced-labor projects," the goal of extermination, he observed, was never really considered in the Soviet Union, despite borderline cases such as the famine in Ukraine in the 1930s.[24] Later, in *Origins*, Arendt also noted the absence of genocidal intent in the Soviet system and emphasized the way that the Gulag system did not rationally serve Soviet economic, military, and strategic purposes.

Macdonald also characterized the historical context as one in which "rationality and system [had] gone mad." Science and technology were in the service of "murder" worthy of "Genghis Khan." But, "once granted the ends, the means were rational enough—all too rational," the very kind of claim that Weber's idea of instrumental rationality was meant to fit.[25] All this clearly anticipated Arendt's emphasis in *Origins* on administrative murder and the industrial nature of the extermination system. In general, then, both thinkers posited the overwhelming contemporary power of state and corporate institutions, within which individuals were forced to make moral and political choices. This led them both to doubt that any idea of collective guilt or responsibility made sense since, as Robert Westbrook has noted,

Germans (and by extension anyone living in a totalitarian society) were severely constricted in their choice and action. It was for this reason, not because of their virtue or courage, that the Germans should not be saddled with the charge of being collectively "guilty."[26]

In addition, Macdonald wrote that "the extermination of the Jews in Europe was not a means to any end one can accept as even plausibly rational."[27] As he noted to a correspondent to *Politics*, one might validly call the enslavement of Jews and other minorities "rational," if the use of their labor contributed to the success of the regime. But even then, it did not mean that the camp labor system was more productive because it made use of slave labor. Rather, as Arendt emphasized later in *Origins*, the camp system furthered the "preservation of the regime's power" through the creation of permanent "fear" and "totalitarian domination."[28] In fact, neither the extermination of the Jews, Slavs, and Gypsies nor the creation of what Arendt would later call "superfluous" human beings, enhanced German military and economic power. If anything, the reverse was the case.

It was the confusing relationship between rationality and irrationality that most readers of *Politics* seemed understandably to have a problem grasping.[29] Overall, Macdonald's article, along with his rejoinders to his readers, proposed several senses in which the totalitarian system was rational or irrational. The first had to do with the distinction between an irrational *end*, the extermination of the Jews, and rational, value-neutral *means* (a well-organized, international rail network) to deliver them to extermination centers. The second concerned the conflict between two rational ends. If the goal were the creation of a pure racial order, then it was "rational" in the sense of "logical" to exterminate Jews, Gypsies, and Slavs. But this rational *end* (new racial order) conflicted with the conventionally rational goal of military survival and economic growth. Especially for the Nazis, there was a genuine conflict between the goal of creating a racially pure society and the goal of military victory. Overall, Macdonald's important achievement was to identify the self-undermining nature of rationality in a totalitarian regime, based on racial and genocidal ideologies, and to anticipate Arendt's similar, but more elaborate, analysis in *Origins*. Arendt failed to explore the rationality versus irrationality issue in relation to the camp system in her 1945 articles and perhaps was influenced by the debate in *Politics*.

Complicity, Guilt, and Responsibility

It was in reference to these moral concepts that Macdonald seemed to take his cues most clearly from Arendt's "Organized Guilt," including the plaintive, "What have I done?" uttered by the paymaster at Auschwitz."[30] Both agreed that the Allied policy of unconditional surrender, the assignment of collective guilt to Germans in general, and serious discussions among the Allies of the Morgenthau Plan drove the Nazi regime and the German people closer together by considering all Germans coresponsible for the crimes of the regime. Anti-Nazi Germans had nowhere to go.[31] Macdonald made this more specific by drawing on Hegel's idea of the "organic state," which conceived of the people and the state as one in essence. This meant that any state action was an expression of the will of the people, since the state was "the personality of the whole."[32] Put another way, as Arendt sardonically commented: "The only way in which we can identify an anti-Nazi is when the Nazis have hanged him."[33] Though Macdonald did not place great emphasis on the peculiarities of German national character,[34] neither did he shy away from noting the unique way that Germans conceived of the state's relationship to its subjects or citizens, a position that Arendt had grudgingly admitted in "Organized Guilt" when she observed that Germans were less "imbued with the virtues of civic behaviour" than other Europeans were.[35]

Indeed this essay was also where Arendt introduced—though she didn't develop—the language of republicanism (civic humanism). At the core of her analysis was the split between public and private spheres in bourgeois life. The situation in which family men and jobholders led a purely "private existence and knowing no civic virtue" was "an international modern phenomenon" and not just a German one. (She would link these traits to the emergence of modern mass society in *Origins*.)[36] To illustrate the point, Arendt introduced Heinrich Himmler as an example of the good bourgeois as *genocidaire*, a role that Adolph Eichmann would later assume in her analysis. Thus, an anticipation of the "banality of evil" thesis was already there in her analysis in the mid-1940s. From this perspective, the Eichmann book was a continuation of Arendt's attempt in 1945 to assess the degree to which questions of guilt and responsibility were still relevant under modern bureaucratic conditions.

Both Arendt and Macdonald vacillated between asking how anyone could be charged with guilt and how anyone could be exonerated from guilt in such situations. Arendt's ironically inflected answer to the paymaster's plaintive question was: "Really he had done nothing. He had only carried out orders and since when has it been a crime to carry out orders?"[37] Yet, as mentioned, the Nazis emphasized the idea that "there really are no differences between Germans."[38] Collective guilt played into their hands. Macdonald captured it well with his "If Everyone Is Guilty, No One Is Guilty," a variation on Arendt similar coinage in "Organized Guilt": "Where all are guilty, nobody in the last analysis can be judged."[39]

How then to straighten out this ethical-historical antinomy, in which everyone and no one is guilty? On her first attempt, Arendt identified three types who were involved in the Final Solution: those who were both "responsible and guilty," those who "share responsibility without any visible proof of guilt," and those "who have become guilty without being in the least responsible."[40] As used here, she assigned responsibility to those who held power, formulated policy, and administered the Final Solution. "Guilt in the stricter sense" was applied to those who actually had pulled the trigger and/or flipped the switch. Such a system of "administrative mass murder," she wrote, "strains not only the imagination of human beings, but also the framework and categories of our political thought and action." Because there is no political solution, "the human need for justice can find no satisfactory reply."[41] The cruel irony of all this later became apparent in the Auschwitz trials at Frankfurt in the mid-1960s when one of the only "good" men at Auschwitz, Dr. Franz Lucas, was sentenced to three years and three months imprisonment, even though he was one of the few men in Auschwitz who had saved lives and helped inmates. He had been whipsawed by the twin, but not always compatible, charges of committing a murder and complicity in mass murder. [42]

Arendt concluded "Organized Guilt" by viewing "humanity" and the burden of equality from a global perspective. This, she contended, was the only alternative to the belief in "race theories," whose "consequence" was belief in "systematic mass murder."[43] But by this point in her essay, responsibility had taken on a positive meaning—it entailed the willingness to address racism in a global context, so that the public "shame" could be combated and "what is left of our international solidarity" could be remembered. Moving beyond the issue of German guilt, the larger lesson was not just of what the Germans were capable but "of what man is capable" in general and "the inescapable guilt of the human race."[44] Now, responsibility and even guilt seemed positive things, future oriented and collective in their manifestations. In this context, guilt was no longer the label attached to those who performed blameworthy actions but was something like a form of moral self-awareness. Still, matters had not entirely come into focus in Arendt's own mind.

In some respects, Macdonald was clearer than Arendt on these matters, though his essay and his exchanges with readers of *Politics* lacked Arendt's complexity. He achieved this clarity by deploying "responsibility" as an all-purpose term, while largely abandoning the use of guilt. This was largely a rhetorical adjustment, since he still worked with a distinction between "moral" and "political responsibility" instead of between "guilt" and "responsibility." In his reply to one reader, Guenter Reimann, he contended that moral responsibility was individual and depended on a modicum of freedom, while political responsibility referred to a collective or shared situation that needs remedying in the present and in the future. Political responsibility, he later replied to Louis Clair (Lewis Coser), involved "criticism from within" and was not about "guilt or punishment."[45]

Macdonald went on to give two examples. While Germans could not be tarred with the brush of collective guilt, that is, moral responsibility, they did have political responsibility for Nazism. Only sharply delineated subgroups such as the SS were collectively guilty, that is, morally responsible. If we applaud collective resistance to domination, he asserted, we must also judge collective passivity and lack of resistance as a failure of political responsibility. For that reason, the German working class should also be cited for this failure of political responsibility. He also noted that people like himself in the North had failed in their political responsibility toward black Southerners, despite the fact that they were not morally responsible for the situation there. But in the South, "actions which are approved by the mores," such as lynching, what he called "people's actions," should be judged in moral terms.[46]

Two further observations here: first, Macdonald stressed the close relationship between self-criticism and moral responsibility. But when he discussed actual cases, for example, the failure of the Germans, including the working class, or the Northern liberal failure to work harder against segregation in the South, the concept of political responsibility sounded a good bit like collective *moral* responsibility. As already observed Arendt came to use responsibility as the collective sense that there was an imperative to right certain wrongs and to prevent something from happening again.

Second, in *The Question of German Guilt* (1947; *Die Schuldfrage* [1946]), Karl Jaspers, one of the few German thinkers or intellectuals to face the unhappy history of his country directly after the war, adopted a distinction much like Macdonald's, except he, rather refreshingly, used the term "guilt" rather than "responsibility."[47] For Jaspers, political guilt referred to that which is incurred in one's name or on one's behalf by a state or political entity: "liability [*Haftung*] of all citizens for the consequences of the deeds done by their state." But, moral guilt, that which involved "conscience," could only be charged to an individual and not a collective. "Following orders" was, then, an example of moral guilt, but only individuals could incur it.[48] Practically speaking, political guilt was always collective, although the degree of guilt among individuals was variable. He summed things up by writing: "To hold liable does not mean to hold morally guilty. . . . Guilt therefore is politically collective as the political liability of nationals, but not in the same sense as moral and political, and never as metaphysical guilt."[49] It is not hard to see ways in which Jaspers's analysis could admit a de facto notion of collective guilt in a political sense, and thus some sort of punishment would be justified. He also identified criminal guilt with the individual's violation of a written law and metaphysical guilt as that feeling incurred for having survived the death of others. Significantly, the only two names Jaspers mentioned as sources for his argument were Hannah Arendt and Dwight Macdonald.

American Relevance

Macdonald's "Responsibility" departed most clearly from Arendt's essays in his exploration of American (and British) hypocrisy. Where Arendt went global with her considerations, Macdonald focused in on local and national implications. As we have seen, he underlined the enthusiasm certain white

Southern communities showed for lynching, along with Northern white aggression against black Americans during, for example, the Detroit Riots in 1943. White Southerners were "collectively responsible in a moral sense," as indicated by their direct involvement and explicit support.[50] Only much later did Arendt connect the guilt/responsibility issue to the situation of Southern whites in the United States, but she never really expanded on it to any great extent.[51] Clearly, Macdonald had identified a situation where collective moral guilt could be assigned, the only question being how far that guilt extended.

Macdonald also argued that if the German people were politically complicit with actions of the German state, then British and American citizens were certainly complicit in the fire bombings of German cities, the mass incarceration of Japanese citizens, the maintenance of racial segregation during the war, including in the armed forces, and the failure to allow "the Jews of Europe to take refuge inside our borders."[52] The complicity among British and American citizens was perhaps even greater than among the Germans since all of these issues had been matters of public knowledge but were never really debated politically. The use of atomic weapons against Japan, to which Macdonald devoted a long lead essay in the September 1945 issue of *Politics*, was a more difficult case. Crucial decisions to develop the bomb had been hidden from the people and never publicly discussed by them, much less approved. But the "scientists" and "leaders" who planned, developed, and used the bomb did bear responsibility for what they had done.[53]

Macdonald's overriding political point in "Responsibility" was that American citizens had gotten a free moral ride. They hypocritically condemned the German people without acknowledging their own complicity, even responsibility and guilt, for actions taken by the Roosevelt government, for whom they had freely voted. Germans clearly risked persecution and prosecution for speaking out against German policy in a way that American or British citizens did not. If there was a mystical or actual bond between the German people and their leader, so there also seemed to be one between Americans and their president, the British and their prime minister. From this perspective, American and British citizens could hardly claim greater moral or political virtue than their German counterparts.

Impact and Implications

These mid-1940s essays by Macdonald and Arendt exerted considerable influence over the next quarter century, at least among independent leftists. Along with Arendt's intellectual contribution, Macdonald enriched one of America's most important contributions to democratic political thought. Dating back at least to the transcendentalists and abolitionists, this tradition historically stressed the role of morality and conscience in politics, the need to view state power with suspicion, and the use of civil disobedience as one of the main weapon in its arsenal of actions. This American anarchism (though not libertarianism) also tended to be much more suspicious of violence than were European forms of anarchism. Yet one need only re-member Henry David Thoreau's apotheosizing of John Brown to see the point of Max Weber's shrewd observation in "Politics as a Vocation" that the politics of conscience could easily end up embracing violence. This tradition of political ethics was revived by Randolph Bourne and then, as suggested, bolstered not only by Macdonald and Arendt but also by post-war intellectuals such as Paul Goodman and, to a degree, C. Wright Mills, both of whom contributed to *Politics*. New Left thinker-polemicist, Noam Chomsky, also belongs in this tradition; indeed, his influential antiwar essay of 1966–67, "The Responsibility of Intellectuals," explicitly acknowledged how much Macdonald's work had shaped his thinking. Moreover, Chomsky concluded his essay by returning to the canonical anecdote supplied by Arendt—the case of the camp paymaster who asked plaintively and un-comprehendingly: "What have I done?"[54] Not only Macdonald's essay but many others printed in *Politics* supplied the moral and political resources on which the New Left drew, especially in its formative years of the late 1950s and early 1960s. Even before Chomsky, another stalwart of the early New Left, historian Staughton Lynd, also acknowledged the influence of *Politics* in his political education.[55]

Arendt herself was struck by the importance that moral questions, and political questions couched morally, had in the thought and action of the 1960s student movement in the United States. Though her own notion of the political had neglected the role of morality in politics as such, in an interview of 1970, she noted with approval the vast importance of "moral

motives" in the movements of the previous decade, along with the realization that "acting is fun," which she connected with the eighteenth-century
notion of "public happiness." In this respect, she and Macdonald were at
odds with the liberal pluralism and social democracy of mainstream liberals
and social democrats figures such as end-of-ideology thinkers, Daniel Bell
and Seymour Lipset. Finally, Arendt's 1968 essay "Civil Disobedience" (to
which I will return in the last chapter) addressed itself to the complex relationship between conscientious objection and civil disobedience, morality
and politics.[56]

The other important transatlantic link that Arendt and Macdonald established in the early postwar years was with the continental tradition of
existentialism, about which she wrote several pieces in the late 1940s and
early 1950s.[57] Arendt was one of the first "explainers" of this new European
philosophical and literary movement to the United States, along with William Barrett, who helped translate Arendt's efforts for *Partisan Review* in
the 1940s and who later published a popular analysis of the existentialist
ethos, *Irrational Man* (1958).[58]

Besides Karl Jaspers, Albert Camus and Jean-Paul Sartre among Europeans, no one explored the issues of action, guilt, and responsibility as
exactingly as Macdonald and Arendt did in the war's aftermath. Camus's
pamphlet *Neither Victims nor Executioners*—which Macdonald translated
and later identified as one of the three most important pieces he published in
Politics—gave reasons for the position announced in the essay's title, while
the title of Sartre's play *Dirty Hands* (*Les mains sales* [1948]) similarly considered the inescapability of the dilemma Camus had thematized.[59] Camus
also explored the moral issues raised by terrorism in several of his plays and
theatre pieces, while *The Rebel* took up the murderous consequences of
deriving a political morality from the teleology of history, a point Arendt
was to make forcefully in her treatment of Marx in *On Revolution* and almost everything she wrote about history. Still, it is important to note one
difference between the American and French approaches to these issues.
Where Arendt and Macdonald discussed them largely in terms of the failure
to resist domination or failure to take a stand against the Nazis, Camus and
Sartre tended to be drawn to questions about the morality of violent action
in revolutionary or extreme situations.

In her short 1946 *Nation* piece on the two Frenchmen, Arendt concentrated on their literary writings, while neglecting the analysis of Sartre's *Being and Nothingness* it deserved. The themes in their work that she focused on were the rejection of the "espirit serieux" of the respectable, the "homelessness of man in the world," and the "absurdity" that is "the essence of things." Their attitude, she concluded, exemplified "the depth of the break in the Western tradition" and, more cryptically, included certain "nihilistic elements." [60] Overall, however, Arendt took the explicitly philosophical work of the two Germans, Heidegger and Jaspers, more seriously than she did that of Camus or Sartre.

Her long *Partisan Review* piece "What Is Existential Philosophy?" was her first public pronouncement about Martin Heidegger after the end of the war. Clearly, his "absolutely and uncompromisingly this-worldly philosophy" had influenced her own idea that political thought should be "worldly" rather oriented toward the transcendent or divine. The great missed opportunity of the essay came near the opening of the piece where she identified "Pragmatism and phenomenology" as "the most recent and interesting of the epigonal philosophical schools of the last hundred years." But she never analyzed the impact of pragmatism at all. Finally, her description of Heidegger as "really (let us hope) the last Romantic" and one "whose complete lack of responsibility is attributable to a spiritual playfulness" deriving from "delusions of genius and in part from despair" was as devastating as it was terse. Besides that, this compact critique was placed in a footnote. Dripping with sarcasm, she also suggested that "his political behavior" was "ample warning that we should take him seriously." It was a harsh evaluation that she would move away from and never really mention again. [61]

Finally, I want to look briefly at what had happened to Arendt's analysis of guilt and responsibility, morality and politics as it appeared in her essay "Collective Responsibility" (1968) nearly a quarter century later. Over the years, Arendt had continued to think about and teach these issues with some urgency, no doubt related to her coverage of the Eichmann and the Frankfurt trials and also by the moral emphasis of movement politics. [62] Clearly, her increasing interest in the moral or ethical per se was a significant supplement to her political thought. She even tended to distance moral (and legal) modes of thought from "intentions or potentialities." With the example of white liberal guilt in mind, she denied that one could feel guilty "without oneself actively participating" in some action. At the same time, as Macdonald had emphasized earlier, one could and should feel responsible for a deed that one had not committed or an action one had not participated in, though responsibility also required that "my membership in a group (a collective)" must be one "which no voluntary act of mine can dissolve." This was the meaning to her claim that "we are always held responsible for the sins of our fathers" but "we are of course not guilty of their misdeeds."[63] In a certain sense, then, responsibility demanded a more rigorous thinking through than guilt.

In her essay, Arendt placed these two ways of evaluating action in historical perspective by linking them to the classical and to the "Hebrew-Christian heritage," respectively. With this, she supplied the underpinnings to her thinking about morality it had lacked in the mid-1940s. For the classical point of view, which she would call political in the broad sense, "the question is never whether an individual is good but whether his conduct is good for the world he lives in. In the center of interest is the world and not the self." But, she went on to distinguish this attitude from what came later. "When we talk about moral questions, including the question of conscience, we mean something altogether different . . . for which we don't have a ready-made word." The only real exception to this, she observed, was Socrates's idea that it was "better to suffer wrong than to do wrong." In fact, Socrates's example emphasized "care for the soul and salvation." In this he anticipated the Christian tradition's emphasis on inwardness, while "care for the world and the duties connected with it" belonged to the classical conception of self and world. Overall, by the late 1960s, Arendt had come to see politics and responsibility as concerned with "the world," while morality and guilt had to do with one's "self."[61] Thus, where her essays of the mid-1940s emphasized guilt and responsibility as two different ways of judging actions, by the late 1960s Arendt was talking of the differences between morality and politics as types of action.

In conclusion, it should be noted that the firm distinction Arendt drew between morality and politics ran the risk of impoverishing both. Arendt did not mean that politics had no principled component, but she made it easier to think so by contrasting morality and politics so starkly. For example, the (moral) principle informing politics was responsibility for the public world and not just the pursuit of self-interest. But her original formulation didn't do justice to the interpersonal dimensions of ethics, which is both about the state of one's soul and about one's relationship to the world, including, of course, others. Similarly, the ethical dimension of politics involves consideration of the states of one's soul in taking certain political actions and decisions, precisely the point Weber was making in his "Politics as a Vocation" essay and the one Machiavelli had earlier made. Unfortunately, Arendt never really discussed the ways in which matters in the private sphere or household could have a political impact. Lacking this, it has always been difficult to see the way to link her thought very easily with the feminist movement as it was emerging in her lifetime.

Finally, the rigid dichotomy between guilt and responsibility, morality and politics can perhaps be dismantled, if we turn the nouns into adverbs and adjectives, the concepts into modes and moods. This would allow us to talk about acting morally or politically without drawing such a hard-and-fast distinction between them, yet retain some basic sense of the differences between morality and politics.[65]

CHAPTER 2

The Origins of Totalitarianism
in America

The Origins of Totalitarianism has enjoyed a remarkably long life and relevance.[1] Though widely hailed at its publication in 1951, by the mid- to late 1960s, conventional wisdom was that Hannah Arendt's big book was an "outmoded justification of the Cold War" in its identification of the Soviet Union with Nazi Germany as totalitarian regimes.[2] However, the concept of totalitarianism enjoyed a new lease on life as perestroika and glasnost took hold in the Soviet Union and before that dissident movements in Eastern Europe began emerging. Political intellectuals working within the various movements of liberation from Soviet domination—Solidarity in Poland, Charter 77 and the later Velvet Revolution in Czechoslovakia, along with dissident groups in East Germany—were shaped by their reading of *Origins* and works like it. As Jeffrey Isaac has noted, the idea of totalitarianism took on a new importance in Eastern Europe as it lost it in the West.[3]

To be sure, there were differences: while Arendt's interpretation of totalitarianism stressed ideology and terror, embodied in the pervasiveness of the camp system of both regimes, totalitarianism in Eastern Europe and the Soviet Union by the 1980s referred more to the stifling of authentic political life and the pervasive presence of the state. Where *Origins* had originally focused on the perpetrators of totalitarianism, the focus now fell on the victims and the complex process through which victims attempted to become political actors. Authentic opposition, in Vaclav Havel's conception, was "moral" rather than "political." The "power of the powerless" was pitted against the sclerotic Communist regimes of the Eastern bloc—and triumphed. Of course, the dichotomy between the moral and the political was a false one, strictly speaking, since what was really at issue were two different concepts of politics.[4]

The publishing history of *Origins* is an interesting reflection of Arendt's assimilation into New York and American intellectual life. It was first published in 1951, in English, with the German edition appearing in 1955, followed by a second American one in 1958. The first British edition was called *The Burden of Our Time*, a title that some in America also preferred.[5] Between 1942 and 1951, Arendt published some twelve essays and chapters that were worked into the book. Her breakthrough year in America was 1944–45, when she published four pieces in *Partisan Review*, two in *Review of Politics*, one in *Commentary*, and one in the *Nation*, a quite variegated brace of publications by anyone's reckoning. At the same time, she reestablished her German ties by sending pieces to Karl Jaspers's German-language publication, *Die Wandlung*, and also to *Merkur*, which was funded by the Congress for Cultural Freedom. By then Arendt's star was clearly on the intellectual and cultural ascent.

Arendt finished writing *Origins* in 1949. The next summer, Arendt and Heinrich Blücher spent several weeks on Cape Cod where they were joined by Alfred Kazin and Rose Feitelson to "English" the book.[6] Kazin later wrote of trying to "de-Teutonize many of its too summary sentences." He even asked literary historian Van Wyck Brooks to take a look at Arendt's manuscript and was immensely relieved when Brooks pronounced that "it will do."[7] That Arendt dared write such a long book in English was testimony to her pride and ambition—and intellectual guts. In fact, those who read her letters in English from the late 1940s will find her English adequate, by and large; occasionally it was eloquent and powerful. But sustaining a readable style over the long haul is hard to manage and thus she called on her friends. Later, Arendt would typically first write her pieces in English and then translate them herself into German when she secured a publisher.

For my discussion of *Origins* in the American context, I will focus on the second edition of 1958. There, she replaced the "Concluding Remarks" of the original edition with a difficult and dense essay titled "Ideology and

Terror," which she first published in 1953 in *Review of Politics* and as part of a Festschrift for her mentor, Karl Jaspers, in the same year.[8] The "Ideology and Terror" piece was a shortcut into the conceptual-philosophical world of *Origins*, particularly the "Totalitarianism" section, the only place she really treated Nazi Germany and the Soviet Union under Stalin together.[9] The 1958 edition was the only edition that included, as chapter 14, "Epilogue: Reflections on the Hungarian Revolution," a historical event of great importance for her. Ironically, then, the book of Arendt's that is least *about* America had significant implications for, and influence on, American thought and culture, as well as the political thinking of the Cold War period—and after. It is to those matters that I will now turn.

The Modernity of Anti-Semitism

Part 1 of *Origins* ("Anti-Semitism") dealt primarily with late nineteenth- and early twentieth-century European Jewry, primarily in Germany but also in France, including a powerful analysis of the Dreyfus affair. Arendt was especially concerned to identify the conditions under which German Jewry, in particular, did or did not assimilate into nineteenth-century gentile society. Most importantly, the book's focus on the modern history of anti-Semitism served notice that this phenomenon would be a central factor in her study; as Steven E. Aschheim has observed, it removed the Jewish problem from the intellectual (and actual) ghetto and placed it at "the storm center of events."[10]

This focus on the tragic fate of European Jewry and the modern importance of anti-Semitism was particularly significant—and exceptional—in the American context. As Stephen J. Whitfield has noted, American Jewish intellectuals were, quoting Lionel Trilling, guilty of a "failure to articulate a commensurate response" to the Holocaust after the war. In symposia and in questionnaires up to the 1960s, Whitfield found surprisingly few responses from younger Jewish intellectuals that "stressed the imprint of the Holocaust on their lives."[11] It took a couple of decades after the war for the commitment to universalism and cosmopolitanism among predominantly left-wing intellectuals to weaken enough to allow sufficient attention to be paid to the religious, ethnic, and racial dimensions of the war. In America, it was also often felt to be strategically, as well as morally, advisable to link anti-Semitism with anti-black racism rather than stressing the horrible uniqueness of the massacre of European Jewry.[12] Peter Novick has also suggested that the crimes of Nazi Germany were soft-pedaled as West Germany became an ally in the emerging Cold War. Besides that, numerous former Nazis were in positions of bureaucratic influence in the Federal Republic. The postwar focus of attention shifted to the other totalitarian country, the Soviet Union. Overall, then, in focusing from the start on anti-Semitism, Arendt played a pioneering role. Yet, by linking Nazi Germany with Stalin's Soviet Union as totalitarian regimes, her book tended to dilute the importance of race and anti-Semitism in the historiography of totalitarianism.[13]

But this is not to say that there was a total postwar silence on the fate of European Jewry as a people, Jewishness as a cluster of characteristics, and Judaism as a theological and institutional entity, to use the tripartite division Arendt deployed. New York intellectuals like Alfred Kazin, Irving Howe, and Saul Bellow turned their attention, over the next decade or so, to their own Jewish-Yiddish heritage. Paradoxically, the emergence of a stronger sense of American Jewish identity after 1945 saw American Jews more prepared to explore the horrible truths of the Final Solution and also more ready to enter fully into American life. Remembering and forgetting stood in a tense but sometimes fruitful relationship. Culturally, American Jews were increasingly counted as charter members of the culture as reflected in the popularity of the rubric "Judeo-Christian." Judaism was accorded one of three places in the triumvirate of American religions in Will Herberg's influential *Protestant-Catholic-Jew* (1951). There, being Jewish as an ethnic or racial fact was deemphasized, while the religious-culture significance of Judaism was played up. Racially, Jews had become "white."[14] Nor was the fate of European Jewry entirely ignored until the 1960s either. Between 1947 and 1952 in older Jewish journals such as *The Menorah Journal* (1915) and *Jewish Social Studies*, which was founded in the 1930s, and then in newer ones—*Commentary*, the *Chicago Jewish Forum*, the *Jewish Spectator*, and the *Reconstructionist*—somewhere around 170 articles dealing with aspects of the Holocaust appeared in print. Many of the authors were refugees from Central Europe and Germany.[15] With all that said, Arendt largely ignored American Jewry in *Origins* and in the rest of her work.

Not surprisingly, Arendt's work on nineteenth- and early twentieth-century German Jewry in part 1 of *Origins* has come under some scrutiny. Her thesis was that modern anti-Semitism differed in kind not just degree from traditional anti-Semitism. For Arendt, modern anti-Semitism had been murderous, while traditional anti-Semitism, though it could tolerate, even sanction, persecution of Jews, never advocated mass murder (or what Raphael Lemkin, Arendt's contemporary, called "genocide"). If contemporary, post-1870s anti-Semitism had to do with race and culture rather than religion, with ideology rather than just a personal belief, and with political rather than just social discrimination, it was much easier to imagine and justify group extermination, to organize political parties around racial oppression or removal, and to galvanize hearts and minds to support causes such as imperial expansion and colonial control, along with racial laws.[16] Arendt's fundamental distinction between traditional Jew hatred and modern, biologically based anti-Semitism became one of the core tenets of the post-Holocaust understanding of anti-Semitism.

But though Arendt's point was intellectually and logically hard to gainsay, even racial theoreticians and Nazi-party intellectuals did not have fully worked out views on the scientific status of racism or anti-Semitism. Clearly, for instance, religious considerations continued to play a role on down into the 1930s and during the war. Dirk Rupnow has recently emphasized that Nazi racial scientists and thinkers never drew "a clear distinction between bodily and mental attributes" of Jews and more often than not "the historical argument—genealogical dissent—was employed rather than one based on physical characteristics." Historians rather than racial scientists were used as authorities when, for example, the attempt was made to classify "Jewish groups" in the trans-Caucuses, Central Asia, and the Crimea.[17] Thus, the distinction between biological and religious-cultural anti-Semitism was not as airtight as Arendt presented it—though her work was invaluable as a way of clarifying what was modern, and thus different, about Nazi anti-Semitism.

Recent work has raised questions about other aspects of Arendt's work on European Jewry.[18] Peter Staudenmaier claims that she sometimes confused "assimilation" and "amalgamation" in the writings of late nineteenth-century Jewish intellectuals and never really worked out her own feelings about assimilation: "She does not want assimilation and she does not want separation." He also suggests that some of Arendt's vacillation and ambivalence on these topics had to do with her own changing feelings about Zionism.[19] (This was also at work in *Eichmann in Jerusalem,* as we shall see.) Arendt also no doubt overemphasized the apolitical nature of Jewish history, though this was a common theme among Jewish intellectuals concerned with Zionism in Weimer Germany, including Leo Strauss. Besides that, she was off base in her suggestion of "Jewish co-responsibility" for their separateness.[20] In addition, Staudenmaier questions the strict separation Arendt made between "social Judaeophobia and political anti-semitism."[21] Where she saw little connection between them, except perhaps an inverse relationship, most students of the phenomenon assume that the former established the basis for the latter. Finally, David Niremberg's *Anti-Judaism: The History of a Way of Thinking* (2013) has challenged Arendt's rejection of the idea of "eternal anti-Semitism," since it is impossible to separate Western thought and culture from certain fixed — and negative — notions of thinking about Jews, Jewishness, and Judaism.[22]

Race and Rights

Part 2 of *Origins,* titled "Imperialism," offered a rich mix of political and economic history, with its focus falling on late nineteenth-century European expansion, the modern intellectual history of race, and the idea of rights. The interaction of expansion overseas with the emergence of racial ideology back in Europe was a genuinely fresh insight that still needs more historical study. Among American reviewers, only sociologist, David Riesman really took explicit notice of Arendt's discussion of European colonization of sub-Saharan Africa.[23] Arendt herself was of the opinion that the United States did "not have a colonial tradition or imperialist ambitions," at least as of the mid-1940s, and most reviewers in the United States probably shared this view.[24] America's own history of slavery and allegedly irresistible westward expansion (anticipating Cecil Rhodes's grandiose rhetoric of expansion in Africa) should have made Americans sensitive on these issues, but it didn't. After World War II, radical African Americans such as W. E. B. Du Bois applied the colonial analogy to black Americans. But most African Americans saw themselves as an oppressed (or discriminated against) racial minority rather than as a colonized people, a position that had never gained much traction when it was part of the Communist Party program in the mid-1930s.[25] By neglecting the ways that American racial politics and warfare tracked the same European phenomena, *Origins* undoubtedly helped confirm the notion of American exceptionalism, particularly when contemplating the horrors of recent European history.

Riesman also tried to persuade Arendt to incorporate more American material into what became *Origins*. But she generally resisted. At only three points did she mention matters in *Origins* that also bore on the America experience. Always distrustful of multiparty systems, an attitude undoubtedly shaped by her Weimar experience, she praised the British (and by extension the American) two-party system as more committed to the stability of the state and the government. It was less prone to encourage fragmentation.[26] Second, she also emphasized that her indictment of modern mass society and politics was not related to equality per se. Indeed, she noted that American national character was further from the "modern psychology of the masses" than any other country.[27] Finally, she contrasted the institution of slavery with that of totalitarianism, as embodied in the camp systems of both totalitarian regimes. Of course, slaves were denied most significant rights or protections. Slavery represented a "crime against humanity" because the slave's status (under modern slavery) was "attributed to nature" rather than considered to be the outcome of historical events. Slaves provided labor power and were thus vital to the survival of the economic system as a necessary commodity. But they also had a "place in society."[28] By contrast, camp inmates could be literally worked to death. As individuals and as members of a given group, they were, in one of her most powerful formulations, "superfluous." Though the Western tradition of law was fully acquainted with the category of slave, the unprecedented nature of the total domination of totalitarian regimes meant that there were no legal protections for the superfluous.

In its sustained analytical acuity, moral engagement, conceptual depth, and historical scope, chapter 9 ("The Decline of the Nation-State and the End of the Rights of Man") was the most powerful single chapter in *Origins*. Since publication, the resonant phrase "the right to have rights" found in it has received considerable attention.[29] Surprisingly, early reviews of *Or-*

igins hardly mentioned it. Yet, just as surprisingly, the phrase did turn up soon in an appropriate context—Supreme Court decisions concerning immigration and citizenship. In *Into the Dark* (1980), Stephen J. Whitfield writes of discovering the phrase "the right to have rights" in a 1955 *Yale Law Review* article by Stephen J. Pollak. This article was cited and the phrase incorporated into two opinions by Chief Justice Warren in the latter half of the 1950s and one by Associate Justice Arthur Goldberg in 1963.[30] Of prime importance was the parallel between the two types of rights/laws implied in "the right to have rights" and the distinction drawn between the constitutional and positive law, a distinction that ultimately went back to the idea of natural or "higher law." In the American context, this double level of law also left the way open for the idea of "judicial review" exercised by the Supreme Court."[31]

Something like the idea of the right to have rights also turned up in two of Martin Luther King's speeches, one at the beginning and one at the end of the classic phase of the Civil Rights Movement. At Montgomery, Alabama, in 1955, King asserted that "the great glory of American democracy is the right to protest for right," while in his final speech in Memphis, Tennessee, on April 3, 1968, he repeated that "the greatness of America is the right to protest for right."[32] But though King's formulation sounds (and is) close to Arendt's, there are two differences. Arendt referred to having rights, while King talked of protesting for them, thus conveying a more active and assertive sense of rights claims. Beyond that, the first use of "right" by King refers to subjective rights, the personal claim on something that may or may not be moral, while the second use of right (not "rights") in each statement refers to a normative concept and is thus closer to the idea of objective right.

In *Origins*, Arendt's "right to have rights" came at the end of a relatively lengthy exposition of the interwar fate of human rights: they turned out to be futile. She sounded both rueful and scornful when she wrote: "The very phrase 'human rights' became for all concerned . . . the evidence of hopeless idealism or fumbling, feeble-minded hypocrisy."[33] She also explored the relationship among a "minority," the "stateless," a "displaced person," the "refugee," and even volunteers for foreign civil wars. The ideas of asylum and repatriation, as well as internment camps, were also added to the vocabulary of human rights talk, along with discussion of the League of

Nations and Minority Treaties. She also contrasted "the rights of man" or "unalienable rights" with "civil rights," not to mention "natural rights" and "human rights." As is typical in Arendt's writing, the conceptual distinctions came thick and fast.

Finally, the final twelve pages of chapter 9, a section called "The Perplexities of the Rights of Man," offered a compressed intellectual history of the loss of foundations—God, history in the sense of customs and traditions, or nature—for those rights. Following on from this, Arendt advanced the claim that the only possible future foundation of human rights was humanity: "Man himself was their source as well as their ultimate goal." After the French Revolution, such rights were understood in terms of "national emancipation" and "the people," that is, group self-determination, not the protection of individuals. Unless one belonged to a state or some sort of political unit, she wrote, "The Rights of Man . . . proved to be unenforceable whenever people appeared who were no longer citizens of any sovereign state."[34]

Arendt's problem, then, was to find a basis for human rights and then to propose a political-legal entity that could implement and enforce those rights. Both were necessary if either was to be viable. Christoph Menke has emphasized that Arendt could not have meant that human rights were just a trumped-up version of enumerated civil rights, as guaranteed by treaties among nations, which a political order (state, polis, republic, etc.) should protect. That is, the "right" that guarantees a place in a political order must be something more than a constitutional one or one based on international treaties or agreements. For that reason, Menke contends that the "one human right" must be derived from, grounded in, humanity, as in "human dignity." However what Arendt specifically refers to is not nature in general but the human capacity for speech, which is intimately bound up with politics. It exists "by virtue of their [humans] being speaking beings" which "means for Arendt . . . political beings." Beyond that, what is necessary is a political order of institutions "integrating diverse populations" and "upholding the rule of law" and/or a "rights-based legal order." Finally, this "one right" is not just a subjective right but an objective right as well; that is, it "is the right thing for human beings" who are the kinds of beings who should have their actions and opinions recognized. As Margaret Canovan once suggested, this right to have rights comes into existence through a performative, discursive act and exemplifies what it advocates.[35]

Again, what is necessary is, to quote Arendt, "a place in the world which makes opinions significant and actions effective" and that satisfies the "right to belong to some kind of organized community."[36] But, as Samuel Moyn has emphasized, Arendt's idea of the one human right goes beyond self-determination and also entails the possibility of challenging state political authority from within.[37] Moyn's term "threshold right" is one way to express what Menke designates by "one true right." Clearly the U.S. Constitution or, specifically, the doctrine of judicial review anticipates this double structure of right and rights, but it is not clear what authorization underlies the threshold right in the American system—perhaps "We the People," since there was no original Bill of Rights when the preamble was written. In the twentieth century, the Fourteenth Amendment has been interpreted to make (some of) the Bill of Rights apply to the states, that is, it incorporates them. In this sense, the Fourteenth Amendment now plays a triggering role for a right to have rights in the American system.

Finally, however, a question remains that Arendt did not answer: does the philosophical anthropological assumption underpinning "the one true right" also cover the cultural anthropological issue of whether (and to what degree) the claim about "the right to have rights" has traction beyond the tradition of the West? In retrospect, we can see that Arendt's "right to have rights" was the conceptual and moral bridge between totalitarianism and her new focus on the sphere where humans can act together, that is, the realm of the political.

Law and Ideology

Part 3 ("Totalitarianism") was a phenomenology of totalitarian domination. Arendt's basic thought was that the big difference between an ideal or normal political order and a totalitarian order lay in the nature of the law that superintended each. The normal purpose of "positive laws" was to protect "beginnings" and to stabilize the world in which they occur: "They guarantee the pre-existence of a common world, the reality of some continuity which . . . absorbs all new origins and is nourished by them."[38] Second, normal law stabilized but also set limits, thus illustrating the point that Philip Rieff made about *Origins*—that evil in her book was about the "absence of limits." Or in Arendt's terms: "Lawfulness sets limitations to actions, but does not inspire them . . . they only tell what one should not, but never what one should do."[39] Strictly speaking, the law is not interested in intentions (good will, purity of heart, benign purposes) but in effects and impacts. When the law does concern itself with inner states, the danger is that, like the Terror, it will attempt to regulate not just behavior but also attitudes.[40]

Conversely, totalitarian law, she asserted, was defined by movement or motion: "It claims to obey strictly and unequivocally those laws of nature or of history from which positive laws always have been supposed to spring." It further "claims to transform the human species into an active unfailing carrier of a law" based on predictable motion: "All laws have become laws of movement." Instancing Marx's admiration for Darwin, she asserted that "nature is, as it were, being swept into history, that natural life is considered to be historical." Put another way, the two totalitarian regimes show that the law of nature (survival of the fittest race) or law of history (the triumph of the working class) "became the expression of motion itself."[41] Their link with movement is as important as their content.

Her rejection of law as motion entailed something more familiar to her thought—a rejection of any logic immanent in history, for example, the coming of the kingdom of God (Christian), the triumph of reason and progress (liberalism), the arrival of a classless society (Marxism), or the triumph of the Aryan race (National Socialism). Nor did she contend, as did many conservative thinkers, that history followed the logic of decline as exemplified by the triumph of historicism and relativism, according to Leo Strauss, or what Eric Voegelin named gnosticism. The effect of identifying the laws of morality with the laws of history or of nature was that "everything is possible." Terror, for Arendt, was inflicted not because some one person or group had violated a positive law of the totalitarian order; rather, they were picked out as an "objective" enemy by virtue of some ideological selection process.[42] Arendt resorts to two tropes to capture the essential nature of a totalitarian order. Like tyranny, it creates a "desert," but, beyond that, it "destroys the space between" human beings; that is, it abolishes the public world. The dominant trope that captures this meaning (and experience) is of an "iron band" (*das eiserne Band*) that abolishes all differences and distinctions.[43]

While terror defined the essence of totalitarianism, the "principle" informing it was "ideology." If, as Abbott Gleason has asserted, totalitarianism was the most important political concept of the first two decades of the Cold War, the concept of ideology ran it a close second.[44] What is often forgotten is that Arendt was the first thinker in postwar America to give such a prominent place to ideology, well before Daniel Bell's "The End of Ideology in the West" essay appeared at the beginning of the 1960s, which has always been the locus classicus of the term among postwar American intellectuals and intellectual historians. In broad terms, three basic meanings of ideology circulated during the Cold War.[45] First there was, as George Lichtheim later wrote, ideology as "the 'false consciousness' of men unaware of their true role." This sense of ideology derived from the Marxist notion that bourgeois ideology (including beliefs, traditions, values, ideals, and ideas) obscured the real, that is, class, interests of those who adhered to it. The second sense of ideology referred to "the consciousness of an epoch," a rough equivalent to "worldview" or "belief system" or "philosophy" of a particular historical period.[46] Third, Arendt and Bell particularly emphasized the manner in which ideology was "a way of translating ideas into action." Bell, however, also linked the concept of ideology very closely to "chiliastic hopes, to millenarianism, to apocalyptic thinking," a move that Arendt always very much objected to. Finally, underlying the "ideology" was a particular "idea" of ideas—they are worldly entities that make a difference in the world, a thoroughly pragmatic understanding of their importance.[47]

But Arendt saw the danger of linking truth claims to political ideas or ideologies, since, for her, politics had to assume the existence of a plurality of human truths/opinions or goods. However, an ideology "assume[s] that one idea is sufficient to explain everything in the development from premise, and that no experience can teach anything because everything is comprehended in this constant process of logical deduction."[48] For Arendt, ideology created the reality, which it then purported to reflect. Her notion of ideology was close to what we might call "frozen consciousness." Arendt also stressed that no concept was ideological per se; nor were all ideologies linked with totalitarianism as such. To paraphrase William James, ideology was something that happens to an idea. Still, as one who rejected a history of ideas approach, she should have stressed more emphatically the way that events and forces had to be part of the mix for an ideological driven movement to become a totalitarian one. In fact, later American policy makers used the distinction Arendt made between totalitarian regimes and authoritarian ones (such as in Fascist Italy or Franco's Spain) to justify support for authoritarian regimes in Latin America against the penetration of allegedly totalitarian ideologies from Castro's Cuba.

The Identity Thesis

At the time of its publication, one of the most contentious issues in *Origins* concerned the formal-functional identity she posited between Nazi Germany and Stalin's Soviet Union, despite their deep-seated historical, political, and ideological differences. As historian H. Stuart Hughes later expressed it, Arendt's view was that Nazi Germany and Stalin's Soviet Union had "essentially identical" state structures, which were devoted to "total domination by means of ideology and terror."[49] In each case, as Arendt emphasized, the central institution was an extensive camp system, which functioned as a laboratory for changing human nature, and operated, as we have seen, by a relentless logic of domination and transformation, possibility and necessity.

No doubt that Arendt's identity thesis fit into the anti-Soviet tenor of the Cold War period and of American foreign policy. Looking back nearly two decades after *Origins*' publication, Les Adler and Thomas Patterson contended that: "Once Russia was designated the 'enemy' by American leaders, Americans transferred their hatred for Hitler's Germany to Stalin's Russia, with considerable ease and persuasion."[50] Not surprisingly, plenty of people, particularly on the left and/or critical of Cold War foreign policy, were skeptical of the identity thesis. If it were essentially correct, they reasoned, there was not a shred of hope that the Soviet Union, however flawed, could provide a model for the achievement of socialism. Critical support of the Soviet Union was discredited and the left considerably weakened. In its place came what has come to be called modernization theory, the view that the most fruitful model of modernization—including the move from a traditional to a modern society, the construction of politically democratic institutions, and the achievement of a secular, urban, and industrial way of life—was found in the representative democracies of western Europe and North America.[51] The United States, in this model, was the prime example of a modern society. Indeed, modernization theory was built on three basic postwar, Cold War assumptions of American political culture—the end of ideology, the elite theory of democracy, and consensus history.[52] But Arendt's story of modernity was anything but a celebration of modernization or economic development, including the emergence of consumer capitalism, at least in the affluent society. If anything, it was the opposite.

Still, one did not have to be a fellow traveler or a pedantic academic to wonder whether Nazism and Stalinist Bolshevism, as examples of "absolute totalitarianism," really shared a common essence.[53] The most compelling and credible set of objections came from French liberal, Raymond Aron. A firm anticommunist, Aron proposed what might be called the "perversion" thesis. On this view, Soviet Marxism was a potential modernizing force, but one that had gone off the tracks. According to Aron, Marxism-Leninism was a grotesque perversion of Marxism, while National Socialist Germany was a frighteningly accurate fulfillment of the racialized vision of the Thousand-Year Reich. As a spin-off of the Enlightenment, Marxism's theoretical commitment to a vision of collective self-realization and equality was something with which people of good will, not just radicals, could sympathize, even though it had become deeply, perhaps fatally, flawed. As Aron noted in his 1954 review of *Origins*, one of the few to appear in France where *Origins* was not translated until the 1970s, the abuses and horrors were "trappings" not the "essence" of the Soviet system.[54] Above all, the ideology of extermination was not part of the Soviet ideological package, however many millions of lives had been lost within the Gulag system and at the Lubyanka Prison.

Another nuanced challenge to the identity thesis came from Herbert Marcuse in his *Soviet Marxism* (1961). There he underlined the "fundamental ambivalence in Soviet developments" where the "means for liberation and humanization operate for preserving domination and submission." Still, Marcuse saw hope and in this differed from Arendt: "Technical progress and the growing productivity of labor make evolution toward the future a rational possibility."[55] For all the abuses and perversions, Marcuse still wagered that the basis for a socialist society had been laid in Soviet Russia. On this view, then, the Soviet experiment was a large-scale and often unspeakably brutal version of modernization, deeply flawed but perhaps at least worth preserving.

Particular attention is worth paying to H. Stuart Hughes's views on these matters. Though he initially praised *Origins* highly, he did note, as did many others, that Arendt's account of total domination was drawn largely from the German case, with the Soviet Union as a late addition. Arendt's knowledge of the Soviet situation also left something to be desired, which Arendt well knew, due in part to the lack of access to Soviet archives, which handicapped everyone.[56] Arendt did not claim that the Soviet Union's descent into totalitarianism was inevitable and, in fact, sharply differentiated the Leninist from Stalinist heritage.[57] But Hughes also observed that Arendt covered very little of the intellectual or political history of Russia leading up to the Bolshevik Revolution. As a result, the Soviet Union seemed to emerge from nowhere in her treatment of it.

Specifically, Hughes challenged Arendt's description of Stalin's first Five-Year Plan as "insanity."[58] He contended that the Five-Year Plan and even the system of forced, that is, slave labor made economic sense, while Aron tended to stress the mixture of rational and irrational factors in the system. "The totalitarian essence did not arise mysteriously, fully armed, out of the mind of History or Stalin," Aron insisted, though he conceded that the great purges of 1936–38 were "rationally useless" rather than the product of historical "circumstances."[59] This went part way to meeting Arendt's most striking claim in *Origins* that both totalitarian systems were marked by a deep incoherence, an antiutilitarian logic that seemed to entail self-defeating policies. The logic of economic production for German military purposes conflicted with the logic of incarceration of political and racial enemies, not to mention racial extermination. Analogously, the Soviet camp system, primarily a system of bound labor, involved a massive waste of time and labor. Rational in conception, in the way that slavery was, it was hopelessly underproductive in fact. Hughes's interesting verdict overall was that Bolshevism was "*both* more totalitarian and more rational than Nazism." This criticism was not entirely incompatible with Arendt's position, since it granted that there was a totalitarian dimension to the Soviet Union, yet

Hughes also stressed the existence of rationality within the Soviet system. Overall, he concluded, Soviet Communism had "greater resiliency and staying power."[60] That is, it was on the winning side in World War II. Later, in his book of 1975, *The Sea Change*, Hughes damned *Origins* with faint—and familiar—praise as "erudite and the most emotionally compelling" account but "overwrought, highly colored, and constantly projecting interpretations too bold for the data to bear."[61]

Arendt knew very well that the ideological origins and historical development of the two totalitarian regimes were significantly different, but she was still struck by how similarly they functioned. That said, her failure to chart the historical emergence of Soviet totalitarianism was certainly an intellectual miscalculation, though she was well acquainted with the varieties of Marxism and Marxists.[62] In her defense, the fact that she claimed that the two regimes shared a totalitarian essence, one of the few occasions when she was a lumper not a splitter, showed that she was offering a phenomenology, not a history, of totalitarianism Her point was that, for instance, ideology worked the same way in both systems, even though one was organized around class conflict, the other, racial conflict. It (ideology) sought to create a new reality, rather than reflecting what existed. Most important, in both totalitarian regimes the camp system was central to their aims of creating a new sort of human being and society. She granted that Nazism had come to power by exploiting the atomization of mass society, while Stalin had had to destroy the fabric of Soviet society and its leadership cadre by means of the terror of the 1930s and the show trials/purges of the last half of the decade. She also had to concede the point about the nonexterminatory intentions behind the Soviet system. But she was a direct challenge to the "perversion" thesis, proposed by Hughes, Aron, and Marcuse. The slave labor camps had been exceedingly unproductive, to the point of irrationality—they were not self-correcting—and came at a cost of millions of lives.

Epistemology and Method

There was a second, more general, area where Arendt's critics were in agreement—the hyperlogicality of her style of analysis, the confusing mixture of fact and value of that analysis, and, by extension, the problematic relationship between theory and reality. Robert Burrowes spoke for the liberal social scientific perspective when he objected to Arendt's failure to separate her descriptive analyses of totalitarian systems from a relentless moralizing.[63] This alleged moralizing, along with her emphasis on historical uniqueness, made comparative studies very difficult and reified totalitarianism. As a result, for instance, she neglected Mussolini's Italy. But Arendt unapologetically rejected an objective, value-free approach to totalitarianism, since, as she retorted to Eric Voegelin: "To describe the concentration camps *sine ira* is not to be 'objective,' but to condone them . . . when I used the image of Hell, I did not mean this allegorically but literally."[64] That said, Arendt insisted on separating what had happened historically from what would have been desirable. There is not even a hint in her work of a "whatever is real is right" standpoint.

Besides the moralizing, Burrowes again led the charge when he noted the way that *Origins* combined "deductive reasoning" with "disregard for data."[65] David Riesman's criticism was that the logicality of totalitarianism was something that Arendt had imputed to it, rather than a quality inherent in it. The danger was "to mistake blundering compulsions or even accidents of 'the system' for conspiratorial genius," to succumb to the "appeal of an evil mystery," and "to imagine social systems as monolithic."[66] In other words, her post hoc, ergo propter hoc style of reasoning made it tempting to describe existing policies and developments as the inevitable result of prior intentions. Yet, against this line of criticism, it should be remembered that Arendt, for instance, never claimed that the Nazi extermination policy of the Jews had been inevitable from the start. Rather, it resulted from a complex mix of ideas and events, intentions and motivations that emerged over time. Riesman's line of criticism really amounted to a reminder that a concept-based analysis could not take into account every detail of historical reality. In fact, nothing could.

In general, Arendt always resisted the idea that history unfolded according to an immanent or transcendent historical logic. The emergence of totalitarianism in both countries was the result of specific historical circumstances not some metahistorical process. At the level of the functioning of specific institutions, however, she was not averse to assuming that it followed an internal logic.

Resistance, Human Nature, and Evil

A final set of concerns of reviewers in America had to do with three closely related philosophical-religious issues: the capacity for resistance to absolute power, the possibility of changing human nature, and the question of evil. All these issues had a certain influence in postwar intellectual and cultural life, for instance, in the study of slavery in the Western Hemisphere or the analyses of genocidal regimes in the latter part of the century. David Riesman first presented "Some Observations on the Limits of Totalitarian Power" at a meeting of the American Congress of Cultural Freedom with Arendt present in 1951. His major concern was that "after greatly underestimating, greatly to overestimate the capacity of totalitarianism to restructure human personality" was a mistake.[67] The common source that had informed the thinking of Arendt and Riesman was Bruno Bettelheim's account of his experience at Dachau and Buchenwald where the systematic destruction of the character structures and values of inmates seemed to be the goal.[68] In *Origins*, Arendt also formulated the stages by which individuals were stripped of their legal, moral, and then personal identity by totalitarian regimes, thus stressing the political and institutional not psychological dimension of total domination. It was by this process that individuals were not just dehumanized but actually reduced to bare humanity, possessing nothing, except their lives—which was all that remained after their worlds had been destroyed.[69]

Riesman's account of resistance to total domination was particularly interesting. He emphasized not the human capacity for dignified and courageous resistance but, rather, the "quieter modes of resistance to totalitarianism," ones revealed, for example, in the tendency of oppressors to yield to "corruption," since the dominated had "long training" in "duplicity, evasion, and sly sabotage," even in "sheer unheroic cussed resistance."[70] Optimistically, what Riesman drew from Bettelheim was not a sense of despair over the destruction of the self, but "the astonishing capacity" inmates had "to wipe away those nightmares." "People," he asserted, "could resist and recover, fight but also simply forget." Finally, he pronounced himself encouraged that a "certain immunity to ideologies seems to me to be spreading in the world."[71] Overall, Riesman was onto something in stressing the nonheroic ways that people resisted domination. Yet, as Arendt emphasized, there was hardly even a minimal space of freedom for such resistance in the camps. As she later developed it in *Eichmann in Jerusalem,* resistance depended more on the decisions of Jewish leaders in the ghettos than it had on the decisions of individual inmates. Yes, Nazi officials and guards in the camp could be bribed about this or that thing, but it made no difference ultimately to the fate of the inmates—which was death.[72]

Émigré philosopher Eric Voegelin challenged Arendt from another direction. He focused on what he considered a philosophical-ontological error in Arendt's suggestion that what "totalitarian ideologies . . . aim at . . . is the transformation of human nature itself."[73] In his 1953 review of *Origins,* he simply assumed that Arendt fully accepted this as a possibility rather than having merely posed it as a "what if." Having escaped Vienna in the late 1930s and by then teaching at Louisiana State University, Voegelin included totalitarianism among the "immanentist creed movements" (what he called gnosticism elsewhere) that aimed at the "idea of immanent perfection through an act of man."[74] Voegelin charged Arendt herself with being a proponent of an immanentist ideology, as though considering the possibility was equivalent to accepting its reality. Still, Voegelin's basic point was hard to gainsay: the project of changing human nature was a "contradiction in terms; tampering with the 'nature' of a thing means destroying the thing."[75] The nature or essence of something is precisely that which we cannot transform. Voegelin, I think, had the better of the argument on that issue.

But Arendt's response had its own strong points. Voegelin made the sweeping charge that "totalitarianism is only the other side of liberalism, positivism, and pragmatism," as was practically everything else in modern "Occidental political or intellectual history."[76] Voegelin's claim taken literally made McCarthyism look positively temperate. Arendt rejected the idea that there was a link between these positions and totalitarianism, even though she did not identify with any one or all of them. Voegelin's liberal baiting was not infrequently found on the postwar right as well as the left. Arendt also rejected Voegelin's approach to historical explanation when she asserted that "I proceed from facts and events instead of intellectual affinities and influences," what she referred to in *Origins* as "the history of ideas" approach to historical reality.[77] Finally, while partially conceding Voegelin's critique of her thesis concerning human nature, her response nevertheless was a powerful one: "It will be hardly consoling to cling to an unchangeable nature of man and conclude that either man himself is being destroyed or that freedom does not belong to man's essential capacities. Historically we know of man's nature only insofar as it has existence, and no realm of eternal essences will ever console us if man loses his essential capacities."[78] Put broadly, Arendt's reply to Voegelin was a deconstruction of the difference between a psychological and a philosophical understanding of human beings.

This question of changing human nature also led to Arendt's introduction of the problem of evil in *Origins*. Besides Dwight Macdonald, only Philip Rieff really took up the issue of evil in Arendt's *Origins*. "In Hannah Arendt's theology of politics, totalitarianism is the burden (punishment) of our time, visited inevitably upon Western man for *hybris*; for a politics whose dynamic is expansion for expansion's sake; for a morality that believes that everything is possible and everything is permitted.... For Miss Arendt evil is the expansion of man to something beyond his limited humanity."[79] In fact, Arendt only offered some brief suggestions as to the definition of evil in *Origins*. Radical evil was a characteristic linked to an institution or the outcome of a policy: "We may say that radical evil has emerged in connection with a system in which all men have become equally superfluous." Central to it was the attempt to change, even eradicate, human nature. It was all this taken together that she thought escaped rational understanding of motives. Radical evil was something that "men can neither punish nor forgive." In conventional terms, the new concepts of "crimes against humanity" and "genocide" would begin to cover this kind of evil, though the creation of superfluous human beings was itself a new idea.[80]

But Arendt didn't really talk of Nazi leaders, including Hitler, as embodiments of radical evil in any direct way. Only later in her Eichmann book, as we shall see, did she shift her focus to the qualities that made a specific person—in that case Adolph Eichmann—evil, but in a different sense than she had used it in *Origins*. In the latter, Arendt mentioned "radical evil" in connection with Kant's notion of perverted will, only to suggest that she did not mean by it what he did. The traditional embodiments of evil she evoked were biblical (rebellion against or disobedience of God), literary-cultural (Milton's Satan's "Evil Be Thou My Good"), Shakespeare's attribution of

"motiveless malignity" to Iago, and Melville's description of Claggart in
Billy Budd as using "cool judgement" for the "accomplishment of an aim in
wantonness of malignity [which] would seem to partake of the insane." [81]

Rieff also wondered whether it made sense to speak of evil without
having a counterpart notion of goodness. Didn't Arendt need to supply
theological or philosophical underpinnings to the concept of evil? Without
the latter, evil easily deteriorated into an all-purpose term of abuse. But
Arendt's concept of evil was nominalist in nature, a set of modern conditions that defied previous notions of political or social theory or practice. In
some of Arendt's letters to Jaspers she sketched in ways that the concept—
and fact—of modern evil could not be adequately understood by Judeo-
Christian notions of evil as "selfishness" or "disobedience"; nor, she claimed,
did the focus on individual will by Kant do justice to impersonal, collective
evil or evil without conscious intent. It would have helped considerably if
Arendt had provided more analysis of evil along these lines in the text of
Origins itself.[82]

Provenance

Finally, an important gap in the early discussions of *Origins* was Arendt's
own intellectual trajectory. Arendt was never one for revealing much about
the sources of her ideas. Someone might have guessed at the importance
of Martin Heidegger and Karl Jaspers, though that sort of issue only began
being raised four decades later in earnest. But few of her early American reviewers, except for Voegelin and arguably Rieff, were philosophically trained
or, come to that, were political theorists. Much of what we now understand
about the seminal importance to her thought of the Greeks and Romans,
the modern transition spearheaded by Machiavelli and Montesquieu, the
enthusiasm for the American Framers, and her confrontation with Marx
were hardly visible in *Origins*. It is possible to see the rudiments of her
later republicanism even in *Origins*, as witness the importance of "the right
to have rights" and her meditation on the nation-state in chapter 9. But in
Origins the sources offered for this discussion were primarily early modern
European thinkers, rather than the Greeks, about whom there was remarkably little in *Origins*.[83]

More recently, Alfons Söllner has clarified the role played by the existentialist strand of modern thought in the shaping of *Origins*.[84] Arendt had read Kierkegaard and heard lectures by Romano Guardini as a teenager. At Marburg she studied theology with Rudolf Bultmann as well as philosophy with Heidegger, even though she was untroubled on a personal level by questions of belief and matters of faith. The reading lists for her courses and the papers she gave in the early 1950s make clearer the thinkers who had influenced her and whom she was still reading, among them Heidegger and Jaspers, along with the French secular existentialists (Sartre, Merleau-Ponty, and Camus) and Catholic philosophers such as Jacques Maritain, with Erich Voegelin also receiving mention. (None of these names, it is fair to say, would have turned up on the reading lists of Oxford or Cambridge philosophy courses or, for that matter, at postwar Harvard.) But it was not until the 1990s that readers paid more attention to Nietzsche's shaping influence on her agonistic notion of politics and the great importance of the Heideggerian roots of her thought. Of Karl Jaspers's influence, there still is more needed.[85]

Beyond that, Arendt took what had already become standard philosophical and spiritual experiences of "modern man" and explored their actual historical origins and implications. Statelessness and homelessness were the social and political equivalents of philosophical concepts such as "worldlessness" and "superfluousness," the term with which Arendt described what others called the "revolution of nihilism." As background to all this, we can also see the importance of debates carried on by thinkers such as Carl Schmitt and Leo Strauss in the Weimar years about political theology, the concern with everything from the relationship of church and state to the idea of political or civil religion to a theological understanding of politics altogether. In all this, there was, of course, much Heidegger at work too. She used one of Heidegger's important terms—"world"—quite flexibly in *Origins* to refer to shared human existence within time and focused its sense to include the public realm or culture ("human artifice") in general. [86]

Among reviewers of *Origins*, H. Stuart Hughes noted the importance of the idea of superfluousness as a component of radical evil, but he was practically the only early reader who paid it much attention. It obviously related to the concept of evil we have just discussed. Arendt later referred to Sartre's novel *Nausea* (1938) as his best work, not surprisingly, since the seminal perception/experience of its central character, Roquentin, was one of being de trop, or superfluous. As George Kateb has much more recently reminded us, Arendt's concerns are rarely straightforwardly about ethical or moral matters, so much as they are existential, that is, concerned with the nature of, and conditions for, human status and stature—what it means to be fully human, which is to say, human in a normative sense, rather than what is the humane or moral way to be or act. From that perspective, what Arendt developed in *Origins* and in her subsequent work was a philosophical anthropology.[87]

Finally, in this context of the existential, the second edition of *Origins* ended with Arendt's exploration of the modern experiences of isolation (*Isolation*), solitude (*Einsamkeit*), and loneliness (*Verlassenheit*). The whole point of the mass society analysis she made part of *Origins* (of which more later) was to give a sociological dimension to the paradoxical state of loneliness in which people live cheek by jowl with others, yet do not share that common world and hence also lack a "common sense." It was this condition that made them vulnerable to the appeal of proto-totalitarian movements that promised to assuage their loneliness and re-create a common world that would bind them together. Loneliness, the qualitative experience of having been left or abandoned (*verlassen* = to leave), was more serious and more loosely related to the condition of superfluousness than to isolation or solitude. "What we call isolation in the political sphere, is called loneliness in the sphere of social intercourse. . . . To be uprooted means to have no place in the world, recognized and guaranteed by others; to be superfluous means not to belong to the world at all."[88] Here works such as Erich Fromm's *Escape from Freedom* (1941) deserve mention for having located the origins of the modern desire for security and community in the midst of apparent freedom produced by the Reformation.[89] At the same time, Arendt considered solitude to be the precondition for human thought and creativity, a condition in which one could be by oneself.

Though I will return to it later, Arendt's meditation on loneliness had a parallel American context that emerged quite clearly in the 1940s and 1950s. In fact, some have speculated that her comments on the topic of loneliness and related matters were triggered by *The Lonely Crowd*, which she read in manuscript and about which she corresponded with David Riesman.[90] Overall, then, Phillip Rieff was onto something when he suggested that Arendt made the crisis of "our times" sound like a religious crisis without being able to point to a new order of belief or creedal support: "Her massive spiritualization of history provides the most sumptuous refuge yet made available to an American intelligentsia in full retreat from Marxism and unable to accept an avowedly theological interpretation of history."[91] He also located her in "the great tradition of conservative social thought" since "man emancipated from his particularity becomes not human but demonic."[92]

Yet, Rieff claimed Arendt for the party of the past a bit too hastily. The charge that her work was conservative was only partly correct. Arendt's fellow New York intellectuals did come largely from Marxist or socialist backgrounds (encompassing everything from communism to Trotskyism to socialism) and so did a good number of postwar academics. Rieff himself had been a young socialist in the second half of the 1930s. And there was a certain religious turn in postwar America, though *Origins* appeared before it really got fully underway. *Partisan Review*'s "Religion and the Intellectuals" symposium of 1950 registered a greater openness to religion among its contributors than would have been the case before the war. Theologian Reinhold Niebuhr and Jewish religious thinker Will Herberg had become part of the American intellectual and religious establishment by the 1950s, while émigré theologian Paul Tillich, a friend of Arendt's, had appeared on the cover of the March 16, 1959, issue of *Time*.

However, what finally tells against Rieff's judgment of Arendt as a conservative is that Arendt sought to call the world back to its own dignity rather than proposing its total transformation or rejection. What she called "worldliness" entailed a commitment to the only world we have. It needed our protection, she thought, against those who act in the "absence of limits" or who demote it in value in relation to the transcendent. Rieff's judgment also foreshadows the extreme reaction of many New York intellectuals against her *Eichmann in Jerusalem* (1963) as the product of a "God(dess) that failed" psychology. Many thought that the Arendt who had defined *their* modern condition and taught them how to make sense of the post-Holocaust world, even in all its senselessness, turned out to be terribly wrong about Eichmann and the Jewish leadership during the Final Solution.[93] Yet unlike others such as Marx, Weber, Freud, and Arendt's contemporary, Leo Strauss, Arendt had no apparent interest in being involved in quasi-political movements or cultivating disciples and encouraging a cult following the way the others had. All this would suggestion the aptness of Rieff's characterization of her as a "prophetess" with "nothing to prophesy." "There is no hope and no prophecy," he added near the end of his review of *Origins*.[94]

Yet as her thought developed over the 1950s, she was opposed to ideologies of progress but not of hope. It was the sense of the precariousness, the feeling that she was walking the knife-edge between sense and absurdity, meaning and emptiness, that lent her work the great urgency and resonance it had. Indeed, if there is a single work of discursive prose and philosophical analysis that manages to capture the modern sublime without being seduced by the threat of total meaninglessness, it would be *Origins*. Most of the complaints about Arendt's tone and style—its overwrought quality, that it is too "colored," and too moralistic—really point to her commitment to a different rhetorical register than most professional readers or academics, especially historians, found comfortable. Her rhetoric was an attempt to do justice to the deep seriousness of her topic—the collapse of the European world. The signal achievement of Arendt was that she managed to repair the worldlessness of that world by re-membering it.[95]

CHAPTER 3

Rediscovering the World

After the publication of *The Origins of Totalitarianism* (1951), Hannah Arendt spent the next decade rethinking the concept of politics and the political, the importance of action, and the nature of political freedom. What Sheldon Wolin said of Alexis de Tocqueville was just as true of Arendt: her "abiding concern . . . was the revival of the political."[1] Surprisingly, the formulation of her political theory was also dependent in a clear, if complex, way on the political thought of the American Framers, which she discovered in this period, too. At the same time, Arendt was also trying to come to terms with what the Holocaust meant for her understanding of the Western tradition and human existence in general. Overall, the intellectual trajectory that ran from *Origins* to *On Revolution* (1963) was constructed from a mixture of ideas, traditions, and experiences, both European and American, past and present.

Trauerarbeit

To what was Hannah Arendt's turn to politics a response? Arendt was always pretty closemouthed about the relationship between her own experience and what she wrote about. In fact, the political turn she made was by no means a common response to the horrors of World War II, the onset of the

Cold War, and the emergence of mass society.[2] A much more likely reaction was to link politics, particularly mass democratic politics, to totalitarianism itself, while looking to some version of civil or political religion for stability and lodging trust in political elites to maintain a stable political order. In fact, a great emphasis on participatory politics seemed to many to be the way to exacerbate not ameliorate the "burden of our time."

There are clues as to what propelled her in the direction she took. In an interview of 1964 with Günter Gaus, she pinpointed the importance of "the day we learned about Auschwitz" in 1943. At first she and her husband, Heinrich Blücher, "didn't believe it." A half year later, their stoic realism had crumbled: "It was really as if an abyss had opened." From then on, the feeling that "this ought not to have happened" and "something happened there to which we cannot reconcile ourselves" dominated their view of the past. Overall, she later remembered that the mid-1940s had not been all bad, hard up as the couple had been in material terms and as refugees trying to get on in their new country and city of residence. What they could not get over was the mass murder of European Jewry: "This was something completely different. Personally I could accept everything else."[3]

The first entry in her *Denktagebuch* (June 1950) reflected her ongoing effort to come to terms with what had happened. There she considered the differences between forgiveness (*Verzeihung*) and reconciliation (*Versöhnung*). What she writes is strikingly similar to what she later told Günter Gaus: "Radical evil is that which ought not to have happened; that is, it is that with which one can not be reconciled." And, in a formulation familiar to readers of *Origins*, she adds that it was something for which "there is no punishment that would be adequate."[4] To her, "reconciliation" was the best term to describe the process of coming to terms with what had happened— that is, with the world: "Reconciliation on the other hand has its origins in the process of coming to terms with destiny [*Geschickten*]. This must be differentiated from a fundamental thankfulness for what is given [*Das Gegebene*]. . . . This 'coming to terms with' [*sich abfinden*] can occur as a kind of basic thankfulness—that there is something like Being anyway. . . . Reconciliation with destiny is only possible if it is based on thankfulness for what is given."[5] The train of thought is complex and allusive; the prose dense. But Arendt seems to suggest that one must be reconciled with the world in general before it is possible to come to terms with what history has presented in particular. Clearly, this is an agonizing process of great difficulty. It is a kind of *Trauerarbeit* or "mourning work" that ideally leads to an "understanding" of the world, a process that she referred to as "reconciliation in action."[6]

It was only by the mid-1950s that Arendt was able to write to her mentor Karl Jaspers that, "actually, only in the most recent years, have I begun to really love the world, and that I must be able to do so."[7] Two things are worthy of comment here. First, to "love" the world was much stronger than being reconciled with the world. Second, Arendt did not then, or ever, suggest that the Holocaust had a meaning or was somehow historically explicable. She could never accept the Christian or Hegelian view of history as a process, of which genocide was an integral part, aimed at a predetermined goal. Worse than finding no meaning to the Holocaust would have been to find that it did have a meaning.

Indeed, the problematic status of narratives of the Holocaust was already on her mind as she began work on what became *The Origins of Totalitarianism*. To her way of thinking, one could hardly tell the story of what had happened without seeming to imply that it was inevitable. As she wrote to her editor at Houghton Mifflin, Mary Underwood, on September 24, 1946: "The problem, briefly is this: the coherence of this book which is essentially a book *against* should not be the coherence of continuity. Each history of . . . is by its very nature a justification and even a glorification."[8] Just why creating a historical narrative entailed a "justification" of what happened historically needed clarification. But it probably derived from the Hegelian and Rankean traditions of historical/historicist thinking so powerful in German intellectual history. In this respect, she joined Karl Popper and Leo Strauss, as well as her late friend Walter Benjamin, in fundamentally rejecting any view of the past that implied an inevitability to the way it *eigentlich gewesen ist.*[9]

Nevertheless, *Origins* represented a major effort at understanding the history of totalitarianism, the term she used at the time instead of "the Holocaust" or "Shoah." In "Understanding and Politics" (1954), she explained that the term "imperialism" had been replaced by "totalitarianism" as a synonym for "political evil" in the late 1940s. It was, in turn, only by the beginning of the 1960s that "Holocaust" came into more general currency, though it had a more narrow meaning than the previous two terms.[10] But Arendt, I suspect, might have been suspicious of the shift away from the use of "totalitarianism," since that term implied a European rather than just a Jewish focus since it also encompassed Stalin's Soviet Union. It was her firm conviction that what had happened to European Jewry desperately needed to be understood by all Europeans, not just Jews.

If we doubt that her early postwar intellectual work was an extended process of mourning, a sentence near the beginning of "Understanding and Politics" explained that she was concerned with how she could live with herself for continuing to live in the world.[11] As she wrote: "To the extent that the rise of totalitarian governments is the central event of our world, to understand totalitarianism is not to condone anything, but to reconcile ourselves to a world in which such things are possible at all."[12] As Arendt was working on this essay, the Nietzschean theodicy of "eternal recurrence of the same" was also very much on her mind: "The will to power is nothing other than the will to live the life I have been 'thrown into' as though I had chosen it."[13]

The distinction she drew between "condoning" and being "reconciled with" was also important for understanding the process of coming to terms with the past. In a 1954 lecture, "Concern with Politics in Recent European Philosophical Thought," she talked about how Hegel had helped make the truth more "worldly," but that the belief that "what is real is rational; what is rational is real" was no longer tenable. No one, she asserted, could now see history as the story of "the realization of more and more freedom. . . . Who would dare reconcile himself with the reality of extermination camps or play the game of thesis-antithesis-synthesis until his dialectics have discovered 'meaning' in slave labor?"[14] It is important to note in connection with her concluding reference to slavery that nineteenth-century white and black Christian ministers, intellectuals, and scholars often did assert divine or providential grounding for the "meaning" of slavery as part of God's plan in the United States.

Arendt also distinguished "understanding" from "knowledge" (the accumulation of information) and from "forgiveness" (close to a condoning of the world). Rather, understanding "was an unending activity by which, in constant change and variation, we come to terms with and reconcile ourselves with reality, that is, try to be at home in the world." "Understanding" is now the term for what earlier she had called "reconciliation" or that which enables reconciliation.[15] Through it we become responsible not for what has happened but for living in the world in the aftermath *of*. As she wrote in her *Denktagebuch*: "One decides to be co-responsible [*mit-verantwortlich*], but under no circumstances co-guilty [*mit-schuldig*]." Reconciliation with the world "presupposes human beings who act and do wrong, but not humans who are poisoned."[16] All this is to say that Arendt's particular brand of theodicy was not a justification of the world but, instead, a way of finding a home in it. Susan Neiman has characterized her position as one in which she was "both determined to defend Creation and deeply troubled about the form any justification could take."[17] The destination of Arendt's line of thinking, as expressed in *Eichmann in Jerusalem* (1963), Neiman continues, was "to help us find our way in the world without making us too comfortable in it.[18] From this perspective, Arendt's 1954 essay was the public version of the letter of 1955 to Jaspers in which she wrote about loving the world.

But, again, how did all this relate to the importance of politics? At the end of her spring 1955 lectures titled "The History of Political Theory" at Berkeley, she posed the question: "Leibniz, Schelling and Heidegger: Why is there anything at all and not rather nothing?"[19] Writing in her *Denktagebuch* that same spring, she posed the political version of the ontological questions about Being. The passage is also striking because it shows us a verbally playful Arendt: "Why is there somebody rather than nobody anyway? That is the question of politics. That is what Augustine referred to when he said 'before which nothing was,' as the void before the creation. People are there to protect creation. Nobody [*der Niemand*] can destroy it. If we destroy it and someone asks us, we will answer. No one [*der Niemand*] did it. The desert of nothingness, populated by the nobody people."[20] Here Arendt is alluding to the life-and-death exchange between Odysseus and the Cyclops, Polyphemus, in book 9 of *The Odyssey*. But even as she played with the riddling question of the relationship of action and identity, she was, of course, deeply serious in her recognition of the human capacity to "destroy" the world and the fragility of personal identity.[21]

Yet another *Denktagebuch* entry (in English) that same spring repeated these questions when she talks of her proposed book, which she planned to name *Amor Mundi* (*Love of the World*): "What is it in the Human Condition that makes politics possible and necessary? Or: Why is there somebody and not rather nobody? (The double threat of nothingness and nobody-ness) Or: Why are we in the plural and not in the singular?"[22] Embedded in the midst of three critical concerns that underpin politics, her words in parentheses strongly reflect the existentialist ethos of her time. They point to Jean-Paul Sartre and Ralph Ellison (the idea of invisibility and hence nobody-ness) as much as they do to Leibniz. They are a sharp reminder of the abyss that, in Nietzsche's terms, "stares back" or of Heidegger's claim that *Dasein* (human being) is the being for whom "Being itself is an issue for it."[23]

Finally, the latter part of "Understanding and Politics" provides an answer to the question of why and how Arendt saw politics as the best response to the Holocaust: "man not only has the capacity of beginning, but is this beginning himself."[24] Human action is the privileged way for something new to appear in the world.[25] For Arendt, then, it was this capacity and courage to begin things anew that desperately needed to be rediscovered if the return of totalitarianism or a more benign form of mass passivity was to be prevented.

Historical Excursus

The central theme of Arendt's master narrative of Western political thought was the failure of philosophy and religion to take the world—and hence also politics—seriously enough.[26] Arendt's premise, in her wide-ranging narrative, is that, since Socrates's condemnation to death, philosophers had regarded politics in wary, even hostile, terms, even though philosophers such as Plato and Aristotle had formulated the basic vocabulary and grammar of Western political philosophy. Philosophy's suspicion of politics arose from the identification of politics with power and self-interest, as well as the temptation of leaders to pander to the opinions of the many rather than to encourage the search for truth and wisdom by the few.

But, for Arendt, politics took the risk of taking the world seriously. Thus, her political thinking (as opposed to political *philosophy*) was not pulled in opposite directions by the dichotomy between the temporal/eternal, material/spiritual, mind/body. Her general claim was that the Greek philosophers "lost sight of man as an acting being" in favor of humans as "animal

rationale and as *homo faber.*"[27] If Martin Heidegger located the forgetfulness of Being at the very source of Western philosophy, Arendt identified a
forgetfulness of the world at the origins of Western political thought. Most
radically, Arendt suggested that philosophy was no longer needed as a war-
rant for political thought or action, a view on which she parted company
with fellow émigrés to America such as Leo Strauss and Erich Voegelin. Less
surprisingly, Christian thought and ethics always assumed an arms-length
attitude toward the world, even though the Roman Catholic Church had
to develop an internal politics of its own and carve out a political place for
itself in the secular world.[28]

Modern political philosophy returned the world to politics and politics
to the world. But politics in the Christian tradition still, she felt, retained
the bad odor of power, self-interest, and/or elitist self-cultivation. It was a
temptation or a burden. The Marxist tradition was very much concerned
with politics and the political realm but, for Marx, the political realm did
not possess the ontological or causal status of the economic realm. According to Arendt, Marx identified the essence of man as with labor and
work (*Arbeit*) not action, the issue that so concerned Arendt in *The Human
Condition*. Similarly, liberal political thought made individual self-interest
and self-development its raison d'être. To be sure, a Thomas Jefferson or
John Stuart Mill showed that liberalism, too, could persuade people to risk
"their lives, their fortunes and their sacred honor" to create their own public
realm. But once established, the ideal liberal polity existed to protect the
pursuit of interests and self-development. It could allow, even encourage,
political participation, but politics was really about creating the possibility
of a good life outside the public realm.

An important article that clarified the master narrative of the political
she was developing in the 1950s was "The Tradition of Political Thought,"
though it was not actually published until 2005.[29] In it, Arendt pointed out
that, to its detriment, Western political philosophy had neglected "three
political experiences": "the experience of action as starting a new enter-
prise in pre-polis Greece, the experience of establishing and maintaining
the foundations of the republic in Rome, and the Christian experience of
acting and forgiving." In addition, all three of these situations testified to
the underlying "fact of the plurality of men."[30]

With this historical claim in mind, we can say that *The Human Condition* (1958) was her "Greek" work. Clearly the most philosophical of her books, it established her reputation as one who looked to the Athenian polis as the exemplary space of political appearance for the rest of Western political thought. She spoke of action as the way of beginning something anew, while the polis was the space where great deeds and words of eloquence could be preserved in memory.[31] *On Revolution*, along with an earlier essay, "What Is Authority?" (1958), was her "Rome" book. Where the Romans claimed to ground their republic in "religion, tradition and authority," these elements were no longer available for the modern republic.[32] This concern with the authority of foundations, she observed, was largely absent from Greek thought. She also admitted that "the Roman experience of foundations" occupied a central position in Machiavelli's thought and thus had not been neglected in the way she had once thought. The questions of authority and legitimacy were also important for modern revolutionary polities and had been a source of deep concern to Robespierre, who proposed that a cult of the "Supreme Being" would help preserve the virtue of the citizens of the French Republic. This essay on authority also saw her discuss the American Revolution for the first time.

Though she never really developed the Christian side of her thought, she did suggest in *The Human Condition* that all political orders had to be founded on "promising" and "forgiveness." Citizens were obligated to work within the framework of laws and for the common good, while the polity dealt with failures and violations of that framework of laws by punishing and forgiving. This represented a partial return to the theme of forgiveness versus reconciliation, except that in *The Human Condition* she concentrated on the system's capacity to wipe the slate clean more than she fixed on individuals or groups.[33] It was only with her two books of 1963—*Eichmann in Jerusalem* and *On Revolution*—that she returned to politics and the problem of evil.

For Arendt, then, the period beginning around the mid- to late 1940s and ending around the mid- to late 1950s was one of intense thinking about and working through (*durcharbeiten*) of the problem of politics. Arendt only began to talk in specific terms of the revolutionary council tradition in her essay on the Hungarian Revolution in 1956 and of the modern revival of the republican tradition in *On Revolution*. In both cases, she was seeking to identify modern counterparts—not so much direct links as analogies—of the ideas of politics forged in Greece and Rome.[34]

Still, later critics such as Benjamin Schwartz would wonder why political action and freedom rather than, say, adherence to tradition or religious belief were the best answer to totalitarianism's nihilistic vision of human superfluousness?[35] Her answer was that politics assumes a shared world with others; in this space citizens can reveal themselves to others and preserve the plurality of human existence by initiating plans and projects without needing to know their inevitable outcome. This was a necessary alternative to the Marxist and socialist traditions, which had shown themselves incapable of preserving political freedom. And to her way of thinking, the republican public realm or council system's idea of decentralized decision making preserved the capacity for political speech and action more clearly than did liberal democracy where citizens handed over their voice to representatives and hence lost the participatory experience.

Yet, could such a vision of politics perpetuate itself? Or was it the fate of the public realm to suddenly appear, as though illuminated by a lightning bolt, only to fall back, as she sometimes said, into obscurity? It is hard to imagine an Arendtian version of Weber's essay "Politics as a Vocation," since authentic politics, as she envisioned it, was such a transitory, even evanescent, experience and the "unforeseen consequences" that flowed from political action were by definition impossible to predict. No one more than Arendt was aware of the contingencies of action, the difficulties of freedom, and the fragility of the public world. The culmination of this preoccupation came in *On Revolution* where her constant concern was with the need to discover or create the "lasting institutions" that would protect freedom.

Worldliness: History and Politics

Arendt was a thinker concerned with political action and an eccentric kind of intellectual historian of politics in Western thought. She was also a "citizen intellectual," who spoke, primarily in print, about the issues facing the American republic, even though she had only been a citizen since 1951.

Indeed, her work as a whole is particularly interesting for the way her theoretical concerns, her long historical narrative of Western politics and the
political, and her engagement with the political issues of her own time are
often all at work at the same time in her writing.

What linked them were the ideas of worldliness and the world. Besides
her "Understanding and Politics" essay, her concern with the concept of
the world was particularly evident in the paper "Concern with Politics in
Recent European Political Thought," delivered at a American Political Science Association meeting and referred to earlier here.[36] Besides Hegel, she
focused attention on her former mentor, Martin Heidegger, whose thought
she had all but dismissed in the late 1940s as having failed to escape the
solipsistic "self," for whom public speech and appearance were inauthentic.[37]
In this paper, she noted approvingly that Hegel, whose work had enjoyed
a revival in France in the 1930s and 1940s, treated "truth" or "reason" as
present within history. Similarly, she suggested that Heidegger's emphasis
on "historicity" (*Geschichtlichkeit*) and "thrownness" (*Geworfenheit*) was
a way of emphasizing the human enmeshment in time and history. The
philosopher could no longer claim the status of "wise man," who somehow
escaped the trammels of history. Indeed, Arendt was always suspicious of
the idea that there were moral experts or elites who possess superior political
or moral wisdom, which was a kind of slap at Leo Strauss avant la lettre.
She had seen too many of her fellow students and former teachers in the
German university capitulate to, or be neutralized by, Nazism to set much
store in elite political wisdom or virtue.

Often associated herself with existentialism, Arendt nevertheless questioned the (predominantly French) existentialist focus on revolutionary
politics as a kind of "salvation" from the absurdity of human existence. She
approved of the way that, for Jean-Paul Sartre and Maurice Merleau-Ponty,
politics stood "at the very center of their work."[38] But she was suspicious
of their idea of political action as a "leap" out of an existential impasse,
without being grounded in any principles or dialogue with others. Even
though French Marxism readily accommodated action, their revolt, she
observed, was usually directed less against "social or political conditions"
than against the "human condition."[39] What Sartre and company lacked
was supplied, Arendt pointed out, by Karl Jaspers, whose work thema-

tized "communication" rather than "solitude." Meaning was found "between" rather than "within" or "above" human beings.[40] In this way, Jaspers avoided a subjectivist or idealist account of meaning production or action.

Drawing on Heidegger's concept of world, Arendt used the term, first, to refer to human affairs in general; second, to the political realm in particular; and, third, to something like culture ("human artifice") where not only action but art as well was accessible to everyone. In this sense, "world" often was preceded by the term "public."[41] The concept of world is contrasted, on the one hand, with nature and, on the other, with the condition of isolation or introspective subjectivity, what she called "worldlessness." Worldlessness could also refer to the condition of having lost the (shared) traditions and structures of meaning that sustained collective life. But people could also choose to retreat from the world, that is, from normal human intercourse. As she later wrote: "The world and the people who inhabit it are not the same. The world lies in between people."[42] Yet not all interpersonal worlds were political. For instance, she recognized that Jaspers's emphasis on communication "has its roots not in the public political sphere, but in the personal encounter of I and Thou."[43] Jaspers had escaped the solipsism of the Heideggerian self of *Being and Time* but had not yet defined the path from interpersonal intimacy to the public world of speech and action where citizens acted on behalf of the public good.

Returning at the end to Heidegger, Arendt also made clear that Heidegger had never made the jump between worldliness and authentic politics, from "throwunness" to political action: "Despite its obvious closeness to the political realm, it never reaches but always misses the center of politics—man as an acting being."[44] This was, she noted shrewdly, apparent in Heidegger's great sensitivity to certain novel historical trends and forces—"technicalization," "the emergence of one world on a planetary scale," and the "concomitant atomization of society." But these insights had not led him to ask "the more permanent questions of political science... such as, What is politics? Who is man as a political being? What is freedom?"[45] Finally, while politics was the realm of freedom, history was where the emphasis fell on the all-determining forces and trends. Still, it was important historically that contemporary ideas of reason and meaning were worldly, not transcendent, in nature.

Between America and Europe

Arendt's measured optimism about contemporary European political philosophy's rediscovery of the world was paralleled by her growing interest in the writings of the American Framers, whom she had read for her citizenship exam, which she successfully completed in December 1951. Writing to Karl Jaspers earlier that fall, she admitted that: "I am always thankful that I ended up here. For my citizenship test, in fact for the ceremony itself, I learned a bit about American constitutional history. Really great [*grossartig*] down to the smallest detail. And much of it still lives."[46] At roughly the same time, an entry in her *Denktagebuch* sketched in what she saw as the "political novelty" of the American system. First, the "highest law" was established by the Constitution against all efforts by "the individual, the few or the many" to gain dominance over the others. It was with the Constitution that a "beginning was fixed . . . without violence, without ruling or being ruled." Second, she noted that the "separation of powers was a division in sovereignty." But it was not the division that Montesquieu had set forth—among executive, legislative, and judicial—but rather the "casual [*unbekümmerte*] division of functions between the federal government and the states that was crucial." Federalism was the most novel form of divided sovereignty. Third, she claimed that not only the Constitution and laws but also "treaties" made up "the highest law of the land." By requiring a two-thirds vote of the Senate, she contended that "for the first time foreign policy had become domestic policy." Furthermore, she added, this "pointed the way toward organizing humanity politically."[47]

In the last year of her life, she delivered an acceptance speech in Copenhagen after being awarded the Sonning Prize. There she reflected on those early sentiments: "What I learned in these crucial first years between immigration and naturalization amounted to a self-taught course in the political philosophy of the Founding Fathers."[48] This is not to suggest that Arendt wasn't interested in America before studying for her citizenship exam. As we shall see, she was reading Tocqueville by the mid-1940s and enthusiastically exchanging opinions about America with David Riesman in the late 1940s. But her reading of the Framers focused her attention specifically on the origins of American political culture and institutions.

Still, Arendt was—and remained—very much European oriented in her thinking. For instance, the effect of studying Rosa Luxemburg on "spontaneous revolution" in the middle 1950s was to infuse her concept of political action with a modern revolutionary consciousness. From this perspective, political action reentered the normal politics of the European nation-state through the revolutionary tradition. Arendt was later to insist that Luxemburg had always emphasized the "republican question rather than the national one." She proposed a "republican program" that emphasized "not only individual but public freedom" for the national parties. From the "revolutionary workers' councils" Luxemburg had "learned" that "revolutions are 'made' by nobody but break out 'spontaneously.'"[49] Most importantly, Arendt's idea of political action (and freedom) now assumed a modern historical shape; no longer could it be thought of primarily in aesthetic and performative terms, which she emphasized in discussing the Greeks. While *Origins* had somewhat defensively proposed "the right to have rights" as a fundamental human inheritance, Arendt recast her idea of the political to accommodate a more active role for public speech and action.[50]

Besides her reading of Luxemburg, the Hungarian Revolution of October–November 1956 redoubled her interest in the politics of freedom. With a renewed faith in the possibility of politics, she wrote a long essay analyzing totalitarian imperialism in the *Journal of Politics* in 1958, which became the epilogue to the second edition of *Origins* published the same year.[51] Despite the pessimism of *Origins*, events in Poland and then Hungary led her to write with a "certain hopefulness." The Hungarian uprising had, she reported, "interrupted these types of automatic recurrences and conscious and unconscious repetitions" that characterize normal history and "brings to mind Luxemburg's 'spontaneous revolution.'"[52] Most impressive about Hungary had been the "sheer momentum of acting-together" evident in the revolutionary and workers' councils. The latter were the best possible answer to the crucial concern, later posed more generally in *On Revolution*: "how to institutionalize a freedom that was already an accomplished fact."[53]

The reemergence of the council system, which had first appeared in the revolutions of 1848 and then turned up again in the Paris commune of 1871, in the Russia revolution in 1905, and in the German and Austrian *Räte* (councils) of November 1918, became for her the main European institutional instantiation of the political freedom she so celebrated. It was the chief "democratic alternative" to the conventional "party systems" of Europe of which she always took a dim view.[54] The twelve days of the Hungarian Revolution demonstrated the "very realistic understanding that freedom resides in the human capacities of action and thought, and not in labor and earning a living."[55] Thus the Marxist and liberal understandings of modern politics (the pursuit of self-interest and self-development) were overshadowed by what happened in Budapest. As she wrote, "While not unaware of the role which the council system had played in all the revolutions since 1848, I had no hope for its re-emergence." With a rare demonstration of humility, Arendt concluded that "the Hungarian Revolution had taught me a lesson."[56] The tradition of the council system was still alive.

Hungary's importance for Arendt is hard to overestimate. She also included a three-page analysis of it in *The Human Condition* and a lengthy discussion of the council system tradition in the last chapter of *On Revolution*. Still, there was an apparent contradiction in her work here and she knew it. Why and how had the workers' movements in Europe, whose entire existence had been bound up in with labor (*Arbeit*) rather than action (*Handeln*), displayed such keen political instincts and the great desire to participate in political action? This contradicted the thought behind her distinction between labor and action, which was that those who were enmeshed in the laboring process had an "incapacity . . . for distinction and hence for action and speech." She also noted that laborers in these political struggles were "more or less suddenly admitted to the public realm, that is appeared in public, and this without at the same time being admitted to society."[57] In this their experience sounded similar to that of pariah people such as the Jews and even to African Americans in Reconstruction and then the 1950s and 1960s.

To her credit, Arendt admitted that the history of nineteenth-century radical politics contradicted her idea that those who were involved with labor were politically incapacitated. In response, she first claimed that there has been a "striking absence of serious slave rebellions in ancient and modern society." This, however, was wrong since there had been a successful Haitian slave revolt between 1792 and 1803.[58] Then in a footnote, Arendt modified her mistaken claim by contrasting ancient slave rebellions that failed to universalize their demand for freedom with modern ones that did, after the French Revolution, universalize their demands. She had to grant that "even" modern slaves had shown themselves quite capable of thinking in political and universal not just economic and particularist terms. Such had been the case on Saint-Domingue and of course also in the United States.[59]

In reference to the labor movement, Arendt tried to salvage something of her original point about the incompatibility of labor and political action by suggesting that the modern labor movement included two separate tendencies: the "trade-union movement," which was concerned with better working conditions and the pursuit of economic issues, and a more political movement, of those who were concerned with "the people's political aspirations," including a concern with the political conditions that would allow participation in the "political realm" as a "citizen."[60] Arendt never really tried to make this distinction stick empirically. In fact, she had landed in this dilemma because she saw no substantive difference between a slave class and a laboring class. Already, in the early 1950s in her *Denktagebuch*, she cited Simone Weil approvingly: "Those who work can not be free."[61] Thus this Greek thinking on slavery set the terms for her discussion of the modern working class, even though the legal and political status of the two was vastly different. According to her analysis, the social sphere overwhelmed the political realm among those who labored, but, historically, this was not the case.

In the same entry, Arendt also proposed that the "American experiment" had succeeded in restoring "human dignity" by, among other things, organizing the work force, lessening the negative implications of work and thus class differences, partially abolishing misery and poverty, and creating a market where "labor power has become the most expensive good." But, she continued, this ran the "palpable danger that all had become equally slaves of necessity" as reflected in the "fearful overestimation of the 'job.'" As she summed it up: "Through the recognition of the 'dignity of labor,' necessity is trivialized and with that everything that one cannot master—death, suffering, etc., the old story."[62] The condition of the modern working class, at least in America, had been alleviated, but at the same time "generalized" to members of all social classes. In addition, she also talked later of the insecurity of the inhabitants of contemporary societies where the majority of people were "job holders" not "property holders."[63]

It is also telling that Arendt failed to pay any attention to another momentous event in the early winter of 1956—the beginning of the Montgomery bus boycott (1956–57). She did mention the independence movements in Africa and Third World in her "Totalitarian Imperialism" article, but mainly to call attention to the way that Third World leaders and intellectuals were enamored with the Soviet Union because "the principle of racial equality is not violated" and "it is not imperialism as they knew it." Arendt's grudging recognition was followed by a warning that there would be no revolution of freedom in the former colonies "so long as former colonial people are color conscious instead of freedom minded."[64] Apparently, her international perspective of the mid-1940s had narrowed, even atrophied. Her one-dimensional contrast between "color conscious" and "freedom minded" seemed designed to deflect rather than encourage political thought.

Still, her failure to show a bit more sympathy for the Third World's rejection of the European colonizers is surprising. Indeed, the essence of colonial rule had been to consign and confine native populations to the realm of labor, while generally excluding them from politics. She was intolerant of the politics of race where and when it appeared in non-European independence movements. But she was not alone in finding the emphasis on race bothersome. After attending the Bandung Conference of nonaligned Asian and African states in 1955, Richard Wright wrote of his bewilderment at the emphasis on race and religion voiced by delegates from neutral nations. At the same time, C. L R. James brought a wider, more comprehensive perspective to the political ferment of the mid-1950s when he linked the Montgomery bus boycott, the independence movements in Africa, and the Hungarian Revolution as three examples of authentic politics in the contemporary world.[65]

The American Political Tradition

Arendt's decision to teach a semester at Berkeley in 1955 put her into direct touch with specialists in American political thought. There she taught two courses, one of which was based largely on the piece on European philosophy already analyzed.[66] She also met a talented group of young political theorists and graduate students there, several whom went on to distinguished academic careers. One of the young theorists, Sheldon Wolin, was on leave, but another, Norman Jacobson, urged Arendt to deepen her interest in American political thought by reading John Adams. One former student in the political science department at Berkeley, Brad Cleveland, suggests that Arendt helped shape this group of young theorists and that they, in turn, played a very important role in shaping some of the leaders of the Free Speech Movement (FSM) at Berkeley in the first half of the 1960s.[67] Though Wolin would later say that he had not read *The Human Condition* when his *Politics and Vision* appeared in 1960, he did acknowledge that Arendt's work had been "enormously liberating."[68] In the future, Wolin and Hanna Fenichel Pitkin, who came to Berkeley in the early 1960s as a political theorist, would explore with great subtlety the political-social distinction so central to Arendt's thought and expand on the history of the political realm in general. Wolin and Jacobson also shared Arendt's distaste for Marxism, liberal pluralist theory, and the newly emerging American conservatism influenced by émigrés such as Strauss and Voegelin. Strangely, she was silent about these contacts in her letters home to her husband, Heinrich Blücher while she was at Berkeley. Arendt also wondered whether there was anything in American political thought that would counteract "the old suspicions of philosophers" about politics.[69]

Later, in *On Revolution*, she would underscore one salient difference between European and American revolutionary political thinking—the American Framers wrote from positions informed by political experience accumulated while active in colonial governments, the lead-in to the independence struggle from 1763 down to 1775–76, and, then, the war itself, which lasted until 1783. They had acquired "the habit of self-government," while most French political thinkers were speculating about the origins of government in the state of nature.

By late in the decade, Arendt had built up momentum in her study of the Framer's political thought. In November 1958, Arendt reported to Karl Jaspers on her preparations for the lectures she was to give at Princeton in the spring of 1959, which she planned to call "The United States and the Revolutionary Spirit": "I am immersed in American history and preparing my Princeton lectures on the concept of revolution. (I'll incorporate this into my book for Piper.) It's breathtakingly exciting and wonderful, the American

Revolution, that is, and the founding of the republic, the Constitution. Madison, Hamilton, Jefferson, John Adams—what men. And when you look at what's there now—what a comedown."[70] A month or so later, she repeated her words of praise for the American Framers and condemnation of contemporary American politicians, regularly paired motifs in her American writings of the postwar period. She then added: "In the meantime I've wound up in the French Revolution. I have a lot to say about that, about Robespierre in particular. But better for another time."[71]Interestingly, Arendt's correspondence is otherwise lacking in any mention of the French Revolution.

Moreover, the fact that Blücher had written to her that summer—"But you know the concept 'republic' must be understood in a new and more decisive way"[72]—pointed both to his significant involvement in his wife's project and to the fact that republicanism was very much on both their minds. Significantly, Blücher was referring to her "Totalitarian Imperialism" piece about the Hungarian Revolution not the American or French revolutions. But the larger point is worth underlining. Both Budapest in the mid-1950s and in Philadelphia in the 1770s and 1780s seemed to teach a republican lesson. Before *On Revolution*, Arendt's essay "What Is Authority?" (1958) contained her longest discussion of the American Revolution up to that date. The theme of the essay was the desire of the Framers to emulate the Romans in their attempt to recover "the experience of foundations" in the late eighteenth-century revolutions. But, as of this essay, Arendt was hard put to assert the novelty of the American Revolution, since many of its structures were in place: it "confirmed and legalized an already existing body politics rather than making it anew."[73] Though Arendt likened the experience of the American Revolution to the Roman experience with foundations, she made no direct mention of the republican tradition. It was only later in *On Revolution* that she radicalized her claim about the way the revolutionary generation created a new beginning.

Later, Sheldon Wolin would suggest that the concept of freedom could refer either to participation or to action, to "taking a share" in or "activating" something.[74] From this perspective, participation in direct democratic rule could be seen as the best way to institutionalize the more dramatic forms of action; in fact, Arendt would later stress the role of civil disobedience as a bridge between action and participation. Another version of this tension in her concept of politics is the difference between the spontaneous emergence of self-organizing groups at the grassroots level (for instance, the council systems) and organizing of conventions to write constitutions. Overall, the tension between creating and maintaining a political world remained unresolved, perhaps fortunately so, in her theory of politics and freedom.

Finally, with the publication of *On Revolution* in 1963, Arendt's great period of exploring the republican idea and experience of revolution, with America as its apotheosis, was essentially complete. After preparing for the 1959 lectures at Princeton, she worked further on what became *On Revolution* at Wesleyan University's Center for Advanced Studies in the fall of 1961 and brought it to completion late that year. She spent 1962 revising the manuscript, while she also worked on her controversial articles on the Eichmann trial that appeared in the *New Yorker* in early 1963 and, later in the same year, as *Eichmann in Jerusalem*. That she was working on both books at the same time is itself an apt reminder of her position between the European past and the American present and future.

Early reactions to *On Revolution* from friends such as Alfred Kazin and Mary McCarthy, from her husband, Heinrich, and from Karl Jaspers were, of course, positive. Jaspers "sense[d] the influence of Heinrich's character and his experience" in the way Arendt linked the "councils" with "revolutions since the American one."[75] Arendt's assessment of her nearly finished book at the end of 1961 was that: "I think it is quite good, at least in passages. What I feel I have been able to do is to clarify certain basic facts about America that people in Europe know very little about."[76] Thus she explicitly saw her book on revolution as part of an ongoing attempt to explain the United States to Europe and even to the world. She wanted to make sure that the American Revolution assumed its rightful place as a major political event of the modern age rather than as an aberration or an exception that appealed to no one else but Americans. In asking if she could dedicate the book to Karl Jaspers and his wife, Gertrud, Arendt revealed her persistent effort to educate Europeans to American realities rather than allowing them to assume that they knew all they needed to know about the United States. *On Revolution* was also, as Young-Bruehl (following Bernard Crick) suggested, an "act of gratitude" from Arendt to the country that granted her, her mother, and her husband refuge from certain death.[77]

As we shall see, Arendt was far from uncritical in her treatment of her adopted country in *On Revolution*. In private letters, she could patronize America with all the assurance of the *echt* European she was. But not long after the book appeared, Arendt reacted to a positive review from Supreme Court Justice William O. Douglas in the *Washington Post* with the observation (to Jaspers) that "even though I took great care with my examination of American institutions, which all go back to the Revolution, I never felt absolutely sure of myself. My interpretations are often very idiosyncratic [*eigenwillig*]."[78] Jaspers put the European perspective succinctly when he expressed the "hope(s) that it will rouse the Americans out of their self-forgetfulness."[79] But, contrary to Arendt's intentions for the book, Jaspers failed to acknowledge that Europe had anything to learn from it.

[**CHAPTER 4**]

Arendt, Tocqueville, and Cold War America

"We take walks each day; I read Tocqueville and Shakespeare and I despair over the hash I'm making of the human rights business."[1] Thus Hannah Arendt described her vacation routine in July 1946 in New Hampshire to her husband, Heinrich Blücher. At the time, Arendt and Blücher were planning a book of readings on America as seen through European eyes, with Blücher handling the background reading and making appropriate selections. But he reported two years later: "It will be more difficult than you believed to make something interesting out of the stuff."[2] A week after that, Arendt replied in a more determined mood: "It will happen because it must happen." After mentioning a few visitors' accounts, plus sections by Goethe and Voltaire, she added that, of the travel writing, only "Tocqueville, Matthew Arnold and Bryce [are] really important."[3] Ultimately, Blücher proved to be correct: the book about America never came to fruition.

Despite Tocqueville's obvious influence on Arendt, she surprisingly never wrote in a sustained way about his thought. This stands in stark contrast with her treatment of Karl Marx, about whose thought she was much more divided, even negative, but with whose thought she spent quite a bit of time.[4] What Arendt and the Frenchmen shared was a desire to develop new ways of thinking about politics, to explore the relationship between the social and political spheres, and, generally, to clarify the complex relationship between equality and freedom.[5] This was all helped along by the appearance of a new edition/translation of *Democracy in American* in 1945. Combined with George W. Pierson's pioneering *Tocqueville and Beaumont in America* (1938), it helped launch Tocqueville as the preeminent analyst of America in postwar America, a period in which Tocqueville and Max Weber replaced Karl Marx as the most important sociologists in contemporary American intellectual life.[6] Arendt's acquaintance, Raymond Aron, was one Frenchmen who clearly recognized Tocqueville's importance, placing him with Weber as one of the founders of the modern sociological tradition itself.[7] For her part, Arendt played Marx and Tocqueville off each other in her *Denktagebuch*: "Tocqueville and Marx: Tocqueville lives in France and only sees the political implications of modernity [*die Neuzeit*]. Marx lives in Germany and England and only sees the economic ones. For Tocqueville the French Revolution is decisive; for Marx, it is the industrial one. Both belong together, something both know. But only Tocqueville demands a new 'science of politics'—not Marx who has the idea of History."[8] Clearly, Arendt was interested in Tocqueville as an analyst of democratic society but also as what we would call a political theorist whose central theme was the relationship, referred to above, between equality and freedom.[9]

For many students of America, Tocqueville's work has always seemed the founding text in American "exceptionalism," even when he was critical of the new republic. For the more somber minded, his penetrating exploration of America in the 1830s seemed to foreshadow the conformist, at times totalitarian, tendencies of modern mass society, especially in America. In general Arendt tended to accept the Frenchman's analysis of America as a conformist culture, but she was also drawn to Tocqueville's more positive view of Americans as a self-organizing people, always ready to create associations and organizations to meet social and political problems. As we shall see, by the mid-1950s Arendt had assumed a certain Tocquevillean role of explaining the New World to the Old and vice versa.

The Odd Couple

Writing in the wake of a profound historical dislocation, Arendt was fond of citing Tocqueville's plangent observation that, "since the past has ceased to throw its light upon the future, the mind of man wanders in obscurity."[10] Arendt herself was among those who tended to read *Democracy in America* as equally applicable to the 1940s as the 1830s,[11] equally full of hope and foreboding. As said, she was aware of the importance of what Tocqueville called "political associations" to counteract the privatism and conformism endemic in a democratic society.[12] On a theoretical level, they also shared the idea that the distinction between the political and social spheres was central in any understanding of the modern world. Like Arendt, Tocqueville was a splitter not a lumper and had the "tendency to think in terms of contraries or pairs in tension."[13]

But Arendt and Tocqueville did not mean exactly the same thing when they referred to the social sphere. Tocqueville tended to see the modern social sphere in terms of increasing "equality of conditions," specifically, the absence of legal distinctions, ranks and titles, along with the egalitarian *moeurs* (habits of mind) that held the society together. Tocqueville's analysis concentrated on social conformity and homogeneity of opinion in a democratic society, but he also emphasized the role that the aristocracy (in France) had played in blocking the total triumph of the state and what he called "democratic despotism."

In addition, Arendt emphasized the uniformity and homogeneity of a society of equals. But she pictured the social realm as made up of, first, people of differing economic and social status. The picture of American society painted by Thorstein Veblen, whose ideas of "conspicuous consumption" and "conspicuous production" she referred to in *The Human Condition*, was not far from what Arendt saw as characteristic of social life in a democratic society.[14] American society was also made up by racial, religious, regional, and ethnic differences that, as she explained to Günter Gaus, were a "natural condition. You belong to some sort of group when you are born, always." A social group seemed to become political when, after choosing to "join or form a group," individuals become self-conscious about "interests." Overall, "whenever men come together in whatever numbers, public interests come into play. . . . And the public realm is formed."[15] Whether that was quite the same as "the political" is not entirely clear.

Tocqueville and Arendt converged in their emphasis on the largely subliminal, even unconscious, nature of socialization, while the political sphere was connected with agency and choice.[16] As Hanna Pitkin has observed (in her discussion of social contract theories), "We do not agree contractually to" follow the "norms, standards, and patterns of our society, . . . we grow into them."[17] In contrast, "the role and character of political action is quite different: it is collective, public, rather than individual, and it is at least partly deliberate and intentional."[18] Pitkin's comparison reveals the subtle sense in which political action is a species of freedom. It is not a negative kind of freedom that emphasizes shedding restrictions as such; rather it is a kind of positive freedom organized around taking the initiative to propose something new that will make a difference.

Still, Tocqueville never treated the social in the pejorative terms Arendt did. His nostalgia for the French aristocracy had to do with the way it had resisted political centralization in France before, during, and after the revolution. He sometimes spoke as though a stronger aristocracy in American would have blocked the power of "public opinion" in the new democratic society. Certainly social virtues and certain habits of mind (*moeurs*) rather than just free action were necessary in Tocqueville's ideal republic. Though Arendt used the phrase "tyranny of the majority" in reference to postwar public education, she did not use the phrase very often.[19] But Tocqueville's pithy observation that there was "no freedom of mind in America" anticipated her own rather low assessment of American intellectual and cultural life.[20]

Nor did Tocqueville place much faith in purely institutional hindrances to the political desires of the majority: "I think, therefore that one must always place somewhere one social power superior to all the others to block the majority."[21] Thus, institutional checks and balances needed social reinforcement. In addition, participation in politics, based on "self-reliance and the habits of free association," was necessary to check the power of the many. Tocqueville was one of the French liberals, according to Larry Siedentop, who were "the first consistent champions of participation in modern political thought."[22] For her part, Arendt placed greater faith in institutional arrangements than in the aristocracy or in political virtue(s). The federal system itself redistributed power away from the center. Federalism was—and would be—an effective antidote to what Tocqueville most feared. But the two were very much in agreement on the importance of protecting and deploying "local liberties" to check the centralization of power that accompanied democracy.[23]

Both also followed Montesquieu in assuming that each form of political rule was informed by a basic principle: fear in the case of despotism, honor in the case of aristocracy, and virtue or "love of the republic" in a republic.[24] While Tocqueville tended to be interested in the political and social psychology of modern democratic society, Arendt studiously avoided any great concern with the individual experience of politics or political education, except for a few pages in "The Crisis of Education" published in the late 1950s.[25] Politics was about creating and maintaining a public world, of seeing to it, for example, that the Constitution was preserved. It was not primarily about satisfying desires, interests, or needs or even about producing citizens.[26]

Still, Tocqueville's general notion of political freedom as a good in itself comported well with Arendt's emerging conception of political freedom and of political action. Later, Arendt would cite his dictum about freedom approvingly: "The man who asks from freedom anything other than itself is born to be a slave."[27] I also suspect that Tocqueville helped show Arendt that action was an essential capacity of free human beings that could be institutionalized as political participation and classified as political freedom. Yet one of Arendt's most important innovations was to separate the political from governmental authority. As a form of political participation, action helped nurture and preserve freedom, equality, and virtue, but its existence did not depend on duly constituted political institutions.

Again, Tocqueville's greater flexibility meant that he, unlike Arendt, could find ways to talk about the mutual influence between the social and political spheres without immediately fearing that the social would always contaminate or compromise the political. According to Tocqueville, participating in political associations gave people the taste for civil associations: "Political associations can therefore be considered great schools, free of charge, where all citizens come to learn the general theory of associations."[28] But he also noted that while rulers feared political associations, they welcomed civil associations, which "distract" citizens from political complaints and "turn them away from revolutions."[29] Thus Tocqueville, like Arendt, could see ways that the social and the political could work at cross-purposes.

All this was linked, at least in one direction, to Tocqueville's observation that the power of social values, along with the desire for economic well-being, contributed to the emergence of "individualism" as a threat to political and public involvement. Famously, he differentiated between "selfishness" and "individualism" by noting that the former is a "passionate and exaggerated love of the self" and of "the self alone."[30] The latter, however, "is a reflective and peaceable sentiment that disposes each citizen to isolate himself from the mass of those like him and withdraw to one side with his family and his friends . . . having thus created a little society for his own use, he willingly abandons society at large to itself."[31] Tocqueville's account of individualism was all the more effective because he recognized its appeal as well as its dangers. At the same time, it is surprising that Arendt didn't make more of the dangers of individualism and the family to the political realm in her writing on modern politics.

One of Tocqueville's more interesting ideas was "self-interest well understood" as a kind of feeling that, though aimed at the well-being of the self, also linked that well-being with willingness "to aid each other and . . . sacrifice a part of their time and their wealth to the good of the state." According to Tocqueville, the dominant idea in America was not that virtue was "beautiful" but that it was "useful."[32] Tocqueville's thinking here clearly captured the paradox(es) of self-interest. The pursuit of self-interest is not always in one's self-interest, while true self-interest entails concern with the wider public interest. Americans, he noted, often acted better than they were willing to admit, an observation that Arendt might well have remembered. Finally, as Hanna Pitkin has observed, Arendt and Tocqueville, even Marx, all were faced with the question of why human beings did not prefer public freedom to the claims of self-interest, even when political freedom was not just a product of self-sacrifice. Perhaps it is because concern for the public realm requires some extra effort and is harder to determine in specific cases. Yet self-interest is arguably as difficult to determine as the public good.

Finally, there were several important issues which the two assessed differently. Surprisingly, it was only in "Civil Disobedience" (1970), her last major essay in political thought, that Arendt linked "consent and the right to dissent" with "action," which was, in turn, the source of those "voluntary associations whose role Tocqueville was the first to notice with amazement, admiration, and some misgiving."[33] While Tocqueville placed great emphasis on the influence of the Puritan tradition and also of religious institutions such as a triumphant Catholic Church in America, Arendt was relatively neglectful of religion's role in American political culture. In "What Is Authority?" and *On Revolution*, Arendt wrote a good deal about religion, tradition, and authority as vital ingredients in the foundation of the Roman republic. She also underlined the fading belief in immortality and the crucial modern loss of "fear of hell" as a blow to political authority.[34] But she was also convinced that religious underpinnings no longer provided much authority and that the attempt to revive them was both futile and dangerous. She was also adamant in rejecting the argument of political philosopher Eric Voegelin and others that contemporary ideological movements (Fascism, Nazism, Communism) were substitutes for authentic religions in the modern, secularized world.[35] Even though a political ideology performed some of the same meaning-imparting functions as Christianity did, this did not mean it was an ersatz- or proto-religion.

Overall, then, Arendt devoted little attention to the phenomenon of political religion in her work. Nothing in Arendt really anticipated the 1960s work, say, of Robert Bellah on American civil religion or helped explain the importance of racial, ethnic, and religious loyalties in creating "democratic religion" as Will Herberg did in his *Protestant-Catholic-Jew*.[36] When citizens functioned as citizens in the public realm, Arendt seemed to think they should check their particularistic allegiances or identities at the door. For all her emphasis on worldliness, her notion of the citizen is culturally and socially underdeveloped. As Mark Reinhardt has noted, her intent seems always to be to "purify" it, to eliminate from it much of what might be seen as its "worldliness."[37] Echoes of the Kantian notion of "autonomy" sound through her idea of political freedom. In general, the dilemma she never worked out was how to escape the determinism of the biological and social without losing the human world, as it were.

Finally, there are two areas where Arendt departed most clearly from Tocqueville. First, there was the Frenchman's claim that America had never experienced a revolution: "The Americans have a democratic social state and constitution, but they did not have a democratic revolution."[38] Later, he repeated that Americans "have arrived at democracy without having to suffer democratic revolutions, and to be born equal instead of becoming so."[39] As Louis Hartz famously noted in the 1950s, Americans were "born equal as Tocqueville said." Lacking a feudal past, he suggested, they could not imagine a socialist future.[40] Of course, by denying that the American Revolution had been a *social* revolution, Arendt went part way toward agreeing with Hartz and ultimately Tocqueville. But finally, she saw the American Revolution as a genuinely political revolution that brought something new to the political world, even though it owed much to the Roman precedent.

They also disagreed, at least implicitly, on the matter of historical inevitability. For Tocqueville, the democratic revolution seemed inevitable and universal. Though he lacked the philosophical interest to develop a full-fledged philosophy of history, he stressed equality as inevitable fact to be realized in the future. Evoking Providence and the hand of God, rather than the "cunning of reason" or the "laws of history," he spoke of the way

> all have worked in common, some despite themselves, others without knowing it, as blind instruments in the hand of God.
>
> The gradual development of equality of conditions is therefore a providential fact, and it has the principal characteristic of one: it is universal, it is enduring, each day it escapes human power; all events . . . , like all men, serve its development.[41]

A few lines later, he wrote of the "sort of religious terror in the author's soul, produced by the sight of this irresistible revolution."[42] Though Arendt mentioned this deterministic/prophetic aspect of Tocqueville's thought in *On Revolution*, she never criticized him for his historical determinism in the way that she criticized Marx for his. To her, such a vision of inevitability made a mockery of political action, the whole point of which was to escape inherited social and historical realities. History with a telos was the enemy of freedom.

It is also here that we must come to the question of race as a historical problem. It is a matter of great irony that just as the first revolution in the equality of social and political conditions was gathering momentum in the European world (circa the 1830s), racially based slavery had become firmly established as a crucial part of the economy of the Western Hemisphere and vital to Europe's prosperity, too. Tocqueville neither saw nor proposed a political solution (as opposed to a violent one) to the problem of race in America; after an eloquent and penetrating analysis, he seemed to confine his conclusions about race and slavery to the margins and never returned to them.[43] Extermination seemed to be the destination of the copresence of the three races in the New World. Historically, the antislavery movement was part of the same system that created enormous empires of inequality, driven by the search for markets and natural resources and justified by ideas of racial and cultural differences.

In *Origins*, as we have seen, Arendt's attention to the growth of biological racism and anti-Semitism in Europe after the establishment of racialized societies in its colonies was important in calling her readers' attention to the centrality of race in modern European politics. For Arendt, the period from circa 1870 to the mid-1940s was the apogee of a civilization-wide conflict over race and racism, including anti-Semitism. Whether one can see this period as a detour on the long road to equality or as the beginning of second stage of the democratic revolution on a global scale is hard to say. Whatever the case, Arendt's *Origins*, like Tocqueville's *Democracy in America*, sought to define the context in which race emerged as a world-historical factor.

Ideology and Americanism

Not surprisingly Arendt was more candid about America in letters than she was in her published work. Arendt could be quite open in her admiration for the political thought, values, and institutions of the American Framers.[44] It is charming, even moving, to imagine that the U.S. citizenship exam had propelled one of the twentieth century's most important political thinkers to immerse herself in the works of the Framers and then to write a book about it, *On Revolution* (1963). As already said, that book was an "act of gratitude."[45] Gratitude is not, of course, a rare or empty emotion among immigrants to any country that has offered refuge against certain death. Yet Arendt was no pushover where America was concerned. She could be *too* dismissive of contemporary American politics and politicians, not to mention American mass culture and society. But, for her, the country's institutions were more impressive than its leaders. She became a citizen not long after Senator Joseph McCarthy began his rampage through American political life and as the House Committee on Un-American Activities continued its work of ferreting out alleged subversives in all walks of American life. German intellectuals as different as Thomas Mann, Theodor Adorno, and Bertolt Brecht decamped for Europe partly because of such threats to civil liberties. At least in New York circles, Arendt was an active participant in the swirl of public controversy over loyalty, subversion, and the meaning of Americanism in. But Arendt neither left nor did she particularly keep her head down, though she did keep a bag packed.

It is interesting to read her lectures, essays, and articles on the postwar crisis of American identity as she sought to apply theoretical concepts such as "ideology" and "fabrication" to current political arguments about loyalty and subversion. For one thing, she drew relatively little on the discourse of liberal rights and freedom associated with American constitutional culture. To be sure Arendt wrote of the "right to have rights" in *Origins*, a fertile idea involving the self-grounding of rights.[46] But she never developed the idea much further. Rather, she emphasized the way that the ability to learn from experience and to think against the grain was restricted by anticommunist straitjackets. Rather than familiar notions such as inalienable rights and civil liberties, she emphasized the "concern for public freedom" and, more generally, the idea of "political happiness" as the core ideas of the American experiment that were manifest in free speech.

Arendt also had a complex attitude toward Marx, the Marxist tradition, and the Soviet Union. Arendt's husband Heinrich had been a member of the Spartacist faction of the German Communist Party until the mid-1920s and three of her most powerful 1960s essays explored the thought of Marxist intellectuals—Rosa Luxemburg, Bertolt Brecht, and Walter Benjamin. But Arendt had no use for Marxism as a theory of history or politics, for communism as a blueprint for the ideal society, or for Marxism-Leninism as the ideology of the Soviet Union. [47] She also disliked the label "anti-Stalinist," since it implied one-time participation in KPD or Communist Party USA conflicts, which she had never been a party to.[48] The most heartening single event in postwar Europe was, as we have seen, the short-lived Hungarian Revolution in 1956 against Soviet domination. This momentous event revealed that, even in a totalitarian situation, political resistance and positive political action were possible. Finally, in response to Gershom Scholem's charge after the Eichmann controversy that she was one of those "intellectuals who come from the German Left," Arendt insisted that if she had "'come from anywhere,' it is from the tradition of German philosophy."[49] In sum, though she could be attracted to and admire communists, she was never attracted to communism.

Yet none of this led Arendt to believe that communism was a serious domestic threat in the early 1950s—certainly not in the way Senator McCarthy was. As a citizen, she involved herself in two ways against the witch-hunting atmosphere of the times. Though the project never came to fruition, Arendt joined a small group of like-minded colleagues such as Mary McCarthy, Dwight Macdonald, Alfred Kazin, and Harold Rosenberg, along with establishment figures such as Richard Rovere and Arthur Schlesinger Jr., to consider founding a magazine based on a "commitment to civil liberties."[50] Otherwise it would be open to contributions from across the political spectrum. Arendt and her colleagues hoped that the magazine would provide an alternative to what they saw as the pernicious influence of *Commentary* intellectuals such as Elliott Cohen, Irving Kristol, and the "unbearable" Sidney Hook, the leading figure in the American Congress for Cultural Freedom.[51] Though not panicky, she was still worried. She wrote to Jaspers that the mood of the times reminded her of the early days of National Socialism with its embrace of "police methods" and encouragement of the "expansion of lawlessness." She warned Jaspers ruefully that it might no longer be possible "to speak without reservation for America" as they had done up till then.[52] In a lighter vein, she added in her next letter that: "You certainly know of the farce of Cohn and Schine; one can follow it best through Shakespeare's Rosenkrantz and Guildenstern."[53] It is also easy to forget that her public involvement took a certain amount of courage, since the recently passed McCarran-Walter Act of 1952 would have made it easier to deport her husband Heinrich, who had lied about his one-time membership in the German Communist Party when he originally entered the United States in 1941.[54]

But her most significant public interventions were the pieces she wrote to be delivered or published in the first decade of the Cold War. One was an unpublished lecture given at the working-class Rand School in 1948, followed by another unpublished lecture called "The Eggs Speak Up" (1951) and an essay published in the liberal Catholic weekly *Commonweal*, "The Ex-Communists" (1953).[55] In these essays, we can see Arendt assume a Tocquevillean persona as the somewhat detached yet concerned commentator on the state of the republic. Indeed, it was her willingness to engage in intellectual and cultural shuttle diplomacy between America and Europe, explaining the one to the other, that helped create her eminence among the New York intellectuals. In her Rand School lecture, she rejected the provincialism and "theoretical inarticulateness" of American left intellectuals, which led them to a blanket rejection of everything American. In fact she called on them to "own up to the American Constitution," since the American political system was better than anything that existed in Europe, something that European intellectuals should also recognize.[56] But American intellectuals also needed to understand that not all anti-Stalinists were democrats (the clearest example of which was Tito in Yugoslavia), while European intellectuals should not consider anti-Stalinists to be servants of the status quo and only interested in Soviet baiting and thus risking Europe's future. The radical rhetoric of Europeans — she undoubtedly had the French intellectuals in mind here — often followed a kind of zero-sum logic: since the Soviet Union was a communist regime and the opposite of communism is fascism, the United States was a fascist nation.[57]

Arendt also used the Rand lecture to sketch in a complex account of the relationship between American society and politics. Specifically, she criticized European intellectuals for their ignorance about America, particularly their lack of awareness of its social complexity. A class analysis simply failed to do justice to an American society in which racial and ethnic distinctions were just as important as class conflict. But the relative lack of class consciousness did not automatically mean that Americans were captives of mass culture and society. She also noted other complicating factors in understanding America. For instance, "social and political forces simply do not match and frequently even contradict each other," while social conformists were often politically knowledgeable and principled.[58] What made all this so difficult to decode, she observed, was that America, a "twentieth-century (and in some respects a nineteenth-century) society lives and thrives on the solid basis of an eighteenth-century political philosophy."[59] The problem ironically was that many American anti-Stalinists had been misled by the "same Marxist theories and therefore, theoretically, cannot believe their eyes so to speak."[60] Moreover, the labels "anti-Stalinist" and "Trotskyist" failed to describe people like herself. In sum, she called on American radicals to abandon the obsession with Bolshevik quarrels and Soviet intraparty struggles.[61] Overall, Arendt clearly considered a Marxist-oriented approach, whether voiced by European or American intellectuals, to be a poor guide to the complex relationship between contemporary politics and social analysis in the United States.

Also of great interest was her analysis of a stock Cold War type, the "ex-Communist" who used "totalitarian means in order to fight totalitarianism."[62] Arendt pointed to what had already become a familiar phenomenon: those who sought to defend America against antidemocratic ideas and illiberal proposals often adopted those very traits to do so. For instance, several key members of the board of the newly organized, William Buckley–led magazine *National Review* in 1955 were former Communists or leftists, who, having recanted, returned to the fray on the side of conservatism rather than liberalism or radicalism. "Anti-liberalism," she noted, was a crucial among ex-Communists.[63] She also shrewdly differentiated "former" from "ex" Communists by noting that "former Communists" had simply left the party behind and moved on, while "ex-Communists" such as Whittaker Chambers continued to construct his post-party identity in terms of his one-time adherence to the party. In short, ex-Communists had left the party but had not left it behind. They were less the polar opposites than secret sharers of totalitarianism. Though Arendt generally disliked thinking in terms of political ideology as political religion, she suggested that ex-Communists were looking for a "substitute for a lost faith."[64] In a Manichean, world-historical manner, new American conservative intellectuals such as Chambers and others like him were convinced that modern history would come down to a conflict between "Communists and Ex-Communists."[65]

But Arendt's most interesting point, particularly in the "Ex-Communists" essay, concerned her objection to the idea of "Americanism" in general. At the time, conventional wisdom was that an explicit American ideology was needed to provide a counterpart to the Communists' intimidating ideological arsenal. In her essay "The Eggs Speak Up" (1951), Arendt expanded on the discussion in *Origins* when she wrote: "Democratic society as a living reality is threatened at the very moment that democracy becomes a 'cause,' because then actions are likely to be judged and opinions evaluated in terms of ultimate ends and not on their inherent merits."[66] Here Arendt used "cause" in roughly the way she used "ideology"—as a hyperintellectual construct that demanded allegiance rather than illuminating the world. Besides the means-end issue, Arendt detected another danger in reifying American democracy when she wrote two years later that: "America, this republic, the democracy in which we live, is a living thing which cannot be contemplated and categorized, like the image of a thing I can make; it cannot be fabricated."[67] "Fabricating" an ideology or image transformed a collection of diverse people into an entity to "make America more American."[68]

Behind this objection to the fabrication of an ideology was the idea she would later spell out in *The Human Condition* (1958)—fabrication of an object (thing, concept, entity) did violence to the raw materials being used. Thus, to impose an ideology on history does violence to the materials of history. When we talk of "making history," she noted, we are suggesting the impossible since, in reality, we confront history as a *given* rather than as something to construct ex nihilo. When we try to force an idea/ideology on historical reality, or try to fit reality into the idea, the process can turn murderous.[69] In more conventional political terms, Arendt was saying that we do violence to people when we conceive of them as components of an idea, in this case the idea of America itself.

This was the source of the title of her 1951 piece, which derived from the old revolutionary adage: "to make an omelet, you've got to break eggs." In fact, Arendt's doubts about the whole idea of "making history"—or constructing an American creed—led some of her early readers to identify her as a political conservative, more akin to Michael Oakeshott in his anti-utopian essay "Rationalism in Politics" or closer to Edmund Burke's hostility to the revolutionary abstractions of the French Revolution, than to Rosa Luxemburg, whom she of course also deeply admired—as she did Burke and Oakeshott.[70] Jacob Burckhardt's description of the aim of Renaissance statecraft—the creation of "the state as a work of art"—prefigured the worst that was to come in the twentieth century. Arendt thought that artists and intellectuals were often so seduced by authoritarian or totalitarian leaders and causes because they admired whoever or whatever could "make history" or "create" a new political order similar to the ways works of art were created—by an imposition of imagination and intellect on the materials at hand.

By way of contrast, she concluded, "acting politically" involved uncertainty and unpredictability. It took creative form by thinking things out in a new way: in action "I never quite know what I am doing," while those who think they are making history are "quite convinced that they know what they are doing."[71] The ideological image of America as a well-ordered polity created a real problem for democratic politics that thrived on difference and plurality, as Arendt was so bent on reminding her readers. Turning loyalty to America or democracy into a creed undermined the idea of America as an experiment and as an ongoing conversation about its own meaning.

The Politics of European and American Relations

September 1954 also saw Arendt publish three essays on the special American-European relationship in the liberal Catholic journal *Commonweal*. Once again she donned the Tocquevillean mantle as an explainer, even justifier and defender, of America to its European critics. Implicitly, she also was explaining Europe to her American readers. It was in these three pieces that she adverted directly and indirectly to Tocqueville more than anywhere else in her work.

Like other postwar American intellectuals and academic specialists in American history and culture, not to mention those who formulated Cold War American foreign policy, Arendt was particularly disturbed by European misconceptions about American politics and culture, especially America's new role in the world, and about the postwar European responsibilities. Underlying all the differences, Arendt contended, Europeans particularly resented the fact of American "plenty" in a world of scarcity.[72]

Especially in the first *Commonweal* piece called "Dream and Nightmare" (September 10, 1954), Arendt's own position closely resembled Tocqueville's. She underlined the idea that other careful readers of Tocqueville shared: "His interest in the workings of democracy as a European possibility—or even necessity—was greater than his interest in descriptions of a foreign country." By understanding how Americans reacted to the new ethos of equality, Europeans would be better prepared for the future "under the unprecedented conditions of equality," as Arendt put it.[73] In fact the American idea of equality was a European idea that had taken root in the United States. Thus, for her, America wasn't exceptional in any permanent sense. Rather, what happened in the United States, foreshadowed the possibilities of a European future. Where America was—and Tocqueville, she contended, felt that "the United States was an older and more experienced country than Europe herself"—there Europe would be.[74]

She was, however, made uneasy by the growing estrangement between Europe and America that flowed from the great disparities in wealth and power between them. This alienation was also fed by the emergent ideology (not simply feeling or impulse) of anti-Americanism generated by a new "pan-European nationalism." Indeed, "the anti-Americanism" is "actually much more dangerous than all the tirades against an imperialist, capitalistic land . . . because it corresponds to a growing 'Americanism' at home."[75] Put another way, Euro-nationalism generated a counternationalism in America and drove the two regions of the world further apart.

In her other two articles, Arendt explored important examples of this growing estrangement. "Europe and the Atomic Bomb" (September 17, 1954) obviously grew out of American use of the atomic bomb to end the war in the Pacific. Though never mentioning Heidegger by name, Arendt was also clearly addressing his concern with the triumph of *die Technik*, which he had explored in lectures and articles between 1949 and 1953.[76] She noted that Europeans had come to see "all technical achievements as inherently evil and destructive and to see in America chiefly, and Russia sometimes, the epitome of destructive technicalization which is hostile and alien to Europe."[77] For her the absurdity of this position was self-evident. Europe and America clearly had shared history of science and technology between them, while, of course, European scientists had largely been responsible for the advanced theoretical work in developing the atomic weapons. That said, she also took aim at what she called the "better to be dead than a slave" mentality in the United States.[78] Its provenance was a pre-Christian one that assumed courage to be the highest virtue. The problem was that courage was useless when nuclear conflagration might well leave no survivors behind to witness that courage. Her larger point was that Europe had to take its own responsibility for the creation and uses of technology and not simply blame everything on America and the Soviet Union.

The other symptom of the estrangement between Europe and America was found in her last piece "The Threat of Conformism" (September 24, 1954). There she noted the irritating European tendency to give "great prominence . . . to everything we have come to include under the name of McCarthyism." Americans were thought to be blindly unaware of a kind of conformity "that conditions each of its members so perfectly to its exigencies that no one knows that he is conditioned." There were two problems with this view, noted Arendt. First, it failed to give due recognition to the actual "opposition to McCarthyism." In fact, many spoke out freely against him and the witch-hunt atmosphere during his period of prominence.[79] Second, because Europeans knew so little about the political and legal culture of civil liberties in America, (along with other sources of opposition to demagogues such as Senator McCarthy), they overreacted when someone like McCarthy came on the scene.

Turning her guns toward Tocqueville, Arendt also questioned the pertinence of his classic European view that America lacked a strong enough society, or needed an aristocracy, to provide a bulwark against political and social conformity. Europeans were ignorant of the fact that the bulwarks against the tyranny of the majority were the "Constitution" and the "institutions of liberty."[80] As she noted, the Tocquevillean line was that "the individual, even if his liberties were violated by the government, could always find a relatively safe refuge in his social and private life."[81] But in America, the situation was reversed. The American "institutions of liberty" derived from the way the written Constitution and the political culture protected individuals against other social and economic (corporate) forces. As already mentioned, she thought that power was best dispersed through the federal system in America rather than amassed at the center. Of course, Arendt's attraction to federalism as a bulwark against centralized state power could cut both ways, since it was federalism, in the form of the idea of states' rights, that the Southern states used to resist the 1954 *Brown v. Board of Education* decision.

She closed by suggesting that Europeans had themselves not been tested by the tyranny of the majority and the conformism of mass societies. Just as

Americans had been complacent about totalitarianism, so Europeans were complacent about the threat of political conformity. Arendt concluded with the extravagant claim that "the history of the two continents is fundamentally the same" and ultimately this is true for "all mankind," an uncharacteristically exuberant position to take in this context.[82] At the same time, she also suggested that what "Europeans dread as 'Americanization' is the emergence of the modern world." Indirectly gesturing toward Tocqueville, she added: "One hundred and twenty years ago, the European image of America was the image of democracy. . . . Today the image of America is modernity."[83]

Overview

Arendt's intervention in the second Red Scare and her negotiation of trans-Atlantic political and cultural tensions testified to a newly arrived at sense of security with her American identity.[84] This, of course, was helped along mightily by the public humiliation of McCarthy by Joseph Welch in the Army-McCarthy hearings in June 1954 and the rapid waning of his political and popular fortunes. By October 1954, her tune had changed in the letters to Jaspers. She commented on the surprising absence of an anti-Semitic component to McCarthyism. (In fact, the McCarthy subcommittee's chief counsel, Roy Cohn, was Jewish.) More interestingly, she also linked her analysis of McCarthyism to the idea of mass society and totalitarianism. The point she made to Jaspers, as Elisabeth Young-Bruehl has pointed out, was that there could be "totalitarian developments" within "mass-society itself," but "without a 'movement' and without a fixed ideology."[85] This was one of the main lessons, a guardedly optimistic one, of the whole anticommunist hysteria of the previous half decade or so.

A year later, Arendt wrote another lengthy letter to Jaspers updating him on her feelings about the country. In doing so, she looked again to Tocqueville to help explain a general "reversal" (*Umschwung*) in "public opinion" that had occurred all across the country. What Arendt had perceived in her time in Berkeley in the spring of 1955 dovetailed with what her husband had noted in New York in the same period. It has been "one of the most interesting and strangest phenomena under the heading of 'public opinion' that I know. Only Tocqueville could have anticipated such a story-line." She went on to observe that "even Eisenhower, who taken as an individual is a 'dummkopf,' is as reasonable as can be." Returning to the political institutions and culture of America, she wrote: "The political tradition of the country has won out, and we were, may God be thanked, with all banners waving and flags flying, wrong." In the same letter, she admitted that the upswing in her mood was also driven by personal feelings: "Only in recent years have I begun to love the world, that I actually have to be able to do so."[86] In general, however, Arendt's basic attitude toward America remained much the same: deep admiration for the political institutions and ideas formulated during the early years of the new Republic and a just as deep suspicion of American social and cultural conformity.

CHAPTER 5

Arendt, Riesman, and America as Mass Society

Just as Hannah Arendt's understanding of America was deeply informed by Alexis de Tocqueville's work, so David Riesman's *The Lonely Crowd* (1950) was a "conversation with *Democracy in America*."[1] In fact, Arendt and Riesman carried on a fascinating correspondence about American society and culture (and the differences from Europe) in the early postwar years. At the time, Arendt was finishing what became *The Origins of Totalitarianism* (1951), while Riesman was concluding a study of "American character and society" for a Yale University–sponsored series, "Studies in National Policy." It became *The Lonely Crowd*, which was published in 1950.[2] But there was nothing inevitable about the way Arendt and Riesman hit it off. He introduced himself to Arendt by letter in February 1947. There, he praised the essays of hers that he had read and expressed hope that she might be lured to the University of Chicago to teach — something, he wrote, that he had discussed with sociologist Daniel Bell who, like Riesman, was also teaching at Chicago.[3] In only six years, Arendt had become part of a network of academics and intellectuals later known as the New York intellectuals.

Still, their backgrounds were quite different. Riesman trained in law at Harvard and clerked for Supreme Court Justice Louis Brandeis. He lacked an academic PhD, but by the late 1940s he identified himself as a sociologist. For her part, Arendt had an allergic reaction to the social sciences that lasted throughout her career.[4] Riesman was also steeped in psychoanalytic theory and conversant with what was going on in psychoanalytically oriented culture-and-personality studies, while Arendt had nothing but bad to say about psychoanalysis as a theory or a therapeutic practice. Thus, when Riesman hoped that she would be willing to work on an historical study of "changing character structures in the western world," he was proposing the last sort of project that she would have chosen to be a part of.[5] Later, in her 1956 preface to *Rahel Varnhagen: The Life of a Jewish Woman*, she characterized "depth-psychology, psychoanalysis, graphology" as forms of "curiosity-seeking" and "modern form[s] of indiscretion" that "aspire to know more than the subject knew about herself or was willing to reveal."[6] Clearly, psychoanalytic theory would have a problem with public speech, perhaps as a form of "acting out." All that said, the exchanges between Arendt and Riesman saw none of these issues openly discussed.

Conversely, there were interesting similarities in the ways Arendt and Riesman conceptualized their materials. Both thought in terms of contrasting types. Both were splitters rather than lumpers, sociological, political, and even metaphysical pluralists who feared the impact of dogma and ideological certainty in politics. Politically, they were strong opponents of McCarthyism. For all her self-confident brilliance, Arendt also needed someone she respected to approve of her approach (and her command of English), while Riesman was clearly stimulated by her comments on his work, including exchanges about Tocqueville. Considering each figure's education and interests, she had a tendency to go abstract, while he inclined toward the specific example and the exception. Riesman's general sensibility was liberal in the best sense: open and inventive, ready to offer criticisms but also to articulate doubts about his own work. He was clearly in awe of Arendt's intellectual prowess, but she, too, could be fulsome in her reactions to his comments. She began a long and rich letter dated June 13, 1949, with: "You are a most wonderful reader."[7] Later that summer, Riesman likened her work to that of Marx and Tocqueville, while contrasting it with the work of a historian, about whom he said: "There is no excitement in reading him or any other historian."[8] Riesman also praised her prose style as she prepared the final draft of her manuscript. His long review of *Origins* in *Commentary* was replete with praise, though he was by no means uncritical.

Later, Riesman acknowledged her thanks by noting that it is "wonderful to be understood and I am glad you feel I did understand."[9]

Their intellectual relationship continued for a time after their "big" books were published. In November 1951, they debated the issue of totalitarianism in a public forum sponsored by the American Congress of Cultural Freedom in New York.[10] They were also coparticipants in a 1953 conference on totalitarianism at Harvard organized by Riesman's mentor, Carl J. Friedrich, who had come to America from Germany in the 1920s. It was attended both by émigrés such as Erik Erikson, Leo Lowenthal (a member of the Frankfurt group and in sociology at Berkeley), and Else Frenkel-Brunswik (one of the *Authoritarian Personality* team), and native-born scholars such as political scientist Harold Lasswell and Riesman. Erich Fromm and Reinhold Niebuhr were invited but couldn't attend.[11] The keynote speaker, George F. Kennan, was already recognized as the preeminent thinker and policy intellectual among American diplomats and State Department policy planners. Arendt did not write a separate contribution for the collection but commented at some length on several papers and participated in the discussion, though one also has the sense that she was holding back, since what was distinctive about *Origins* doesn't come through as clearly as it should in her comments.[12] Still, other than a note to Arendt saying that he looked forward to seeing her at her Walgreen Foundation Lectures in Chicago in the spring of 1956 and a reference to *The Human Condition* in his 1961 essay on Tocqueville, Riesman fell quiet about Arendt and her work subsequent to *Origins*. They were, it's fair to say, never close friends, but more like friendly acquaintances who appreciated what each had done for the other without taking it much further.

Social and Political Typologies

One important thing the correspondence with Riesman reveals is her persistent curiosity about American society and culture, along with her concern with developing a distinct idea of the political. Riesman's new typology of American social character, especially his idea that contemporary American society had witnessed the emergence of a new "other-directed" social type, particularly interested her. This led her to suggest that Riesman's great fondness for Tocqueville derived from the fact that the Frenchman had done more than anyone else to "think through the inherent implications of a society of complete equality."[13] When she asked if the other-directed individual believes that the "other" is the "ideal man" and thus makes the "average" into the "norm," she went on to add that, though individuals no longer believe in original sin, they think they are "sinners," in the "privacy" of their own thoughts. In her comments on the ethics and epistemology of American identity, her emphasis fell on the role of the ideal other. Less abstractly, Arendt wondered if Americans didn't derive their sense of self from their perception of the way others perceived them rather than cultivating independence in its own right. All this echoed the role theory of American psychoanalyst Harry Stack Sullivan and of sociologist Erving Goffman, not to mention the earlier work of George H. Mead. Yet there is no evidence that she had read them.[14]

Most interestingly, Arendt wondered how Riesman's concepts of inner- and other-directedness differed from what Tocqueville had observed about Americans in the 1830s:

> I have been wondering where the similarity between Tocqueville and your discoverings [sic] ends, and it seems to me that this craving [of Americans] for being loved and accepted is new after all. It seems to indicate a being lost in the world that is similar from [blacked out] the (otherwise very different) situation of my mass-men in Europe. What struck me in your paper is that people are not (even if they say so) satisfied with respect in their community, that they want more; they want here again the impossible, they want the active approval, amounting to friendship, of exactly everybody. And, of course, make friendship impossible because of this.[15]

Several things about Arendt's rich cluster of observations are worth unpacking. First, other-direction, for her, was not just a tendency to orient oneself to the reactions of others. It also involved the active attempt to solicit a positive response from them. Specifically, Americans desired not merely "respect" but to be "accepted," to receive "approval," and even to be "loved." Her use of the phrase "lost in the world" also sounds a common concern with loneliness among American intellectuals at the time. Interestingly, Arendt made these comments before Riesman's book assumed its final title, *The Lonely Crowd*. As late as June 14, 1949, Riesman was referring to his work in progress as "Passionless Existence in America," a title that hardly reflected a positive view of American society. Overall, Arendt's suggestion that Americans tried, in a self-defeating fashion, to compel affection or love was also a striking one.

Riesman's response to Arendt's close questioning indicated broad agreement. Regarding the question about average and norm, he agreed that Americans think "the average is the norm in the normative sense. And each feels he doesn't quite measure up. As against this, the European feels that his very non-normality is an achievement."[16] Thus where Americans felt guilty about standing out, Riesman contended that Europeans were proud to be different. Later, in his 1960 foreword to *The Lonely Crowd*, he elaborated on Arendt's comments on the American desire to be loved: "The other-directed person wants to be loved rather than esteemed; he wants not to gull or impress, let alone oppress, others but, in the current phrase, to relate to them; he seeks less a snobbish status in the eyes of others than assurance of being emotionally in tune with them."[17]

Yet by the 1960s, Riesman was eager to downplay the negative connotations of other-directedness, since many—including Arendt—considered his book a defense of old-fashioned nonconformity and the individualism associated with the fast disappearing inner-directed type. As he noted, "The negative aspects of these qualities [other-direction] have been overemphasized by many readers of *The Lonely Crowd*, and the positive aspects underemphasized."[18] Riesman's desire to right the negative balance here reminds us of his own ambivalence about other-directedness. As Wilfred McClay has emphasized, Riesman was powerfully affected by his exposure to Arendt's mass society analysis.[19] Erich Fromm's "marketer" or "marketing personality" was another source of Riesman's other-directed character type.[20] Clearly, Fromm was more negative about the marketing type than Riesman was about the other-directed individual. Yet, in his best seller, Riesman referred to the other-directed person's tendency to "overconform."[21]

Part of the problem here arose from the tension between the value-free language/jargon of other-direction and the morally (and politically) charged notion of conformity. Riesman was every bit as concerned with the problem of social conformity as Arendt was, but she also bridled at Riesman's acceptance of a certain social determinism behind the idea of other-direction. Of course, as Daniel Bell wrote in the mid-1950s, "no one in the United States defends conformity."[22] To remedy the lack of a normative character type in his schema, Riesman added the ideal of the "autonomous" character type, which assumed a certain distance from the constraints of social roles (other-directedness) *and* from the subtle strictures that went with introjected identities (inner-directedness). The problem was that autonomy lacked the social and historical groundedness of inner- and other-directedness. Riesman used the term "autonomy" as roughly synonymous with "self-consciousness," but it still seemed abstract and a bit bloodless.

For our purposes, the way Riesman and Arendt treated American politics and political culture was highly significant. As already noted, Arendt was always struck by "the fundamental anti-intellectualism [*Ungeistigkeit*] of the country." Indeed, the role of the intellectual was to resist the social conformity that permeated American life. Yet she praised the commitment to "freedom" in the United States and emphasized the way that ethnic pluralism helped protect dissenting political and social opinion. She was also impressed (as Tocqueville had been in the 1830s) with the way that Americans "felt responsible for public life in a way that I know of in no European country." Overall, her verdict was that the "fundamental contradiction of the country" lies in the coexistence of "political freedom" with "social servitude [*Knechtschaft*]."[23]

Arendt was particularly interested in the political typology Riesman had developed, specifically an early distinction between political "indignants" (what he later called the "moralists") and the "apathetic." In a letter of May 21, 1948, she speculated that the indignant type (not to be confused with the "politically concerned") was easily seduced by totalitarian movements because she or he placed too much faith in politics itself: the indignant "no longer conceives of politics as a limited affair." Arendt also suggested that the Soviet sphere had produced a third "functioning" type who transcended both moralizing and apathy. By simply learning to fit into the system, "spontaneity no longer exists."[24] Arendt would later refer to bureaucracy as "rule by Nobody."

More importantly, Arendt firmly rejected Riesman's identification of politics with the "personal satisfaction" of desires, including even the satisfaction derived from political participation. According to her, it was not as individuals seeking "personal satisfaction" but as "citizens" who "inhabit a common world" that we should act politically. "In politics," she asserted, "we are always concerned with something that 'transcends' the individual."[25] All this contrasted quite clearly with Riesman's liberal pluralist conception of politics as about power and interest satisfaction. Clearly Arendt's quasi-republican comments foreshadowed what was to come in her thought — the idea of the primacy of the political over the social, of the public over the private. The point of politics was not to work out the way to satisfy economic and social interests, much less to pursue individual happiness; rather it was a way of insuring that there was a public realm in which one could speak and act about public concerns. Politics was its own justification.

Later, in *The Lonely Crowd*, Riesman's "veto group" account of American politics assumed that, since the turn of the century, a coherent "business ruling class" had been replaced by a series of groups who competed for an "amorphous distribution of power."[26] Any notion of what C. Wright Mills would call a "power elite" was absent. In fact, Riesman was more sympathetic to John Kenneth Galbraith's idea that the American system was a system of "countervailing powers," most obviously the corporations, the unions, and the activist state.[27] The dominant ethos of inner-directed politics that stressed "morality" and/or "well-defined interests" had been superseded by what Riesman called the "inside dopester," the dominant political type within a liberal, other-directed society. In such a political culture, the average citizen assumes a detached position and revels in political gossip disseminated by inside dopesters and/or sees him or herself as part of a "veto group." Tolerance of competing groups rather than demonizing of opponents was the rule in other-directed political cultures, though this claim about the pluralist political culture was hardly an accurate prediction of the McCarthyite ethos of the 1950s.[28]

Yet, Riesman later admitted that veto-group liberalism could stifle political creativity and encouraged a quietism in which people "lack the conviction that things could be done any other way."[29] He also granted that the politics of morality was not without its value; and while apathy served as a form of resistance in a totalitarian context (a point he stressed against Arendt), it was less than desirable in a representative democracy. Finally, both Riesman's veto-group politics and Daniel Bell's nonmoralistic, "end of ideology" politics represented a serious misjudgment of the importance of a moral dimension in politics then and in the ensuing decade. As we shall see, Arendt was one of those who were favorably impressed by the New Left's reintroduction of moral concerns into American politics in the 1960s. As Riesman noted, minority rights in the veto-group conception of politics was a matter of each social group's ("Negro, Jewish and labor union defense organizations") organizing to defend its interests, with only the ACLU left to look out for the rights of the "stateless" and for "human rights."[30] That is, there was no overall protection of the public interest in veto-group liberalism.

Arendt and Mass Society

The theory of mass society has been largely forgotten since the 1960s, despite Daniel Bell's claim at the time that "Marxism apart, it is probably the most influential social theory in the Western world today."[31] In chapter 10 ("The Classless Society") of *Origins*, Arendt, whom Bell identified as a theorist of mass society, organized her account of the rise of totalitarianism and the revolution of nihilism around a mass society analysis.[32] Clearly Arendt needed a political sociology to underpin her political thought, a sense of how social forces and structures related to political values and institutions. With her mass society analysis, Arendt tried to wed a descriptive theory of society with a normative idea of politics and the political. Not surprisingly, there were problems with this since it was hard to see how her normative vision of politics could be realized in a mass society where conditions were so inimical to its realization. To complicate matters further, Arendt had a "hard" version of mass society analysis as it applied to the Europe catastrophe and a "soft" mass society analysis as it applied to postwar America

Though Bell identified mass society theory with a "romantic conservatism," there were clearly critiques of mass society and culture from the left—for example, from the Frankfurt School in exile in America. But what the radical and conservative critique shared was an objection to "the liberal individualism of the center" of contemporary Western society.[33] Bell's Columbia colleague, the radical sociologist, C. Wright Mills, also devoted a chapter in *The Power Elite* (1956) to an analysis of America as a mass society, which he pictured as one in which "the loss of a sense of structure and the submergence into powerless milieux is the cardinal fact." Moreover, Mills suggested that the "transformation of public into mass" entailed "the idea of an elite of power." In general, then, the theory of mass society assumed the coexistence of, but muffled conflict between, "elite" and "mass" rather than open class conflict.[34] Only with the reestablishment of a politics of publics could elite domination of politics be checked. Arendt's analysis was, if anything, closer to Mills's than to the cultural orientation of the Frankfurt School or to the conservative critique, which saw mass society as too democratic.

But most mass society analyses of postwar America fell in the liberal middle of the political spectrum and saw the "central problem" of a mass society to be one of "social alienation, or the distance between the individual and his society."[35] Mainstream mass society theory assumed that routine politics remained class and interest based. It was only in times of crisis that politics assumed a more ominous set of characteristics and potentialities. For instance, the anticommunist hysteria of the McCarthy period, the so-called second Red Scare, showed how the politics of irrationality, organized around symbolic, cultural, and psychological tensions, could overwhelm economic and social interests.[36] This helps explain, as H. Stuart Hughes has noted, the "tone of moral urgency" to much mass society theory, which was "prompted by anxiety and a sense of intellectual disorientation."[37] Arendt herself saw some value in such an analysis, since at least interest-group politics was still "worldly" in the way psychological and symbolic politics was not.

Indeed, a conservative version of an American critique of mass society involved a nostalgia for lost community, small town and rural cohesion, the town meeting, and a distaste for large-scale institutions of all sorts. Most dramatically, mass society was, Bell suggested, the society of "lonely crowds." From the perspective of mass society theory, "the United States," as Bell observed, "ought to be exceptionally vulnerable to the politics of disaffection . . . urbanization, industrialization, and democratization have eroded primary and community ties on a scale unprecedented in social history."[38]

Bell also suggested that there was a fascinating, if apparently contradictory, coexistence in mass society between "interdependence" among all sectors of society and a pervasive sense of alienation.

But Arendt's analysis was more intricate when she talked of the preconditions for the emergence of totalitarian movements. In the lengthy letter to Riesman of June 13, 1949, she suggested a greater American experience with the preconditions of mass society. "In Europe they had not yet time to develop their own character structure. The difference between America and Europe, is among others, that Europeans became 'masses' without developing a 'mass psychology'; this psychology was developed artificially by the totalitarian movements whose ideology fitted the objective conditions better than the individual psychology."[39] Her analysis here implies that Europeans were less prepared than American society for the emergence of a mass society, composed of "the fragments of a highly atomized society whose competitive structure and concomitant loneliness" were no longer assuaged by "membership in a class."[40] Such a society had emerged out of the rubble of World War I and included a relatively new phenomenon—large numbers of stateless and homeless people. In such a situation,

> masses are not held together by a consciousness of common interest and they lack the specific class articulateness which is expressed in determined, limited, and obtainable goals. The term masses applies only where we deal with people who either because of sheer numbers, or difference, or a combination of both, cannot be integrated into any organization based on common interest, into political parties or municipal governments or professional organizations or trade unions.[41]

She concluded from this that the social psychology of mass man was not characterized by any greater amount of "brutality and backwardness, but isolation and lack of normal social relationships."[42] Mass men were largely immune to the normal politics of (class) interests, incapable, as it were, of social reality testing. Thus, mass society was formed by a "great unorganized, structure-less mass of furious individuals." They were marked by "self-centered bitterness" combined with "Selflessness." They had the "feeling of being expendable" and had "contempt" for "common sense." Curiously, they had a "passionate inclination toward the most abstract notions as guides for life."[43] That is, the class consciousness of mass men was replaced by paranoia-tinged, comprehensive ideologies. This social psychological profile of European mass men and women also fit the protofascist writers and intellectuals, who often allied themselves with what she referred to as "the mob." She described the ideology of these "armed bohemians" as a "kind of political expressionism."[44] Lacking a stable world of shared values, intellectuals vacillated, as men of action, between the "primacy of sheer action and the overwhelming force of sheer necessity."[45] The result was the emergence of a political culture of terrorism in which political action was defined by violence not speech.

And yet Arendt made clear in *Origins* that this ideological and cultural situation was primarily European. In fact, she insisted that the hard version of mass society theory did not apply to America; nor was mass society another name for egalitarian societies, not, at least, America's. Evoking Tocqueville's "equality of condition," she wrote: "The masses, contrary to prediction, did not result from growing equality of condition, from the spread of general education and its inevitable lowering of standards and popularization of content. America, the classical land of equality of condition and of general education with all its shortcomings, knows less of the modern psychology of masses than perhaps any other country in the world."[46] Clearly, Americans had been inoculated, as it were, against the panic reaction to the collapse of European society, though Arendt never spelled out exactly how Americans escaped the extreme effects of having become a mass society. There was also certainly nothing in Arendt's analysis that recalled Martin Heidegger's proclivity for seeing America (and the Soviet Union) as the very symptom and source of the decline of the West.

Not surprisingly, critics of mass society analysis have always objected to its minimizing of class differences, especially when analyzing the social bases of National Socialism. Specifically, as Peter Baehr notes, the claim about the "dissolution" of classes and social de-structuring was not supported by empirical evidence from interwar Germany. Rather, support for the Nazis "cut across class lines."[47] Of course, Arendt never identified the masses with any one class and certainly not with the working class. The psychology of living in a mass society was fueled by, and generated *ressentiment* and anxiety across class lines. What it registered was the waning of explicit class consciousness not the disappearance of classes as such. This social and psychological anxiety found expression in symbolic issues and/or matters of cultural and racial identity (anticommunism, racial and ethnic prejudice, rural-urban cultural tensions, secularization): in sum, it was bound up with a hostility to cultural modernity.[48]

Riesman was fascinated by the mass society idea and showered Arendt with examples that he thought showed the similarities between America and Europe on this matter. His long handwritten letter (thirteen pages) of August 26, 1949, contained a flurry of topics and suggestions: the possibility of including more material on American Jews; discussions of race and class; the American Civil War; British colonialism in India; musings on Marx, class, and state; thoughts on Lionel Trilling's novel, *The Middle of the Journey*; and the phenomenon of "proletarian worship." As he said in a further (typed) set of remarks he wrote that same day: "Much is to be said for using your footnotes for analogies of this sort to contemporary America," though he recognized how long Arendt's manuscript had already become.[49]

Two of his subsequent letters that autumn suggested that the Okies in the 1930s and the Puerto Ricans in postwar New York were examples of the "superfluous" people Arendt argued were present in a society vulnerable to totalitarian rule. Riesman also speculated about the possible relationship between the passage of the Johnson-Reed Act of 1924, restricting the number of immigrants into America (and favoring northern Europeans), and the subsequent difficulty the superfluous peoples in Europe, for example, Jews and Roma, had in finding refuge in the United States. He compared Theodore Roosevelt to T. E. Lawrence as a kind of "adventurer," not a million miles away from the "secret agent and imperialist" whose world Arendt analyzed in *Origins*.[50] As late as September 1949, Riesman was still wondering whether conformity was "bred into the new type of character" or "to what extent is it merely a matter of behavior."[51]

From Mass Society to the Social

But Arendt generally resisted these European-American parallels. Still, aspects of Arendt's mass society analysis, in both its soft and hard versions, paralleled the political sociology of McCarthyism and the radical right as they emerged in the 1950s.[52] The rhetoric of mass society theory turned up sporadically in Arendt's writings after *Origins*, but she didn't really develop it much further. In her controversial essay on the Little Rock desegregation crisis, first written in 1957 but published in 1959, Arendt identified the way mass society "blurs lines of discrimination and levels group distinction." Conformity, she granted, was present in any society, but it is more threatening in an ethnically diverse America where "social conformism tends to become an absolute and a substitute for national homogeneity."[53] This was a plausible, even shrewd, point, though she didn't speculate as to why some groups, such as African Americans, were excluded even more decisively when ethnic lines became generally blurred.

The concluding paragraph of her essay "The Concept of History" (1958) struck an even more somber note. There she spoke of the "twofold loss of the world—the loss of nature and the loss of human artifice in the widest sense which would include all history." Echoing her earlier piece "Ideology and Terror," she characterized mass society in terms of "desperate lonely separation," of being "pressed together into a mass," a formulation that (rather awkwardly) yoked Riesman, Thoreau, and her own work together. One of her more explicit characterizations of mass society described it as "nothing more than that kind of organized living which automatically establishes itself among human beings who are still related to one another but have lost the world once common to all of them."[54] There is little difference between this kind of diagnosis and the quest for community theme that was so common in postwar American thought.

Yet, it is hard to see where Arendt could have gone with the mass society analysis as such. The history of the politics of freedom that emerged in *On Revolution* (1963) put the focus back to the late eighteenth century before the historical emergence of mass society. Besides the Greek polis and the Framers' republican vision, Arendt suggested near the end of *On Revolution* that the participatory impulse of the workers councils would be "the best instruments, for example, for breaking up the modern mass society" and "pseudo-political mass movements." But writing later, in the mid-1960s, Irving Howe noted that Arendt's mass society analysis in *Origins* "lacked a sense of the dynamic that might lead to a disintegration from within or transformation from without."[55] On her account, America as a mass society was hardly fertile ground for participatory politics. And, as already mentioned, Arendt had a hard time spelling out at what point and in what way a social group or movement became a political group acting for the public good.

Surprisingly, Arendt responded positively to Raymond Williams's largely favorable, but somewhat critical, review of *Between Past and Future* in the fall of 1961. In his review, Williams noted two different definitions of mass society in Arendt's writing, one stressing a general loss of faith that formerly linked members of a society together and one stressing a society becoming more democratic and inclusive. More importantly, Williams noted her failure to mention the causal importance of capitalism in the emergence of mass society. Arendt took the trouble to thank him for his review: "How re-assuring to see that one has spotted my illegitimate use of 'mass society.'" "Nobody ever caught me" before, "my trouble" being "that I don't quite understand it" and "don't know what to do with it." With this kind of uncertainty, no wonder the idea of a comprehensive analysis came a cropper. (It should never be said that Arendt was incapable of taking criticism).[56] Still, Arendt was hardly alone in failing to spell out the conditions under which something like an authentic politics was possible in a mass society. Not only Mills, but also Paul Goodman and Herbert Marcuse diagnosed the problem with considerable power and insight yet offered no way out of the dilemma. Thus well into the 1960s, despite the way the Civil Rights Movement and the emerging New Left chipped away at America's self-congratulatory image, fundamental change seemed hard to imagine.

One thing missing in all these analyses was the idea of a key social group that would play the role that the proletariat once had in Marxist analyses of bourgeois society. Later, the New Left would spend much time and thought on trying to identify a new *Träger* (carrier) of fundamental change. At times Arendt seemed to assign great importance to the critical spirit of intellectuals. Yet she had already been deeply disappointed by the failure of German intellectuals and academics, especially Martin Heidegger, to resist the Nazis and the reluctance of left-wing intellectuals to ignore the seductions of the Soviet idea. Philosophers, she thought, were incapable of dealing with political matters. In the 1960s, she was quite sympathetic with the student movement, but she saw it mainly as symptomatic of contemporary political and social frustration and hardly the stuff from which revolutions were made.

What happened was that Arendt gradually recast (and renamed) her mass society analysis without dropping the terminology entirely. What she had once called "mass society" was incorporated into her concept of "the social" in *The Human Condition* and *On Revolution*. Assuming a greater significance but more vague meaning, the social became a placeholder for all that Arendt considered negative about contemporary life. Originally, for her, the bourgeoisie was the enemy, while the working class had been neutralized and fragmented under totalitarianism. In fact, Riesman called her out on her "animus" against the "bourgeoisie and the liberal."[57] The other destination of her critique of modern society was in her analysis of the bureaucrat-manager of the Final Solution, Adolph Eichmann. Instead of authentic politics, bureaucracy—the rule by Nobody—exercised faceless power without personal responsibility. Large-scale bureaucracy seemed destined to be the chief form of rule in mass society. Eichmann, the "desk murderer," was a sign of what was to come. Yet this reading of Eichmann, to which we will come, was never really developed to any degree by Arendt either.

Perhaps Europeans such as Arendt were particularly prone to forget that race, ethnicity, and religion had historically been among the main social sources of meaning, companionship, rejuvenation, cultural stimulation, even protection to individuals and groups in America (and elsewhere). Arendt did important work with the Jewish-owned and -run Schocken Press in the 1940s and her efforts at retrieving the stolen culture treasures of European Jewry late in the 1940s were invaluable, but Arendt never identified with *American* Jewry as a cultural community. Loyalty to Judaism or Jewishness came too close to something like racial loyalty, which was anathema to her. At best, she could imagine others choosing to be so committed but not really herself. As already seen, Gershom Scholem accused her of a certain "heartless, frequently almost sneering and malicious tone" toward Israel in her writing about Eichmann. There was in it "little trace of" what Scholem called "love of the Jewish people."[58] He was wrong here, but Arendt's specific interest in American Jewish life—aside from the examples already noted—was pretty hard to detect.

My larger point here is that even radical politics in America has been intimately related to religious and racial-ethnic experience, to the social in an extended sense, right from the beginning. If the idea of a strict separation of church and state became constitutional doctrine over the course of the nineteenth century, American politics has always been marked by an overlap between religion and politics. The Puritan "errand into the wilderness" and the "covenant" concept, the religiosity of the Protestant-led abolitionist movements of the mid-nineteenth century, and the black-led Southern Civil Rights Movement of the 1950s and 1960s all exemplified the way that the initial goals of religious and/or racial groups could be transformed into values identified with legal and political universality. Finally, the intimate connection between the social and the political spheres throughout American history itself suggests, against Arendt, that the relationship between the two spheres was, and is, complementary rather than as adversarial.

CHAPTER 6

Arendt and Postwar American Thought

Hannah Arendt's relationship to the postwar American intellectual and academic scene was hardly straightforward. She had been thoroughly disillusioned by the craven response of German gentile academics to the rise of National Socialism and the expulsion of Jews from academic positions. Having also been shaped by the freewheeling intellectuality of Weimar Germany and finding a similar atmosphere among New York intellectuals, she tended to view a regular academic position as a way of playing it safe.[1] Generally, her postwar publishing history shows a largely fruitful tension between her role as a public intellectual aiming for a general audience such as that of the *New Yorker* and as a political theorist whose articles appeared in academic journals. For instance, not only was Arendt's *The Origins of Totalitarianism* reviewed widely in academic publications, she even appeared on the cover of the *Saturday Review* (March 24, 1951) when it was published.

When Arendt did begin part-time teaching in the 1950s, she tended to teach political theory/thought in political science, government or politics departments rather than in philosophy departments. For her, this choice had to do with the conflict between what she saw as the worldliness of politics and Western philosophy's orientation to the transcendent and eternal, that is, its otherworldliness. "Kant," she insisted, "is the exception."[2] About politics, one had to take sides and make judgments; with metaphysics or natural philosophy this was not necessary. Her work was located at the intersection of politics and sociology, history and philosophy and in this resembled Machiavelli's *Discourses* on *Livy's History of Rome*, Montesquieu's *The Spirit of the Laws*, Burke's *Reflections on the Revolution in France*, Tocqueville's *Democracy in America*, and *The Federalist Papers*.[3] Such works were hybrids that located themselves within the world that she so valued. Besides that, logical positivism and then analytical philosophy swept into power in American philosophy departments in the early postwar years, and Arendt would certainly not have felt at home in them. Symptomatic here is the fact that the work of Martin Heidegger was brought to America by theologians such as Paul Tillich and the Protestant divinity schools rather than by mainstream philosophers.[4]

After the war, there were further splits within political science departments between political theory, on the one hand, and, on the other, political science, dominated by the "behavioralists" who concentrated on study of "voting behavior, political parties, interest-group activities, decision-making in institutions." (The terms "positivist" and "empiricist" were rough synonyms for behavioralism.) The behavioralists sought to make their work compatible with a broadly scientific approach involving "objectivity, detachment, fidelity to fact, and deference to intersubjective verification by a community of practitioners."[5] Not surprisingly, they were less than enthusiastic about the value of political thought, political theory, or political philosophy. Clearly Arendt's work belonged with the political theorists, such as émigrés Leo Strauss and Eric Voegelin, and a growing number of younger scholars including Sheldon S. Wolin and, slightly later, Hanna Fenichel Pitkin, Judith Shklar, and Michael Walzer. By the 1960s, there was also a (less serious) split within the theory camp between the epic or narrative approach to political thought, which typically began with the Greeks, and those who were influenced by analytical philosophy, such as Pitkin and her use of Wittgenstein, Shklar and her grounding in American and modern French political thought, and a rare example of a theorist grounded in socialist and Marxist thought, Walzer.[6]

Yet there was also a broader tradition of twentieth-century American thought with which Arendt also needs to be connected. Clearly by the late 1950s the progressive-liberal tradition of American thought was on the wane and there had been a new conservative turn, as analyzed by Morton White.[7] This raises the question of how Arendt's thought stood in relationship to these homegrown figures and movements of the 1950s, particularly with pragmatism in light of the historical tension between American and German thought.

Arendt as a Counterprogressive

American political and social thought underwent a sea change after World War II. It had already come under fire in the 1930s from Marxists for its bourgeois individualism and opposition to socialism; from conservative, often Catholic, traditionalists offended by its relativism and naturalism; and from many European émigrés who brought a decidedly antiliberal bias to the New World. In particular, it was the philosopher of pragmatism, John Dewey, along with sociological jurisprudence and legal realism, economic interpretations of history and culture, and positivism in the social sciences that bore the brunt of the criticism. The most important work to seriously address this shift in the intellectual orientation of the postwar period was Morton White's *Social Thought in America: The Revolt against Formalism* ([1949] 1957). In it, the Harvard philosopher examined five figures— Dewey; the jurist Oliver Wendell Holmes; economist and cultural analyst, Thorstein Veblen; and two "progressive" historians, Charles Beard and James Harvey Robinson—who formed the backbone of the tradition of progressive/liberal political thought from the late nineteenth century down to the 1950s. Though differing among themselves, their body of work had been broadly devoted to challenging the social inequality that resulted from class and economic conflict. They basically believed in the power of the social sciences to chart the best path to social progress and they believed in the use of state power to implement the changes needed to make American society a more equal one.

However, White made the point, particularly in the 1957 edition of his book, that this tradition was increasingly out of touch with the mood of the country as reflected in the emergence of an intellectually respectable conservatism and a liberal realism that owed more to the Reformation than to the Enlightenment. As higher education in general and specialized research in particular flourished, America's philosophy—pragmatism—was also losing its place of honor in university philosophy departments. Perhaps because White was a philosopher doing intellectual history, he slighted the historical context related to the Cold War and the aftermath of the Holocaust as possible explanations for the change in mood in the country.

White's assessment of liberal-progressive thought was far from uncritical, but he was clearly sympathetic with the broad vision informing it. Each figure had challenged late nineteenth-century formalistic modes of thought, that is, the mind-set that emphasized deductive logic and internal consistency over concrete historical realities; abstracted ideas from their historical context; and concentrated on the origins rather than the development of an idea. The formalist style was linked, he proposed, to "logic, abstraction, deduction, mathematics and mechanics," while being opposed to history, the idea of "cultural organism," and "life, experience, process, growth, context, function."[8] Antiformalistic liberal thought contrasted "real" with "formal" freedom and was "deeply concerned with the economic aspects of society."[9] Philosophically, liberal/progressive thought identified the "real" with underlying social and economic forces and structures. The purpose of social analysis, then, was to penetrate to that reality in order to better understand how change could be brought about.

White's 1957 edition of *Social Thought in America* also contained a new preface and a long (thirty-three-page) epilogue that discussed new conservative trends in political and social thought. By the 1950s, Dewey's instrumentalism and Holmes's realist demystification of the law, Veblen's bracing skepticism about idealism and philanthropy, and Beard's hard-nosed analysis of the motives of the Framers of the Constitution were being marginalized by two ideas in particular—"original sin" as proposed by Protestant theologian Reinhold Niebuhr and "natural law" as championed by one-time progressive intellectual and journalist, Walter Lippmann. Underlying these two concepts, suggested White, were two basic questions: "what is man like?" and "what man should do?"[10]

Niebuhr especially claimed to be offering a new realism about human nature to challenge the "soft-headed, complacent, dreary, secular liberalism" of Dewey, even though the debunking mentality of a Beard or Veblen would have presented more of a challenge to Niebuhr.[11] Symptomatically, where progressive social thought once identified realism with social change, realism now referred to a skeptical attitude toward social, political, and economic reforms. Niebuhr's Christian realism in foreign policy (and moderate liberal stance on domestic issues, including civil rights) comported well with the perspectives of intellectual-diplomat George F. Kennan and German-Jewish émigré Hans Morgenthau (a friend of Arendt's) that stressed the limits to American power at home and abroad but also the need to contain Soviet expansion. More importantly, where liberal Christian theology had once been identified with the homegrown Social Gospel—a theological and institutional movement that emphasized the importance of Christianity in abolishing social inequality and bringing about a more just society—postwar theology now found its bearings from Swiss theologian Karl Barth's neo-orthodox theology. The gap between God and human beings and a prudent realism, not the quest for social justice, were features of the new Protestantism. Catholic intellectuals were attracted to the neo-scholasticism that underpinned the authority of the Catholic Church, while Jewish social theorist Will Herberg was close temperamentally and theologically to Niebuhr.

Not surprisingly, Dewey's most pugnacious follower, Sidney Hook, saw this postwar resurgence of religion as a "failure of nerve," while liberal David Riesman praised postwar utopian intellectuals such as Paul Goodman for having "the nerve of failure."[12] Still, where the scientific method, guided by experimentalism and fallibilism, had once provided the model for intellectual work, a newly emergent natural law tradition looked to the metaphysical/religious origins of morality and the epistemology of "self-evidence" in moral and speculative matters.[13] All this was a far cry from the hostility to natural law and natural rights of Oliver Wendell Holmes Jr., one of the founders of legal realism. For Holmes, such notions functioned as protection for private and corporate property and were metaphysical moonshine. In fact, for Morton White, Lippmann's commitment to natural law was a form of dogmatism that did not, because it could not, argue the case for self-evidence. White's nice throwaway judgment was: "It is not self-evident that there are self-evident principles of natural law."[14]

With this retreat to theological and metaphysical ideas duly noted, where did Arendt fit into this story of the rise and fall of modern liberal thought? It is not easy to say. One problem was that White's choice of the two new conservatives was a bit puzzling. It may have arisen from the fact that both Niebuhr and Lippmann were once progressives, even socialists, or that both were American thinkers rather than Weimar refugees. Otherwise, the émigré political philosopher, Leo Strauss, as reflected in *Natural Right and History* (1953), was a more intellectually formidable proponent of natural law than Lippmann and either Richard Weaver or Russell Kirk was a more interesting, and genuinely conservative, thinker than Lippmann. Still, Arendt's commitment to rethinking the Western tradition and her rejection of teleological conceptions of history distanced her from the idea of progress associated with American progressivism.[15] Her emphasis on the unintended consequences of political action and policy anticipated a central claim of the neoconservatives of the 1970s. Generally, the cast of her thought brought to mind the Spanish philosopher José Ortega y Gassett's pronouncement: "Hence I no longer believe in any ideas except those ideas of shipwrecked men."[16] With the exception of William James in certain moods and possibly Oliver Wendell Holmes, most American liberals and progressives simply did not seem to be "shipwrecked men." Certainly none of them focused on the political relevance of evil or thematized the loneliness of modern man and the appeal of totalitarianism. Both Arendt's mentors had been critical figures in creating the crisis vocabulary of modernism.[17] Needless to say, the experience of most (white) American thinkers bore little resemblance to what she experienced as a Jewish refugee from Hitler's Germany.

Not a few readers of *Origins* thought that her commitment to a mass society analysis betrayed a certain skepticism about egalitarian ideals and democracy. Yet, as we have seen, Arendt refused to equate American egalitarianism with mass society as such and thus rejected the easy conservative (and often European) claim that equality in America led inevitably to political disaster. As she observed once, "the fact, indeed, that a travesty of equality prevails under all despotic governments has led many good people into the error of believing that from equality springs tyranny or dictatorship."[18] Yet, Arendt *was* suspicious of the strong state so feared by the new American conservatives and old liberals on both sides of the Atlantic, going all the way back to Tocqueville.[19] Moreover, her controversial piece questioning forced school desegregation in Little Rock in 1957 revealed an admiration

for American federalism, which was close to the hearts of American conservatives, insofar as it diffused, rather than concentrated, state power (and,
for Southern conservatives, protected segregation). Like a certain type of
sophisticated conservative, she was also suspicious of grand abstractions and
the attempt to cut the cloth of society and polity to fit those abstractions.
As Margaret Canovan has put it, Arendt shared with Michael Oakeshott
and Edmund Burke (and I would add Philip Rieff) a political vision "that
is concerned with limits: limits to natural processes and to human hubris."[20]

Moreover, Arendt rejected the Marxist and the progressive-liberal tendency to identify the real with what lay below the surface or behind the
appearance of things. Hers was not a three-story model of the universe;
rather, both reduction down to material reality and idealization up to spiritual reality were "unworldly" to her and thus inimical to the political. In
other words, Arendt was always suspicious of the claim that reality was
somewhere else than *in* the world. This meant that she might have been
suspicious of a certain cynicism in Holmes's thought. Though her library
included nothing by Holmes, she did own a copy of Veblen's *The Theory
of the Leisure Class* (1899), whose influence was detectable in her critique
of consumer society in *The Human Condition* in 1958. Beard's *Economic
Interpretation of the Constitution* (1913) was also in her library, but she was
put off by Beard, who was, she noted in *On Revolution*, "obsessed by the
unmasking of the Founding Fathers." This reminded her of the attacks
on hypocrisy that helped create the climate within which "The Terror in
the French Revolution" flourished.[21] Where Beard's interpretation of the
Framers' work stressed the politics of self-interest, Arendt basically ignored
the economic interpretation of the Declaration of Independence and the
Constitution. Her conclusion was that the Founders had been uniquely
creative and liberating political thinkers/actors. In fact, she lacked a concept
such as ideology (Marx) or defense mechanisms (Freud) or *ressentiment*
(Nietzsche) that could generate a totalizing critique of the world.

Arendt's commitment to the primacy of the political also worked against
the grain of progressivism's and liberalism's emphasis on social and economic reform. Like many of her Weimar compatriots, Arendt was suspicious
of "party and interest politics."[22] While *On Revolution* stressed the dangers
of a politics devoted to the social question, progressive political thought

assumed that both the law and politics were instruments to alleviate, even abolish, poverty and want. More surprisingly, Arendt lacked a strong concept of social justice.[23] Had she pronounced on it, she might have characterized liberal political thought as an ideology of public housekeeping that could easily grow less benign when it sought to reconstruct reality, a sure recipe, she thought, for the triumph of authoritarian forces.

And yet there were (and are) problems with seeing Arendt as a conservative too. She was hostile, to the emergence of consumer capitalism in postwar America, what Lizabeth Cohen has called "the Consumer Republic," and in *Origins* blamed European imperialist expansion on the European capitalist economies.[24] She also took her cue from Montesquieu, making equality the central principle in the political realm and arguably desirable in the social sphere.[25] More importantly, her essay on Hungary made clear that Arendt's master ideal was political action/political freedom. Her discussion of politics in terms of participation and new beginnings presupposes, rather than rejects, revolutionary contexts—the great late eighteenth-century revolutions; the council system of government that kept appearing in nineteenth- and twentieth-century Europe; and self-organizing grassroots movements in the United States, Latin America, and Africa, particularly South Africa. Her concept of freedom was implicitly, if not explicitly, democratic, though she preferred to call it republican. In short, it was, and is, difficult to formulate any sort of conservatism that would accommodate Arendt's normative theory of politics.

Nor did Arendt, a nonobservant Jew, set much store in the various revivals of religion, which have been at or near the top of conservative wish lists, despite Philip Rieff's shrewd analysis of *Origins* as a book that announced a religious, not just a political and cultural, crisis.[26] To some, the weight she placed on the cultural implosion of European moral stability after World War I sounded conservative. But it says volumes about the intellectual limitations of the secular view of the world that it could never quite understand why the modern loss of moral and religious certainty was such a problem for large numbers of people and left them vulnerable to the totalitarian temptation. In commenting on Eric Voegelin's view that totalitarianism was a "substitute for the lost creed of traditional beliefs," she suggested that "those who conclude from the frightening events of our time that we have got to go back to religion and faith for political reasons seem to show just as much lack of faith in God as do their opponents."[27] From this perspective, Lippmann's commitment to natural law and Niebuhr's to original sin, along with the later idea of civil religion proposed by Robert Bellah, appeared to Arendt as equally unsatisfactory solutions to real problems. For instance, the defense of civil religion clearly reflects a pragmatic judgment of religion, which must justify itself in terms of its use value.

Nor, as a Jew did she set any store by the Christian idea of original sin that Niebuhr made so much of, even though she revived, almost single-handedly, a concern with evil in a secular world. Original sin really explained too much and too little, though her analysis of Melville's *Billy Budd* showed a fascination with the possible effects of evil on a body politic. White himself noted that it was hard to see how the idea of sin actually influenced Niebuhr's politics; some have asked a similar question of Arendt's concept of evil. But Arendt's notion of evil was not a religious one that depended on transcendent justification. She formulated it in situ, as it were, and then waited for challenges—which did in fact arrive. She did come close to a metaphysical sense of "humanity" in proposing the idea of a right to have rights and helped put the idea of "crimes against humanity" into general circulation in her book on the Eichmann trial. But unlike Strauss or Voegelin, Arendt never spent much time trying to find or develop philosophical foundations for these notions. After all, this was what she meant when she said that people had to learn to think "without bannisters."

Arendt was well aware that she was suspected of being a conservative, since she was a firm opponent of progressive education and a conservative in cultural matters. But, she distinguished these positions from being a political conservative when she wrote that "in politics . . . this conservative attitude—which accepts the world as it is, striving only to preserve the status quo—can only lead to destruction, because the world, in gross and in detail, is irrevocably delivered up to the ruin of time unless human beings are determined to intervene, to alter, to create what is new."[28] Thus, for Arendt, it was precisely the worldliness of the world that clinched the argument against political conservatism. But it was only really with *On Revolution* (1963) that her political stance as a modern day republican became clear.

Arendt, Dewey, and Pragmatism

But there were aspects of Arendt's thought that placed her in close proximity to John Dewey and the pragmatists without making her one of them. Except for a short review of a minor Dewey text in 1946, Arendt seems to have shied away from his work. In her review, she expressed bafflement at Dewey's tendency to focus exclusively on the evils of laissez-faire economics and the minimal state, when the experience of totalitarianism had taught that "hell can be properly established only through the very opposite of laissez faire, through scientific planning." She also questioned Dewey's unquestioning attitude toward the application of science as a kind of deus ex machina to human affairs, as though humans themselves weren't the creators of science.[29] For her, Dewey seemed to either say the unexceptionable or the unacceptable.

Otherwise, the strongest Arendtian statement against what she took to be pragmatism came in her 1958 essay "Crisis in Education," where she took a broad and extended swipe at progressive education. Arendt considered her essay to be a way of clarifying her thoughts on "education in a mass society" and under the sway of the "concept of equality." For her America was a society where parents were estranged from their traditional roles and there was a general loss of institutional loyalty and cultural traditions.[30] Moreover, progressive education, which was firmly mainstream after 1945, began to come under steady attack for the failures of American children to learn to read (*Why Johnny Can't Read*) and the way Soviet science had outstripped America by launching Sputnik in 1957. Specifically, John Dewey had already come under attack before the war for allegedly weakening the national will to resist fascism and totalitarianism.[31] Yet, as Robert Westbrook has insisted, Dewey had not been actively involved in rethinking American education for quite a while and by the late 1930s he was writing that "it is unrealistic to suppose that schools can be the main agency" of change in American society.[32]

In contrast with Richard Hofstadter's head-on attack on Dewey in his *Anti-Intellectualism in American Life* (1964), Arendt did not mention Dewey by name, but she did explicitly refer to progressive education and to pragmatism. She described her position as "conservatism in the sense of conservation." Formal education should be conservative so that students would be equipped to know the world they would later want to change. Adults should "teach children what the world is like and not . . . instruct them in the art of living." The ultimate goal of education was one of "renewing a common world."[33] Specifically, she objected to three things about progressive education. First, there was the assumption that the school is "a child's world and a society formed among children." Child-centered education privileged the group over the individual child and the children over the teacher. It was "the tyranny of the majority" in action. Child centeredness arose in a society where conventional roles based on parental and adult authority had collapsed.[34] Second, Arendt explicitly referred to "modern psychology and the tenets of pragmatism" in her objection to the way that teaching had become "wholly emancipated from the actual material being taught." Under progressive education, a teacher was "a man who can simply teach anything; his training is in teaching, not in the mastery of any subject."[35] This led, she asserted, to problems, particularly in public high schools, where knowledge becomes specialized and subjects or disciplines need to be clearly demarcated.

Her third criticism was directed at the assumption that found "its systematic conceptual expression in pragmatism"—"that you can know and understand only what you have done yourself." At issue here was the substitution of "doing for learning" and the replacement of "knowledge" with "skill." In addition, "play" instead of "work," a distinction usually couched in terms of activity versus passivity, was emphasized. Overall, her most damning point was that, instead of preparing children for the world, progressive education meant that children were "debarred from the world of grown-ups." (This was later to fuel the claims about the "generation gap" in the 1960s).[36] Thus, by its own standards, progressive education failed and, according to Arendt, pragmatism bore some responsibility for it.

As already noted Arendt emerged as an intellectual force in American life just as pragmatism was losing its intellectual prestige in general. One problem was that pragmatism had come to mean whatever people wanted it to mean. As John P. Diggins has stressed, pragmatism came to mean so many different things by the 1950s and 1960s that it is hard to arrive at a single, agreed on meaning. Besides being a philosophical position, it was a form of pernicious relativism to conservatives, synonymous with opposition to "ideology" to liberal Cold Warriors, and just another name for political realism in defense of the war in Vietnam. Moreover, the Cold War was a time for certainties rather than openness. Thus, as Louis Menand has observed, "tolerance," which he placed at the heart of pragmatism, seemed passé in the postwar political climate. Among New York intellectuals, Dewey had a certain amount of influence over the years but not enough to receive a major defense from that quarter. His main champion, Sidney Hook, and Arendt did not get along, to put it mildly. Daniel Bell, with whom Arendt was on good terms, identified Dewey as one of his "masters," and Howard Brick notes that Bell "embraced John Dewey's philosophy of 'democracy as a way of life.'" Beyond that, Paul Goodman was a firm defender of radical forms of progressive education, but perhaps was too radical for Dewey, while C. Wright Mills had written his PhD on the sociology of pragmatism.[37] But one way or the other, Dewey and pragmatism had lost their cachet.

Indeed, no one then or now would have ever taken Dewey and Arendt for intellectual soul mates. Dewey was a lumper, who never encountered a dualism he didn't want to deconstruct, while Arendt was someone who insisted on making the kind of distinctions, especially between public and private, the ethical and the political, and the social and the political, that Dewey most decidedly rejected. Though Arendt was interested in modern science and technology, she was suspicious of their direct application to human affairs. But there were enough similarities between Arendt's thought and pragmatism, especially Dewey's version, to make comparisons interesting. She most resembled the pragmatists in her objection to combining politics with final truth and fixed dogma and in her commitment to pluralism. What Dewey called naturalism, Arendt referred to as worldliness. Richard Bernstein has recently referred to the tradition they shared as "pragmatic fallibilism."[38] Both Arendt and Dewey tended to consider the vocation of thought to be one of discovering meaning not truth. As Dewey put it: "Meaning is wider in scope as well as more precious in value than is truth, and philosophy is occupied with meaning rather than with truth. . . . Truths are but one class of meanings."[39]

Most saliently, Arendt and Dewey made the concept of action central in their thought. Dewey's contrast between (positive) freedom as "action in accord with the consciousness of fixed law" and freedom as "meaning a universe in which there is real uncertainty and contingency, a world which is not all in, and never will be" where we continually "make this new experiment and that fresh effort"[40] chimed with the spirit of Arendt's thought with its concern with new beginnings and unknown outcomes. To be sure, she never used the trope "experiment" to describe what action was *like* and *for*. But the emphasis on contingency was similar. Still, while Dewey tended to stress the instrumental value of acting, Arendt emphasized its self-revelatory value and as a good in itself in her early conceptions of action. She was more likely to associate instrumentalist activity, a concern with means and ends, with the realm of work rather than with action. Yet later, when she became more concerned with political and moral judgment, she stressed not the intentions behind but the impact and implications of action, including its chances of success. In terms of institutional considerations, Robert Westbrook has underlined Dewey's strong interest in "non-statist radicalism," as contrast to his one-time image as a big-government, strong-state man. Specifically Dewey evoked Jefferson's "proposed ward system" in which "every man would then share in the government of affairs not merely on election day but every day." Readers of *On Revolution* will know that Arendt saw the failure to incorporate mechanisms of ongoing participation as the great failure of the Constitution—and made direct reference to Jefferson's idea of the ward system. And like both Arendt and C. Wright Mills, Dewey bemoaned "the eclipse of the public."[41]

There were other areas where similarities (and differences) show up. Even though Arendt rejected history as the story of progress, thus putting her at odds with the spirit of progressivism, her emphasis on natality, the appearance of new human life, meant that much of her thought and action was oriented toward the future—and the present. But, for her, tradition and the past in general were also repositories of exemplars that could inform and inspire the present. Constructing a story of the past was a way of preparing to act toward the future. One might be able to get something like this out of pragmatism, but that was by no means a natural way of interpreting Dewey's consignment of much of the history of philosophy to the scrap heap.

The liberal-progressive rejection of formalism and Arendt's rejection of ideology bore a certain similarity. Ideology, which tended toward extreme logicality, was a kind of abstraction run rampant. One of the key terms of pragmatism and liberal political thought—"experience"—was also important for Arendt. Yet, it is hard to find in Morton White's book, or in any other postwar pragmatist's work, much awareness that the postwar decline of liberal/progressive thought had any connection with the experience of totalitarianism. Writing in the early 1950s, Arendt also seemed to fear that a nascent version of the "stringent logicality" marking totalitarian ideologies could find its way into a pragmatism heavily influenced by "the new logical movement in philosophy," which itself "grew out of pragmatism." But she went on to say that pragmatism preserved contact with "experience" and hence remained in touch with "common sense." Thus pragmatism entailed action (not contemplation) as "truth-revealing." In this particular discussion, Arendt seemed to vacillate between seeing pragmatism as a form of opportunism that stressed success above all else and pragmatism as a more or less philosophical position.[42]

This reminds us, I think, of the gap between Arendt's experience of the world and what a Dewey or James might have experienced growing up in America as white, Protestant, well-educated, and privileged. (With W. E. B. Du Bois and Alain Locke, who had strong links with pragmatism, the differences were not, perhaps, as great.) In the history of America constructed by pragmatists and progressives, formalists were conservative members of the Supreme Court; Arendt's ideologists were servants of the party, architects of mass murder in Poland or of mass deportation to Siberia. Disagreements in liberal thought were settled by an agreement to disagree; in the world Arendt had barely escaped, disagreement was settled by incarceration, exile, or execution. Louis Menand was also onto something when he criticized pragmatism for its failure to pursue certain questions to their limits. A "deficiency" of pragmatism was, he asserted, that "wants and beliefs can lead people to act in ways that are distinctly unpragmatic"; indeed, there are those "for whom ideas were things other than instruments of adjustment." The problem is that "pragmatism explains everything about ideas except why a person would be willing to die for one."[43] In other words, pragmatism and American progressive thought had little experience with "shipwreckedness." Arendt, of course, had lived in and reconstructed a world in which the pursuit of self-interest by political actors was at cross purposes with their motivations or values. Common sense was not an adequate way of negotiating the world of totalitarianism.

But, what is true of the Deweyan version of pragmatism—its tendency to avoid death, worldly evil and suffering, and the political implications of isolation, solitude, and loneliness—was, and is, by no means true of much American poetry and fiction. Philosopher Stanley Cavell has even wondered: "Why has America never expressed itself philosophically? Or has it—in the metaphysical riot of its greatest literature?"[44] Despite Arendt's indifference, at best, toward pragmatism, she did not reject all expressions of American (high) culture. In "The Crisis in Culture" (1961), she suggested, for instance, that "American literature and painting has suddenly come to play such a decisive role in the development of modern art" because it was free of the snob value associated with other national literatures and artistic traditions. It was simply less encumbered with considerations of prestige and status. It seemed much fresher.[45] She was very much taken with American fiction and poetry, William Faulkner and Herman Melville being her two favorites. In Faulkner she found a writer who understood the way that the telling of the story of the past was a way of coming to terms with it and how memorialization was central to that process. In Melville's *Billy Budd*, she found a post–French Revolution exploration of the danger, not only of evil but also of goodness, in politics. By implication, it may have been the absence of such issues and ideas that Arendt most keenly missed in philosophy, including pragmatism, in the New World.

American versus German Thought?

But Arendt was far from alone in her prejudices against American philosophical thought. A couple of other examples point toward a general European, specifically German, attitude here. First, the Frankfurt School thinkers, with whom Arendt had relatively little in common philosophically or politically, also found it hard to appreciate pragmatism as anything other than an American version of logical positivism, while the New York intellectuals, according to Thomas Wheatland, thought the Frankfurt philosophers were just doing more of the same German "thing"—metaphysics.[46] At the same time, while Arendt and the first generation of the Frankfurt School largely ignored pragmatism, Jürgen Habermas (b. 1929), who received his philosophical training at the reconstituted Frankfurt School, not only used Arendt's work but also acknowledged the writings of American pragmatists such as Dewey and George H. Mead. Such theoretical bridge building within German thought and between German and American thought was exceedingly valuable in building transatlantic bridges in the postwar world.[47]

Over two decades ago, Hans Joas suggested that the German reception of pragmatism was marred by blatant anti-American stereotypes, especially the view that Americans allegedly had no philosophical talents or traditions. This attitude, as we have seen, was manifestly clear in Arendt's own attitude.[48] Arendt largely shared the view that pragmatism was a philosophical expression of "instrumental reason" (Weber's *Zweckrationalität*), the attempt to rationalize the world via means-end calculations or a way of calculating chances of success in a given context. It treated everything in terms of use value not truth value. For Martin Heidegger, such an attitude expressed the inner essence of technology, one in which human beings were treated as "standing reserve [*Bestand*]" material to be used to achieve certain external purposes.[49] Conversely, when Arendt did write a short piece on Ralph Waldo Emerson, she described him, as we have seen, as a "humanist" rather than a "philosopher."[50] This characterization typified what Stanley Cavell was later to see as the standard European (and even American) philosophical reaction to Emerson—to deny his status as a philosopher. Overall, then, Germans and Europeans tended to condemn pragmatism as a form of Enlightenment-derived instrumental reason, as a counter-Enlightenment form of irrationality (a form of *Lebensphilosophie*), or as a kind of harmless humanism. It couldn't win. [51]

Despite Joas's own favorable attitude toward the pragmatist tradition, he also admits that several of the German thinkers most knowledgeable about American pragmatism were ideological outriders of National Socialism. They were attracted to pragmatism as "a philosophy of action" and the way it seemed, at least, to encourage "enthusiasm for decisiveness, action, and power." The problem was that in the German context the "democratic ideal" was all too easily jettisoned for the idea of a "national racial community."[52] But Joas also notes that not only Arendt but also Ernst Cassirer, Ernst Bloch, and Alfred Schütz as philosopher-émigrés to America were either indifferent toward or seriously distorted the meaning of pragmatism. Thus Arendt was not alone among German émigrés in missing the value of the work of James, Peirce, Dewey, and Mead.[53]

With this in mind, Arendt's attitude toward pragmatism seems less personally capricious. There are other ways that Arendt might have interpreted pragmatism that would have made it more acceptable. For instance, Joas's own idea of adaptation, a key term in Dewey's thought, did not need to imply that one was conforming to reality; rather, it could suggest a way of adjusting reality to one's needs and desires, as a kind of "situated creativity." Such an emphasis shifted the sense of pragmatism from an instrumentalist one, in which pragmatism is a way of fitting into existing reality, to pragmatism as a modification of things as they are. Later, Richard Rorty would often use the term "redescription" to depict what the pragmatist did. Dewey, Charles S. Peirce, and George H. Mead also emphasized that pragmatism pursued a "cooperative search for truth."[54] On this Arendt would have been divided. She tended to emphasize the solitary nature of genuine thought but she agreed on the cooperative nature of political argument and debate. Indeed Mead's interactionist theory of the self also suited Arendt's (underdeveloped) idea that the self arises in the context of acknowledgment by others.[55]

Coda

In the context of postwar American intellectual history, the question might be turned around—why did so few pragmatists respond to Arendt's work or that of the other émigré thinkers, including the Frankfurt School on the left and Leo Strauss and Eric Voegelin on the right? There has been a long tradition of American reflection on German thought, beginning at least with Emerson, but also including Santayana, Dewey, and Veblen in the twentieth century. As Morton White points out in *Social Thought in America*, Dewey and Veblen took the occasion of World War I to criticize German thought as divided uneasily among a certain unworldly and apolitical idealism (in both senses of the term), an enthusiasm for science and technology that stimulated industrial production, and a tradition of hard-nosed *Realpolitik*. Some of this is reminiscent of Thomas Mann's critique of German romanticism and inwardness and ultimately traces back to the Kantian dualism between the phenomenal and noumenal realms. White also notes the way the war forced Dewey and Veblen to reassess upward the English concept of "intelligent self-interest" in light of what they saw as the ethic of "duty" in German public life and politics.[56]

Among post-1960s pragmatists, the two figures whose interests and contacts were particularly transatlantic were Richard Bernstein and Richard Rorty. Rorty never really addressed Arendt's work, though he planned for a time to write a book on Heidegger in the 1980s, while Bernstein's engagement with Arendt's work, as well as with Habermas's and Hans-Georg Gadamer's, has been exceedingly fruitful. The story of his link with Arendt is an interesting one. In the first half of the 1970s, Bernstein wrote two studies of contemporary social and political philosophy, *Praxis and Action* (1971) and *The Restructuring of Social and Political Theory* (1976), but consigned Arendt to one footnote in each book, even though both books were centrally concerned with action. They only became friends after she sought him out to discuss his *Praxis and Action*, of which she thought highly, and she also tried to help get him hired at the New School for Social Research.[57]

Over the next decade and a half, however, Bernstein wrote substantial essays on Arendt's concept of judgment, a central concern in pragmatism as well, and on Arendt's distinction between the social and the political, especially her claim that Marx neglected the distinction between labor and work. Though highly critical of her treatment of Marx, Bernstein also noted that Arendt's concept of action and equality in the public sphere had radically democratic potential and thus could transform the meaning of the social itself.[58] Finally, in an essay on Heidegger and technology, published in *Constellations* (1991), Bernstein touched on Arendt's thought in his long, probing essay on Martin Heidegger's theory of technology, his outspoken condemnation of the spirit of *Die Technik*, and his silence on the Holocaust.[59]

Bernstein has always made clear that he does not share Arendt's entire philosophical vision. But his two large books after the early 1990s, *Hannah Arendt and the Jewish Question* (1996) and *Radical Evil: A Philosophical Investigation* (2002) clearly take up Arendt on two of the central issues in her work.[60] Bernstein's recent book *The Abuse of Evil* (2005) grouped

Arendt with Canadian philosopher Charles Taylor and with Habermas, as belonging to the tradition of pragmatic fallibilism. Bernstein also noted the failure of pragmatists to admit that they had avoided dealing with the problem of evil and that the pragmatic virtues of "deliberation, diplomacy, and persuasion" might not always work in the face of obdurate evil.[61] Very recently, Bernstein has also marked out Habermas, Arendt, and Dewey as three thinkers whose central concern is with the survival or revival of "the public sphere," which, for all its limitations in historical reality (the descriptive dimension), contains a "promise" of free speech in an idea of politics grounded in authentic, not manufactured, public opinion. In all three thinkers' cases, the notion of the public sphere is detached from the nation-state.[62] Overall, Bernstein's critical writings on Arendt are import-ant reflections in their own right. But they suggest that, for all the parallels and overlaps, neither Arendt nor the pragmatists in general (have) availed themselves of each other's best insights.

CHAPTER 7

Reflections/Refractions of Race, 1945-1955

Hannah Arendt was one of the first (white) thinkers to locate race and racism (including anti-Semitism) at the heart of Nazi totalitarianism. In the first decade or so after the war, most analysts located the essence of totalitarianism in politics (theories of state formation, mass leadership, and consent; the power of ideology); massive historical dislocation (escape from freedom or mass culture and society); or, finally, the spiritual-cultural crisis of modernity (the death of God, historicism, gnosticism)—or some combination of these three.[1] Ironically, her application of the term "totalitarian" to both the Nazi and Soviet regimes made it easier to sidestep the importance of anti-Semitism, not to mention racism or the colonial experience, to totalitarian regimes in Europe. Theodor Adorno and Max Horkheimer were partial exceptions to this generalization, at least in *The Dialectic of Enlightenment* (1947). But when Adorno and his colleagues later explored the nature of racial, religious, and ethnic prejudice in the massive postwar study, *The Authoritarian Personality* (1950), the title itself betrayed a shift in emphasis—away from anti-Semitism to the social psychology of obedience and away from Europe to the United States. Another Frankfurt School contribution, Franz Neumann's *The Behemoth* (1942), raised the issue of anti-Semitism in National Socialism but only to dismiss its ultimate importance.

Yet, for Arendt, it was the specifically racial nature of Nazi totalitarianism that placed the "administrative mass murder" of the Nazis beyond comprehension and thereby "strain[ed] the framework and categories of our political thought and action." Such racialized mass murder was "the true consequence of all race theories and other modern ideologies which preach that might is right."[2] In the wake of Arendt's work, no longer could anti-Semitism be considered a premodern phenomenon and National Socialism a conservative movement.[3] After World War II, race and ethnicity gradually became privileged terms of political and social analysis, rivaling and often outstripping class conflict, particularly in the United States. For much of this, Arendt was at least partly responsible.

Ambiguities of the Global and Local

Arendt's prescient 1945 essay "Organized Guilt and Universal Responsibility" adopted a "cosmopolitan" perspective in the wake of the war's horrors.[4] She saw belief in fundamental human equality as the great test of postwar good faith but also speculated that it would not be easy to face "the terror of the idea of humanity and of the Judeo-Christian faith in the unitary origins of the human race."[5] An entry in her *Denktagebuch* of April 1951 expands on these remarks by providing a universalist grounding for human equality. Discussing the "difficulty of grasping the idea of human plurality," she speculated that, in the "Judeo-Christian creation-myth," "human beings . . . derive from one Human Being ['*ex uno homine*'] and have in this origin 1] the guarantee of a likeness to God, because God is also One; and 2] the guarantee that peoples do not degenerate or need to degenerate into races. In the 'from one Human Being' [*ex uno homine*], in the fact that plurality is secondary, lies the guarantee of humanity [*Menschlichkeit*]."[6] Thus the unity of the human race was the presupposition of Arendt's idea of human plurality. This meant that plurality could not be racialized or used to justify racial separation. It is also significant here that Arendt grounded equality in the religious heritage of the West not the secular Enlightenment's assumption of universal equality.

However, a sense of "how great a burden mankind is for man" caused some, she observed, to "become more susceptible to the doctrine of race,"

since the idea of mankind as such entailed "an obligation of a general responsibility which they do not wish to assume." Prophetically anticipating
the collapse of European colonialism, she also predicted (pessimistically/
realistically) the difficulty of adhering to "a non-imperialistic policy and
maintain[ing] a non-racist faith."[7] Clearly the voice speaking in this essay,
as well as in *The Origins of Totalitarianism* (1951), was one that rejected the
ethnic and racial ideologies that justified the nation-state in Europe and colonialism around the globe. Yet racial and ethnic self-consciousness became
important in the non-European world after the war. Once having challenged
the scientific claims for racial inequality, the colonized people of Africa and
Asia then affirmed racial and cultural identities in the process of throwing
off the white man's yoke. For example, what struck African American writer
Richard Wright when he attended the Bandung Conference in 1955 was the
surprising proliferation, not the disappearance, of appeals to race and color.[8]

Yet a more realistic and less visionary side to Arendt in those early postwar years emerged pretty quickly. Her argument for the global equality of
people (and cultures) was not based on a claim about a human capacity
for rationality or on natural, historical, or divine law. Nor did she embrace
liberal or Marxist notions of historical progress that foresaw the eventual
triumph of equality over racism, tolerance over bigotry. All foundational
or metahistorical supports for human equality had crumbled. Rather, she
stressed the "inescapable guilt of the human race" and an "elemental shame"
at "being human" as remnants of a solidarity forged in the shared—and
shattering—experience "of what man is capable."[9] Indeed, one of the most
striking aspects of *Origins* was her indictment of the international community, ostensibly committed to natural or human rights, for utterly failing to
protect legal, political, religious, and racial minorities in the chaos of the
interwar years and of World War II itself.[10]

It was this Arendt who saw little point in working to strengthen the
fledgling United Nations and paid little attention to the intellectual and
moral commitment to protect refugees, minorities, and displaced persons.
She seemed to settle for the limited idea of defending the rights belonging to
humans by virtue of their humanity itself—what she referred to, as we have
seen, as "a right to have rights."[11] In contrast with cosmopolitan contemporaries such as Raphael Lemkin, who formulated the idea of genocide in the

1940s, Arendt, notes Seyla Benhabib, was "quite skeptical that declarations of human rights, conventions, and the like" could be efficacious.[12] She paid little or no attention to the Nuremberg Trials, since radical evil involved "crimes which men could neither punish nor forgive."[13] Nor did she ever explicitly comment on the rights regime established by the United Nations, including the Universal Declaration of Human Rights or the Convention on the Prevention and Punishment of the Crime of Genocide of 1948, perhaps because such measures seemed to be merely more of the same.[14] Ironically, then, Arendt's insistence on the radical nature of totalitarian evil all but deprived her of any way to carry out an intellectual reckoning with that evil.

Yet by the time of the Eichmann trial in Jerusalem in 1961, Arendt, notes Benhabib, had rediscovered some of her intellectual and moral engagement and saw the value of some sort of super- or international idea of law.[15] For instance, Arendt would have preferred that Adolf Eichmann be charged with "'crimes against mankind' committed on the body of the Jewish people" rather than the genocide charge of "crimes 'against the Jewish people.'"[16] Her formulation refined the context and, to a degree, the content of Lemkin's ideas of genocide: all genocides were instantiations of a crime against humanity, but not all crimes against humanity involved genocide. Another sign of the persistence of the universalist dimension to her thinking about race was evident in her biting comment on the failure of the Catholic Church to protect converted Jews in Nazi Germany in a 1963 letter to Jaspers: "It is evident in purely theological terms that racism is a true heresy: if the sacrament of baptism cannot make a Christian out of a Jew—and that means the fact that one can not even officially protect baptized Jews—, then they can simply pack it in."[17] Overall, then, Arendt's universalist perspective won out over a more particularist, defeatist view of such matters.

Only in America

Despite the somber perspective that Arendt brought to her discussion of race, her experience in America moved her to optimistic, at times enthusiastic, assessments of how her new home dealt with race and ethnicity in the context of politics and citizenship. As she explained not long before her death, "What influenced me when I came to the United States was precisely the freedom of becoming a citizen without having to pay the price of assimilation."[18] Though Benjamin Barber exaggerates when he suggests that, like other refugees, Arendt "seemed to forgive nothing associated with Europe's recent past while exonerating America of just about everything others might regard as dark in its history," she was prepared to give America the benefit of her doubt, at least on issues having to do with race, whether at a personal or historical level, and always stressed her gratitude for having ended up in the United States.[19]

The fullest account of her early thoughts on race and ethnicity is found in a long letter to Karl Jaspers on January 29, 1946. Having only regained contact with Jaspers in late October 1945, the January letter was replete with sharply expressed judgments and written in a lively, sometimes allusive, and even breathless style. It played a major role in reestablishing the bond with her *Doktorvater* and with the "other" Germany of *Dichter und Denker* (poets and thinkers) not *Richter and Henker* (judges and hangmen). For all the attention that has been lavished on Arendt's relationship with Martin Heidegger, Jaspers had a moral stature that neither she nor anyone else ever found in Heidegger as a man or a thinker. Arendt prefaced her critical remarks to Jaspers by insisting that "freedom" was something more than a "delusion" (*Wahn*) in the United States. She attributed it to the absence of a "national state" and an "actual national tradition" that commanded great loyalty. American society remained divided among various ethnic groups: "The melting pot is for the most part not even an ideal, not to mention a reality." Yet this pluralism was also a valuable source of dissent from public opinion. She was impressed, too, that Americans "felt responsible for public life in a way that I know of in no European country."[20] The stark juxtaposition of political freedom and social separation was clear in the example of the New England family with whom she lived for a time. They wrote irate letters to their congressmen protesting the law interning the Nisei Japanese in California, though they never had any Japanese American friends. She also mentioned a young Jewish woman who had only first actually met gentiles in the home of this same family. Of course, she admitted, "social anti-semitism" existed; but "this is not to say that one would not defend Jews politically; only that socially on both sides people wish to be 'with their own.'"[21] In a later letter to Jaspers, she observed that people who might be reluctant to stay in the same hotel with Jews would be "astonished and outraged if someone tried to deprive their fellow Jewish citizens of their vote."[22] Indeed this last point concluded a passage in which Arendt turned more critical and worried about the combination of social conformity and racial exclusivity in her new home. American society "organizes and orients itself according to race [*rassenmässig*]," regardless of social class or status. That America was a "nation of immigrants" provided one explanation, she granted. But racialization was also "accentuated to an unhealthy degree by the Negro question—that is, America "has a real 'race problem' and not just an ideology."[23]

Several things deserve comment about Arendt's often shrewd analysis in the letter to Jaspers. Her position was broadly similar to the "cultural pluralism" identified with Randolph Bourne and Horace Kallen in the 1910s.[24] This position sought to preserve cultural differences in the face of the assimilationist tendencies of the WASP culture, while affirming the virtues of the American political and legal system. She observed that the lack of a strong central government in America did not extinguish the desire to participate in public affairs (voting and holding office) and to secure equality before the law. In fact, this analysis from the mid-1940s already contained the distinction between the political and the social that she explored in her analysis of Tocqueville and her exchanges with Riesman and that became central to *The Human Condition* and *On Revolution*. For instance, in a later letter to Jaspers (June 30, 1947), she described the United States as an "a-national republic" in which "nationality and state are not identical." Nationality, that is, ethnicity, "has only social and cultural meaning but politically it is meaningless."[25] As sociologist J. M. Cuddihy once observed, the confusing attitudes Arendt expressed about "society" in general reflected the persisting ambivalence of many Jews toward assimilation into modern (gentile) society.[26]

Overall, she thought that the right balance between society and politics had been struck in America. In *Origins*, she had contrasted Jews who sought social assimilation (parvenus) with those who remained independent (pariahs),[27] a distinction she would later use in reference to African American assimilation too. By implication, she seemed to be saying that Jews in America had been more aware than their European counterparts of the need to secure legal and political rights, including participation in political parties and the labor movement, and, perhaps, less concerned with social and cultural acceptance by gentiles. Thus race and ethnicity were also integrally bound up with the distinction between the social and the political sphere so central to her work.

Though Arendt spent little time on the "Negro problem" in the letter to Jaspers, she did emphasize two important things. First, the respective situations of American Jews and of African Americans were problematic, but in different ways. She did not spell it out explicitly, but she obviously knew that African Americans had been deprived of their voting rights in America, while the political rights of Jews and other European ethnic groups in the United States were secure by the post-1945 period. She also noted the incarceration of the Nisei Japanese, a fate suffered by none of the European ethnic groups in America, particularly Germans or Italians, except for a short time. Strangely, she didn't make more of this massive violation of civil liberties and civil rights and the construction of concentration camps on the West Coast. Second, the obscure distinction she drew between a racial "problem" and a racist "ideology" derived, I think, from her perception that there were real differences in conditions between black and white Americans, while such differences were diminishing among white ethnic groups and between them and the old stock Americans.[28] That is, a social and cultural reality underpinned the ideology of differences between the races.

One particular problem with Arendt's analysis has to do with the relationship between social conformity and racial-ethnic diversity in America. It is difficult to see how she could square the fact that the United States allowed groups to maintain their inherited cultural identities (and enjoy political and legal equality) with the idea that American society was rampantly conformist. Why *was* a consensus on political institutions and traditions a good thing, while social conformity was looked down on? Overall, she never really developed a convincing explanation of intellectual or cultural conformity in America. At times she seemed to suggest that ethnic and racial diversity helped moderate conformity, while, in her analysis of the role public schools in America, she suggested that conformity was stronger in ethnically and racially diverse societies.[29] Her claim of a higher sense of civic involvement in America than in Europe was probably proposed with

Germany in mind, but otherwise she never really followed out this claim either. Overall, the charge that Americans were conformists was a standard, even monotonous, observation from Europeans since Tocqueville at least. It is one that she, and we, will return to repeatedly.

Race and Racism: New and Old World

For all its path-breaking importance, *Origins* took little account of the devastating history of race and racism in the Western Hemisphere, specifically in the United States. The book contains one short discussion of race and slavery and one paragraph on the status of being a Negro that plausibly refer to North America.[30] For her, racism and ultimately genocide were scandals of the European world, and intricately bound up with European colonialism and imperialism. As already noted, she denied that America had an imperial or colonial tradition of thought or experience. As she wrote in her Little Rock essay, America's race problem was not one that "grew out of the colonialism and imperialism of European nations—that is the one great crime in which America was never involved." Rather the "color question was created by the one great crime in America's history" and that was slavery.[31] America's indigenous population of Native Americans was invisible in a way that Africa's was not.

For Arendt, racism was not just the name of negative feelings toward, and discriminatory treatment of, one people by another. There was nothing unique about the West in that respect. "Others" have been feared and placed at a disadvantage in practically all human societies. Nor was racism an enduring human phenomenon: there was no such thing as "eternal anti-Semitism." Rather, race and racism had a history. Specifically, racism was a modern idea that served to justify late nineteenth-century imperialism and it marked a break with what she called the "race-thinking," which had originated in the early eighteenth century. "Race," observed historian Ivan Hannaford, "is not everywhere."[32] Race-thinking assumed the coexistence of races, with their own peculiar traits (strengths and weaknesses) supplied by culture (including, especially, religion and language), geography (including climate), and occasionally biology. But racism took the horizontal relationship of the races in race-thinking and rotated the axis ninety degrees so that the races were now ranked in terms of their various capacities for, and achievement of, culture/civilization. Thus the differences among races thematized in race-thinking (what George Fredrickson would later call "romantic racialism" and K. Anthony Appiah "racialism") was now, according to racism, the superiority of one race over another. In Europe, this shift from descriptive to normative differences happened in the mid- to late nineteenth century. Whatever the validity of her distinction for Europe, widespread racism in the sense of coherently formulated ideas of racial superiority was present a good deal earlier in the United States than she claimed for Europe. For instance, Thomas Jefferson's writing about race proposed the highly probable superiority of whites to blacks in his *Notes on Virginia* in the 1780s, and there was an American school of racist anthropology in the mid-nineteenth-century United States.[33]

As mentioned in chapter 2, this specifically modern rank ordering of the races was bolted into place by three shifts in thinking that transformed religious anti-Semitism (what she called traditional "Jew-hatred") into a secular ideology. In this worldview, race, not class, became the moving force in human history. Second, late nineteenth-century Europe also witnessed the emergence of political parties that introduced anti-Semitism into the mainstream political life of Europe, while the United States also saw racial politics enter the mainstream and explicitly racist laws were put in place at the state level, particularly, though not exclusively, in the South. Racism was no longer a merely personal prejudice of individuals or the particular belief of small groups. This was the politicization of anti-Semitism. And most uniquely modern was the biologization (or naturalization) of race. This also probably set in earlier in the United States than in Europe. In this development, race was what philosophers were later to call a "natural kind."

Arendt also made the important point in her analysis of European anti-Semitism (which was no monopoly of the Germans) that Jews were increasingly described (and described themselves) in terms not of beliefs, ceremonies, rituals, and sacred texts — that is, the religion of Judaism — but in terms of shared characteristics, namely, a shared physiognomy, psychology, and culture — in short, "Jewishness." This also meant, fatefully, that no longer could a Jew convert to Christianity. Being a Jew was a natural not a religious fact. Paradoxically, then, as the culture became less religious and more secular, a new kind of racism grew in strength. What we would now call racial prejudice was considered a normal reaction to group differences rather than an aberrant form of thought and behavior. Racism was blind to its own existence. But while such deep-seated racism began coming under attack in the United States and Britain in the interwar years of the twentieth century, there was a resurgence of anti-Semitism in Germany. We know the rest of that story.

Finally, for Arendt, the intellectual pedigree of biological racism and secular anti-Semitism were of little or no interest, since they came out of the gutter not the mainstream of the culture. On a personal level, she always condemned racism in America in the strongest terms and declared her sympathy, for instance, for "the cause of the Negroes as for all oppressed or underprivileged peoples."[34] If we follow her own definition of racism, she was not a racist. She advanced no biological explanation for group differences; she rejected any political role for the idea of race, from any quarter (as can be seen later in the 1960s when she objected to black power); and she certainly did not think of race as central to her view of the world. To be sure, she once noted that, "if one is attacked as a Jew, one must defend oneself as a Jew," but this was a polemical point and a situational reaction. Originally, she was, for instance, against the establishment of the state of Israel as a "Jewish" state.

However, as critics have noted, Arendt's discussion of the peoples of sub-Saharan Africa in *Origins* assumed they were inferior to Europeans in cultural terms.[35] On this issue, at least, she seemed to hold to some version of cultural evolution, since she certainly did not deny that Africans could *become* "civilized" in European terms. Her descriptions are worrisome in large part because we generally hold a different set of assumptions on these matters than was quite common circa 1950. But when placed besides her European, German, and American contemporaries, Arendt looks much better than most. She was never an apologist for, or advocate of, colonialism or imperialism and was dead set against basing any political order on racial or ethnic criteria. To be a citizen, moreover, was to belong to a group of equals, and thus differential citizenship made no sense.[36]

As far as theoretical assumptions are concerned, Arendt was particularly influenced by Eric Voegelin's idea of treating race as an "idea" (or a "symbol") within history. On this view, to take account of the influence of race in history was not to accept the reality of race as a causal factor in itself, but to determine how racial beliefs affected action and thought.[37] The proper concern of the historian or the social scientist was the function not the truth claim about race. Still, Arendt hardly remained neutral when she treated race as the last of a series of forces that had been advanced to explain human nature and human behavior. For her, the resort to race in philosophical-anthropological terms had been an intellectual and moral disaster that foretold not the "beginning of humanity but its end." Indeed, those who thought and acted in terms of the determinism of nature, for example, as expressed in racial explanations of events or achievements, contributed to "the natural course of ruin."[38] This inevitability of decline and death as part of nature bore a certain resemblance to the idea of entropy. It is important to remember that, though trained as a philosopher, Arendt nevertheless rejected the view that ideas were the prime movers in history.[39]

Overall, despite her disclaimers about the status of race in Western thought, Arendt's work clearly invited future investigators to see race as a suitable topic for the intellectual historian, while rejecting the idea that history was the fulfillment of the race idea. In *Origins*, Arendt was concerned with the way racial theories justified economic expansion and imperial domination by European powers. In general, she avoided analyzing the racist mentality in sociological or particularly psychoanalytic terms, two of the most important ways in postwar America of understanding such matters, as found in the work of Adorno and Horkheimer or of Bruno Bettelheim. Overall, then, *Origins* was one of the first books to give the idea of race crucial explanatory weight, not as a real thing but as a weapon in the hands of historical actors.[40] Finally, Arendt's view on race and racism was unclear on the matter of what Stephen J. Whitfield has referred to as the "indivisibility" of racism. As we have seen, she obviously recognized that anti-Semitism and color-coded racism did not have the same object of historical address and differed in their context of occurrence, but her reluctance to analyze the internal logic of racism(s) meant that it was not clear whether she saw them as essentially the same, but with different historical objects, or as essentially different, but overlapping in their effects and implications.[41]

Anthropology and Race

As already stated, Arendt assumed the ontological and hence normative status of human plurality. But how did this square with her rejection of racial differences and the primacy she gave to the political? Where philosophy and theology assumed, she asserted in her *Denktagebuch* (August 1950), the primacy of the single type, *Man*, politics was most importantly concerned with how *Men* lived together.[42] Beyond that, Arendt identified two enemies of plurality and hence of politics. The first was the premodern tendency for the "family" to be the template for the organization of "political bodies." This, she thought, was the "downfall of politics." The idea of kinship emerged from the centrality of the family model and led "to the fundamental perversion of politics, because it abolishes the basic quality of plurality, or rather forfeits it by introducing the concept of kinship."[43] The family model represented the polity as a pseudo-unity but denied individuality and posited permanent hierarchies of power. Politics, which was for her the realm of equality, was swamped by society as the realm of inequality. Arendt might also have mentioned the centrality to modern liberalism of John Locke's rejection of Robert Filmer's idea that the ideal society/polity should be modeled on the family. The family appeals to inherited traits and is constructed along hierarchical lines, with the inherited roles of parent and child at its center. All this helps explain why, for Arendt, "the social" is the realm of determinism, in this case by fixed roles and hierarchies of power. Put another way, family histories (or genealogies) are the history of the nonpolitical.[44]

In addition, Arendt also argued that racism was a form of biological determinism and that it denied the equality of citizens necessary for authentic politics based on real choices. Race as collective lineage, history as the story of race, nature historicized and history naturalized: all are ways of rejecting the possibility of freedom. As she wrote near the end of *Origins*, if the Negro is defined as "a Negro and nothing else," he or she loses "freedom of action," since "his deeds" are now explained as "necessary consequences of some 'Negro' qualities."[45] For her, racism was as much "about" the denial of freedom (and not just liberation) as it was of equality; analogously, when those oppressed because of race react by embracing racial consciousness, they run the danger of assuming a false freedom.

Arendt also considered the modern attempt—she, of course, has Marx in mind—"to transform politics into history, or to substitute history for politics" in which "the multiplicity of men is melted into *one* human individual, which is then called humanity" to be a denial of freedom. Thus both nature (family and kinship) and history (as the movement of forces and groups toward a particular goal) are incompatible with politics, since both are hostile to plurality and to freedom. Politics, she insisted, recognizes difference: it "organizes those who are absolutely different with a view to their *relative* equality and in contradistinction to their *relative* differences."[46] It is important to note that Arendt seems hostile to the idea of humanity, even though she had spoken positively of the global unity of humankind in her "Organized Guilt" essay and even though, in the Eichmann book, she referred several times to "crimes against mankind" or against "humanity" (*Menschheit*). It was not that such crimes were gratuitously brutal or inhumane but because they somehow violated "the human status."[47] Overall, what Arendt really wanted to do was, on the one hand, undermine the idea that humanity had a teleology built into it, that is, that it was something to be fulfilled, but, on the other hand, also affirm the equal worth of all human beings as members of the same species.

At the end of chapter 9 of the second edition of *Origins*, Arendt offered several pages of ruminations on the three-way tension within the shared public world: the "human artifice," where all are equal and common; the "private sphere," where "everything [that] is merely given" and all is "difference and differentiation"; and the "alien" as the "symbol of the fact of difference . . . of individuality as such."[48] The discussion is knotty and hard to follow but what she seemed to be saying was that human existence must be maintained without any one of the three spheres gaining the upper hand. The more "at home men feel within the human artifice,—the more they will resent everything they have not produced." In other words, they resent the "the given" or the natural. But she also contended that, "wherever public life and its law of equality are completely victorious," there will be "complete petrification." In such a situation, the realm of the other preserves our differences. There a person "becomes a human being in general. . . . *and* different in general."[49] Such human beings become aliens, without a self-description, and the danger comes from strangers within not without, ones that don't belong to the public world—in a word, barbarians. The whole thrust of her thought is that we are most fully human when we appear in a public world. And yet, the "dark background of difference" and the private realm must also be preserved as balancing forces.

Coda: What's in a Name?

Despite Hannah Arendt's pioneering role in introducing race and racism into the history of totalitarianism, many readers, as mentioned, have been uneasy with the way she talked about non-European peoples, particularly those from sub-Saharan Africa, not to mention her controversial essay opposing school desegregation in Little Rock, Arkansas, in 1957, and, finally, her willingness to be extremely critical of radical black politics and culture in the 1960s. Blücher, having accepted a full-time position at Bard College in 1952, remained behind in New York when his wife took the train to Berkeley to teach the spring term of 1955 (roughly February into June). Besides being a delight to read, their letters to each other reveal something about the difficulty in getting race talk "right" in an alien setting and also raise questions about the strict separation Arendt tried to maintain between judgments in the public and private spheres.[50]

Arendt's early February trip across the continent exposed her to the striking qualities of the Western plains and mountains. Her descriptions reveal an unexpected visual sensitivity and a readiness to respond with the rhetoric of the sublime. Adjectives such as *ungeheuer* (colossal) and *unbegreiflich* (ungraspable) abound in the passages containing her visual impressions. She later told Heinrich of excursions to see redwood forests in the Bay Area with Leo Lowenthal, one of the Frankfurt School in exile who taught sociology at the University of California. Once at Berkeley, she set about dissecting the strange behavior and customs of her host university, its faculty and students, and West Coast America in general. Among other things, these letters present us with a snapshot of Arendt as an enthusiastic student of the flora and fauna of the continent and an anthropologist of American academic life.

Though Arendt and Blücher enjoyed kvetching about everything, she just as clearly enjoyed herself at Berkeley. Their letters are chock-full of sharp opinions and anecdotes, with Blücher tending toward long-windedness and Arendt expressing herself in an informal, vigorous way. They leapfrog from topic to topic and exchange candid, and irreverent, opinions about friends as well as foes. They also refer to each other with affectionate, if untranslatable, nicknames. Her German is lively, sometimes colloquial, and nothing like the "deep" prose of Heidegger nor the abstract system building style of a Kant or Hegel.

Like most political science departments at the time (and perhaps still), Berkeley's was divided between theorists and behaviorialists. As we have already seen, the Berkeley department included a strong contingent of young political philosophers whose impact on Arendt (and vice versa) was considerable.[51] Strangely Arendt mentioned none of this really to her husband. The impression she gave in her letters to him was that she existed in splendid isolation with only her students—and a few social contacts—to keep her company. Her letters also reflect an ambivalence about teaching, undoubtedly linked to a certain distaste for public exposure, which, ironically, Arendt found hard to bear for very long. Casting back over her experience as the semester neared its end, she wrote: "I cannot write and teach at the same time . . . teaching has overstimulated me."[52] Of course, there is a "she doth protest too much" quality about her experience of teaching. Her willingness to see students outside, as well as inside, class, to extend her office hours, and to offer private tutorials has the ring of truth to it. She was a popular teacher and lecturer. She had already characterized her teaching experience as "hellish fun, or better still, fun in hell," and complained to Blücher about "this damned popularity . . . I feel like an infernal scoundrel for wanting to go home as soon as possible."[53] In fact, Arendt did not teach regularly until well into the 1960s.

But I focus here on Arendt's letters from Berkeley to her husband because they include some casual, but revealing, comments about the way Arendt thought and talked privately about race. These comments are reminiscent of the ambiguities that mark her discussion of sub-Saharan Africa in chapter 7 of *Origins*. Specifically, in a May 5, 1955, letter, she wrote to Heinrich in passing that "I just got back from the private lesson in Kant that I give to a little fuzzy-head [*Wuschelkopf*] whom I like very much and who's learning a lot."[54] Just over a week later, she mentioned him again: "In the afternoon my little fuzzy-head to do some Kant reading."[55] Finally, her

May 19 letter reports that: "Yesterday in my seminar the usual report was given by a gentleman from Kenya, presumably a member of the Mau Mau, who had to leave the country. It was the best report given in this seminar. The young man understands everything, and has a facility for order and presentation that makes my graduate students look like pipsqueaks. Isn't that nice, dearest? He's as black as black can be, and yet as well known among the students as if he had come from some Western country. What is happening in the world to make this possible! Beautiful world!"[56] What is there to say about Arendt's racial views after reading these three passages? How do her condescending nickname, her report of the young man's achievement, and her strikingly joyous celebratory attitude toward "the world" in which race is forgotten fit with one another?

First, there is Arendt's use of "fuzzy-head." Arendt had lived in America for fourteen years, but she used a German term, not an American colloquialism like "colored boy" or the cruder "Sambo" or something that could have been even worse. Historically, there have been controversies over the public use of such terms by prominent people. In the late 1950s, historian Samuel Eliot Morrison had been "taken to task," noted Stanley Elkins in his *Slavery* (1959) "for his use of the name 'Sambo' to refer to plantation slaves" in volume 1 of *The Growth of the American Republic*.[57] Ironically, Elkins was also attacked later in the 1960s for using the same term "Sambo" in his book, even though he deployed it in clearly stipulated ways. There are also examples like Arendt's of intellectuals using casual terms of denigration in private correspondence. In June 1897, William James wrote brother Henry to urge him to "read the darkey Washington's Speech, a model of elevation and brevity."[58] Closer in time to Arendt, Isaiah Berlin referred to "my old friend Dr. Bunche, a negro from Washington, a good nigger," in a letter of August 3, 1947.[59] It is another irony that Arendt, James, and Berlin used a jokey but derogatory term, while praising the individual in question—the young Kenyan, Washington, and Bunche, respectively.

There are some uncertainties here. I am not sure that the young black student she was tutoring was the same person who gave the excellent seminar report. The passage in German refers to "den Gentleman aus Kenya." This should be translated as "the gentleman from Kenya" NOT "a gentleman from Kenya" as it appears in English. If it had been translated "the," it would imply a further description of the African student of Kant she was tutoring. But as it stands, the translation using "a" suggests that there are two different Africans involved. Nor am I sure what to make of the reference to the "Mau Mau[s]." It might be a plausible supposition, but Arendt could as easily have offered it in a semi-joking spirit to allude to his exotic aura. The adverbial qualifier "presumably" suggests that the Kenyan student did not tell her this.

There are clear, as well as subtle, shifts in tone among her statements. The first two references are conventionally and mildly derogatory. Not only does she use "fuzzy-head," she also precedes it with "little" and "my little," a usage that adds patronization to derogation. To be sure, she adds that she "like[s] him a lot," but clearly she (or anyone) can "like" someone whom they also consider inferior. Conversely, the young African was also a student and the forty-nine-year-old Arendt was never shy about her own importance. She might very well have used "little" and "my little," even if the student had been white. Arendt sometimes referred to her students as "the children." Another problematic usage is of "gentleman" to refer to the Kenyan student. I hear it as a somewhat arch (and humorous) term to refer to men (she used the English "gentleman" not German "Herr" in the letter). There is a similar usage in a letter to philosopher Glenn Gray where she refers to Heidegger and Benjamin as "gentlemen" who never took the trouble to read Hitler's *Mein Kampf*.[60] After all these observations have been made, the overwhelming sense of the paragraph is a positive one. The Kenyan was not only very smart but well liked, not only by her but also by the students.

But, Arendt also intended to report on something historically momentous in relating this incident to Blücher. That spring in Berkeley was one year after the May 17, 1954, *Brown v. Board of Education* decision of the Supreme Court and, also, anticolonial movements such as the Mau Mau had emerged in Africa. In this context, this small event in her seminar seemed a very encouraging sign. Clearly, the woman who considered naming her 1958 book *Amor Mundi (For Love of the World)*, not *The Human Condition*, saw this episode as an example of why, despite the horrors of Holocaust, the world was occasionally worth affirming. It also illustrated her (and our) need, as Susan Neiman has put it, to "find our way about in the world without making us too comfortable within it."[61] In a real sense, she had earned the right to conclude her observations with: "Beautiful World."

More generally, this anecdote forces us to ask how we are to weigh the relative importance of Arendt's private versus her public utterances. Are we just being prudish and politically naive in squirming over the term she used to refer to a young African student? And are we judging her utterance by the standards of sixty years later? Her own hermeneutic clearly privileged the public over the private sphere. As an example, writing privately to his wife on July 15, 1946, Blücher savagely characterized Karl Jaspers's *The Question of German Guilt* as "Hegelized, Christian, pietistic/hypocritical nationalizing piece of twaddle."[62] To Blücher's way of thinking "outer cleansing is more important. The Germans don't have to deliver themselves from guilt, but from disgrace . . . so let us speak about disgrace. That is a worldly thing. . . . Now before God we are all sinners. But among ourselves, there is a difference between honor and disgrace."[63] Arendt was never as critical of Jaspers as Blücher was here, but the distinction between guilt and shame fits her own thinking. For both of them, German pietistic *Innerlichkeit* diverted attention from the need for Germans to respond to their past with concrete action rather than wallowing in guilt. Arendt disliked psychoanalysis for many of the same reasons.[64] The point is that Arendt probably agreed with the intent of her husband's harsh words but would never have told Jaspers what Heinrich had said.

In thinking about ethics and actions, Arendt also came to resist the tendency to privilege intentions (and sincerity) in evaluating actions. According to Susan Neiman, Arendt wanted a "moral theory that locates guilt and responsibility in something other than intention."[65] Actions were between people, "in the world" as it were, while intentions were (initially) private and often not fully known to those who acted on them. Judgment is a crucial moral and political capacity that is by definition worldly. It is related to her "strong distinction between public and private."[66] This emphasis on actions not intentions suggested a kind of consequentialist, or pragmatic, theory of judgment, since the effects, not the origins, were most important in evaluating political action.

From this perspective, whether President Lyndon Johnson referred to African Americans as "niggers" in private is irrelevant in evaluating his accomplishments in securing the civil rights of African Americans and improving the economic lot of poor Americans in general. Politically, we would still have to judge his efforts as a success and certainly praiseworthy, while condemning the language that he used in describing what he was doing. Similarly, the term Arendt used—not at all as serious as Johnson's term— reflected an endemic sense of cultural superiority. But as long as it didn't affect her judgment of his performance, then the term she used in a private letter was politically irrelevant. Indeed, only because of the assiduousness of modern scholarship has the letter become public. In that sense, it is a kind of unwanted knowledge—except that it isn't.

Such a view should not go entirely unchallenged either. Just because Arendt viewed psychoanalysis with distaste does not mean that we should. In fact, psychoanalysis assumes that psychological change is possible only when a private experience or desire is made public to someone else by narrativizing it. It is often, perhaps almost always, impossible really to separate private and public judgments, but ethical or political considerations may make it politically necessary. In principle a Christian has to subject desire or intention to the same sort of scrutiny as she or he judges the effects of actions. (In traditional Christian terms, to look on a woman with desire carries the same moral weight as immoral sexual relations with her, as witness Jimmy Carter's confession in the presidential campaign of 1976 that he had looked on women with "lust in his heart.") Overall, private intentions and motivations can be separated from public action, but for the historian or the political analyst both realms need to be taken into account, if only to better judge the relationship between intentions and actions in the career of a particular political actor or thinker. We will return to this issue of intention and action in discussing the Eichmann case.

In the case at hand, then, several important things were, and still are, at issue. First, our primary concern here is with how Arendt's published writings might have shaped the racial views of others. As mentioned, the language of description and evaluation she applied to sub-Saharan African cultures in *Origins* presented them as culturally backward, but she also characterized the Civil Rights Movement in positive terms in her late essay "Civil Disobedience" (1970). Second, when we place her public use of patronizing terms about people of African descent side by side with her public condemnation of racism and, in the case at hand, her private praise of the African student(s), we are witnessing a person and a culture deeply divided in the way to think and talk about race. Third, though unseemly private expressions can be kept separate from acceptable public ones, the question as to which is the more important or authentic or real is not an empirical but a hermeneutic one. Fourth, contra Arendt, we should ask why it invalidates the political and moral status of the public world to also try to understand how private intentions and motivations relate to public utterances and actions? That Arendt did not call Africans or African Americans "fuzzy-heads" in her published writings—but did in a private letter to her husband—testifies to the fact that she herself tacitly understood the borderland between private and public in these matters. At the same time, that dividing line was, and is, neither self-evident nor self-reinforcing. Rather it must be constantly patrolled and assessed.

[CHAPTER 8]

Arendt, the Schools, and Civil Rights

The 1954 *Brown v. Board of Education* decision of the Supreme Court ushered in a period of constitutional "refounding" that saw the United States undergo a "minority rights revolution."[1] Hannah Arendt's "Reflections on Little Rock" (1959) was intended to call attention to what she saw as the disturbing implications of the Warren Court's epoch-making decision. Though she sometimes talked of race and rights in global terms, the occasion for "Reflections on Little Rock" was a very local controversy: the desegregation of Little Rock Central High School in Arkansas in the fall of 1957. Her article, which expressed doubt about the principles behind the *Brown* decision, the strategy adopted by local black leaders in Little Rock, and the wisdom of President Eisenhower's commitment of federal troops to enforce the desegregation order in late September 1957, was finally published in *Dissent* magazine in 1959, after having been rejected by *Commentary* magazine early the previous year. As Norman Podhoretz later wrote, the piece was rejected "on the basis of various high sounding pretexts but actually because they were too controversial." Besides that, the troubled reception of her essay was, in Ralph Ellison's words, a "dark foreshadowing of the Eichmann blow up" of 1963–64.[2]

Why did Arendt want to grapple with the issues raised by the Little Rock crisis in the first place? "The point at stake," she wrote in "Reflections," was not "the well-being of the Negro population alone, but at least in the long run, the survival of the Republic alone."[3] This decision traced back to her shock at seeing the photograph of one of the nine black students, Elizabeth Eckford, surrounded by a mob of screaming white people as Eckford approached Little Rock Central the morning of September 3, 1957.[4] In addition, the essay itself made clear that what happened to the students at Little Rock was, in her mind, a recognizable replay of—or at least a variation on—familiar patterns from the history of postemancipation Jewry.

Arendt's experience with the South and knowledge of its history was very minimal. At the beginning of "Reflections," Arendt explained her attitude toward the South: "I have never lived in the South and have even avoided occasional trips to Southern states because they would have brought me into a situation that I personally would find unbearable."[5] As she went on to note, this was not unusual for a European who had not grown up with race as a constant presence in her life. She seems to have been relatively ignorant of the historical circumstances in which Little Rock Central High was desegregated. "Reflections" includes very few references to the history of Supreme Court decisions on racial matters or the history of race relations in the South or the nation. Meili Steele's judgment that Arendt's work has swung between the "rich, historically detailed accounts of the world under totalitarianism" and "historically thin and idealized discussions of the retrievals of the Greeks and the thinkers of the American Revolution for their momentary achievement of freedom" clearly fits the historical "thinness" of "Reflections on Little Rock."[6]

Audience and Expectation

How did Arendt's "Reflections" comport with liberal opinion on racial matters in the mid- to late-1950s? *Commentary*'s readership, for whom it was first intended, was a largely northern, highly educated, liberal, and Jewish one. The magazine had been founded in 1945 as an organ of the American Jewish Committee. In addition, *Commentary* paid well for contributions. *Dissent* had been founded by Irving Howe and Lewis Coser in the early 1950s as a "quarterly of socialist opinion." It was generally close to the American labor movement, more radical politically, and did not pay well. When

Arendt's piece appeared in the winter 1959 issue, the editors prefaced it with a disclaimer making clear that the magazine was publishing the piece in the name of "freedom of expression," not because the editors and the board agreed with it.[7] Overall, the core contributors to the two journals (along with *Partisan Review*) were drawn from the same cultural and political pool and constituted the core membership in the New York intellectual group.

Surprisingly, the New York intellectuals included relatively few experts on American race and ethnic relations. *Dissent* sent a young Michael Walzer to cover the sit-in movement in the South in early 1960 and Southern historian C. Vann Woodward of Johns Hopkins contributed articles to *Commentary* about the white South as civil rights activities heated up in the late 1950s. But except for James Baldwin and Ralph Ellison (and arguably Anatole Broyard), there were very few African Americans among the contributors to any of the journals where the New York intellectuals published. There were certainly African American social scientists and historians active in the 1950s, for example, Kenneth Clark, E. Franklin Frazier, John Hope Franklin, and Oliver O. Cox; young black writers such as LeRoi Jones (later known as Amiri Baraka) and Lorraine Hansberry; and an impressive cadre of visual artists and jazz musicians in New York City. But they did not run in the same circles as the New York intellectuals.[8] Later, in the 1960s, Harold Cruse emerged as a leading black public intellectual in New York, but he was a veteran of the Communist Party USA and had contributed to *Freedomways* not the *Partisan Review*. The aging W. E. B. Du Bois moved into the anticolonial, pro-Stalinist orbit in the postwar years and thus his politics were hardly congenial to that of the New Yorkers. Trotskyist C. L. R. James, an admirer of Arendt's work and sometime correspondent with Daniel Bell, Dwight Macdonald, and various ex-Trotskyists, did not publish in the New York journals and had been expelled from the country for passport violations in the first half of the 1950s. Thus there very few people in Arendt's circles who might have set her straight on matters having to do with the South or with race.

This matter of Northern public opinion and historical knowledge is no abstract historical concern. Specifically, Arendt's relationship with her *Commentary* "handlers," George Lichtheim and Norman Podhoretz, along with the editorial board, especially Martin Greenberg, was replete with miscommunications, mutual recriminations, occasional apologies, and tension all around.[9] Lichtheim, an associate editor, was a Berlin-born, freelance intellectual who later wrote histories of Marxism, socialism, and imperialism. He usually lived in England, but in the late 1950s, he was in America for an extended period. He also had a distinct talent for rubbing Arendt the wrong way (and probably vice versa). It all began when Arendt submitted a piece to *Commentary* in the fall of 1957. In an early letter to her, Lichtheim boasted that, in the *Commentary* editorial board meeting to consider her submission, he had transformed what was originally the totally negative position of his colleagues into a qualified approval of her article — "under the condition that Sidney Hook, or someone else, would be requested to publish an annihilating counter-critique [*vernichtende Antikritik*] in the same issue . . . you seem to have threatened several sacred cows of the country."[10] Though he later suggested that his tone was deliberately jokey, this was not a very shrewd tactic to pursue. In fact, Lichtheim was known for his "biting irony," which, on the evidence here, he found hard to control. He also observed that Arendt's article specifically "affronts American Jewish-Liberal sentiment in some respects."[11] The problem here was not the warnings but the breezy, know-it-all tone. He also mentioned the need for minor rewritings and urged her to reconsider positions in her article that might give too many hostages to fortune. Most wrongheadedly, he seems to have assumed that, because Arendt was not a native, she shared his skepticism about the whole American political scene.

None of this went down well with Arendt, who refused to distinguish between the credentials of "natives" and her own as a naturalized citizen. As she wrote (in English): "In political matters I am as much of a native as any other American." As a citizen and a political scientist, she felt that her "judgment has at least as much weight as the judgment of journalists." Of course, Arendt was hardly known for her sense of humor, which may explain why she failed to "get" the joke about "annihilating" criticism: "I never heard of a magazine that wishes to publish an article for the sole purpose of having it 'annihilated.'"[12] Lichtheim's mention of Sidney Hook as a possible hatchet man would hardly have reassured Arendt that *Commentary* would stand behind the piece if it were subjected to Hook's considerable polemical talents. The term *vernichtende* itself may have jarred considerably, trailing, as it did, a whiff of the Final Solution. Still, Arendt also made an attempt to apologize to Lichtheim and invited him to her apartment for drinks.

But after these contretemps of late November and early December 1957, Lichtheim had the sense to turn to an admirer of Arendt, Norman Podhoretz, then on editorial staff, to take over working with Arendt. Meanwhile, the *Commentary* board, led by Martin Greenberg, vacillated and even showed the article to the David Sher, the chair of the publication committee, for approval. Podhoretz seems to have been ill, and Lichtheim reentered the picture. Finally, in February 1958, Arendt withdrew the article from consideration, but then reinstated it. In the end, it became a dead issue after more charges and countercharges were exchanged. After her withdrawal, one rumor was that she had "chickened out" because she couldn't face Hook's dissection of her article.[13] Hook's original response was later published as a pamphlet by the *New Leader* where he (rightly) took exception to Arendt's reference to his piece in her preface to the *Dissent* version of "Reflections" in 1959.

As a coda to the whole messy affair, Lichtheim wrote to Arendt in February 1959 to compliment her on her courage in allowing *Dissent* to publish the piece. This, he felt, would help discredit the rumors that she had been afraid to expose it to public scrutiny and rebuttal. Yet he diluted the effect of what seemed a generous apology by adding that he should never have doubted that she would want the piece published since "it gave you the chance to (a) mention Tocqueville."[14] In fact, it is easy to read his whole letter as an exercise in sarcasm if the final sentence in the first paragraph is any measure: "I was altogether mistaken about you, and I am the first man to proclaim it. You really do shrink from nothing. It was all our fault at *Commentary*."[15] Lichtheim concluded by repeating his more radical-than-thou agnosticism about the whole affair: "As I pointed out to you on the very first occasion when we talked about it, my own position is rather perversely noncommittal, since I frankly don't believe that any important problem can be solved in this century on the basis of liberalism, democratic or otherwise."[16] Lichtheim's ambiguous and ambivalent apology, along with a certain condescending liberal baiting, suggests that he was hardly the best person to have been Arendt's original editor for that piece.

Constitutional Ambivalence

But Arendt was not entirely alone in her unease with *Brown*. It is tempting to see *Brown* as the inevitable outgrowth of a post-1945 consensus that racial segregation contravened what Gunnar Myrdal called the American Creed and thus violated the spirit of the laws as well as the Constitution. On this account, the *Brown* decision ratified, rather than created, an emerging consensus among white Americans that segregation was wrong. In fact, the nation as a whole divided pretty evenly on *Brown*, with interesting variations noted, as, for example, "73% of college graduates approved of Brown, but only 45% of college dropouts did." Another example: when *Brown* was first argued in 1952 before the Court, the law clerks at the Court were all but unanimous in their support of the plaintiffs, the lone exception being future Chief Justice William Rehnquist, who was Justice Robert Jackson's clerk. None of this quite cinches the matter, but for legal historians like Mark Tushnet, it is "quite likely that something would have happened in the South without *Brown*."[17]

The problem in all this was the fickleness of public opinion and the sheer length of what came to be called the second Reconstruction. Public attitudes can remain static for a long time and then suddenly lurch into motion overnight. White Southern support for desegregation had all but disappeared by the time of the Little Rock crisis in 1957. Neither President Eisenhower nor the Senate, held to ransom by the threat of a filibuster from the Southern delegation, could be counted on to provide much leadership on the issue. Yet 1957 did see majority leader Lyndon Johnson steer the first civil rights bill since Reconstruction through the Senate and win approval by the Congress, though it was not a bill liberals were very happy with. Surprisingly *Brown* failed to hold the headlines for very long after it was announced on May 17, 1954, since Senator Joseph McCarthy was just beginning his last stand at ferreting out subversives from the federal government and the armed forces. But the white South was still very much paying attention, with billboards springing up around the region calling for the impeachment of Earl Warren and charging the Court with being anti-American, anti-Christian, and pro-Communist.

However, if such demagoguery was largely foreign to the North, some of the nation's most respected constitutional experts were surprisingly uneasy about the arguments behind the Court's decision in *Brown*. It is no wonder since the case itself and the ensuing controversy involved the two most problematic constitutional principles in the American system—states' rights and judicial review. The two legal thinkers chosen to deliver the prestigious Holmes Lectures at Harvard in 1958 and 1959—Judge Learned Hand and Herbert Wechsler of Columbia Law School, respectively—expressed serious doubts about the constitutionality and/or wisdom of the decision. On the one hand, Hand questioned the principle of judicial review, which allowed the Supreme Court to invalidate laws duly passed by Congress or other elected bodies. It was this active use of judicial review that led many observers, and not just Southerners, to see the legal-constitutional stance staked out by the Warren Court's decisions as only dubiously democratic and certainly politically unwise. Where the legal realist tradition sought to free majority views to express themselves in legislation (despite a conservative Court), the Warren Court set about rendering those laws unconstitutional that blocked minority rights, while affirming principles that expanded civil liberties and corrected distorted schemes of political representation (malapportionment).[18]

In his dissenting opinion on the wisdom of *Brown*, Wechsler asked whether a constitutional principle could be formulated that could be applied without having the desired outcome already in mind, that is, could constitutional reasoning ever be anything but an elegant form of special pleading? Was there an algorithm or neutral constitutional logic to justify *Brown*? Key concepts such as "equal protection" or "color blindness" were hardly neutral principles to be applied automatically. Finally, Alexander Bickel, one-time law clerk for Justice Felix Frankfurter, published an article in the *Harvard Law Review* in the mid-1950s based on background historical research he had done for the *Brown* decision. Bickel expressed serious doubt that those who wrote and supported the Fourteenth Amendment intended to outlaw segregated public schools. With this, Bickel raised not so much a theoretical as an empirical-historical question about the intentions behind the Fourteenth Amendment.

Not all of the nation's intellectuals outside the South were enthusiastic supporters of *Brown*, either. Like Wechsler and Bickel, some approved of the Court's ruling in principle but didn't agree with the constitutional reasoning behind it. Theologian Reinhold Niebuhr feared that the decision would needlessly alienate the white South and wondered, even though he approved of the decision, if the pace of desegregation wasn't too fast and the introduction of the 101st Airborne to oversee desegregation of Little Rock Central hadn't won the battle but lost the war. In his books *Segregation* (1956) and *The Legacy of the Civil War* (1961), poet, novelist, and critic Robert Penn Warren criticized the unthinking white Southern resistance to racial equality but also the smug self-righteousness of Northern liberals who had no real understanding of the meaning of racial change in the South.[19] Many others feared that enforcement of the *Brown* decision would discredit Southern progressive forces for years to come. Indeed, Justice Hugo Black of Alabama, one of the leading supporters of *Brown*, raised this very question and may have supported the milder *Brown II* because of this fear. Thus, though Arendt's approach to the issue was idiosyncratic, she was not alone in being troubled by the constitutional issues raised by the desegregation order of the Supreme Court.

The Issue of Discrimination

The position Arendt articulated in "Reflections" followed from her division of the world into three spheres of human interaction—the political or "body politic"; the social or "society"; and the "private" or sphere of intimacy. Each sphere or realm was guided by a single principle: "What equality is to the body politic—its innermost principle—discrimination is to society," while "the realm of privacy—is ruled neither by equality nor by discrimination but by exclusiveness." Much of Arendt's concern derived from her worry about the prospects of life in mass society. As we have seen, Arendt felt that conformity was especially strong in America, where it "tends to become an absolute and a substitute for national homogeneity."[20] But the assumption of hers that made such a huge difference was that public schools belonged properly to the social, not to the public-political, sphere. This meant that parents possessed "the private right over their children and the social right to free association."[21] Since discrimination was proper in the social realm, the social composition of a particular school might validly reflect parental choice as to whom their children associated with.

Though this may seem an unfamiliar way to analyze the constitutional and political issues involved in Little Rock, her distinction between the social and the political spheres was the rough equivalent of the public-private distinction familiar in American constitutional law at least since the *Civil Rights Cases* of 1883, which differentiated private, that is, nongovernmental institutions and actors, from state institutions and public actors, responsible to elected authorities. Where Arendt departed from the American liberal position was in reversing the valorization of the two spheres. While liberalism privileged private life and the pursuit of interests under the aegis of (negative) freedom, Arendt gave pride of place to public-political speech and action as something closer to (positive) freedom. She was not entirely consistent about the central principle informing the body politic or the political realm. She often identified "freedom" as its central point, but she also followed Montesquieu in identifying "virtue" (public-spiritedness) as the animating principle of a republic, while in "Reflections" she identified "equality" (equal legal status) as the crucial principle of the body politic. Certainly "Reflections," shows us Arendt as a kind of republican or civic humanist rather than an American liberal or a conservative.

As we have seen several times, the social in Arendt's thought covered several aspects of group life. "Reflections" was concerned not with the economic aspects of the social sphere but with the social as it related to forms of association, such as religious, racial, ethnic, and religious groups, along with voluntary clubs and societies. Such institutions were built on discrimination, which she saw as the essence of the social.[22] "Reflections" is also practically the only place in her work where she defends the social sphere in its American incarnations. She failed to see why private clubs or exclusive resorts should not be allowed to exclude those who did not fulfill the particular criteria of group membership or association. As she put it, the "moment social discrimination is legally enforced, it becomes persecution" but "the moment social discrimination is legally abolished the freedom of society is abolished."[23]

But Arendt had been here before. In discussing late-nineteenth-century European Jewry in *Origins* (and earlier), she claimed that postemancipation German Jews had been so preoccupied with acceptance into gentile society that they failed to defend their political and legal rights. In fact, she claimed (in a private letter) that in the German-Jewish experience there was an inverse relationship between social and political-legal equality.[24] Arendt's European-derived distinction between pariahs and parvenus was one of the lenses through which she judged Southern race relations Those Jews who succumbed to the seductive lures of gentile society—and tried to force, including buy, their way in—she called "parvenus," while those who maintained a self-chosen distance from it, she named "pariahs," a positive term in her conceptual vocabulary. For Arendt, it all seemed an "affair of social climbing," whether in Königsberg in East Prussia or in Little Rock in Arkansas.[25] In fact, black Americans did worry about whether they should try to force their way into social situations from which they were excluded informally or even legally. Many felt that they "had too much self-respect to go where they were not wanted."[26]

So, it was her proud pariah self-consciousness that explained her in-comprehension of, bordering on contempt for, the National Association for the Advancement of Colored People (NAACP) and the Supreme Court in sending black students into the teeth of the angry white mob. She was also disappointed with the parents themselves. She felt that the assumption behind school desegregation was a false one. Again, blacks should not seek to intrude into those settings where they were not wanted. It was this that seemed so demeaning to her. In response to the critics of "Reflections," she explained her reactions to the photo of Elizabeth Eckford: "My first question was: what would I do if I were a Negro mother? The answer: un-der no circumstances would I expose my child to conditions which made it appear as though it wanted to push its way into a group where it was not wanted. . . . If I were a Negro mother, I would feel that the Supreme Court ruling, unwillingly but unavoidably, has put my child into a more humiliat-ing position that it had been in before."[27] As illuminating as that distinction could be—the familiar terms "Uncle Tom" or more subtly "Oreos" (black on the outside but white on the inside) are cognate terms for "parvenus"— the novelist Ralph Ellison called her hand on it as we shall see.[28]

But what of the political sphere and state—as opposed to private— institutions? Since, according to Arendt, equal citizens occupied the political sphere, there was no justification for black disfranchisement in the South. As she wrote privately: "Rigorous enforcement of the Negro franchise would do more good than this whole educational adventure."[29] But, surprisingly, there was no mention in "Reflections" of the body politic as the realm of action and speech or as the realm of freedom, which she so stressed in *The Human Condition* (1958). In "Reflections," she also stressed that public services such as transportation, hotels, restaurants, museums, and theaters should not be segregated since these facilities were part of the "public domain" and should be open to all equally. Segregation in such public areas illustrated the "most inhuman and conspicuous" aspects of segregation and deserved to be targeted before the schools.[30] Arendt's objection to segregation in the public sphere proved inadvertently prophetic, since, after February 1960, the Civil Rights Movement shifted to attacking segregation in public establishments with consumer-initiated actions such as sit-ins and the freedom rides. More generally, her concern with balancing discrimination and equality arose from her anxiety about the stifling effects of conformity in a mass society, one of her constant worries that had nothing to do with race as such. These Veblenian and Tocquevillean motifs remind us that, as James Bohman has insisted, the tension between equality and diversity is a crucial line of thought running through "Reflections."[31]

Finally, there is the third sphere, one of privacy or intimacy. Arendt spoke from her own experience of having married a German gentile when she expressed her repugnance at the laws forbidding racial intermarriage in the South. Many liberals thought that raising this issue was a sure way to be consigned to irrelevance, but it wasn't the capricious claim that some readers took it to be. Mentioning it also showed that Arendt was not advancing racial or cultural arguments against desegregating schools. Rather, her defense of segregated schools was situational and principled. Besides, antimiscegenation laws, finally ruled unconstitutional by *Loving v. Virginia* (1967) after years of the Court avoidance of the issue, *were* outrageous.

And yet, she seemed bent on spoiling her case. First she alluded to Gunnar Myrdal's *An American Dilemma* (1944), which had reported interracial marriage as low on the list of black American priorities. That showed, she asserted provocatively, that "oppressed minorities were never the best judges on the order of priorities in such matters." Ironically, the confused priorities she had in mind here were those that arose in the history of postemancipation European Jewry as she had traced it in *Origins*. Her statement that "there are many instances when they preferred to fight for social opportunity rather than for basic human or political rights" was a reference to the Jewish parvenu behavior.[32] Had she simply said that Jews had also made mistakes in setting their goals, the irritating effect of her know-it-all attitude would have been lessened. Instead her statement looked like a put-down of African Americans, about whose lives she knew little. In addition, Arendt's reluctance to approach a political and social issue in psychological terms led her to neglect the sexual underpinnings of the segregationist ideology. Nor did she make enough of the glaring contradiction between segregationist sponsorship of antimiscegenation laws and the Sumnerian insistence that "stateways cannot change folkways."[33] Clearly, there had been nothing automatic about the full emergence of segregation in the post-Reconstruction era as C. Vann Woodward's *The Strange Career of Jim Crow* had made clear. Yet Arendt often sounded as though the existing order were somehow an unchanging given.

Ironically, Arendt's distaste for school desegregation also showed a kind of prescience, though perhaps for the wrong reasons. After the simmering three-year Little Rock school crisis, followed by desegregation of public schools in Atlanta and New Orleans in the early 1960s, the activist wing of the Civil Rights Movement shifted its efforts away from the schools as the main arena in the struggle for racial equality. Protracted court cases were simply too costly for the movement to afford and voter registration in the deep South seemed a better path to progress.

Critiques and Implications

Sphere Theory

Arendt's sphere theory was vulnerable on several grounds. Not surprisingly, her three main critics—David Spitz and Melvin Tumin in *Dissent* and Sidney Hook in a *New Leader* pamphlet—attacked the idea that human existence could be conceptualized in terms of three separate spheres of existence. Spitz saw Arendt's model as a somewhat baroque version of John Stuart Mill's distinction between the political and private but found it wanting: "Society is the web of all human relationships; the political and the private are at most distinguishable, but not separable strands within the greater fabric." For Hook, equality was as much a social and economic as a political and legal ideal.[34] Surprisingly, none of the critics referred to Arendt's *The Human Condition* (1958), where she spelled her position out in in greater detail.

But the criticisms of Spitz, Tumin, and Hook begged the question of the status of the social itself. Conventional wisdom on the left assumed the priority of the social over the political sphere, with self-interest defined largely in economic and social terms, and a thin notion of the common good. But it was precisely Arendt's point to challenge such understandings. None of the critics mentioned her worry that a consumption- and status-oriented citizen body provided shaky foundations for a republic to be erected on. Hook's specific criticism was harder to meet in empirical terms, since social and economic inequalities had real effects on the ability of citizens to act politically. But Arendt's positing of a dominant principle animating each of her spheres—equality in the political; discrimination in the social; and intimacy in the private—was a normative judgment not a descriptive claim. Her critics also missed the fact that she wanted to rethink the idea of equality as such.[35] Thus Arendt's project had dimensions to it that her critics seemed unaware of, restricted as they were by the terms of American political and legal culture and their failure to have read her other work.

Arendt's argument was, in fact, most vulnerable in its claim that public schools were social rather than political institutions. In the remarks prefacing "Reflections", Arendt recognized that she was on shaky grounds in this matter when she mentioned that a friend (probably Mary McCarthy) had also criticized her position.[36] Contrary to Chief Justice Earl Warren's claim in the *Brown* decision that, "today, education is perhaps the most important function of state and local governments," and thus clearly a "right which should be available to all on equal terms," Arendt focused on the parents' (social) right to choose a school for their children. She granted that the state could require school attendance and that curricular matters should reflect the "right of the body politic to prepare children to fulfil their future duties as citizens." However: "This public world is not political but social, and the school is to the child what a job is to an adult."[37] Arendt also referred readers to her 1958 essay "The Crisis in Education" for the broader rationale behind the Little Rock essay. (She had written it after the brouhaha with *Commentary* had blown over and before *Dissent* picked up "Reflections.") Along with the critique of progressive education found in it, she also wanted its readers to consider American education in the context of a decline in (parental) authority and tradition.[38] Second, in condemning politicized education in a specific sense, she nevertheless saw the task of education as one of conserving of the nation's traditions and preparing students to enter and, if need be, to "set right anew" the shared world. It was, she insisted, "exactly for the sake of what is new and revolutionary in every child [that] education must be conservative."[39]

But how did her arguments connect up with Little Rock? First, there was something to be said for Arendt's strong objection to politicizing education and making the schools into the battleground of desegregation with the children as foot soldiers. But the real danger at Little Rock was not from overly politicized black students but from the white students, who harassed them over the whole school year of 1957–58. Some of this was fed by resurgent ideologies of states' rights and also the blatant racism emanating from the Ku Klux Klan and the White Citizens' Councils all over the region. By the same token, Arendt's objection to the abdication of parental responsibility would have been better directed at the parents of hostile white students than the black ones.

Again, one can understand Arendt's immediate outrage at the way Elizabeth Eckford "obviously, was asked to be a hero—that is, something neither her father nor the equally absent representatives of the NAACP felt called upon to be."[40] But Arendt's claim here conflicts with other accounts. The black parents of the nine black students certainly were concerned about protecting their children. In fact, several of them had been very doubtful about allowing their children to participate.[41] But they had been assured by the authorities that protection would be forthcoming—and it was, but only after the fiasco of September 3, when Elizabeth Eckford was isolated and alone. Local NAACP leader Daisy Bates's account indicates that, on the night of September 2, all the parents and children were told by phone to stay away from the school the next day. But the Eckford family did not have a phone and Bates forgot to contact them in some other fashion. Elizabeth and her parents were not aware that Governor Faubus had decided to post

National Guard troops around Central High to keep the nine black students out, not protect them as they went in. Thus, when Elizabeth showed up the next day, she was unprotected.[42]

Still, there is more to be said in reference to two aspects of the situation here. First, Arendt's own experience in Königsberg helps explain the stress she placed on parental responsibility for their vulnerable children. Born in 1906, Arendt grew up in a secular, middle-class, educated household. She was one of three or four Jewish pupils in her year of a largely middle-class, gentile Gymnasium (secondary school) and thus, in American terms, attended an "integrated" public school. Arendt later remembered that her mother always insisted that "you have defend yourself" against anti-Semitic slurs from gentile classmates. But if such slurs came from a teacher, directed at her or other Jewish children, "eastern Jewish students in particular," Hannah was to leave class immediately and report it to her mother: "These were rules of conduct by which I retained my dignity, so to speak, and I was protected, absolutely protected, at home."[43]

Yet the differences between Königsberg and Little Rock were as important as the similarities. A firm protest from Arendt's mother would probably not have endangered her or her daughter. The likelihood was much greater that a parental protest would have drawn reprisals against black parents and their children in Little Rock and certainly in the rural and deep South in the 1950s. Also, if we accept Arendt's argument for the social nature of public schools, the Christian majority might have validly excluded her and her Jewish schoolmates from the state-run school she attended or made it distasteful to apply for admission to such a school in Königsberg. That kind of thing may have happened elsewhere in Central Europe or Russia, but it didn't happen to young Hannah. It is important to emphasize here that Arendt not only did not believe in ignoring insults, she was no advocate of nonviolence in every situation. The right and duty of individual and collective self-defense were self evident to her.

However, in 1965, Ralph Ellison criticized Arendt's "failure to grasp the importance of this ideal [of sacrifice]" and claimed that she had "no conception of what goes on in the minds of Negro parents when they send kids through the lines of hostile people."[44] Certainly, most others who have commented on "Reflections" have agreed with Ellison's criticism of Arendt's position on this issue, though Ross Posnock, in particular, has also stressed the similarity between Ellison and Arendt. Both spoke, he notes, with self-designated "Olympian authority"; neither had much use for the social sciences; and both stressed the need to act (Arendt politically and Ellison artistically) in the face of oppression.[45] More recently, Ellison's emphasis on the training in disciplined courage that black children received from their parents has been related by political philosopher Danielle Allen to the important idea of citizen "sacrifice" and mutual trust in African American and the general American political culture.[46]

Because the image of the "unwelcome child" was etched into Arendt's consciousness by this episode, it is only fair to honor, as it were, her sense of outrage at the image of a scared and beleaguered Elizabeth Eckford.[47] Undoubtedly Arendt didn't entirely get it and backed away from the charges she'd leveled about social climbing.[48] But she did get some of what Ellison himself neglected to mention. It is clear that African Americans, before and after this incident (for instance, at Birmingham in 1963), were far from united on the wisdom or morality of using children in public protests where their lives might be endangered. Moreover, not only Arendt but also black novelist and anthropologist Zora Neale Hurston thought forced integration was damaging to black self-respect. Later, Malcolm X, too, echoed Arendt's distaste for the way black parents and civil rights organizations in general were using children to fight the battles the adults ought to be leading.[49] To that extent, Arendt was speaking for those black parents who had serious doubts about the wisdom of sacrificing their children. Ellison's self-righteousness on this whole issue seems to me unjustified.

In private, at least, Arendt also distinguished between the dignity/identity of a person and the psychological well-being that arises from his or her acceptance into a group. The former, she wrote in her response to Matthew Lipman, was "not injured by discrimination, it cannot even be touched by it." In contrast, the negative feelings about the self that arise from being rejected "has nothing to do with human dignity." Rather, these feelings derive from "pushing, or rather being pushed into pushing, one's way out of one group and into another."[50] The distinction Arendt makes here between dignity and well-being is too absolute but nevertheless worth thinking through. It needs qualification in the same way her indictment of African American parents does. Overall, the matter of inclusion and exclusion as it had to do with the individual sense of self was one of the few issues she allowed herself to psychologize about, but not publicly.

Schools: Social versus Political

Arendt's basic mistake regarding the public schools was that she could only see the social dimension of them. (If all you have is a hammer, everything looks like a nail.) But if schools were primarily political in origins and purpose, that is, open to all under the aegis of public authorities, then the black children and their parents weren't pleading to be let in. Public schools did not belong just to white people near where they were lived and it didn't matter whether black people were welcome or liked. They were only asking for what was rightfully theirs as citizens, not begging for a favor. Thus, Arendt's categorization of schools as social can be criticized from an Arendtian point of view. If schools were public-political entities, then the crisis was the occasion for Little Rock's black citizens to become politically visible. What also happened during public protests was that the public realm itself was illuminated and revivified. Arendt had likely finished *The Human Condition* (1958) by the time she submitted "Reflections" in the fall of 1957 and published an early version of "What Is Freedom?" in 1960, so her concept of political action was pretty fully worked out by 1959. From this perspective, one could argue that Arendt failed to emphasize the fact that Little Rock's black residents were citizens in her "Reflections". It is an omission that makes her Little Rock essay seem strangely apolitical.

But there was something historically true about Arendt's claim concerning the social function of public schools. As she noted in "Crisis in Education," public schools in the United States had functioned in a more strongly "social" manner than schools in Europe. The American public school aimed to erase, or at least diminish, social and cultural differences (ethnicity, language, culture, and eventually status and class). Yet that weakened Arendt's defense of education as essential to the preservation of tradition. For, the purpose of assimilation was not to conserve the immigrants' traditions but to transform, or rather to undermine, them in order to make Americans out of them. Arguing against this assimilative function, Randolph Bourne, a disciple of John Dewey and William James, suggested in the 1910s that the schools should help immigrants preserve their old traditions as well as learning the new American ones. But whatever was the case in the Jewish section of Manhattan—Hester Street and the Lower East Side—white children in the South were legally separated from black children, solely on the basis of race not religion or national origins. If anything, segregated schools strengthened rather than overcame the differences between the two groups. While the social-cultural function of the public schools in America encouraged the assimilation of immigrant children, the assimilation of black Southerners into white society was legally blocked in all sorts of ways. Thus Arendt failed to take into account the way Southern public schools differed in function from Northern ones and how they stymied the transmission of the nation's traditions.

Arendt also had a strong point when she suggested that schools provided a focal point for the community in which they were located. The invocation of "neighborhood schools" by white parents and of "community schools" by black parents during the era of desegregation testified to the powerful hold that the public school as a social institution has had on Americans of both races. In the South, the (racial) discrimination allowed in the social sphere had overwhelmed the egalitarian principle that was to govern the political sphere. As Walker Percy once observed, the South (by which he meant the white South in general) was a very friendly place until "outsiders" interfered in its affairs. At that point, the South would reimagine itself as a vast racialized family (or kinship group) based on skin color and begin excluding those who differed from them.[51]

In fact, one of Sidney Hook's most effective criticisms of Arendt was that she never spelled out a way to distinguish between "justifiable" and "un-justifiable" social discrimination. Which, if any, social differences deserved preservation and which ones ought to be condemned and/or forbidden?[52] There is nothing in her analysis to explain why difference in appearance—skin color—is more (or less) valid than religious beliefs (churches) or a shared past experience (veterans organizations) or cultural heritage and language (ethnicity) as the basis for discrimination. One way to distinguish valid from invalid differences might be that discrimination based on voluntary or chosen differences (religion) or man-made ones (having served in the army) is different from discrimination based on ineradicable differences (skin color). Or perhaps there is no unjustifiable criterion of social discrimination, unless it violates the law in some other respect.

Finally, the role of education that Arendt most treasured—conserving and maintaining tradition—also implied that American public schools should teach some version of the idea of equality. In the United States, in contrast with East Prussia, the normative political tradition of the country was founded on political and legal equality. If children were taught about the Declaration of Independence and the Fourteenth Amendment, what would it mean to study them in a situation of legally enforced segregation? If Arendt stressed anything throughout her essay, it was that social discrimination should never be mandatory. Yet segregation in public schools in the South was legally mandated, not just allowed by law. No wonder many of her readers came away confused.

States' Rights

Another thing that particularly stuck in the craw of Arendt's liberal (and Northern) readers was her defense of states' rights. It was on the historical role that states' rights doctrine had played in the history of regional and racial conflict that Arendt was tone deaf, even though she granted that the idea of states' rights was a "ready-made subterfuge of 'Southern reactionaries.'"[53] Yet the fact that she had fled Hitler's totalitarian regime, where "power, like sovereignty, was indivisible," meant that she was more appreciative of a system of decentralized power than were homegrown American liberals. What followed from her great fear of concentration of power and unified sovereignty was that no country, particularly one the size of America, could or should be ruled exclusively from the center. This was the meaning of her claim that power, by which she meant popularly supported authority rather than brute force or violence, was augmented rather than diminished by being divided: "The point is that force can, indeed must, be centralized in order to be effective, but power cannot and must not."[54]

Yet, constitutionally, the executive branch had a duty to enforce federal court-ordered desegregation. As David Spitz pointed out, it was simplistic to imply, as she did, that the issue was about a federally imposed tyranny of the majority over a state- or region-based minority, that is, the white South: "The conflict is rather one between a national majority and a national minority *and* between local majority and local minority."[55] With this, Spitz meant to remind Arendt of the rights, not just the responsibilities, of the black parents. Still, Arendt's defense of states' rights was at least worth making, since it challenged conventional liberal wisdom. That said, the era of "massive resistance" in the South was not the best historical moment to remind liberals that states' rights had constitutional and political merit, despite its use by segregationists. Like judicial review, the idea of states' rights was an exceedingly problematic one when examined more closely.

But there was a more subtle confusion about federalism in her essay. The doctrine of state action (articulated in the *Civil Rights Cases* of 1883), established the public-private distinction, which only permitted federal authority to intervene in the public (governmental) rather than private (nongovernmental) sphere. But because public schools traditionally fell under state and local rather than federal control, they appeared—for example, in Little Rock—to derive their legitimacy from the intentions of private individuals acting as part of a social interest group. Segregationists could trade on the aura local schools had of being private social institutions, illegitimately threatened by an invasive federal presence. In truth, however, both federal and state law created and maintained the school systems. But, as already mentioned, segregation was also a conscious legal creation, a prime example of social engineering by state and local governments. In sum, the thrust of Arendt's essay was to associate state law with the social sphere, while associating federal power with the mandate of equality, that is, the tyranny of the majority and the power of the state.

Race: (In)visibility, Equality, and Difference

In "Reflections," Arendt tended to focus less on race from an ideological standpoint than from a phenomenological one, as the way black Americans appeared in the world. Later, this same trope of visibility occurred in the truncated discussions of race in *On Revolution* (1963) and was cryptically linked to poverty in notes Arendt prepared for a lecture at Emory University in 1964: "The poor man is never seen: Visibility achieved in revolutions.

Slavery prevented Social Question: Negroes did not appear."[56] In fact, this cryptic observation linking poverty, (in)visibility, revolution, slavery and race was prefigured in the opening pages of "Reflections." There Arendt wrote of the way "the Negroes stand out because of their 'visibility'" and she linked that to the way immigrants, for example, Jews and Italians, were once judged negatively by their "audibility."[57]

Furthermore, though visibility is a matter of surfaces, it is not a superficial thing but, rather, is freighted with symbolic importance. In time, immigrants came to sound less loud to the dominant white society, but African Americans never seemed to become less visible. Sound differences fade, but color differences don't. Returning to the discussion in *Origins* of the alien: "The 'alien' is a frightening symbol of difference as such, of individuality as such, and indicates those realms in which man cannot change and cannot act and in which, therefore, he has a distinct tendency to destroy."[58] Difference is an integral part of the human condition, but it may also be experienced as a threat to political order and even to political equality.

This brings us back to Ellison versus Arendt, this time on the issue of invisibility, in terms of which Ellison famously characterized African American existence. For him, color seemed to make it impossible for white people to see what a black person was really like—that is, who she or he was. Thus it was not only an epistemological issue but also an ontological one: invisibility led to nonbeing. In experiencing themselves as not seen, African Americans were neither recognized nor acknowledged. They counted for nothing.[59] For her part, Arendt emphasized that the very visibility of blackness created an almost instinctive reaction against black people, not initially because white people were ideological racists but because African Americans took on the literal otherness of being a different color. While Ellison claimed that invisibility was experienced by black people as meaning they were nothing, the heightened visibility of black people to a predominantly white society meant that they were opaque, rather than invisible. Whites thought it was impossible to "read" blacks because of their color, whereas, in the Ellisonian analysis, white people could not read black people because they didn't take the trouble to see them.

In a basic sense, then, Arendt's analysis described the immediate reactions of white people, while Ellison's idea of invisibility was closer, perhaps, to the way black people experienced nonrecognition from whites. Where Arendt's concept of visibility has most purchase is in the simplicity of its claim—to stand out is to be vulnerable; those who are vulnerable stand out. Elizabeth Eckford would not have attracted the mob of heckling whites if she had not been so visible as a young black woman. Of course the Ellisonian point (deriving from the appearance-reality distinction) is that Elizabeth's real qualities were invisible to the mob. And that, of course, is true. But the further Arendtian point is that in a politicized setting Eckford's color symbolized her otherness. She was perfectly readable, not as Elizabeth Eckford but as "one of those black students." In that setting, the white crowd was quite "right" to key on her appearance, which had become politicized.

In "Reflections," Arendt also echoed *Origins* in noting that "the principle of equality, even in its American form, is not omnipotent; it cannot equalize natural, physical characteristics. . . . The more equal people have become in every respect, and the more equality permeates the whole texture of society, the more will differences be resented, the more conspicuous will those become who are visibly and by nature unlike the others."[60] In other words, the modern emergence of equality seemed to have a zero-sum quality to it: the more class differences and legal inequalities were lessened, the more the temptation of racial discrimination grew. From this she reasoned that the social sphere must be cordoned off from the political realm where equality should be the governing principle.

What should we make of Arendt's thesis, which runs counter to the modern idea of the historical inevitability of equality and freedom? Arendt, like Tocqueville, seemed to suggest that a deep human impulse drove individuals and groups to distinguish themselves from, and make themselves superior to, the other. The dynamic that drives Hegel's account of interpersonal confrontation is the drive for recognition of one's freedom, that is, of one's superiority—or in some cases equality—to the other. Not to mention Thorstein Veblen's positing of an instinct not just of workmanship but also of emulation in human beings. Indeed, what Arendt emphasized in the politics of the Greek polis was the desire to outshine others and amass glory in the public realm. For Arendt, like Tocqueville, it was not simply, or mainly, economic inequality that underlies racial prejudice or discrimination. Rather it is the quest for a way of distinguishing "me" from "you" and "us" from "them."

In all this, what remains difficult, as Arendt admitted, was the distinction between equality and sameness and between inequality and difference. One could frame the political issue, as Margaret Canovan has suggested, to say that a political-legal framework of equality should be established within which difference can be protected, even flourish.[61] Arendt largely shared this cultural pluralist ideal. But in practice, inequality and difference are often hard to separate. In Arendt's warning that "the more conspicuous will those become who are visibly and by nature unlike the others," is the "visible" that which is "by nature unlike the other"?[62] Are there other sorts of "natural" differences that count? And is it possible for a political order to recognize natural or cultural differences without either penalizing or privileging them? Is color blindness the only answer or no answer at all? These are only a few of the thorny questions that "Reflections" insists we confront and explore—though it was something that the piece itself failed to do.

Finally, much—but not all—of what made Hannah Arendt's challenge to school desegregation difficult to come to terms with were the kinds of arguments she used. She made no real attempt to link her position to, or contrast it with, *Brown* and previous Court decisions. As her biographer, Elisabeth Young-Bruehl, has noted, Arendt might also have defused some of the criticism of her "Reflections on Little Rock" by acknowledging from the start her strong objections to putting school children on the public firing line, not to mention a fuller explanation for her opposition to antimiscegenation laws. One of the moderate positions at the time called for efforts to secure the black vote in the South rather than trying to begin with school desegregation. Privately, she indicated agreement with this position. Yet Arendt did not make it a key point in her article, though it would have been consistent with her commitment to the priority of the political. Finally, the historical and cultural experience in Germany that she brought to the Little Rock crisis illuminated—but also hindered—a full understanding of the historical and cultural complexities involved there.

CHAPTER 9

The Eichmann Case

The American intellectual public was well primed for *Eichmann in Jerusalem: A Report on the Banality of Evil.* In turn, Arendt's most controversial book was crucial in shaping the contours of understanding of (and disagreements about) the Holocaust from the moment of its appearance until now. Between the translation of *The Diary of a Young Girl* (later *The Diary of Anne Frank*) in 1952 and the Six-Day War in 1967, numerous works touching on what was now called the Holocaust began appearing.[1] This was not just true in the academic world or with freelance intellectuals but also in popular culture. Otto Preminger's movie *Exodus* (1960), a story of Israel's founding, originated as a best-selling 1958 novel by Leon Uris. It was followed by Sidney Lumet's *The Pawnbroker* (1964), which explored the experience of a Holocaust survivor as he sought to overcome the emotional detachment incurred during his time in a Nazi camp. Nor was the irony lost on anyone when the Selma-to-Montgomery civil rights march in Alabama was violently disrupted by nightstick-wielding state troopers and ABC-TV interrupted Stanley Kramer's *Judgment at Nuremberg* (1964) to show footage of black Alabamians beaten to the ground on "Bloody Sunday," March 7, 1965.

It was within this context that the capture of Adolf Eichmann in Argentina on May 11, 1960; his trial in Jerusalem between May and December 1961; the appearance in February and March of 1963 of a five-part report in the *New Yorker* by Arendt on the Eichmann trial; the publication of these articles as *Eichmann in Jerusalem*; and an ensuing public controversy over the next couple of years had a profound cumulative effect on thinking about the Holocaust as "an entity in its own right" and as a "distinct thing" as opposed to "Nazi Barbarism in general."[2] The initial reactions to Eichmann's capture and trial were fascinating too. Newspapers, journals, and magazines across the political spectrum weighed in, often in criticism of Israel's kidnapping of Eichmann. Some critics called for the trial to be an international one, while others thought (West) Germany was the proper venue/jurisdiction for trying the former SS officer. Cold War issues were less prominent than they once had been, but many still feared such a trial would remind people that Germany, America's ally during the Cold War against the Soviet Union, had been responsible for the mass murder of European Jewry. Some talked of the whole affair as demonstrating the "difference between Christian forgiveness and 'Jewish vengefulness.'"[3] If there was ever a time when criticism of Israel was not off limits, from liberals as well as conservatives, Protestants, Catholics, and Jews, it was then.

Near the end of the public controversy in 1965, Arendt herself underlined the ready availability of works on the Holocaust to the reading public. Speaking at the University of Maryland in April of that year, she challenged the conventional wisdom that Western governments and societies had failed to take cognizance of what was going on in the death and concentration camps during the war. Instead, she insisted, the scandal was the failure of any of these governments to act on the knowledge they possessed. It was a failure not of European humanism per se but specifically of "European liberalism (socialism not excluded)." All across Europe, governments had uniformly failed to take political and military action to stop the massacre of European Jewry.[4] She also disputed the contention that there had been a "continuous silence" since the war about the Holocaust from writers, historians, and intellectuals, thus challenging preemptively historian Peter Novick's central thesis in *The Holocaust in American Life* (1999) that nearly two decades passed after the end of the war before a direct confrontation with the Holocaust took place.

Even more saliently, Arendt focused on the relationship of the humanist tradition (specifically the German version of it) to the Nazi genocide when she asked rhetorically: "Is it really an argument against Hölderlin or Beethoven to be read and listened to, perhaps even appreciated, by the commanders of *Einsatzgruppen*?" Arendt avoided further engagement with the question by suggesting that the biggest worry was a "new class of intellectual" who seemed more "swayed by public opinion" and "less capable of judging themselves than about any other social group." Overall, her assessment of the Western humanist tradition was not that it had been actively complicit but that it was "in the danger of becoming *irrelevant*."[5]

As always, Arendt avoided singling out German culture for special condemnation. She refused to blame, say, the tradition of German romanticism, as did some émigré scholars (though she herself had little affection for that tradition), or to see a line of continuity linking Martin Luther to Hitler, as did Thomas Mann or an Americans such as Peter Viereck. This meant, however, that she never grappled, not out loud at least, with the relationship between culture and barbarism raised by her friend Walter Benjamin. Instead, she tended to argue publicly that totalitarianism and nihilism had found their sources in the "gutter," not the mainstream of the Western tradition. She never suggested, as did Theodor Adorno, that poetry had somehow been rendered impossible or more difficult "after Auschwitz"; nor did she join George Steiner in wondering if the German language had been fatally corrupted by Nazi rhetoric and barbarity. And yet, as we shall see, she did suggest that Eichmann had been rendered incapable of moral self-reflection by the distortions in usage caused by Nazi political and racial rhetoric.[6] Her emphasis on the corruption of language as crucial in explaining Eichmann's failure of conscience is central to her understanding of what made Eichmann so important to understand.

The works she mentioned as available to the reading public had various origins. Two of them were by German writers—Günther Grass's novel *The Tin Drum* (1959) and Rolf Hochhuth's *The Deputy* (1963), a play that explored the complicity of Pope Pius XII in the Holocaust and thus attracted the same kind of obloquy as her Eichmann book had. Of course *The Origins of Totalitarianism* (1951) had focused attention on the mass murder of European Jewry, while American journalist William Shirer's *The Rise and Fall of the Third Reich* was a best seller in the early 1960s, though only 2–3 percent of its pages were devoted to the Holocaust.[7] French novelist André Schwarz-Bart's *The Last of the Just* (1959; English translation,1960) attracted much attention in Anglophone countries as well as in France where it was originally published. And of course, *The Diary of Anne Frank* became a major Broadway play and film and sold millions of copies as a book.

Several academic works at the time revealed the emergence of Holocaust awareness in the American academy. Historian Kirsten Fermaglich has focused close attention on the work of four Jewish scholars or intellectuals that owe their existence to the gradual but pervasive effects of the Holocaust on the spirit of the times—and beyond. The first of these is historian Stanley Elkins's *Slavery* (1959), which was an extended—and eventually controversial—comparison of life in New World slavery and in the Nazi concentration camps. Arendt thought highly of his book. The second book Fermaglich focuses on is Betty Friedan's popular classic *The Feminine Mystique* (1963), which controversially used concentration camp imagery to describe the situation of mostly middle-class women in suburban America, while psychologist Stanley Milgram—author of the third work singled out by Fermaglich—analyzed the willingness to inflict pain on alleged subjects in a psychological experiment. Milgram's scholarly articles were eventually expanded into *Obedience to Authority* (1974), and Milgram explicitly acknowledged the influence of *Eichmann in Jerusalem* on his work. Finally, Fermaglich looks at *Death in Life* (1967) by psychoanalyst Robert Jay Lifton, who studied "survivor guilt" in Japan with one eye obviously on the burdens carried by Holocaust survivors as well.[8]

Finally, with the Vietnam War heating up in the mid-1960s, Norman Fruchter wrote one of the most dispassionate and conscientious surveys of the Eichmann controversy in *Studies on the Left*. His "Arendt's Eichmann and Jewish Identity" (1965) focused on questions of post-Holocaust Jewish identity and especially obedience to morally and politically compromised political authority. Young American men clearly faced the problem of serving in a war in Southeast Asia that many had already rejected as illegitimate and unwise, a position Arendt agreed with by the mid-1960s.[9] Thus the issues that Arendt's book on the Eichmann trial explored—especially the obedience to authority and the resistance to state power—found increasing resonance and amplification in 1960s America.

Arendt did not come to cover the Eichmann trial accidentally. First, she saw the Eichmann trial as the successor to the Nuremberg Trials of the early postwar years, yet she also recognized its ambiguous status somewhere between the universalism of the Nuremberg Trials and the particularist emphasis of the Israeli government. One of her criticisms of the Israeli government was that while she thought that Eichmann should be tried for "crimes against mankind committed on the body of the Jewish people," the prosecution wanted to conduct the trial with specific reference to his "crimes against the Jewish people."[10] This was closely connected with her charge that the Jerusalem trial was a kind of a "show trial," that the Israel government wanted to demonstrate not just that justice could be done to Eichmann, but finally another, more important kind of justice would be done for the suffering of the Jewish people and the state of Israel as their representative.

There was a personal dimension to all this as well. As she wrote in her application to the Rockefeller Foundation for financial support to attend the Eichmann trial, "I missed the Nuremberg Trials," while also noting that "to attend this trial is somehow, I feel, an obligation I owe my past." Originally she thought that Eichmann would best be tried in an international court of justice, but she came to accept Israel's legal competence to try him, despite her belief that the law was unable to deal satisfactorily with such radically nihilistic forms of human behavior.[11] She did not think that Eichmann should be spared the death penalty either. The idea that Arendt was uniformly hostile to Israel's decision to put Eichmann on trial or that she did not think he had had a fair trial are myths that were put into circulation at the time but they are without foundation.

Even before the whole Eichmann affair, Arendt had written to Karl Jaspers that she had come to see the great value of legal concepts and judicial trials, possibly, she observed, because she had been "infected with anglo-saxon attitudes" (*angelsächsisch angesteckt*).[12] What she meant was that, as she wrote in the postscript to *Eichmann*, trials made it "well-nigh impossible to evade issues of personal responsibility." On one level, the trial was about whether Eichmann was a mere "cog" (the defense argument) or "the actual motor" of the Final Solution (the prosecution's case). Though she rejected the "cog" argument, Arendt noted that even when people like Eichmann were considered cogs, they were "transformed back into perpetrators, that is to say, into human beings" when they actually took the stand. For her, accompanying factors and forces were "circumstances" but that by no means was a way of "excusing" the crime.[13] Finally, Arendt returned in her postscript to the issues she had raised in her 1945 essay "Organized Guilt and Universal Responsibility"—the strange relationship between guilt and responsibility. As in that essay, she contended in *Eichmann in Jerusalem* that "it was usually the inmates and the victims who had actually wielded 'the fatal instruments with [their] own hands,'" while those higher-up kept their hands clean, as it were. However, in fact, *"the degree of responsibility increases as we draw away from the man who uses the fatal instrument with his own hands."*[14]

One contributing factor to the great controversy around Arendt's report had to do with her choice to focus on a single figure, whom she considered simultaneously unique and representative of the German (European) life of his time. Specifically, she suggested that Eichmann's "conscience" had been "in perfect harmony" with the milieu he had inhabited as an active Nazi. Like Eichmann, she said, Germany "had been shielded against reality and factuality by exactly the same means, the same self-deception, lies, and stupidity." In both cases, "mendacity," self-deception, and a kind of culpable innocence that "peace with [his] former enemies" could be achieved were all too obvious.[15] When one adds to that the great importance of the party and state bureaucracies within which Eichmann functioned, the idea of offering a simple account of guilt or responsibility seems quite daunting.

Finally, the trial itself was the first of the war crimes trials that made victim/survivor testimony crucial in the deliberations. Thus it was a watershed moment in the historical remembrance of the Shoah. Arendt thought the vast majority of survivor testimony was irrelevant, since it did not bear on the question of Eichmann's direct responsibility. Strictly speaking, she contended, the trial was about "justice" in the case of Adolf Eichmann, not about the genocide exacted against the Jewish people of Europe. It was the latter that was, she thought, part of the show trial aspect of the whole production. She was struck in the "endless sessions that followed, how difficult it was to tell the story." In her postscript, however, Arendt changed direction and expanded on what she hoped could be gained through hearing the personal testimony of the survivors. Where she had earlier spoken of "holes of oblivion" into which human deeds and events would disappear forever, she now believed, she told her good friend Mary McCarthy, that "the holes of oblivion do not exist" and at least "one man will be left alive to tell the story." Though each survivor's story had an intensely personal dimension, she was most interested in those accounts that understood the "lesson" derived from a retelling of their experience, "that under the conditions of terror most people will comply but *some people will not*" and "'it could happen' in most places but *it did not happen everywhere*."[16]

A Question of Character: Between Good and Evil

The single most contested idea to come out of *Eichmann* was the idea— though she insisted it was a "factual matter"—of "the banality of evil." Many of Arendt's readers strenuously resisted the notion of the banality of evil, as though it trivialized the immense suffering and unprecedented attempt to eradicate European Jewry. It is worth remembering here that the problem of evil and goodness was at issue in both books Arendt published in 1963—not only the Eichmann book but also *On Revolution*. But each book approached the topic very differently. While Arendt's purpose in *On Revolution* was to show, using Herman Melville's novella *Billy Budd*, the danger that either pure "goodness" (Billy Budd) or pure "evil" (John Claggart) posed for a political order, in *Eichmann in Jerusalem* she sought to revise received wisdom about the nature of evil in general.[17] There was really no Budd-like figure in *Eichmann in Jerusalem*, unless it was Anton Schmid, a sergeant in the German army who had helped the Jewish underground with "forged papers and military trucks."[18]

But there are other links between her exploration of evil and the literary tradition. It is highly likely that Arendt knew the 1939 poem "Herman Melville" by her friend W. H. Auden, though she and Auden did not meet until 1958 and they never mentioned it to one another. In its second stanza, Auden explored the conflict between good and evil as it appeared in Melville's *Billy Budd*. One of the central themes of Auden's poem is the relationship between the "everyday" and that which radically disrupts or undermines it. Here is its third stanza:

> Evil is unspectacular and always human
> And shares our bed and eats at our table
> And we are introduced to Goodness every day.

Even in drawing-rooms among a crowd of faults;
He has a name like Billy and is almost perfect
But wears a stammer like a decoration:
And every time they meet the same thing has to happen;
It is the Evil that is helpless like a lover
And has to pick a quarrel and succeeds,
And both are openly destroyed before our eyes.

Though clearly alluding to *Billy Budd*, Auden also rings some crucial changes on it. Most strikingly Auden seeks to demystify evil, to rob it of its charisma or shock value, which, as we shall see, was part of the effect of Arendt's analysis of Eichmann as well. In fact, in the story, Claggart's evil closely resembles traditional representations of evil as "motiveless malignity," Coleridge's description of Iago's actions. Yet Auden also evokes something only suggested by Melville's story—that Claggart is taken by Billy's beauty and thus "helpless like a lover." Auden turns same-sex erotic attraction in Melville's work into a trope for how opposites attract, yet end by destroying each other. If she did know the Auden poem, it is not that Arendt "applied" Auden in both her works of 1963, but that the cluster of motifs arising in the second stanza of his poem may have stimulated her efforts to explore the various ways evil appears in the world.[19]

Of course, by introducing the concept of radical evil near the end of *Origins*, Arendt took a first step toward re-instating the binary evil/good to a position of importance in modern thought, from which Nietzsche had expelled it. As historian Steven E. Aschheim once noted, Arendt played "a crucial role in the formulation and creation of the ubiquitous postwar 'discourse on evil.'"[20] At one level, Arendt's revival of the idea of evil was a retrograde move in a world that had allegedly lost its capacity for "god talk." But her concepts of evil and good were underpinned by no religious or theological claims or experience. They were thoroughly worldly phenomena or "facts" as applied to action and/or to the character of a human agent (individual or collective).

In certain ways, Arendt had to reimagine a person, Adolf Eichmann, who took his place as a character in her book. This is not to say that she created Eichmann out of whole cloth, but it is to say that the facts at her disposal could have been arranged in other ways—and have been. In Eichmann's case, his own testimony, along with historical documents she had at her disposal, were sources of information. But as we shall see, they were not all the information. Arendt's central problem was how to create a character who could have done what he did and yet also be convincing. He had to seem merely human rather than "demonic" (a term she used quite often in reference to radical evil near the end of the Eichmann book and afterward). Arendt's Eichmann emerged as a failed self, one lacking in capacity to think about others or himself with any insight. This incapacity could be traced back to the "language rules" (*Sprachregulung*) that the clichés and euphemisms of state and party rhetoric reflected. Most notorious here were concepts such as the Final Solution (*Endlösung*) and other terms referring to the process of extermination, such as "evacuation" (*Aussiedling*) or "resettlement" (*Umsiedlung*). As she observed, the "language rule" itself was a euphemism for "what in ordinary language would be called a lie."[21] Arendt's interest in Eichmann's use of language was no exercise in literary showing off, not a put-down of a cultural and intellectual inferior. It was absolutely central for Arendt, since Eichmann's banality had to do most prominently with how he thought about and then justified what he had done. What his language revealed to her was a self that had not yet acquired, or had long since lost, an authentic sense of itself. On one level, Arendt succeeded brilliantly in re-creating Eichmann. Without making evil interesting, she succeeded in sustaining our interest in it, something that fiction writer Flannery O'Connor once wrote was difficult, even impossible.[22] But there were problems, of course—too many people could remember the difference between the smartly dressed and intimidating Eichmann in Budapest and Eichmann in his glass box in Jerusalem, a pedantic, almost clownish, nervous, and twitchy figure.

After the publication of the book in the spring of 1963, much of critical discussion settled on the explosive phrase "the banality of evil," which were the last four words in the original text and also part of the subtitle. Besides the "holes of oblivion" issue, Arendt wrote to Mary McCarthy that *Eichmann in Jerusalem* "was much less influenced by ideology than I assumed in the book on totalitarianism." She had come to feel that "the content of anti-semitism [*sic*] for instance gets lost in the extermination policy" and that the "phrase: 'Banality of Evil' stands in contrast to the phrase I used in the totalitarianism book, 'radical evil.'"[23] As she said earlier in the book "his was obviously also no case of insane hatred of Jews, of fanatical anti-Semitism or indoctrination of any kind" and "he did not enter the Party out of conviction."[24] In this respect, Arendt thought that Eichmann was less driven by anti-Semitism, pure and simple, than by his obligation to carry out the orders to exterminate European Jewry, particularly from Hungary. That Eichmann disobeyed Heinrich Himmler's orders to shut down the extermination process in the fall of 1944 was not "proof of his fanaticism, his boundless hatred of Jews." Rather it was "his very conscience that prompted Eichmann to adopt his uncompromising attitude."[25] He felt an obligation to obey orders that continued the Final Solution, which would presumably outlast even the extermination of the Jews.

Moreover, in her next letter to McCarthy, Arendt also underscored the peculiar nature of her book as a "report," a genre that "leaves all questions of why things happened as they happened out of account."[26] The refusal of the "why" question meant that she did not develop or explore evil further in her book. She was interested in *how* Eichmann appeared and functioned, not especially why he chose to act as he did. From this perspective, her failure to spell out the idea of evil as banality was not an example of coyness: "When I speak of the banality of evil, I do so only on the strictly factual level."[27] Moreover, Arendt's challenge to the idea of Eichmann as a vicious anti-Semite was made easier by her suspicion of the venerable Zionist assumption of "eternal anti-Semitism."

Overall, in her Eichmann book, Arendt went beyond the traditional meanings of evil that she had set forth, however briefly, in *Origins*. Banality of evil implied that the evil that Eichmann manifested did not arise from a deep commitment to, say, eliminationist anti-Semitism or racism; nor was Eichmann a psychopath, a serial killer in an SS uniform. One way to get at this notion is to think of the idea of a "conformist" racist as someone who can live a normal existence without being involved in racist persecution or violence against people of other races or cultures. Yet, if called on, such a person can formulate or carry out orders that entail massacres, atrocities, or genocide. In turn, this conformist racist can return to a normal existence of law-abiding, respectable behavior when the situation allows it. This type manifests what Arendt had earlier identified in the bourgeois personality as a profound split between public and private morality. As we have already seen, it was in her 1945 essay "Organized Guilt and Universal Responsibility" that she linked this idea to Heinrich Himmler, as the prototypical bourgeois as *genocidaire*. Much of her analysis in that essay points directly toward the banality notion as she applied it to Eichmann.

If we look at the qualities associated with banality, then the title of Robert Musil's multivolume novel *Der Mann ohne Eigenschaften* (*The Man without Qualities*) captures something about this type of evil. Arendt thought of banality in qualitative not quantitative terms. It did not mean "average" or "normal." "Mediocrity" is close to this sense of banality as Arendt used it. To German journalist Joachim Fest, she noted that "there's nothing deep about it" or about Eichmann. He was no "fallen angel" like Lucifer; there was nothing "demonic" to him, no hint of the anti-human about him.[28] This was as close as Arendt comes to touching on what Susan Sontag later referred to as the aesthetics of evil, which arises at the intersection of eros and thanatos, sex and death, of bodies massed and leaders standing out.[29] But there was little or nothing of the patina of black leather and SS regalia about Eichmann, not at least in Jerusalem.

A related cluster of associations that Arendt also linked with banality had to do with superficiality and evanescence. It is rarely remarked that, in her response to Gershom Scholem, Arendt briefly mentioned banality as a characteristic of evil itself, not just a way of describing the actions, statements, or personality of a perpetrator of evil. Evil could be, she had decided, "extreme," but never "radical."[30] For example, what happened after the war was not that Germany deteriorated into a place of evil and lawlessness, an antirepublic run by former Nazi functionaries where life was cheap. Rather, it was quite a law-abiding parliamentary democracy that developed a consumer economy via the *Wirtschaftswunder*. A nation of ideological fanatics had over night, as it were, become a body of men and women with moderate, even nonexistent, political convictions and moral values. Closely linked with this notion of banality is, as mentioned, the absence of any sense of the "demonic" about Eichmann and of Germans in general in the postwar world. The "wholly other" or the satanic did not take up lodging in the Federal Republic of Germany.

The lesson that many drew from Arendt's analysis is that there is a so-ciology of evil, with the banality of evil being a peculiarly modern phenom-enon encouraged by large-scale bureaucracies. In the "rule by Nobody," as Arendt put it, large-scale bureaucracy could easily carry out "administra-tive massacre" run by "desk murderers."[31] Seyla Benhabib's suggestion that Arendt might better have spoken of "the routinization of evil" belongs in the same sociological tradition that arises from the work of Max Weber and the Frankfurt School.[32] Dutch novelist Harry Mulisch, to whom Arendt re-ferred favorably in her conversation with Joachim Fest, stressed the way that Eichmann's life was devoted to following "the order." Once committed to obedience to a person or institution, he would obey whatever was ordered, whether it was Adolf Hitler or Albert Schweitzer. Or as Mulisch observed: "He is less a criminal than he is someone who is capable of anything."[33] Arendt also saw this quality in Eichmann, one that helped explain his loyalty to the party, his need to belong somewhere and keep faith with it. In this area, Arendt was also redeploying some of her observations from *Origins* where she depicted mass men as strangely nonideological and willing to act against their own self-interest. Erich Fromm captured this psycholog-ical state early and memorably with his idea of "escape from freedom." All that said, Arendt never did much to develop the idea of the close link of bureaucracy and modern evil, other than continuing to allude to it. In fact, it seemed to push her analysis toward the "cog" theory of Eichmann's im-portance in the Final Solution, which she firmly rejected.

Yet another set of associations with the banality of evil emerged in the 1965 postscript to *Eichmann* (and later). It became the one sense of the phrase that she tended to return to in ensuing years. Eichmann showed what Albert Camus once referred to as a "lack of moral imagination."[34] As Arendt formulated it: "He merely, to put the matter colloquially, never realized what he was doing" and with that demonstrated a "lack of imagination" and a "sheer thoughtlessness."[35] There was an "extraordinary shallowness" but not "stupidity" about Eichmann. This "thoughtlessness" did not have to do with conventional morality or lack of rationality as such. He was a decent father, husband, and businessman, not a lone wolf or psychopath. Rather, as already mentioned, the language rules prevented him from thinking in terms of the other (the internal dialogue of the self) and thus blocked the development of a universalizing conscience as well.[36] As a result, he could only fall back on hackneyed phrases and worn-out sentiments, which meant that any sort of independent moral or political judgment was effectively nullified.

Complicity and Cooperation

Perhaps even more explosive in Arendt's report was her charge that the *Judenräte* (Jewish Councils) cooperated with the Nazis in facilitating the Final Solution. If Arendt's critics thought the banality of evil made the Nazi perpetrators less evil, Arendt's charges against the Jewish Councils seemed to minimize the resistance of European Jewry to the Nazi's Final Solution. Specifically, she was charged with blaming the Jewish people for going like sheep to their deaths. For example, Marie Syrkin noted how she criticized the Jews for cooperating, yet then also attacked them for not being better organized.[37] Nevertheless, Arendt was well aware of the horrible complexities of Jewish-Nazi contacts and of how easy it was "to cross the abyss between helping Jews escape and helping the Nazis to deport them." Charges of "Jewish self-hatred" were also frequently directed against her, even by knowledgeable critics such as Syrkin.[38] One of the most egregious distortions from her critics was to claim that Arendt tarred the whole Jewish people with the brush of passivity. But Arendt was quite explicit that her quarrel was with the Jewish leadership and that she was not blaming the mass of European Jews with lack of resistance.

Arendt's attitude to the leadership of Zionist organizations and movements, indeed to the nineteenth-century German Jewish bourgeoisie, had always been deeply ambivalent. Even before World War II, she felt that the Jewish people had often been ill-served by their leaders, who were parvenus or philanthropists, but rarely skillful political leaders. Moreover, the Israeli government was anxious that the whole issue of the Jewish Councils not be aired in public during the trial. In truth, her discussion of it took up around ten pages at the most and concluded with the oft-cited verdict that aroused considerable anger: "The whole truth was that if the Jewish people had really been unorganized and leaderless, there would have been chaos and plenty of misery but the total number of victims would hardly have been between four and a half and six million people."[39] Though this statement has had a particularly incendiary effect on many readers, such a judgment cannot be dismissed out of hand, though as with all counterfactuals it is impossible to answer conclusively. But as Susan Neiman later emphasized, Arendt's judgment on this matter was not about the intentions or good faith of the Jewish Councils; it was about their decision to cooperate with the process by which the Nazis put the Final Solution into effect.[40] Most plausibly, their hope had been that the historically venerable relationship of gentile to Jew would continue to include bargaining for their very lives. In this, they were wrong.

Overall, Arendt's whole discussion of the role of the Jewish Councils in *Eichmann in Jerusalem* should be set against the background of Dwight Macdonald's observation of 1945 that more harm was done by those who followed orders than by those who disobeyed them. Or as Arendt paraphrased Kant when she was interviewed by Joachim Fest in 1964: "Kein Mensch hat bei Kant das Recht zu gehorchen" ("For Kant no one has the right to obey") was the best riposte to Eichmann's allegedly Kantian justification of his obedience to authority. Other than the better known "the right to have rights," few of Arendt's aphoristic pronouncements have the same paradoxical cogency as "Kein Mensch hat das Recht zu gehorchen" ("No one has the right to obey").

Still, Arendt made the same mistake on the issue of the complicity of the Jewish Councils that she had in her discussion of the banality of evil. She failed to provide a nuanced and complex discussion of key terms and examples. Because her discussion was too short, her judgments seemed dogmatic and immune to criticism. For instance, she might have incorporated her wartime celebration of the Warsaw ghetto uprising—that it meant Jews were "claiming equal rights, joined the ranks of other European peoples in the struggle for freedom," and added "Honor and Glory" to the "political vocabulary of our people."[41] This was, of course, perfectly consistent with Arendt's advocacy of the formation of a Jewish army and her rejection of the idea that it should be left to someone else to free the Jewish people from the Nazis.

At several points after the war, she discussed the councils with understanding and nuance. For example, her review of Leon Poliakov's *Breviaire de la Haine* in *Commentary* in 1952 acknowledged subtleties and gradations among the various Jewish communities as they tried to resist the Nazis. In discussing the *Judenräte*, she praised Poliakov because "he neither accuses or excuses, but reports fully and faithfully what the sources tell him—the growing apathy of the victims as well as their occasional heroism, the terrible dilemma of the *Judenräte*, their despair as well as their confusion, their complicity and their sometimes pathetically ludicrous ambitions." While hardly a paean to communal heroism, Arendt clearly sympathized with the dilemmas facing the *Judenräte*, though she concluded with a comment about how "German Jews, in this respect too, served the Nazis as guinea pigs in their investigation of the problem of how to get people to carry out their own death sentences."[42] But none of this made its way into *Eichmann in Jerusalem*. One explanation for Arendt's nuanced discussion of the Jewish Councils at this early date might be that Raul Hilberg's *The Destruction of European Jews* (1961) was not yet available to her, since it made clear the degree of cooperation between the Jewish officials in Hungary and Eichmann. As Rainer Schimpf has noted, "The role of the Jewish Council in Hungary and the Kasztner Affair were probably the best proofs of her thesis."[43]

The Kasztner affair is a very complicated matter, but basically Rudolf Kasztner, a Hungarian Jew, had done a deal with Eichmann in the spring of 1944 to get 1,685 Jews out of Hungary in exchange for money, gold, and diamonds. In 1953 in Israel, Kasztner was accused of collaboration by one Malchiel Gruenwald and the government sued Gruenwald, on Kasztner's behalf, for libel. Gruenwald was exonerated of the charges and, at least indirectly, Kasztner was now seen as guilty, though in 1958 Kasztner's crimes of collaboration were largely overturned. Before that, however, on March 4, 1957, Kasztner was assassinated. The libel trial itself lasted two years and brought down the Israeli government. All this meant that the Ben Gurion government was bent on keeping this kind of issue from coming up at Eichmann's trial. There were also charges that Kasztner agreed not to tell the Jews scheduled for deportation to the "East" where they were headed and what their fate would surely be. With the publication, then, of Hilberg's *The Destruction of the European Jews* in 1962, Arendt's case was much stronger against the *Judenräte* than it had been before. It is also important to underline that in Israel the arguments over collaboration had been intensely public and had even brought down a government, while American Jews who objected to Arendt's charge were largely ignorant of the whole discussion. But clearly the collaboration of the Jewish leadership with people like Eichmann was an explosive topic.

There is a little remarked passage in *Eichmann in Jerusalem* where Arendt points to the disastrous impact of the failure of Jewish leaders to tell their people what was coming. In fact, some people even "volunteered for deportation from Theresienstadt to Auschwitz." Beyond that, however, she offered the examples of three leaders that showed that not all ghetto leaders conducted themselves in the same way in the antechamber of hell. One was the notorious Chaim Rumkowski in Lodz, who set up his own empire, as it were, in the ghetto there. Another was Rabbi Leo Baeck, who seemed to see the positive side of any situation, for instance, that "Jewish policemen would be more 'more gentle and helpful,'" which they weren't. Heroic as he was in not abandoning his people, he nevertheless failed to warn those in Theresianstadt what the future held farther east. Finally, she mentioned the poignant example of Adam Czerniakow, who, as chairman of the Warsaw Ghetto Council, committed suicide rather than carry out orders. Arendt also noted in her reply to Gershom Scholem about her Eichmann book, that though after a point "there was no possibility of resistance," still "there existed the possibility of doing nothing" and for that "one did not need to be a saint."[44]

Of most interest are Arendt's remarks about the behavior of Jews in the camps when she spoke at the meeting already referred to at the University of Maryland in College Park in April of 1965. In general, she blamed Gideon Hausner, the prosecutor at Eichmann's trial, for raising the whole issue of Jewish resistance in the camps, and her remarks at College Park were perhaps the only place where Arendt expanded on the question of Jewish behavior in the camps. She always made it clear that once Jews had been rounded up, sent to the camps, and then organized for hard labor and/or extermination, Jews "behaved like all other groups in the same circumstances."[45] Discussion of group resistance, she thought, should be confined to the situation prior to transport to the camps, not in the camps themselves, though there were, of course, some camp uprisings. But once it was a question of behavior inside the camps, resistance was, really, too late. This helps explain her strong objection at the way Prosecutor Gideon Hausner raised the issue at the Eichmann trial.

But she went on to explore what might have been the considerations of those faced with certain death. First, she noted that, for some, quick death was better than the living hell of death-in-life in the camps. Second, citing Polish writer Tadeusz Borowski, a gentile, she wrote of the negative role played by hope, which she characterized as "destructive of the very humanity of man" in the context of the camps. People waited, hope against hope, that something, anything, might deliver them. And they were marched into the gas chambers still hoping. Finally, she thought that the very innocence of the Jews (and others) led to an apathy that was "the almost physical, automatic response to the challenge of absolute meaninglessness." As Bruno Bettelheim, who always supported Arendt publicly, had written during the war, camp inmates were stunned by the sheer lack of connection between their lives and the punishment that now faced them in the ghettos and then the camps. They could literally not believe what was happening to them.

Finally, Arendt suggested that the Jewish leadership had had three options, since it was "objectively hardly less helpless than the Jewish masses." First, they could have admitted to their followers that "all is lost, *sauve qui peut*" ("run for your life"). Second, they could have accompanied the people to the east and "suffer[ed] the same fate" of extermination. Or, finally, as in some cases in France, the Jewish Councils could have become de facto resistance centers. She also repeated charges that the plight of the Jews in the bloodlands of eastern European could have been publicized more assiduously by Jews in the West, thus, perhaps, putting more pressure on the Allies to try to disrupt the steady flow of Jews to Auschwitz. She concluded by suggesting that a "normalization" of the situation of European Jewry—a declaration of war, organization of a Jewish army, and a "recognition of the Jewish people as belligerents"—would have been the best response.[46]

Had Arendt clearly developed such lines of thought in *Eichmann in Jerusalem*, her case against the Jewish Council would not have left so many hostages to fortune. It is important to say that there is nothing in Arendt's original account in *Eichmann*—or in her other discussions of Jewish behavior—that blamed the victims or shifted moral responsibility away from the Germans or suggested that she preferred the Germans to the Jews or blamed the ghetto mentality or some other failure of Jewish group character to act otherwise. Whether elaborating, as I have suggested, on her position regarding resistance would have satisfied her critics—and enemies—is another matter. Finally, according to Arendt, she had asked more people than usual to read her manuscript before its publication. A peculiar fact: Arendt reported that at least 50 percent of those she asked were Jews but "not a single one of them voiced the reaction that came subsequently—they didn't even hint at it." "I was," she reported, "quite unprepared."[47]

Only in America?

Eichmann in Jerusalem was not translated into Hebrew for four decades after its publication, and only in the 1990s did Arendt begin to receive respectful attention from Israeli academics and intellectuals. Because of her book, she lost the friendship of her beloved older friend, Kurt Blumenfeld, and that of the greatest scholar of Jewish history, Gershom Scholem, both of whom lived in Israel. *Eichmann in Jerusalem* was translated into French in 1966, while *Origins* was translated in three sections in three different years—1972, 1973, and 1982. In general, however, she was associated with a conservative, pro-U.S. position in France, where there was comparatively little debate, aside from two pages of letters in the *Nouvel Observateur* on the occasion of the translation of the Eichmann book into French. Its headline read "Hannah Arendt, est-elle une Nazi?"[48] It was only with the waning of pro-Soviet political opinion under the influence of Alexsandr Solzhenitsyn's Gulag books that her work began to be considered more widely in Francophone countries. In Germany, the debate was also muted but hostile. Her Eichmann text was not translated until 1964, and some of the key documents, including Arendt's supplementary remarks, were not available. There was considerable resentment of her dismissal of the German resistance against Hitler and she was, as usual, subject to charges of being arrogant and a purist. Golo Mann thought her treatment of the resistance "contained shocking defamation" and argued that she blamed the Jews more than the Germans. But, as Wolfgang Heuer has written, none of her critics really addressed her substantive claims. Later in the 1980s, Wolfgang Mommsen and Alexander Mitscherlich came to Arendt's defense, the former suggesting that even historians had something to learn from Arendt.[49]

Nor was there debate of the issue in Great Britain nearly as widespread as in America. Leading academics and public intellectuals such as Hugh

Trevor-Roper and Isaiah Berlin attacked the book and/or helped build up hostility to it behind the scenes.[50] But it was in the United States that something like a "civil war" (Irving Howe's words) was touched off, particularly within the New York intellectual community, American Jewish organizations and publications, and some of the nation's colleges and universities. Friendships—with Harold Rosenberg and Hans Jonas—nearly went by the boards. Alfred Kazin reported being incredibly "irritated with Irving Howe's attack on Hannah" at the public forum in October 1963, organized by Howe's *Dissent* magazine and attended by nearly five hundred people. Howe, who had once worked for Arendt at Schocken Books, wrote of "the surging contempt with which she [Arendt] treated almost everyone and everything connected with the trial." It is hardly surprising that his relationship with Arendt never really recovered.[51]

Initially, she thought that the wrenching controversy reflected a split between Jews and gentiles within the New York intellectual community, a split that had already shown up in a greater support for civil liberties among gentile than Jewish intellectuals during the McCarthy period.[52] Arendt's strongest supporters were her good friends Mary McCarthy and Dwight Macdonald, along with poet Robert Lowell, all of them gentiles. As she reported to Jaspers: "What is serious about it is that since then all non-Jews stand with me, and that not a single Jew has dared to openly support me, even if he absolutely is 'for me'" (*für mich*).[53] She also reported that she was receiving a positive reception from students at the colleges and universities. This suggests what Norman Fruchter also observed—that there was a generational difference in the reception of the Eichmann book, with students tending to side with Arendt in the argument. Arendt's biographer reports that at the peak of the crisis, University of Chicago faculty, except for people like Hans Morgenthau and Richard McKeon, avoided sitting with Arendt in the faculty club. She also reported that, after one of her talks, she spoke at length with an Israeli consul, who admitted that "of course everything you say is true. We know that. But how could you as a Jew say this 'in a hostile environment.'"[54]

Obviously, then, Israel in the broadest sense was also an important factor in the public controversy in America. In fact, the prosecutor in the Eichmann case, Gideon Hausner, delivered an address to the Bergen-Belsen

Survivors Association in New York in May 1963, where he was joined by Na-
hum Goldman of the World Zionist Organization. In the address he spoke of
"Hannah Arendt's bizarre defense of Eichmann," an ominous indication of
the level at which many of Arendt's opponents would carry on the debate.[55]
In addition, Arendt, at various times, suspected Isaiah Berlin and Leo Strauss
of stirring up enmity against her in academic circles and among reviewers.
In Berlin's case, at least, this certainly seems to have been the case. But on
the matter of Jewish-Christian tensions, Arendt undoubtedly exaggerated.
Admittedly Kazin was a reluctant supporter and only spoke up for her at the
end of the *Dissent*-sponsored forum. Hans Morgenthau reviewed Eichmann
very favorably in the Chicago *Tribune*, while Daniel Bell and Raul Hilberg
spoke for her as members of the panel at the *Dissent* forum where they faced
off against Lionel Abel and Marie Syrkin, who spoke for the prosecution.
Psychoanalyst Bruno Bettelheim was always one of Arendt's stoutest defenders in the pages of the *New Republic*, though he didn't take part in the
Dissent debate, while the editorial staff of the *New York Review of Books*, a
mix of Jews and gentiles, was on her side. And so it went . . .

Yet there was another social dimension to the controversy that may also
help explain its vituperative quality. I refer here to the long-standing class
and cultural differences within the New York Jewish community between
Ostjuden and German Jews such as Arendt. These tensions do not explain
the harshness of the debate by themselves, but they undoubtedly contributed to the extremity of tone. In fact, there was a fascinating reversal of
positions among Jewish intellectuals in America between the 1930s and
the 1960s. In the interwar years, and on into the war, Jewish leftists were
hostile to all claims of religion and ethnicity, embraced a cosmopolitanism
suspicion of nationalism, and very much desired to "break out of the Jewish
immigrant ghetto."[56] All this was no doubt linked up with the secularism
and internationalism of the Marxist and socialist traditions that had shaped
them. In addition, many of these Jewish intellectuals came from immigrant
(Eastern European and Russian), working-class backgrounds.

Arendt had the best available philosophical education in contemporary
Western culture, came from a solid middle-class family, and was a product of
German *Bildung*. She arrived in New York in 1941 as a kind of independent
Zionist with leftist commitments. Politically and psychologically she was a

refugee, a stateless person, a type about whose fate she was to write in *Origins*. Once in America she wrote regularly for the Jewish periodical *Aufbau* and pushed for the organization of a Jewish army to fight in Europe against Nazism. This clearly contrasted with many New York intellectuals, who had opposed U.S. entrance into the war or were lukewarm toward participation in it. Even those intellectuals around *Partisan Review* who supported the war displayed a "remarkable silence" regarding the fate of European Jewry.[57] Almost alone among New York intellectuals, Alfred Kazin broke that silence in a *New Republic* piece in 1944, a cri de coeur that concluded with a general condemnation of "all our silent complicity in the massacre of the Jews. . . . For it means that men are not ashamed of what they have been in this time, and are therefore not prepared for the further outbreaks of fascism which are so deep in all of us."[58]

After the war, Arendt took a stand with those like Judah Magnes, who argued against the idea of a Jewish state in Palestine and thought a much wiser goal was the establishment of a Jewish homeland. Otherwise there would be an excluded minority at the heart of the new Jewish state and that could only lead to trouble. Also during this time, many of the New York intellectuals moved to embrace Cold War America enthusiastically and also demonstrated a new interest in Jewish culture, particularly, as with Saul Bellow and Irving Howe, in the Yiddish culture of Eastern Europe. As Arendt was staking out a kind of universalist position, which was attracted, for instance, to the new idea of "crimes against humanity," many New York intellectuals cut back on their cosmopolitan cultural and universalist political commitments and began exploring their Jewish heritage. Thus, to cut a long story short, *Eichmann in Jerusalem* seemed to many New York intellectuals, American Jews, and Israelis, too, to be a betrayal of her Jewish heritage and an example of Jewish self-hatred. This undoubtedly helps explain the animus and sheer hysteria behind the attacks from American Jewish intellectuals and publicists on what they saw as her hostility to Israel. To Arendt and her supporters, such attacks lacked credibility, coming as they did from those who had only discovered their Jewish identity after the war and felt guilty about their lack of concern during the war for the fate of European Jewry. In addition, few if any of them came close to knowing as much about the history of the Zionism as did Arendt.

Of course, the Israeli dimension was important here too. As already noted, Israeli officials, citizens, and intellectuals found it easy to read *Eichmann in Jerusalem* as somehow questioning the existence of the very state that had provided a home for the remnant of (European) Jewry and insured the survival of Judaism. Arendt's earlier support for a homeland, not a state, looked soft-headed from their perspective. Jews could debate the Kasztner issue among themselves, but her book, published in America for all the world to read, seemed a needless exposure of excruciatingly painful Jewish matters to an uncomprehending gentile world. In the United States, Jews such as Howe wondered how the upper-middle class WASP readers of the *New Yorker* would react to Arendt's articles about the massacre of the Jews and noted also that the *New Yorker* had no letters to the editor column where objections to Arendt's articles could be registered.

Specifically, Arendt was at odds with strong Zionists on two different but related issues. First, she never accepted the basic Zionist assumption of "eternal anti-Semitism," which after the massacre of European Jewry seemed unarguable to many. This meant that the existence of Israel came to be an absolute value in Jewish life, the necessity of its existence an article of faith. This was increasingly true not only of Israelis but also diaspora Jews, particularly in the American Jewish community. Thus Arendt's charges against the *Judenräte*, along with her objections to the way the state of Israel conducted the trial, seemed an onslaught against the raison d'être of the nearly fifteen-year-old state, not just a difference of political or historical judgment.

A particularly poignant example of the conflict of perspectives can be seen in the intense correspondence Arendt carried with Leni Yahil, a German Jewish Israeli, between 1961 and 1963. Born in 1912, Yahil had come to Palestine in 1934. Her doctoral thesis was titled "The Jews of Denmark during the Holocaust," and she later published a book *The Holocaust: The Fate of European Jewry, 1932–1945*. Arendt and she met at the beginning of the trial but the basic issue that eventually ended their friendship concerned the meaning of Israel. In her first letter (from Basel), Arendt set forth her position to Yahil: "What terrifies me is simply that this people, which when all is said and done has after all believed for several thousand years in the God of justice, is starting now to cling to what in its religion Heine rightly called the unhealthy faith of ancient Egypt, because it helps them 'believe in the Jewish People,' in other words, in itself. And this, if I may say so, is real idol worship. However pleasant the idol worshipers may be, as your friend is and was."[59] Arendt added that perhaps they would talk about it when they met again.

One important thing to note here is that the "friend" Arendt refers to in her letter was Golda Meir and the reference is to the conversation Arendt had with Meir that Yahil helped arrange. Later, Arendt mentioned this same incident in her reply to Gershom Scholem when he charged her with failure to love the Jewish people sufficiently. It opens with Meir's words:

> "You will understand that, as a Socialist, I, of course do not believe in God; I believe in the Jewish people." I [Arendt] found this a shocking statement and, being too shocked, I did not reply at the time. But I could have answered: The greatness of this people was once that it believed in God, and believed in Him in such a way that its trust and love toward Him was greater than its fear. And now this people believes only in itself? What good can come out of that?—Well, in this sense, I do not "love" the Jews, nor do I "believe" in them; I merely belong to them.[60]

Though much has been said about this passage, it is important to note that that Arendt's words to Yahil were used as the lead-in to her response to Scholem's charge. Her basic point was that no state or its people should be absolutized or worshiped. To do so was to commit idolatry, which she mentions in her letter to Yahil but not to Scholem.

Yahil gave as good as she got and replied with her own set of probing questions/assertions to Arendt. First she noted that the purpose of "idol worship" was generally "self-affirmation." But she went on to suggest that it was not what but how this "belief in" was expressed that was crucial. Put another way, Yahil quite cogently distinguished between "belief in" and "idolatry." Her final important point was that there "is also idol worship of principle."[61] The correspondence continued but foundered once Yahil read Arendt's *New Yorker* articles in 1963. In one of her last letters, she posed to Arendt the question: "What was or is your innermost intention that you were pursuing? Whom do you think you were serving in this way?" She went on to wonder if Arendt didn't think that Israel had "the right to exist as a nation among the nations?"[62] First, Arendt replied in a conciliatory fashion: "Let's remain friends—and fight." She also went on to suggest that the question about "innermost intention" was a "stupid" one that was also asked when Eichmann was captured.[63] In her next to the last letter, Yahil stayed with the theme: "How deep does your self-criticism reach? . . . what about unconscious ones (unspoken intentions)?" Her evocation of a psychoanalytic approach undoubtedly put Arendt off and the correspondence ceased.[64] Eight years later, Yahil contacted Arendt to ask if she could give her student, Richard Cohen, her (Arendt's) address and the letter indicated that she (Yahil) would like further contact.

Finally, besides the tension among American Jews and between Arendt and Israelis over Arendt's conception of loyalty to Israel, there was the long-standing gender tension that undoubtedly contributed to difficulties in the overall debate. On this issue it is tempting to be reductive, to use gender it as an all-purpose explanation. It should also be kept in mind that Arendt had little interest in feminism and disliked being considered one. Yet, as Judith Ring has noted, Arendt was a "*woman* raising issues about the effectiveness of Israeli and New York Jewish men"—though she also attacked Golda Meir.[65] Her criticism of the failure of American Jewish intellectuals to speak out for Jews during the war and of the failure of Zionist and Jewish leadership to stand up to the Nazis was bound to be filtered, consciously or subliminally, through a gender frame of reference. Particularly, Scholem's assertion that those who had not undergone the experience did not have the right to criticize the behavior of the Jewish leadership implied a kind gender rank pulling.

Two considerations in this context make judgments complicated. First, though Raul Hilberg came in for some criticism in his depiction of the Jewish leadership in *The Destruction of the European Jews*, he received much less vehement criticism, including blatant insults, than did Arendt.[66] Second, Arendt seems to have come in for very harsh criticism from other Jewish women when *Eichmann* was published and later. Responding in *Jewish Frontier* in May 1963 to the *Eichmann* book, Marie Syrkin described Arendt's account as one that ended by being an "indictment of the victims," made mention of Arendt's "polemical vulgarity," claimed that Arendt saw

Eichmann as "a cog in a machine," which she explicitly didn't, and suggested that Arendt was filled with "Jewish self-hatred."[67] In a book review in the *New York Times Book Review* in 1966, the celebrated historian Barbara Tuchman thought that the book's treatment of Eichmann arose either from "remarkable naïveté or conscious desire to support Eichmann's defense."[68] She decided that the latter was the more probable explanation. Two decades after *Eichmann in Jerusalem* first appeared, Gertrude Ezorsky constructed a lawyer's brief in *Philosophical Forum* to call Arendt to account. Like Syrkin's review, hers often made valid points (e.g., concerning the confusing nature of evidence about Eichmann's sanity vs. his normality). But the disdain she expressed and oversimplifications she resorted to made her article sound as though it had been written in the heat of the original controversy and that, otherwise, she had nothing new to say.[69]

Finally, political theorist Judith Shklar, also writing in the first half of the 1980s, mixed appreciation for Arendt's life and career with some important insights about the politics and sociology of American Jewry. She noted that the "politics [of émigrés] were 'so dreadful' because they deal in 'recriminations.'" In addition, she raised the issue of the survivor guilt of American Jews "for having done less than they might to help" but she also noted their suspicion that German Jews were not "genuine Jews" and wondered if "their ability to get on in the gentile world" was perhaps a "sign of their innate disloyalty."[70] According to Shklar, *On Revolution* was "embarrassing," without further explanation. To top that, she declared that *Eichmann in Jerusalem* was an "awful" book in which Arendt, claimed Shklar, asked "why . . . had the East European Jews not behaved like Homeric heroes?" Like others she accused Arendt of distaste for Jewish passivity when what Arendt was angered about was the complicity of the Jewish leadership. To Shklar, Arendt's Eichmann book, like her piece on Little Rock, was an example of "uncomprehending arrogance." Overall, Shklar considered Arendt as the last of the German Jews, the *Yeckes*, whose aristocratic manner and sense of intellectual entitlement, elevated them, in their own minds, above the crude *Ostjuden* around them in America. "American Jewry is a flourishing community, she wrote, "while German-Jewish culture died with Hannah Arendt."[71] Thus the shrill tone of the debate over Arendt's book derived from a tension not just between men and women but among women intellectuals and between an emerging American Jewish culture and a waning German-Jewish culture, which had seen its base eradicated.

What does the whole Eichmann case/affair show us about Arendt and her place in America? As we will see later, Arendt's reputation survived the Eichmann years (roughly until 1966), perhaps not intact, but certainly as still formidable. For Kazin and others, Arendt remained a figure of "moral steadfastness." She had "a definite gift for seeing the moral implication of a position" and an ability to "always put them [her judgments] into a wider and deeper context." Yet she was given to descending into an "imperiousness of outlook" and arrogance, though undoubtedly she had a lot to be arrogant about.[72] Indeed, no small amount of the negative feelings against Arendt had to do with her alleged inability to accept criticism or admit she was wrong.

And yet, that is not the whole story either. The experience of Norman Podhoretz shows us something different, at least as he tells it. His review of *Eichmann in Jerusalem* was quite critical of (and not a little perceptive about) Arendt's "intellectual perversity" and "pursuit of brilliance." "Originality," he later wrote, "was not so great an intellectual virtue as I had once thought." But he and Arendt never had a final blowup and they spent several hours discussing the book face to face in the privacy of her apartment.[73] Indeed, he was one of the few critics from "the other side" that she would agree to appear with, as she did at the University of Maryland in April 1965. Among her closer friends, philosopher J. Glenn Gray voiced extraordinarily penetrating criticisms of her work in letters to her in the 1970s, which she seemed to have no problem accepting.

Princeton historian Anthony Grafton has reported on yet another sort of reaction to criticism on Arendt's part. His journalist father, Samuel Grafton, made an abortive attempt to write a long piece for *Look* magazine on Arendt's reactions to the Eichmann controversy, even as it was still underway.[74] But after the elder Grafton had drawn up a series of questions for her in September 1963, to which she responded at some length, negotiations somehow failed and the article never appeared. Undoubtedly, Arendt was gun-shy, hard to deal with, by this point, not to mention the toll that the serious illness of her husband Heinrich and her injury in an automobile accident in 1962 had taken in the meantime. At one moment she would answer things straightforwardly; at the next, she would, according to Grafton, practically insult his father for the allegedly low-level questions he had posed to her.

It is hard to know what to make of the charge concerning her intolerance of criticism. To the extent that it is true, it points to her tendency to lose a sense of proportion when she thought her standards had been violated or the topic was just too highly charged for her to treat it with equanimity. It is hard not to share her sense that the level of public debate about her Eichmann book was woeful, as witness the insults leveled at her by Barbara Tuchman. Some observers, Grafton's father for one, thought Arendt's claims about the complicity of the *Judenräte* in the Final Solution and her banality-of-evil thesis were historically premature; they had come "too soon." Of course, even fifty years later, Arendt's claims still arouse heated opposition, as witness the discussions of Margarethe von Trotta's 2012 biopic of Arendt, to which we will return in the conclusion.

Others point to her Olympian detachment, her nearly super- or inhuman objectivity to important problems. Exhibit A is her response, already discussed, to Scholem's charge that her Eichmann book was marked by an absence of "love for the Jewish people" and an "almost sneering and malicious tone." Arendt granted that she did not love any single group per se but beyond that asserted that "generally speaking the role of the 'heart' in politics seems to me altogether questionable."[75] Such a statement would fit with Richard Sennett's claim that Arendt sought to detach herself from natural impulses and to escape the "prison of subjectivity." Indeed her thought, he noted, revolved around the contrast between the "human animal," which is "slave to its own instincts and emotions" and "human being[s]," who "detach themselves from slavery to their bodies." Once again, Arendt's suspicion of the natural comes to the fore. Sennett's larger point was that Arendt demanded too much of self and of others, while teaching suspicion of virtues such as "pity, compassion and empathy." What the uproar over her Eichmann book and her Little Rock essay demonstrated, Sennett thought, was that "she could not connect."[76] From this perspective, her "beyond good and evil" was not the usual call for liberation from an interdictive morality but, instead, a call for an ethic of pitiless responsibility for the world.

And yet, Arendt's private life seems to have been all about nurturing friendships. As she told Scholem, she thought disaster ensued when private virtues such as pity or compassion were made public and acted on in that context. Politically, they often entailed absolute demands, undermined a needed perspective on things, and involved patronizing the objects of pity. These were, as we have seen, the points she made in *On Revolution*, the other book she published in 1963. What also emerged in her response to Scholem was her insistence on individual responsibility. No one "gets a free pass" in Arendt's world—except, some would say, Martin Heidegger. This attitude, suggests Isaiah Berlin's biographer, Michael Ignatieff, helps explain Berlin's intense dislike of Arendt, since his uncle occupied a position of responsibility on the *Judenräte* in Latvia under Nazi occupation. An admirer of both figures, Ignatieff has suggested that we may seriously question Arendt's lack of sympathy for those who were faced with making decisions while the Final Solution was underway, but her judgments were never facile or made to score moral or intellectual points.[77]

Overall, where Arendt, I think, fell short in *Eichmann in Jerusalem* was in her lack of intellectual consideration for her readers. The banality of evil is a difficult and paradoxical notion, but it is not impossible to understand and is quite rich in implications. It may be the closest thing we have to a new idea in the last part of the twentieth century. Similarly, the history of the Jewish Councils was an incredibly difficult issue to sort out, with huge implications for understanding some hard truths about life under extreme oppression. I think we need to credit the general idea that she wanted to get a debate going about these two issues in particular. In this respect, she was partly successful. But she was also remiss, I think, in not making her argument clearer and the evidence more compelling. If doing this did not fit into the "report" format, as she kept insisting, then so much the worse for that format. The issues were too important to be left where she left them, with the range of meanings of evil in the Western tradition unspecified and a firmer sense of the range of behavior of various *Judenräte* unexamined. In fact, she knew that the concept of the banality of evil needed more thinking about, including the complicated relationship among conscious rationality, moral imagination, and ethical decision making. She returned to this concept several times in pieces after

Eichmann in Jerusalem but somehow it didn't stick in quite the way her analysis of these problems had in the historical context, with real history figures, which had compelled and fascinated and infuriated her readers. Nor did she ever really return to the Jewish Councils after the first stage of the Eichmann debate had ended by 1966. In the context of the mid-1960s, everyone seemed to have burned out on the issue. The dispute was not settled—merely abandoned for a while.

CHAPTER 10

Against the Liberal Grain

Among Hannah Arendt's major works, *On Revolution* (1963) has received the most uneven treatment.[1] Perhaps because Arendt scholars have tended to be historians of political thought or philosophers and most lack grounding in American history or thought, they have missed the drastic interpretive-historiographical shift Arendt's book proposed. It called into question historian Richard Hofstadter's contention that the American political tradition had always been a "democracy in cupidity," challenged Louis Hartz's claim about the exclusively Lockean nature of American political culture, scuttled historian Charles Beard's emphasis on the economic motivations of the Framers, and largely ignored the nascent New Left (to be) emphasis on the "from the bottom up" sources of colonial revolt against British rule. In fact, her challenge came *before* American historians Bernard Bailyn and Gordon Wood advanced their own interpretation of the Radical Whig, Country versus Court, republican and/or civic humanism origins of American political institutions.[2]

The concerns of Arendt's book were also strikingly echoed in the emergence of the Civil Rights Movement, the Free Speech Movement at the University of California at Berkeley, the anti–Vietnam War movement, and the New Left generally. Uniting these phenomena was the idea of participatory democracy, a contemporary expression of the "public freedom" and "public happiness" she made central to *On Revolution*. While figures such as Paul Goodman, C. Wright Mills, and Herbert Marcuse are generally regarded as intellectual progenitors of 1960s radicalism, Arendt's *On Revolution* provided the political insurgency of the 1960s with a historical pedigree.[3] As Straussian political philosopher Harvey Mansfield later observed: "I would say it is because of her that the Left in America no longer attacks the American Revolution."[4]

Republicanism versus Liberalism

Though Arendt did not influence it, she certainly anticipated the "republican turn" or "synthesis" that was initiated by Bernard Bailyn and Gordon Wood in the late 1960s. Neither man seems to have read, or drawn on, Arendt's work. Among professional historians, only J. G. A. Pocock acknowledged her work as a source for his monumental history of civic humanism, *The Machiavellian Moment* (1975), which covered the classical world, then Renaissance Italy, before moving on to early modern English political thought, and coming to rest in the lower thirteen British colonies in North America. In his final chapter, Pocock cited *On Revolution* in a footnote on republican "renewal" or "renovation": "In terms burrowed from or suggested by the language of Hannah Arendt, this book has told part of the story of the revival in the early modern West of the ancient ideal of *homo politicus* (the *zoon politikon* of Aristotle)." For her part, Arendt's primary interest was not in historiographical debates. It was rather to bring to light a modern example of politics that would constitute the center of an alternative revolutionary tradition in the contemporary world. [5]

Though Arendt devoted more attention to the Roman republic than the Athenian polis in *On Revolution*, the latter remained the ur-source of political freedom for her. As she later described it, "the Greek polis," would "continue to exist at the bottom of our political existence—that is, at the bottom of the sea—for as long as we use the word 'politics.'"[6] But she did not seek to "resuscitate the way it was" in a historicist sense. The purpose of historical retrieval was a monumental rather than an antiquarian one: to recover some particularly luminous moment in the past and bring it to bear on the present.[7] That is, certain historical moments, events, or phenomena may be relevant to the present even though no causal chain between that specific past and this specific present exists. In this case, Arendt was not interested in the way history explained the present but in the way it was a source of examples that might enrich it.

What did Arendt mean by the term "republic"? Despite her dependence on the classical world for examples, Arendt also linked the emergence of modern republicanism to the two revolutions of the late eighteenth century. Their goal had been to create a republic whose constitution, a "tangible worldly entity," provides the authority to protect freedom and to counterbalance the power invested in the people.[8] Thus, for her, "the seat of power . . . was the people, but the source of laws was to become the Constitution." Checks and balances at the federal level and the divided sovereignty of federal-state relations were ways of augmenting, not undermining, power. When she wrote that "the greatest American innovation in politics as such was the consistent abolition of sovereignty within the body politic of the republic," we can see the importance she placed on federalism.[9] Power was not a zero-sum concept but a self-augmenting one.

Judith Shklar's suggestion that, by the last part of the eighteenth century, there were two extant versions of republicanism in circulation—the small communitarian model and the extended representative model—is very much to the point here in understanding Arendt.[10] Arendt was attracted to aspects of both models. On the one hand, the communitarian model was appealing since it eschewed, among other things, representative democracy and preferred direct, participatory democracy. On the other hand, she liked the emphasis on a written constitution to check unalloyed popular democracy and to encompass diversity in the extended republic. Like James Madison, she saw that the extended republic model was of greatest relevance in the new republic.

Arendt's republicanism, of course, assumed the primacy of the political and challenged the liberal understanding of politics and human nature. Her most innovative conceptual move was to emphasize "political" or "public happiness" more than civic virtue as vital to politics.[11] If any single idea/experience of the founding years of the American republic excited Arendt, it was being a "participator in the government of affairs," to use Thomas Jefferson's phrase. The conceptual, rhetorical, and political tragedy, as she saw it, was that Jefferson did not publicly incorporate the "public" part into his phrasing of the Declaration, even though the term "public happiness" was relatively commonly used to refer to something like "the citizen's access to the public realm, in his share in public power." The cognate term in France was "public freedom." The crucial comparative point here is that the love of public freedom and the experience of public happiness were central to the American experience, while it was "the hatred of masters" and the desire for revenge that drove the republican dynamic in France.[12]

In his role as an American Montesquieu, concerned with the best way for power to check power, John Adams was also clearly exhilarated by his involvement in the public business. It was this experience of politics, even before the revolution, that explained revolutionary stability in America: "Americans knew that public freedom consisted in having a share in public business" and that "John Adams was bold enough to formulate this knowledge time and again."[13] Another dimension of public happiness appeared in Adams's emphasis on the "passion for distinction" and the pleasure individuals take in appearing in public affairs.[14] The passion for distinction, however, did not always have positive effects and included envy and jealousy. However, not only was the language of public happiness not incorporated into the founding documents, Jefferson's idea of the "ward system," also championed by John Dewey, was omitted from the Constitution. This was the second great failure of the new American Constitution: "The elementary republics of the wards, the only tangible place where everyone could be free, actually were the end of the great republic whose chief purpose in domestic affairs should have been to provide the people with such places of freedom and to protect them."[15] Thus, there was a participatory deficit in what was an otherwise admirable set of republican institutions. The new American system was organized around a representative government in which elected officials stood in for the citizens. Perhaps the reason Madison played less of a role than expected in Arendt's story of American republicanism was that he assigned to representatives the task of refining and filtering popular views, thus minimizing direct participation by citizens.[16]

But these crucial characteristics did not exhaust the normative meaning of republic for Arendt. Her emphasis on establishing institutions to protect freedom reflected the crucial value she placed on a republic of laws not men, one grounded not in a general will and indivisibility of power but in the separation of powers, federalism, and a written constitution. Her constant refrain in *On Revolution* and elsewhere was that power could and should check power. Sovereignty neither was nor should be "indivisible" in the new American republic; rather, it was dispersed throughout the system. Furthermore, Arendt revealed her commitment to modernity when she suggested that "what saved the American Revolution from this fate [collapse in the face of modernity] was neither 'nature's God' nor self-evident truth, but the act of foundation itself."[17] "Action," as Frederick Dolan has said in reference to the American founding, "creates principles rather than derives from them."[18] Only because of the Judeo-Christian concept of law as a transcendent command and the Roman preoccupation with foundations for their republic did modern political thinkers search for absolutes to underpin their new republics, rather than locate their origins in action in concert.

A final, crucial aspect of Arendt's idea of modern republicanism concerned the durability of the republic, a preoccupation of the civic humanist/republican tradition. Despite its worldliness, the ideal republic—Arendt's "public realm"—could withstand the ravages of time and the specifically corrosive effects of luxury and corruption by a periodic return to origins and by a beginning again. But Arendt also identified the modern republican revolution with an openness toward the future. History was not just "about" decline or repetition; it was also the vehicle of future possibility. But she did not propose a notion of automatic historical progress closely linked to liberal and later to Marxist notions of historical teleology. Rather history was, and is, where "novelty" might emerge and "new beginnings" could be attempted.[19] In the final chapter of *On Revolution*, Arendt also admitted that "the absence of continuity" between the various moments of freedom in history made a continuous narrative of revolutionary freedom, in the sense she meant it, extremely difficult to construct.[20]

Arendt constructed her normative concept of republicanism from a variety of materials. She read a fair amount of the history of political thought, especially works in American political thought from the second half of the eighteenth century. A secondary work such as Caroline Robbins's *Eighteenth-Century Commonwealthman* (1959), which influenced Bailyn, Wood, and Pocock, was not in her bibliography, but Zera Fink's pioneering book on republicanism was. *The Classical Republicans* ([1945] 1962) covered the history of republicanism running from Aristotle and Polybius in the ancient world to Machiavelli and Montesquieu in the early modern period. It was the latter whom Fink considered to be the link between English republicanism and the U.S. Constitution.[21] Fink also foregrounded John Milton, James Harrington, and Algernon Sydney as central figures in modern Anglosphere republicanism. Among historians of America, Arendt drew on Clinton Rossiter, Forrest McDonald, Merrill Jensen, Perry Miller, and Edmund Morgan, along with Max Farrand's edition of the notes of the Constitutional Convention, not to mention Edwin S. Corwin on American constitutional thought, Carl J. Friedrich on constitutional government and democracy, and Lewis Mumford on the history of the city. She also consulted scholarly articles in three languages.

As already mentioned, it was the thinkers of the Roman Republic such as Cicero, the Roman historians, and later Virgil, rather than Pericles or Plato and Socrates, who guided her extended discussion of tradition, authority, and religion in republicanism. Clearly Machiavelli and Montesquieu drew more from Rome than Greece.[22] Machiavelli had been the "first to visualize the rise of a purely secular realm" that would be "a permanent, lasting, enduring body politic." Though he was, perhaps, the "spiritual father of revolution" and emphasized the role of violence in politics, while stressing "the task of foundation," Arendt held him to be only almost modern, since he had not yet conceptualized the modern notion of revolution as open toward the future. In this, she parted company with those like Leo Strauss who saw Machiavelli as the one founder of modern "political science or political thought," whose interest was not how "man ought to live" but how "men actually do live."[23]

Following Fink, Arendt also singled out Montesquieu's influence on the American Framers, claiming that it "almost equals Rousseau's influence on the course of the French Revolution." It was the former who identified the crucial importance of "equality" and "public spirit" (or "virtue") in a "democratic republic," while emphasizing that the way "the constitution of liberty" was constructed determined the stability of a republic.[24] On the importance of Montesquieu, both Gordon Wood and Bernard Bailyn would seem to concur. Wood, for instance, affirmed the centrality of Machiavelli and Montesquieu when he notes that "eighteenth-century English political thought perhaps owed more to Machiavelli and Montesquieu than it did to Locke."[25] In his "General Introduction" to *Pamphlets of the American Revolution*, Bailyn included Montesquieu among those European thinkers constantly cited in the political writings of the best-known Framers and in the pamphlet literature of the radical Whigs.[26] Pocock, of course, emphasized the key role played by Machiavelli and also by James Harrington in Anglosphere civic humanism. Arendt mentioned Harrington enough for him to count as an important source of republican thinking for her, as well as among the radical pamphleteers canvased by Bernard Bailyn.[27] But Harrington certainly did not play as important a part for her as he did for Pocock. She also made fairly frequent reference to Edmund Burke and Tom Paine, whose debates took off from the comparison between the two transatlantic revolutions.

From the postrevolutionary era, the thinker who most influenced Arendt was, not surprisingly, Alexis de Tocqueville. As we shall see in the next chapter, Arendt's understanding of the French Revolution was powerfully shaped by Tocqueville's claim that the revolution completed the centralizing work of the ancien régime, a theme that was anticipated in the debate between Anne-Robert-Jacques Turgot and John Adams about political centralization. Most important, though, was Tocqueville's fear that the drive for social equality ("equality of condition") would eventually undermine political freedom ("equality by virtue of citizenship"). Along with that, he underlined the susceptibility of democratic historians to the "doctrine of necessity," something which was anathema to Arendt. And the Frenchman's fundamental insight that political liberty is the first thing that perishes in a revolution helps explain the chastened, even pessimistic, tone of *On Revolution*. But, as Arendt herself noted, Tocqueville scarcely dealt with the American Revolution itself and denied that America had really had a revolution, a conclusion later adopted by Louis Hartz.[28]

But if it was the attempt to solve the social question, that is, poverty and want, that derailed the French Revolution, what historical factor corrupted the republican ethos in the American system, besides the failure to include a participatory dimension in the Constitution? *On Revolution*'s message is that America's weakness was not the temptation of dictatorship and terror but the pursuit of wealth and the habit of consumption, the triumph of self-interest over public interest, of private over public happiness. As we have already seen, this was a constant leitmotif in Arendt's contemporary analysis of the emergence of the citizen-consumer in the mass society. Clearly, what she did in *On Revolution* was read the economic and social developments of the post-1945 period back into the history of nineteenth-century American politics.

Overall, her historical narrative dovetailed nicely with Wood's thesis that the Constitution, as the expression of the new "American science of politics," meant the defeat of republicanism and the classical model. For Arendt, the Constitution established a representative democracy that undermined participatory freedom.[29] As she summed it up: "The Bill of Rights contained the necessary restraints upon government; it shifted, in other words, from public freedom to civil liberty, or from a share in public affairs for the sake of public happiness to a guarantee that the pursuit of private happiness would be protected and furthered by public power." In addition, it meant "the right of citizens to pursue their personal interests and thus to act according to the rules of private self-interest. . . . *The outcome of the American Revolution, as distinct from the purposes which started it, has always been ambiguous, and the question of whether the end of government was to be prosperity or freedom has never been settled.*"[30]

Clearly, then, Arendt's view of the origins of American political culture was not Louis Hartz's: America had not been born liberal; it became so. Its political experience had been forged in the crucible of republicanism, but what emerged over time was a new form of liberalism. In the context of the early 1960s, her lack of enthusiasm for liberal political culture made her sound too radical (or unrealistic) for the postwar political settlement based on the Madisonian politics of self-interest; the centrality of negative freedom as formulated by thinkers like Isaiah Berlin; and the chastened view of human nature proposed by Arthur Schlesinger Jr. channeling Reinhold Niebuhr. Nor, as we have seen, did she share the suspicion of popular political participation voiced by sociologist David Riesman. Overall, it is possible to understand *On Revolution* as an unalloyed celebration of the American founding. But that would be a mistake. In all, she located three serious flaws at the heart of the American experiment: the failure to entrench the ward system in the Constitution; the failure to cultivate the idea of public happiness; and, finally, the classical corruption of the republic brought about by the triumph of private interests over the common good. Surprisingly, unlike Pocock, Arendt either did not see or was not interested in the survival of republican political culture after the 1790s.[31]

Significantly, the text itself of *On Revolution* repeats the republican *ricorso*, the attempt to recapture the lost spirit or experience of republicanism. In it, Arendt becomes not just a political thinker but also a citizen-participant in the effort to renew the republic by retelling its origins. Her ambivalence regarding temporality reflects not so much the split between tradition and modernity, as the split within modernity itself over whether the Framers were involved in "founding 'Rome anew'" or "founding a 'new Rome.'"[32] What is regression and what is revolution, what is starting "it" over and what is beginning "it" anew? Contrary to the conventional wisdom about America—as a place of the future where people shed their pasts and redefine themselves—Arendt's exploration reminds us that America's prototypical response to crises (and all times are crisis times in a republican ethos) is to return to the original republican moment, which is usually the wrong way to resolve crises.

Thus *On Revolution* was an exploration of the permanent inner division in the politics of temporality. Though she did not systematically explore the range and complexity of the thought of John Adams, Thomas Jefferson, or Tom Paine, she took them seriously as political thinkers, something which Hartz's thesis of a liberal "American general will" discouraged with its emphasis on ideological homogeneity.[33] By combining thought and action, ideas and experience, theory and practice, such figures helped create a politics of freedom. But it was a flawed one.

Spectrum Analysis: Radical to Conservative

Most interpreters of Arendt can be found on the liberal-left end of the political spectrum. Yet *On Revolution* staked out several positions that defied the conventional wisdom of progressive thought. First, Arendt expressly rued the greater historical impact of the French Revolution (and, in the twentieth century, the Russian Revolution) than that of the American Revolution. She also objected to the way that the Jacobin-Bolshevik tradition demoted political freedom in the name of ending want and poverty, the rule of *Ananke* (necessity). With Marxism's valorization of historical necessity went the acceptance, even encouragement, of political violence as the way to force the hand of history. Her distaste for this view was clearly evident in her suspicion of Third World revolutionary tradition as articulated by Frantz Fanon and inspired, in part, by Jean-Paul Sartre later in the 1960s.[34]

Certainly some Old Left figures had a tough time with *On Revolution*. Her former sparring partner, George Lichtheim, objected, with certain plausibility, to Arendt's neglect of the religious factor in explaining the differences between the American and French Revolutions. The French Revolution also appealed more widely in Europe, according to Lichtheim, because political despotism had been more entrenched there and not because the revolution dealt with the "social question" as Arendt claimed.[35] Historian Eric Hobsbawm admitted that he was "not able to judge her [Arendt's] contribution to the study of the American revolution," but nevertheless proceeded to suggest that it was "not great." He also argued that Arendt's book was mainly relevant to "the classical zone of Western Europe and the north Atlantic" not "China or Cuba," while more research should have led her to examples of the "council system" and the idea of a "cooperative commonwealth" prior to the late eighteenth-century revolutions.[36] Actually, Arendt did mention "medieval townships, Swiss cantons, the English seventeenth-century 'agitators.' . . . and the General Council of Cromwell's Army" as earlier anticipations of the council system, but she devoted no further attention to them. Again, it was a fair point for Hobsbawm to make.[37]

Still, it is puzzling that figures sympathetic to Marx would draw invidious contrasts between Arendt's "metaphysical" approach to revolution and that of empirically oriented professional historians or sociologists, as though Marxism was an empirical science.[38] At issue in *On Revolution* was not the conflict between a normative and descriptive approach to revolution but between two normative notions of revolution—the republican and the Jacobin-Bolshevik ones. Clearly, Hobsbawm applied the term "actual" to revolutions only when they fell into the Jacobin-Bolshevik tradition.[39] Overall, the reactions of Lichtheim and Hobsbawm exemplified the way that the dominant model of revolution based on the French and Russian experience had long since hardened into orthodoxy by the early 1960s.

Despite their left-wing credentials, Lichtheim and Hobsbawm missed what Sheldon Wolin saw as an elitist cast to Arendt's republican political vision. Writing in the early 1980s, Wolin (and Hanna Pitkin) criticized Arendt for her neglect of "power and justice" as political problems. In separating the political from the social realm and underplaying the importance of the state in meliorating inequality, *On Revolution* reflected her "antipathy toward material questions" such as social justice. Like Lichtheim, Wolin underscored her neglect of religious tradition(s) in American political culture (from the Puritans on) and her indifference to other cultural resources that (American) citizens drew on when organizing and acting politically.[40] Strangely, none of these critics from the left wondered how the institution of slavery comported with the "constitution of liberty" established by the Framers. But Arendt's particular version of republican politics has also been defended from the left. Jeffrey Isaac, though taking note of a kind of elitism near the end of *On Revolution*, stresses the "political ethic of revolt" in the book, as well as the important affinities of her work with that of Albert Camus and John Dewey.[41] From Isaac's perspective, there is no great problem in reconciling Arendt's vision with participatory politics of a democratic sort. A veteran of the New Left, Dick Howard also "gets" Arendt in a way that Lichtheim and Hobsbawm do not. His essay about *On Revolution* emphasizes not just Arendt's focus on citizen participation but also her idea that a fragmented or divided idea of sovereignty (or "general will") was also a vital ingredient in the "spirit" of American politics.[42]

The most immediate challenge Arendt's book posed was to the hegemony of the liberal political tradition in early American political history. Postwar, post-Progressive American historiography emphasized the consensus — not conflict — among Americans on the basic political, economic, cultural, and social values that characterized American politics. Nor did one have to be a Cold War liberal to believe in the centrality of liberalism in American political thought. In fact, both Louis Hartz and Richard Hofstadter were often severe critics of the liberal tradition, while at the same time emphasizing its intellectual and cultural hegemony.

Consider the different ways Hofstadter and Hartz handled the republican component of American political culture. Hofstadter's introduction to *The American Political Tradition* (1948) sketched in his own version of the American political consensus: "a democracy in cupidity rather than a democracy in fraternity" that defended "the sanctity of private property, the right of the individual to dispose of and invest it, the value of opportunity, and the natural evolution of self-interest and self-assertion . . . into a beneficent social order."[43] But surprisingly, his profile of the Framers in the first chapter, "Age of Realism," also described them as "intellectual heirs of seventeenth-century English republicanism with its opposition to arbitrary rule and faith in popular sovereignty." Aristotle, Harrington, and Montesquieu are cited in the book's bibliographical essay, along with Hobbes and Locke. He also notes the general importance of the idea of "balanced government" as derived from Aristotle and Polybius, who were, of course, canonical sources of republican thought.[44] In the area of political economy, Hofstadter underscored the centrality of property and self-interest in the Framer's thinking but also emphasized the way that the Founders saw representative democracy as a check on the masses. Overall, then, Hofstadter accepted the Framers' "image of themselves as modern republicans standing between political extremes" as "extremely accurate."[45] But though his emphasis was surprising, it had the effect of transforming the republican tradition in America into something compatible with hard-nosed liberal realism avant la lettre, absent any utopian component. Near the end of his *The Creation of the American Republic*, Gordon Wood spoke of "a republic which did not require a virtuous people for its sustenance."[46] Analogously, *The American Political Tradition* presented a republicanism shorn of its visionary dimension and thus compatible with the new American liberalism.[47]

With Louis Hartz, however, it was liberalism all the way down.[48] He only mentioned republicanism once, at least in the opening several chapters. He granted that James "Harrington was one of their [the Framers'] favorite writers" but "much as they liked Harrington's republicanism, they did not require a Cromwell, as Harrington thought he did, to erect the foundations for it. Those foundations had already been laid by history."[49] Less allusively, Hartz was saying that republican political institutions and the centrality of private property were already in place in the New World, since there was no court and crown to revolt against on American soil. Hartz did join Arendt in presenting the United States as the place "where the social questions of France did not exist and the absolutism they engendered was quite unthinkable."[50] In such a situation, no Marxists need apply, since Tocqueville, a particular favorite of Hartz's, and Locke had supplied the requisite conceptual means to understand the American world.

With broad but deft strokes, Hartz suggested why Americans did not need to look beyond John Locke for guidance: "One also found letter-perfect replicas of the very images he used. There was a frontier that was a veritable state of nature. There were agreements, such as the Mayflower Compact, that were veritable social contracts. There were new communities springing up in *vacuis locis*, clear evidence that men were using their Lockian right of emigration."[51] Thus, there was a well-nigh perfect fit between the Lockean ideology and American conditions. No wonder Hartz considered the American Revolution "no revolution at all" but something that merely "codified what had previously been taken for granted."[52] Only in the South had the Lockean ideological hegemony failed to find a place in the hearts and minds of its residents.[53]

While the liberal interpretation of American politics tended to neutralize or ignore republicanism, it is difficult to pinpoint a consistent conservative attitude toward *On Revolution*. Robert Nisbet, the maverick conservative sociologist, once praised the book as a "political classic," though he also suggested that the social question was more pervasive in the thirteen colonies than Arendt allowed and that the American Revolution had had much more influence in Europe than she granted. Like Arendt, Nisbet was influenced by Tocqueville's idea of intermediate institutions, though Nisbet saw community as a social rather than a political concept. His emphasis on totalitarianism's refusal to acknowledge limits was a position that Arendt shared. Shared also was Nisbet's agreement with her that Nazi Germany and Stalin's Soviet Union were both totalitarian regimes.[54]

After *On Revolution*, it became much harder for conservatives to claim Arendt for the antimodern camp, as some had been inclined earlier. Perhaps this is why early American Straussians seemed to ignore *On Revolution*. The core of Leo Strauss's original position, as first set forth in *Natural Right and History* (1953), was a rejection of Machiavelli, Hobbes, and Locke in the name of a classical natural right thinking. Strauss's grand narrative of Western political philosophy emphasized the way that the "first wave" of modernity represented by these three figures paved the way for a protoscientific rationalism and emphasized the political importance of the passions and interests; established the modern split between normative and descriptive political thought; and shifted the focus from virtuous citizens and wise rulers to the individual's quest for self-preservation and self-interest. Liberalism was the wedge of modernity that pushed classical political thinking to the margins.

Nor could Strauss's narrative of modern declension be easily mapped onto Arendt's open-ended narrative of modernity.[55] Arendt focused much less systematically on the canonical thinkers of (early) modern political philosophy and also paid more attention to the Romans than Strauss did. Strauss and his followers were at one with Louis Hartz in assuming the Lockean basis of the American republic, but Locke hardly made an appearance in *On Revolution*. Indeed, his status was one of the main casualties of the republican synthesis as it emerged in the late 1960s and on into the 1970s.[56] Finally, Arendt rejected a "history of ideas" approach that emphasized the causal primacy of ideas in history, while this approach was at the heart of the Straussian vision of history.[57]

Among themselves the Straussians argued not over whether but which Locke was the most influential source of American political thinking. Strauss himself considered Locke's thought to be only slightly more palatable than Hobbes's emphasis on self-preservation, but Straussians, such as Thomas Pangle, later found a natural law/natural right component in Locke, thus making him—and American political culture—more acceptable to the Straussians. Clearly, the Locke of the Straussians was not the one apotheosized by Louis Hartz. Specifically, Pangle's strategy in *The Spirit of Modern Republicanism* (1988) was to accuse Bailyn, Wood, and Pocock (and Arendt) of offering an incoherent view of the republican tradition. Their republican synthesis had overemphasized the premodern nature of republicanism. Nor were the Anti-Federalists the true republicans in the debate over the Constitution; radical Whig ideology was found on both sides of the debate. Shrewdly, Pangle reversed terminological fields by naming Lockeanism—with its emphasis on the "Natural Equality and Rights of Men, including the right of resistance or revolution; religious toleration and freedom of conscience; and 'No taxation without representation'"— the "new republicanism."[58]

For our purposes, the most interesting aspect of Pangle's explication of what he called the new republicanism was his critique of *On Revolution*. It is often severely critical, and sometimes glib. Yet Pangle also acknowledges the power of Arendt's reading of the American Revolution, which emphasized "the civic dimension." He labeled her a "popularizer" of "Heidegger's political broodings," but at the same time acknowledged that she "belongs on a level quite above that of the scholars" who came after her. She was "too much a journalist and even a café intellectual," yet there was "something in her writing that transcends scholarship and reveals the authentic touch of philosophy." Shorn of the easy jibes ("journalist," "café intellectual," and "popularizer"), Pangle's core criticism was that Arendt had bought into Heidegger's "profound disillusionment with reason or rationalism in all its previous forms" and particularly his "radical historicism," the ultimate Straussian sin.[59]

Of course, Arendt had been a student of Heidegger. But Pangle's critique made it sound as though he had been the only modern thinker to register the loss of a substantive notion of reason and the only philosopher to influence Arendt. Yet insofar as Strauss and the Straussians were committed to an understanding of human beings based on "nature and reason" and were engaged in the "quest for universal, natural standards of human and political right discoverable by reason," they kept a lonely vigil, joining Christian thinkers, especially Catholic ones, in their rejection of modernity.[60] Pangle's use of the term "quest" was a hedge on his part, a covert admission that, for the Straussian tradition, all that remained of metaphysical rationalism was the idea of its possibility.

Still, Pangle was right—there were real differences with Arendt on these philosophical issues, not to mention Strauss's more militant anticommunism and conservative foreign policy. Her commitment to the worldliness of politics meant that she rejected metaphysical rationalism as an underpinning for politics. Nor did she really believe in something called "human nature," in the sense of a fixed and final "nature or essence." It needed a "God" to know that. But she clearly posited certain permanent "conditions of human existence" and capabilities such as labor, work, and action as developed in *The Human Condition*.[61] All this led her to believe that the twin mistakes of modernity lay in its assumption that "everything is possible" and that history developed along predetermined pathways. But whatever the influence of Heidegger on Arendt—and it was considerable—hers was never a Heideggerian view of politics and the political. In normative terms, her political thought owed about as much to Karl Jaspers's emphasis on communicative dialogue, while the influence of the French republican tradition, including Tocqueville (ironically, a Straussian favorite), was also considerable—not to mention the American Framers. Arendt simply outgrew Heidegger in her political thinking.

Pangle's second major charge focused on Arendt's misreading of the Greek commitment to civic virtue. Civic virtue, he insisted, was not the highest form of virtue for the Greeks. It was "a deficient form of virtue" in comparison with moral or ethical virtue. Indeed, the "superiority of the philosophical way of life" and "the nature of man conceived as a part of the whole of nature" were central to the Greek contribution to the Western tradition.[62] Insofar as Arendt did claim that the Greeks gave priority to political virtue, then Pangle was right. But the main thrust of *her* thought was to emphasize the centrality of politics in maintaining a shared world, particularly a common public world, as the site where human beings were most human. Neither Plato nor Aristotle, transcendent reason nor nature, ancient nor modern could provide a worldly foundation for the political realm, which was what she was committed to. Perhaps Arendt did underestimate the dangerous implications of Machiavelli's moral-political realism, but what attracted her to his thought was the worldliness of his ethics.[63] Certainly, these were fundamental differences between Arendt and Strauss.

Concerning America, Pangle also objected, rightly so, to Arendt's neglect of the religious dimension in American political culture, though Pangle himself emphasized Lockean liberalism's commitment to "the God of Nature" and not "the God of Scripture."[64] Second, Pangle also rightly criticized Arendt for failing to deal with the content of the Declaration of Independence as a philosophical statement that thematized rights, though how this was also a way of downgrading reason is unclear.[65] Finally, Pangle charged that the distinction Arendt drew between political and civil liberty and ultimately between republicanism and liberalism was closer in spirit to Robespierre's thought than to American republicanism.[66]

But his claim that Arendt always preferred action to "rational political thought or argument" is not quite right. To her the logos of political action emerged in the dialogue among political actors rather than from deductive reasoning or metaphysical rationality. Or one could reverse things and suggest that Pangle's emphasis on rationalism and the importance of truth in politics comported well with the dogmatic spirit of the French Revolution and its decline into terror. Also, Arendt raised the point about the difference between civil and political liberty to emphasize the similarity of the two revolutions in their early stages. In both revolutions, the social question—want and necessity in France or consumption in America—trumped the attractions of public liberty. Most of all, for Arendt, revolutionary terror was not the realization of public freedom—something Arendt favored—but its perversion. Robespierre was not a hero.

Overall, Pangle's razor sharp critique of Arendt's On Revolution revealed the fundamental disagreement between her and the Straussians. For the Straussians, the abandonment of the belief that the political sphere was founded on reason and nature marked modernity's decline, while for Arendt the Western tradition of politics would not recover its vitality until it realized the importance of the human artifice, including a space of political speech and action for all citizens. Other Straussians looked to Tocqueville's idea of "self-interest rightly understood" as an acceptable substitute for civic virtue in America's commercial republic. Political historian Harry Jaffa championed an American political tradition that chose both Jerusalem and Athens as sources to strengthen the American republic. Indeed, Jaffa carried on a furious debate with Walter Berns and Pangle over whether the Founders were religious or not. (Jaffa thought they were.) But he jettisoned Strauss's commitment to the classical belief in human inequality when he insisted that "the democracy of the American regime" was based on "the natural equality of all mankind."[67] For Jaffa, the central principle of the American experiment was "the consent of the governed," a powerful weapon for those who opposed chattel slavery.[68]

Indeed, Jaffa, along with most Straussians and scholars across the ideological spectrum, assumed that there is something like an "underlying principle" (Richard Primus's term) that linked the antislavery intentions of the Founders, the antebellum abolitionist and antislavery indictment of chattel slavery, and the Lincoln administration's successful steps to end to slavery in 1861–65. According to this view, says Primus, "The Civil War and Reconstruction redeemed the promise of the Founding in areas like race and slave labor."[69] This was not a matter that Arendt pronounced on one way or the other, but I suspect she would have been suspicious of such a convenient moral-historical teleology that made the end of slavery an inevitable fulfillment of the Framers' intentions.

Furthermore, the Straussians and Arendt dealt with the Framers quite differently. The former tended toward close explication of the canonical texts of the Framers, while Arendt treated the Framers as political actors as well as thinkers. Straussians tended to underplay the importance of institutional solutions to the problems of politics, while emphasizing the importance of ethos and character. Arendt's republicanism placed heavy emphasis on institutional matters, for example, the importance of checks and balances and separation of powers at the federal level and between national and state governments.[70] Certainly Arendt's emphasis in *On Revolution* fell on the Framers as a founding elite, but her ultimate concern was with how they created and maintained a public realm where political speech and action could flourish. Strauss, and early Straussians in particular, had no strong concept of political participation. However, recent Straussians such as Michael Zuckert have studied the republican tradition more closely and echoed Arendt's emphasis on the importance of Jefferson's ward system.[71]

Moreover, where Straussians stressed the natural right/law foundations of the American republic and looked back to classical Greece primarily and to natural law themes in medieval Scholasticism, Arendt assiduously explored the way Romans deployed myths and stories to authorize the founding of their republic.[72] But her ultimate conclusion was that the authority of the Constitution and the legitimacy of the American republic derived from "the act of foundation itself" as articulated in the performative utterances of the Constitution and the Declaration of Independence. This contrasted with France, where the Jacobins felt compelled to found a "Cult of the Supreme Being" and/or a religion of reason to justify their more radical revolution. John Adams himself insisted that governments in America were based not on "gods" or the "inspiration of Heaven" but the "use of reason and the senses," that is, purely human thought and historical evidence.[73]

Still, as mentioned early in the chapter, *On Revolution* was not primarily intended to be an exercise in historical reconstruction and contextualization. Leaving aside over two centuries of debate, Arendt believed that a considerable gap separated the two founding documents. But the Constitution's flaw was one of omission not commission—the ward system. As mentioned, Arendt thought federalism was as important as political participation in defining modern republicanism. Indeed, Lisa Disch claims that Arendt "told a quintessentially Federalist story of the American Revolution, yet defended an Anti-Federalist conception of democratic representation."[74] Similarly, according to George Kateb, Arendt's early view was that establishing a representative government rather than direct democracy "basically spelled the end of true political action."[75] This meant that, for Arendt, "the survival of the spirit out of which the action of foundation sprang, to realize the principle which inspired it . . . was frustrated almost from the beginning."[76] On this view, it is entirely plausible to link Arendt's position with that of the Revolutionary War generation, which later made up, more or less, the Anti-Federalist position. The problem with all this, however, is that Arendt rarely mentioned the Federalist/Anti-Federalist division in *On Revolution*. It was not a major issue for her.

Arendt was making a historical not a metaphysical point. The Constitution could have been the crowning achievement of a successful revolution; the importance of representative institutions was not finally a fatal flaw. Indeed, Jeremy Waldron has objected to the way that Kateb concentrates too heavily on Arendt's "agonistic" (self-disclosure) and "irregular" (council) forms of political action, while underestimating Arendt's concern with the proper, ongoing functioning of a constitutional government. Indeed, such constitution maintenance was, as we have seen, one form that authentic politics could take. He also notes that Arendt came to see the close relationship between civil liberties and even civil disobedience, on the one hand, and constitutional politics on the other.[77] Still, for Arendt, the basic failure of the American Revolution and the Framers was due not to forgetfulness of classical politics but to the inability to find ways to preserve participatory freedom in, as Herman Melville put it, "lasting institutions." They ultimately failed to create the institutional prerequisites for a modern republic, in America's case ones that would preserve the actuality of political freedom and resist the impact of things like mass consumption by the twentieth century.[78]

Coda: The Problem of American Political Thought

Near the end of *On Revolution*, Arendt wondered why "this interest in political thought and theory dried up almost immediately after the task had been achieved." She explicitly rejected Daniel Boorstin's emphasis on "the colonial experience" of self-rule and his neglect of the importance of political ideas. In fact, Arendt emphasized both experience and ideas as crucial in a tradition of political thought. But the neglect of American political thought after the founding generation, due to the loss of its "revolutionary spirit," contributed to the failure of America's revolutionary inheritance to spread very widely beyond its borders.[79]

How should we assess Arendt's low opinion of American political thought after the founding? First, it is an opinion shared, for instance, by Louis Hartz who claimed that the "law has flourished on the corpse of philosophy in America." That is, constitutional interpretation, including the whole archive of Supreme Court decisions, rendered political philosophy irrelevant per se. Indeed, Hartz sounded a good bit like Boorstin when he asserted that the triumph of American pragmatism as a philosophical movement shows that it is "only when you take your ethics for granted that all problems emerge as problems of techniques."[80] This is a severely constricted view of pragmatism, but his point was that deep thinking about political matters was hardly in high demand in a political culture marked by a consensus on its basic political institutions and values.

Closer to the present, both Judith Shklar and James Kloppenberg have echoed Arendt's observation about the lack of political theory but then added that America has had its own set of political problems that needed thinking about, even if the style of thought doesn't match the grand (European) manner. In the early 1990s, Shklar expressed impatience with the constant harping on the inadequacies of American political thought. She argued that it "did not suffer a single fall from grace, as some now claim, when it abandoned a premodern republicanism in favor of an amoral, atomized individualism. Nor, finally, need we continue that endless Jeremiad about the absence of socialism and conservatism. I believe that when we take a good look at our actual tradition of political theory, we will find something better than a drab and cheerless heritage, a poor thing, but our own."[81] Similarly, when Kloppenberg writes that "students of American political theory should examine the meanings of public texts rather than limiting their attention to a canon of abstract political philosophy," it is hard not to think that Arendt would approve. Though system building in American political thought has been hard to find outside the writings of John C. Calhoun (whom Arendt *had* studied), American intellectuals, politicians, and thinkers have had to confront all sorts of "practical questions of democratic governance," including federalism and citizenship which Arendt also took very seriously.[82] Like Shklar, Kloppenberg offers few examples of American political philosophers who have grappled with these issues, though Dewey would have to head up any accurate list.

Arendt's comment on the failure of Americans to remember their own intellectual history presupposed that political ideas help us remember and thus perpetuate a collective experience. The American "failure of thought and remembrance" has meant that America had been vulnerable to seduction by all sorts of "fad and humbug" from Europe, "particularly in the social and psychological sciences." (Here she clearly has psychoanalysis in mind.) Of the original republican political experience, little remained, as is obvious in the work of Hofstadter, Hartz, and Boorstin in her own time. Rather, the liberal consensus view stressed the legacy of "civil liberties, the individual welfare of the greatest number, and public opinion"—in other words, the liberal tradition in American.[83] For Arendt, then, the real shortcoming of American political thought was not that it failed to imitate the European political thought but that it failed to perpetuate in "thought" and "memory" the same political originality of the republic's founding.

But there is an irony at work here, since Arendt also ignored a dimension of American political thought that lifted it above the politics of interests and opinion. I refer here to the rights tradition that Pangle and Zuckert, among others, have emphasized and that reemerged in the Warren Court of the 1950s and 1960s. On reason is that the American tradition of natural rights, with its emphasis on subjective individual rights, was ostensibly at odds with republicanism's location of political principles within the political tradition itself, not in the individual conscience or in nature. In the case of American progressivism and pragmatism, rights claims were identified with the conservative defense of private property and corporate power, not to mention assertions of purely individual rights. Nor did Hartz's American liberalism thesis place much emphasis on "rights talk" in the Lockean tradition. Not until it was resurrected by the Civil Rights and the anti–Vietnam War Movements, particularly in reference to civil disobedience, did American political theorists once again begin to take rights seriously.[84]

Also in the mid-twentieth century, another tradition of thinking about rights began linking them to assertions of difference and opposition on the part of citizens, who are due "equal concern and respect" (Ronald Dworkin's words). In this sense, rights are the signifiers of our equality as citizens and thus "trump" positive laws. Historically, some basic rights and liberties have helped maintain a public sphere where even the law may be broken through action respectful of the law. In this tradition, rights derive from those foundational documents that define the republic rather than from transcendent sources or God's will. Within the American political tradition as a whole, the Constitution is the "higher law" that stands over and against positive law. In John Rawls's terms, rights are political not metaphysical entities, deriving not from the laws of nature, as the Straussians contend, but from the political culture itself.[85] All this suggests, as well, that the strict bifurcation between the republican and the liberal traditions seems to be the result of retrospective conceptualization rather than a reflection of historical reality at the time of their emergence.[86]

To develop this line of thought about the rights tradition, I want to refer to Richard Primus's contention that American political and legal thought has seen three great periods of concern with rights—the founding of the republic, the Civil War and Reconstruction, and post–World War II America. Each of the periods has had a dominant focus—home rule, labor and legal status, and antitotalitarian concern with "higher law" or "human rights," respectively, though each stage also retains aspects of the previous stages. Interestingly, Primus cites Arendt as part of the post–World War II effort to find something like a principle with universality that protects the dignity of the self and groups. Thus, like Samuel Moyn, Primus locates the origin of authentic human rights thinking in the post-1945 period.[87]

Strangely, he doesn't mention Arendt's one clear reference to rights in her work—"the right to have rights." Otherwise the attention she paid to the issue of rights was strangely minimal. She refers to rights in the Declaration of Independence when she explores the idea of "public happiness" as a needed corrective to "the pursuit of happiness." But she pays no attention to the whole period between circa 1770 to 1800, which was teeming with rights talk on both sides of the Atlantic, expressed most saliently in the Declaration of Independence and the French Rights of Man.[88] From its inception, the former was used by petitioners against slavery, since the peculiar institution obviously violated the right to liberty, life, and certainly happiness. In fact, on the issue of slavery, the conventional Lockean phrasing of the triumvirate—life, liberty, and property—offered, if anything, a more direct way to challenge slavery, since everyone's first piece of property was his or her body. But Arendt wrote almost nothing on these matters.

More broadly, rights in the American system have been linked with freedom and citizenship, not just interests and individualism. Whether the original intention behind rights was the protection of property or whether their origin was in nature, in the Platonic realm, or in the historical past, and whether they were best found in the declarations of legislative or judicial bodies or in philosophical texts, rights eventually emerged as something a person had to argue and even fight for. They had no fixed or static meaning. They fluctuated between, for example, being authorizations of action (we have a right to vote) and the objects of action (we act to secure our rights). In sum, they had to be taken and/or realized and, paradoxically, needed to be recognized by those who had previously withheld them. They were not just something the private individuals enjoyed but were entities in need of public validation and defense. As it developed over the first two-thirds of the nineteenth century, rights talk was one of the idioms within which the actual master-slave relationship was articulated. In the transition from slavery to freedom, from slave to citizen, the pursuit of rights was tightly bound up with freedom and citizenship. Rights, as they evolved in the American setting, were used to claim those rights that everyone else claimed, the American version of Arendt's well-known phrase "right to have rights."

Aside from this Arendtian formulation, as already mentioned, Harry Jaffa has identified the great principle of self-government in the American system as "the consent of the governed." But though she never directly addressed Jaffa's celebration of this principle, Arendt would have recognized it as an example of the vertical contract in which the people hand over their fate to rulers and a fixed hierarchical relationship between ruler and ruled is established. For Arendt, the basic principle of the American republic was not just "the consent of the governed" but the idea that government is based on "reciprocity and presupposes equality" or, as she later said, "mutual promise and common deliberation," with the emphasis falling on "mutual" and "common" as descriptors of a horizontal relationship.[89] Rights *became* aids to, and authorizations of, speech and action among potential equals. From this perspective, rights liberalism, rightly understood, provided a framework within which ideas of action, recognition, and citizenship could develop. This was what the history of the Civil Rights Movement (1954–68) was all about, even nearly two hundred years after the Declaration of Independence.

The second great founding moment for rights was the addition of the Bill of Rights to the Constitution in 1791—specifically, of course, the First Amendment. If the Anti-Federalists in general were outgunned and outclassed by the Federalists, the addition of a Bill of Rights was the price they—and numerous Federalists, too—demanded for support of the new constitution. Indeed Christopher Duncan has suggested that the Bill of Rights were not originally a charter of individual rights or libertarian principles but a declaration of republican principles, inhering in citizens as a body.[90] Now known generally as "civil liberties," First Amendment rights have a narrower range than the great triumvirate found in paragraph two of the Declaration. They bear on specific kinds of activity, both private and public, in relation to religion and religious institutions, freedom of expression (speech or press), and freedom of assembly and petition. They are a mixture of negative liberties (Congress shall make no law . . .) that forbid obstacles to citizen actions and beliefs and empowerments to do something ("right peaceably to assemble and petition"). The First Amendment is not just made up of regulatory principles or commands but also defines the kind of actions that people have a right to engage in, especially political activities in the public realm.

But an important contradiction in Arendt's *On Revolution* arises in this context. Near the beginning of the last chapter, Arendt refers to "the truly political freedoms, such as freedom of speech and thought, of assembly and association." This would seem to be a clear statement of the connection between First Amendment rights and political freedom, in her strong sense of the term; that is, the First Amendment has a republican dimension to it. Yet a page later, Arendt asserts that there "should be no reason for us to mistake civil rights for political freedom."[91] She is even more deflationary when she asserts that "The Bill of Rights in the American Constitution forms the last, and the most exhaustive legal bulwark for the private realm against public power."[92] This assertion seems to deny that the First Amendment, which is one of the Bill of Rights, enumerates liberties linked to political freedom.

Which is the authentic Arendt here? It is hard to say, but clearly First Amendment rights presuppose a public sphere where they can be exercised. The rights to assembly and petition make explicit that these activities are not just restricted to the individual in his or her own private conscience or desires. Except for the "free exercise" clause having to do with religion, these rights and liberties assume the copresence of other people and allow us to think of group action ("establishment of religion," "assembly," "speech and the press," and "petition") as protected as well. Excepting religion, which is explicitly excluded from state action and public purview, the right to speak in public and to the public, the right to assemble and petition, establish where "speech and action" about the public business can take place.

In general, then, Arendt's failure to elaborate on the "right to have rights" in the American context and to underline how the First Amendment augments, not undermines, the republican "right" to be a "participator in government" was a serious omission. The more obvious set of political rights—the right to vote and hold office—had to wait for the Fifteenth Amendment (1870) to be adopted, along with civil rights (Fourteenth Amendment) as distinguished from political rights. Later, the doctrine of incorporation, whereby the First Amendment was understood to apply to state and not just to federal laws, elevated the First Amendment to full importance as a charter of political freedom. Overall, the First Amendment was just as powerful a contribution to political freedom as either the ward system or the idea of public happiness would have been had they become enshrined in the basic documents of the republic. What Arendt failed to recognize was that the struggle for rights throughout American history had changed the meaning of rights, in ways that neither European political theorists nor American legal theorists have taken full cognizance of.

CHAPTER 11

The Revolutionary Traditions

Besides exploring the tension between republicanism and liberal constitutionalism, Hannah Arendt also explored the differences between a political and a social revolution in *On Revolution*.[1] Arendt's basic thesis was that the "obscurity" of poverty in America allowed the American Framers to avoid the "social question," which the French Revolution, especially during the Terror (1793–94), placed at the center of its concerns. Arendt's republican interpretation of the American Revolution has been reasonably well-examined, but her explanation for the Terror has found few takers. Generally, Lynn Hunt has placed her in the tradition of Alexis de Tocqueville and François Furet that makes the distinction between the social and the political central to an understanding of the revolution, while Patrice Higonnet has emphasized Arendt's analysis of the Jacobin-led Terror in terms of pity. Still, among historians and political theorists of the French Revolution her work has received relatively little attention.[2]

What was the importance of the French Revolution to Arendt? First, she emphasized its far greater influence on Europe and the rest of the world than the American Revolution, though this clashed with R. R. Palmer's emphasis on the shared nature of "the Democratic Revolutions," at least in the late eighteenth century. What fascinated her was that the French Revolution had tried to create an absolute break with the past. Not only social and political life but also human nature itself was to be redefined. For her, this foreshadowed a similar, albeit more extreme, impulse in the totalitarian regimes of the twentieth century. The Declaration of Independence was written with "decent respect for the opinions of mankind," but Jefferson's rhetoric sounds sober and lawyerly in comparison with the idea that the French Revolution was, according to Tocqueville, like a "species of religion" that sought to universalize its revolutionary ideas and institutions, the goal being the "regeneration of the human race."[3] That it was not just a revolution for France, or even Europe, was confirmed, as it were, when the only successful slave uprising in the modern world began in the French colony on Saint-Domingue, that is, Haiti, in the early 1790s.[4]

What Arendt meant by the social question was not simply poverty but the all-pervasive presence of "misery and want."[5] In the year of the Terror (roughly midsummer 1793—midsummer 1794), the "biological imagery which underlies and pervades the organic and social theories of history" locked into place. This was, she claimed, the origin of the tendency of modern theories of politics and history to "see a multitude—the factual plurality of a nation or a people or society—in the image of one supernatural body driven by one superhuman, irresistible 'general will.'"[6] Arendt's mention of the general will here links up with what she saw as the pernicious role of Rousseau's thought in creating a politics of compassion and pity, while her use of the term "irresistible" suggests the way that Marx later yoked together a modern teleology of history (historical necessity) with the eradication of want and misery (biological necessity).

That Marx was "much more interested in history than in politics" led to "the abdication of freedom before the dictate of necessity." Because "freedom and poverty were incompatible," the latter had to be abolished before the former could be realized. Initially, Marx "had denounced economic and social conditions in political terms" but came to see that "it was just as possible to interpret politics in economic terms."[7] Overall, Arendt's verdict was that Marx changed the meaning of revolution: "The role of revolution was no longer to liberate men from the oppression of their fellow men, let alone to found freedom, but to liberate the life process of society from the fetters of scarcity so that it could swell into a stream of abundance."[8] From this, she drew the controversial conclusion that "the whole record of past revolutions demonstrates beyond doubt that every attempt to solve the social question with political means leads into terror."[9] Thus revolutions go wrong when they pursue the chimera of economic equality.

Arendt and Revolution

How did Arendt's view of modern revolution fit with those of her Anglophone contemporaries? Almost alone among contemporary students of revolution, Crane Brinton commented briefly but pointedly on *On Revolution* in the 1965 edition of his *The Anatomy of Revolution* (1938), while Barrington Moore's influential *Social Origins of Dictatorship and Democracy* (1966) was silent on Arendt's work, in large part because Moore's book explored the economic and social forces underlying the emergence—or failure to emerge—of modern democracy, which was what Arendt was bent on not doing. Where *The Origins of Totalitarianism* paid ample attention to historical events, economic factors, and social forces and rejected a history of ideas approach, *On Revolution* certainly paid ample attention to the historical impact of the intentions, ideas, and affective states of political actors (Jefferson, Adams, Madison; Robespierre) and the ideas of Machiavelli, Montesquieu, Rousseau, and Tocqueville. For example, chapter 2 of *On Revolution* presents a kind of *Begriffsgeschichte*, one that explores the states of mind, emotions, principles, and ideas that produced the Terror and introduced the repertory of moral-political terms that accompanied her work over its last decade and a half. Included were compassion, pity, and solidarity; evil, goodness, and virtue; will and necessity versus public spirit and consent; suspicion and hypocrisy; rage, vengeance, power, violence, and terror. Her exploration of these concepts and the states of mind accompanying them was intended to illuminate the political landscape of modern politics, including that of the contemporary world.

Brinton's brief mention of Arendt in the 1965 edition of *Anatomy* mixed perfunctory praise with sharp, even dismissive, criticism.[10] He referred to *Origins*, along with Orwell's *1984*, as one of the "profound and persuasive analyses" of totalitarianism, except he quite clearly did not consider to totalitarianism to be "new on earth." In fact, his assumption was that the English, French, and, to a degree, American Revolutions belonged with the Russian

Revolution rather than being distinct from it. The Bolshevik Revolution was, then, an extreme case of a familiar phenomenon. Put another way, Arendt's focus on the historical exceptionalism of the Soviet regime went against the grain of Brinton's "natural history" approach to modern revolutions.[11] Indeed, his approach exemplified what she found so frustrating about the social scientific attempt to deal with totalitarianism—it too easily assimilated a historically unique phenomenon to a tradition of revolution. Also, by grouping the Bolshevik Revolution with the other revolutions in the "democratic tradition," Brinton had great difficulty in dealing with conservative upheavals such as the "German Revolution," which the Nazi revolution itself was an outgrowth of.[12]

Arendt's strong critique of the French Revolution and sympathetic treatment of the American republican revolution were clearly too normative for Brinton. He preferred to analyze modern revolutions in terms of the way they fit his framework, not in terms of independent moral or political criteria. Brinton all but admitted that the American Revolution hardly fit the model of revolution proposed in his schema and agreed with Arendt when he asserted that in America there was "no class ground down with poverty."[13] Like Arendt, Brinton was also interested in the "revolutionary ideal" that dominated each revolution: "no ideas, no revolution."[14] And neither spent time with non-Western revolutions. Overall, Brinton's thesis was that the European revolutions "began in hope and moderation, all reach a crisis in a reign of terror, and all end in something like dictatorship—Cromwell, Bonaparte, Stalin."[15] But, to Arendt's way of thinking, grouping these three leaders together was a deep mistake.

Ironically, Brinton's developmental model revealed the exceptional nature of the American Revolution and thus reinforced the belief in the greater affinities between the French and Russian Revolutions. Indeed, by the 1930s, the Trotskyists were particularly concerned with the parallels between the Terror in each country (1793–94 and the early 1930s, respectively) and the nature of the Thermidorean reaction that followed thereafter (the Directory and Stalin's consolidation of power, respectively).[16] For Brinton the two revolutions resembled one another insofar as both followed the path of revolutionary development his schema proposed—which was itself largely derived from the original French example. Yet conceptually speaking, Brinton's model implied that the Russian Revolution, for instance, would have reached a Thermidorean stage, even had the French Revolution never existed. For him, revolutions developed along parallel tracks without necessarily being related causally.

For her part, Arendt saw a causal relationship between the French and Bolshevik Revolutions. Each revolution sought to address the problem of want and poverty. But the awareness of the movement in the French Revolution from the Terror to the Thermidor was one that fascinated, even obsessed, the participants in the Bolshevik Revolution. Generally, as R. R. Palmer has explained, Brinton's "pattern of revolutionary process" did not entail that "the French Revolution was "a kind of origin, partial cause, or distant prefiguration of the Russian Revolution." But Arendt's analysis certainly did assume that.[17] Arendt made no pretense of preserving (social) scientific neutrality on the matter of revolution; Brinton's medical trope suggested that revolution was a kind of "fever" that had a course to run, while Arendt's open-ended view of history avoided the determinism dictated by Brinton's framework. Neither Brinton nor Arendt sought to identify one or more underlying causes of any or all four of the revolutions, aside from the reasons and intentions voiced by the revolutionary leaders themselves. But without a teleological concept of history, Arendt could only see a successful revolution as a decidedly tenuous achievement. Perhaps this is what Brinton meant when he drew the line in the sand in the 1965 edition of *Anatomy*: "Emotional, intellectual, full of existentialist despair, poles apart from the approach attempted in this book. . . . If Miss Arendt and Mr. [Eugen] Rosenstock-Huessy make sense, this book is nonsense; the converse, one hopes, may also be true."[18] The differences could hardly have been sharper.

How does Arendt's work fit into the historiography of the French Revolution, as it stood in her time? Not surprisingly, she belongs with Tocqueville (and François Furet) in focusing on the underlying tension between the social and the political realms in the French Revolution. Arendt undoubtedly shared Tocqueville's love of political freedom, as witness his statement in *The Old Regime and the French Revolution*: "The man who asks of freedom anything other than itself is born to be a slave." She also followed him in seeing the tragedy of the French Revolution as the triumph of the search for (social) equality over the republican idea of (political) freedom and of centralization over dispersion of power.[19] This is broadly the "political" interpretation of the French Revolution, the central concern of which is: "When did the Revolution go wrong?"[20]

But an interesting contradiction begins to emerge at this point. In the classic, left-wing historiography of the Revolution, Albert Mathiez, Georges Lefebvre, and Albert Soboul were crucial figures. According to William Doyle, Mathiez, needing to direct revolutionary violence against the enemies of the Bolsheviks, sought to rehabilitate Maximilien Robespierre and, more broadly, the Terror. In turn, Lefebvre's work of the 1930s focused attention on the economic dimensions of the Revolution and the coming to power of the bourgeoisie, with the Terror seen as a reaction against the counterrevolutionary efforts of the aristocracy. Finally, Soboul added a focus on the sansculottes and popular participation and distinguished the sansculottes both from the Jacobins and from the proletarians. Furet's critique of Soboul was that he joined "an analysis of causes carried out in the economic and social mode to a narrative of events written in the political and ideological mode."[21]

The irony here is that Arendt's normative vision was profoundly shaped by the Tocquevillean perspective, yet her claim about the centrality of the social question in the French Revolution derived primarily from the work of the Marxist Soboul and his coauthor Walter Markov, who edited a 1957 collection of documents dealing with the sansculottes published in East Germany, and from J. M. Thompson's biography of Robespierre published in 1939, respectively. That is, she depended on the work of the classic/Marxist school to support her idea of the prominence of the social question among the Jacobins, yet gave that prominence a negative rather than positive spin. As Lisa Disch has put it: "In effect, Arendt perpetuated a Marxist interpretive line even as she aspired to displace Marxism from its place of pride in political theories of revolution."[22] Overall, Arendt treated the Marxist interpretation of the Revolution as though it were fact, which she then used to support her claim that the politicization of the social question could only lead to disaster.

Critiques and Comparisons

The French Revolution has a complex and sophisticated intellectual history. By no means uniformly hostile to the French Revolution, R. R. Palmer once asked "Why was [it] so radical at the very beginning?"—a query more recently echoed in Simon Schama's escalated claim that "from the very beginning—violence was the motor of the Revolution," including the urge and the urgency to die a "patriotic death."[23] Why did the execution of the king of France seem to lead inexorably to the Terror, while the execution of the king in England lacked the same sort of shocking—and demoralizing—effect in seventeenth-century England? Why did the American Revolution see no political executions at all, though plenty of Tory property was confiscated?

Or has too big a deal been made of a relatively simple matter? For some analysts of the French Revolution, then and since, the Terror was justifiably directed, wrote Barrington Moore in 1966, against the correct enemies—the "nobility and the clergy" along with "wealthier commercial interests." In this respect, he concluded that "by and large the consequences [of the Terror] were rational." They were most obvious where resistance was strongest, though there were doubtless "tragic and unjust aspects" to the whole process. Moore also suggested that simply counting the lives lost in The Terror makes it too easy to forget the violence exacted over the years of the ancien régime: "To dwell on the horrors of revolutionary violence while forgetting that of 'normal' times is merely partisan hypocrisy."[24] With this in mind, is there any need to wrack our brains for explanations in terms of intellectual history, once we understand the long pent-up need to retaliate for long-standing oppression?[25]

Yet the French Revolution was, more than the American Revolution, an intellectual's conflict. In our context, the post-1945 debate about totalitarianism quickly became a root-and-branch assessment of the Marxist tradition and the Soviet experiment, which had once seemed the future that "works" (Lincoln Steffens). Arendt's *Origins* was central to that reassessment in the first decade after the war. With *On Revolution*, she turned to the French Revolution to see if it, perhaps, offered a clue as to what had gone wrong in the Soviet Union. As already explained, Arendt thought the fatal misstep of the French Revolution had to do with the use of state power to try eradicate want and necessity. Yet, in fact, what she proposed in *On Revolution* also drew heavily on two other traditions of critique of the French Revolution.

Abstractions and Ideas versus Experience

Perhaps the most venerable explanation for the failure of the French Revolution was that it imposed Enlightenment plans and ideas on complex historical and social realities, for which they were inappropriate. The classic expression of this position was voiced by Edmund Burke, whose *Reflections on the Revolution in France* (1790) objected to the attempt to shape the social, political, and cultural traditions of France (and by extension England) to fit novel sorts of abstractions such as rights. Specifically, Burke contrasted the French political revolutionary tradition with the British political tradition, which saw the British "claiming their franchises not on abstract principles 'as the rights of man,' but as the rights of Englishmen, and as a patrimony derived from their forefathers."[26]

In the wake of the great period of the French Revolution, Hegel's *Phenomenology of Spirit* (1807) also tried to assess what had gone wrong with the Revolution. Unlike Burke, Hegel never totally abjured the revolutionary legacy of 1789, but, like Burke, he saw that the claims of absolute reason drained actually existing religious institutions, classes, estates, and other structures of existence of their legitimacy. As a result, the individual was swallowed up by the new revolutionary order, which left no room for competing identities or loyalties, that is, to the church, for example. In such a situation, the individual became dominated intellectually and morally by revolutionary virtue and could appeal to nothing except the "religion of the State" which had banished other forms of transcendence.[27] The politics of absolute principle trumped political debate and deliberation, as well as undermining the claims of tradition. As a result, he wrote that "the immediate realization of the general will culminates only in the Terror."[28] Another post–World War II voice was added to the attack on revolutionary abstraction when Albert Camus, a latter-day advocate of rebellion as opposed to revolution, observed in *The Rebel* (1956) that "truth, reason and justice," when applied in a revolutionary situation, "have ceased to be guides in order to become goals." Detached from the historical process, they become something to be realized at the end of history.[29] In the revolution, of course, time and history were radically reconceived to fit revolutionary imperatives. To "force" time, to construct a new form of history (e.g., a new calendar), revealed the level to which the idea of revolution itself suffused collective as well as individual subjectivity.[30]

In certain respects, Arendt embraced this tradition that stressed the destructive power of abstractions. Surprisingly, the Hegelian analysis is highly reminiscent of her analysis of totalitarian law in the "Ideology and Terror" section of *Origins*. There she claimed that terror resulted from the direct application of the law of history or race to the individual, absent any institutional buffers or the protective stability of positive law. But Arendt saw political experience as the main buffer against abstract ideas. For her, the American Framers developed their political thinking in consonance with their experience of political action. By way of contrast, in France, intellectuals were prepared conceptually but not experientially: "The preparation of the French hommes de lettres who were to make the Revolution was theoretical in the extreme. . . . They had no experiences to fall back upon, only ideas and principles untested by reality to guide and inspire them . . . except 'memories from antiquity.'"[31] It is important to note that Arendt's appeal here is primarily to experience, not tradition as such. Except for Tom Paine, the chief architects of the new republic in North America had exercised power and made political decisions. Overall, Arendt's analysis is also shadowed by her suspicion of political intellectuals, including philosophers, since they rarely are at home, she thought, in the public world. Whether on the left or right, their capacity for political reality testing, compromise, and patience was underdeveloped.

Another example of American success with mediating institutions was the written constitution as it related to positive laws. On one level, this mirrored the conceptual relationship of natural right(s) to positive law. In the American system, the "higher law" did not work in unmediated fashion on the individual but was articulated through human-made documents and institutions.[32] But Arendt noted that the French Rights of Man referred to basic "rights of life and nature" rather than referring to the "rights of citizenship and freedom" as the American Bill of Rights did.[33] The implication was that the rights in the latter were political; in the former they were metaphysical. Rights were intended to protect individuals against the government in the American system, while the French Rights of Man were more like principles of morality. According to Arendt in her analysis of

Billy Budd, when "an absolute . . . was incorporated into the Rights of Man" and "was introduced into the political realm," disaster followed.[34] However, she still did not really explain how the appeal to "inalienable rights" in the Declaration of Independence (not the Bill of Rights) was not an appeal to a source outside the political order, such as nature. Perhaps, it was that nature checked rather than reinforced the undivided will in the American system, while nature and the general will were practically synonymous in France.[35]

Totality and Centralization

Overall, the American Revolution conceived of sovereignty and of "the people" in different ways than the French Revolution did. An idea such as the general will and/or an equivalent idea of "natural right" that operated according to the "logic of unmediated nature" provided the foundation for the new revolutionary order and the constitutional republic in France.[36] Tocqueville's historical claim in *The Old Regime and the French Revolution* that the Revolution completed the old regime's project of centralization also testified to the importance of unity and consolidation in the Revolution. In constitutional terms, the general will, which reconciled individual will with the common good, entailed undivided sovereignty. From this it was but a short step to Louis de Saint-Just's claim, cited by R. R. Palmer, that the "only citizens in the Republic are the republicans," while those at odds with the general will, such as royalists, "had no rights."[37]

Arendt's hostility to Rousseau was based on her view that the legitimacy, and thus power, of government arose from popular "consent," which had "overtones of deliberate choice and considered opinion" rather than suggesting a holistic notion of coincident wills. Where republics should be based on consent from "worldly institutions," she thought, the French Revolution was grounded in "the will of the people themselves," unmediated by institutions. As already suggested, undivided sovereignty implied a self-evident "unanimity" that could brook no debate or discussion.[38] In general, R. R. Palmer noted in his classic study of the Terror that it was not Robespierre's economic and social views but the "tragic misconception" of the people that lay at the root of the Revolution's mistakes. The people were not "all compact of goodness . . . not peculiarly governable by reason" and "not even a unitary thing at all."[39] Believing that they were, Robespierre, in an Arendtian reading, could only consider dissent as treason or hypocrisy.

Overall, then, the emphasis on political unity and totality was a salient difference between the political cultures of France and the United States.[40] The very existence of the United States depended on the retention of a modicum of power, or sovereignty, by the individual states. Arendt rested much of her confidence in the wisdom of the Framers on their commitment to a federal republic, while in France the "federalists" were usually the enemy of the Revolution. As the American Framers saw it, their task was to strike the right balance between national and state governments, without abolishing either. The federal constitution institutionalized a system of what Lisa Disch has called "layered authority."[41] In retrospect, however, the historical problem was, of course, that federalism became the best conceptual and political way to protect slavery, since it placed slavery under state not federal jurisdiction. I will return to this issue later.

One of Arendt's most interesting discussions in *On Revolution*—the French Revolution's obsession with unmasking hypocrisy and the fear of conspiracy—is also relevant here. The revolutionary attack on hypocrisy assumed the "rottenness" and "corruption" of society, as contrasted with the supposed virtue of the people. But the attack on hypocrisy, the stripping away of the mask, left the person a merely natural being: "It equalized because it left all inhabitants equally without the protecting mask of a legal personality."[42] Nor was the political culture of America lacking a conspiratorial dimension, which was the political counterpart of the obsession with hypocrisy. Bernard Bailyn's pioneering work on the prerevolutionary political culture of dissent made the idea of a "conspiracy against liberty" central to American political culture, a tendency that foreshadowed what Richard Hofstadter called the "paranoid style" of American politics that emerged, he thought, in the 1790s.[43] One big difference is that in America the "paranoid style," the tendency to believe in conspiracies, has been lodged on the right not the left end of the political spectrum.

One of the distinctive aspects of the new American political culture was the idea of holding special constitutional conventions, the results of which were subject to popular approval, whereupon the convention dissolved itself. R. R. Palmer describes the overall process thus: "The sovereign people, which, after acting as a god from the machine in a constituent convention, retired to the more modest status of an electorate, and let its theoretical sovereignty become inactive."[44] What was perhaps good for stability was, as Arendt recognized, a blow to direct participation in government. Still, once the constitution was accepted, the American political system tended to lodge sovereignty in various documents and institutions. This thwarted the possibility of one or a few individuals speaking in the name of the people. Put another way, in the American system, the idea of "the people," as Arendt says, "retained . . . the meaning of manyness, of the endless variety of a multitude whose majesty rested in its very plurality."[45] Generally, the conventions were grounded not in a transcendent or foundational source but in the act of self-constituting itself. A people gave a law to itself and took responsibility for it.

The French were by no means totally oblivious to this issue. Even the Jacobins made the right kind of noises about operating under a stable constitution written by a national convention, which had replaced the revolution with a republic. But, Robespierre felt it necessary in the late autumn/early winter of 1793 to suspend the constitution and reestablish a revolutionary dictatorship under the Committee of Public Safety. Faced by enemies abroad and domestic, Robespierre stated in December 25, 1793, that "Faction" is the "chief menace to the Revolution." Specifically, "The aim of constitutional government is to preserve the Republic. The aim of revolutionary government is to found it." Palmer concludes that "Robespierre regarded dictatorship as an interim phase, necessary rather than desirable." It was an acceptable, if provisional, alternative to constitutional government.[46] Still, constitutionalism was not as strong a tradition in France as in the United States. Furthermore, since the general will was embodied in the sovereign state, there was less need to actually consult the people about decisions. This contrasted sharply with U.S. political history where, even in the midst of the Civil War, the presidential election of 1864 proceeded as normal.

The Social Question

As already mentioned, Arendt's interpretation of the French Revolution clearly identified the economic-moral impulse to eradicate poverty and want as the prime cause of its failure.[47] In general, her emphasis fell on the conscious intentions of Robespierre and the Jacobins rather than the working of social forces to explain the rise and fall of the Jacobins. But she did take into account the appearance of the sansculottes and the Jacobin clubs on the public scene as crucial in creating revolutionary public opinion.

But how did Arendt's emphasis on the Jacobins' obsession with the social question fit with the understanding of the causes of the Terror at the time she was writing? One thing to note is that the Jacobins (led by Robespierre and Saint-Just) occupied the center position among the radicals in this period of the Revolution (1792–94). In his classic, *Twelve Who Ruled* (1941), which Arendt praised highly, R. R. Palmer noted that, during the year of the Terror, the Jacobins regulated economic affairs "through a policy of "preemption," something close to "requisition." They still maintained private rights, including property, and did not support "economic equalization." Indeed, Palmer emphasized that it was a myth that "he [Robespierre] was an early friend of the proletariat, about to embark on economic revolution when he fell."[48] Palmer also observed that the Jacobin leader "paid little attention to the economic demands" but did support them in general. However, he was not a radical on these matters.[49]

Regarding the social sources of revolution, Marxist historian Albert Soboul "did claim social forces to be the driving factor in the French Revolution, [but] he emphasized that the sans-culottes were neither homogeneous nor predominantly poor."[50] Barrington Moore summed up the relationship between Robespierre's faction and the sansculottes by emphasizing the distance Robespierre took from the sansculottes: "Robespierre and the Montagne took over a large part of the program of the *sans-culottes*, including the Terror on a massive scale, tried to use it for their own purposes, and in time turned the weapon back against popular forces."[51] Overall, Patrice Higonnet summed it up as follows in the late 1990s: "The Jacobins' instinct was to favor the crowd.... But like their monarchic predecessors, they had no intention of ever losing control of the social and political machine." Indeed in 1793, the Jacobins had "decried" the justification of the food riots by "enraged leader Jacques Roux" and in the summer were accused by the sansculottes of "being too tolerant of greed and insufficiently universalist."[52] All this is to say that the Jacobins by no means were willing to give the populace a blank check.

That said, there is some evidence that the Jacobins grew more radical in 1793 and on into 1794 as the economic situation worsened. William Doyle notes the gradual emergence of a proto–planned economy based on price and wage fixing, a kind of tax on the well-off and some confiscation of land. Still, the Jacobins were not levelers nor did they want the abolition of private property: "They sought to raise the poor to their level rather than to lower the rich to some draconian average."[53] But none of these historical analysts, representing a range of opinion on the Revolution itself, provide much support for Arendt's view that Robespierre and the Jacobins developed a strong politics of pity and/or compassion. Rather, what stands out in Palmer's profile is his emphasis on Robespierre's goal of creating a "moral republic."[54] On this reading, Robespierre's central goal, as announced in early February 1794, was to secure democracy through "virtue and terror: virtue without which terror is murderous, terror without which virtue is powerless."[55] Eventually, the logic of the process overtook Robespierre himself in the summer of 1794 when he fell to the guillotine.[56]

Still, there is something compelling about Arendt's critique of Rousseau's ethic of compassion and pity. It, more than the idea of the general will, was what Arendt saw as truly dangerous about Rousseau's impact. Arendt's line of thought ran something like this. Rousseau had posited compassion as a natural reaction (instinct) among humans, but, to Arendt, compassion was destructive of the distance between political actors that allowed them the objectivity to test the world and the reactions of others. Like love (as she suggested in *The Human Condition*), compassion should be confined to the sphere of intimacy and not allowed in the political realm. In addition, the objects of pity were seen as inferiors and part of a collective whole rather than in their "singularity."[57] Arendt uses the term "boundless" to characterize the power of such sentiments when they appear in the public realm as, for example, with Robespierre. As such "pity-inspired virtue" is a far cry from political virtue.[58] Arendt contrasted the politics of pity with the moral psychology of the American Framers who were, she claimed, moved by "solidarity." The latter, she thought, was something like a detached involvement that was required to assess friends and enemies, as well as the wisdom of policy. It was not driven by passions and emotions (including hate and suspicion). As she sums up her position: "Terminologically speaking, solidarity is a principle that can inspire and guide action, compassion is one of the passions, and pity is a sentiment."[59] Whereas, solidarity maintains a connection across the space between people and thus preserves the possibility of a political relationship, compassion and pity act on behalf of, but not with, the other.

And yet, the idea of solidarity also helps explain why the Framers never felt compelled to take on the issue of slavery. Their ability to be detached was stronger than their capacity for compassion or even pity, the occurrence of which is foreign to their writings—as Arendt recognized. Finally, her analysis leads the reader to wonder if Terror as policy didn't arise from a sense of weakness and impotence as much as from a feeling of absolute freedom. In the terms Arendt developed in *On Violence*, violence as policy may betoken the lack of popular support and collapsing legitimacy rather than political self-confidence and strength.[60]

In fact, Arendt provided the materials herself to complicate her claim about the centrality of the social question to the Terror. First, she turned briefly but importantly to a discussion of the importance of "the revolutionary municipal council, the Commune of Paris," along with the "great number of spontaneously formed clubs and societies." Their existence testified to the powerful force of "public spirit," which was identical with "revolutionary spirit," according to Robespierre in September 1791. Overall, these groups and clubs were the "very foundations of freedom." In fact Lisa Disch has suggested that Arendt's evidence for organized public debate among the populace in France is more compelling than what she found in the thirteen colonies. Yet Arendt also observed that, by the summer of 1793, Robespierre had come to see the existence of various revolutionary societies negatively, as evidence that "there could be no unified opinion." This led Robespierre to betray the spirit of the republic for the sake of consolidating a unified national will. She records that Saint-Just also reversed course in a similar manner.[61] Clearly, then, even Arendt agrees that the will to unity and fear of plurality of opinion were important in the emergence of the Terror.

Moreover, Arendt presents the Jacobins both as creating a unified regime based on virtue and as seeking to deal with the social question. The clubs and societies were pushing the solution to the social question as "pressure groups of the poor," as well as presenting their demands as "participators in government" in the spirit of Jefferson's ward system.[62] The situation during 1793–94 can be divided into three separate components. First, there was the fight for republican "public freedom" versus the sansculottes push to alleviate "private misery." Second, there was the conflict between the Jacobins' appeal to "unified public opinion" and the fact of "public spirit" grounded in "diversity." Third, the government monopoly of power was challenged by the "federal principle" with "its separation and division of power," a principle that was admittedly "practically unknown in Europe."[63] In this complex situation, the social question certainly did not play the only role, despite Arendt's general thesis about the relationship between the social question and the terror.

Overall, Arendt's thesis concerning the two great revolutions can be understood in one of two ways. The reading she stresses is that the American Revolution focused on the political sphere, while the French Revolution emphasized the social sphere. Robespierre, Saint-Just, and the Jacobins took a different path from Adams, Jefferson, and the American Framers and led the Revolution resolutely away from its original aim of freedom. But, Arendt also presents evidence of a deep conflict between two different concepts of the political, which has been present in Western politics and thought since then. On one view, politics is concerned with the ability of the state to amass power and create a unified will/sovereignty to pursue its goals, whatever they might be, including its own perpetuation. The opposing view of the political gives priority to the public/political space in which participatory speech and action for the public good are primary. Arendt used the council system of government in modern Europe, including periodic upwellings of spontaneous self-government, to illustrate this latter notion of the political. In this context, virtue was not about moral stringency or compassion and pity but was concerned with acting on behalf of "the public thing." But, in France, and most everywhere else, the state as unified sovereign triumphed over the state as an institutionalized public realm of participation. From this perspective, the issue wasn't so much whether the Jacobins would pursue the social question or not, but whether they would concentrate power in the state guided by a unified purpose or whether they would allow a public realm of diverse opinions and participatory impulses to emerge and continue to exist.

Finally, my guess is that Arendt's emphasis on the social question was also linked with a desire to make the connection between the French and the Russian Revolutions, specifically, between the Jacobin Terror of 1793–94 and the Stalinist Terror of the 1930s, with the former foreshadowing, perhaps even inspiring, the descent into the proto-totalitarianism of the Stalinist regime. Useful here is François Furet's distinction between a revolution "as a historical process, a set of causes and effects" and revolution as a "mode of change, a specific dynamics of collective action."[64] In the former, the concern is with specific historical events and developments in a particular country, a position that comes naturally to the historian who looks for singularities and differences among revolutions. The second sense of the term, more associated with the social scientist and political philosopher, develops an ideal or normative type of revolution as a way of being and acting. What Arendt did in *On Revolution* was move from a comparison of the specificities of the American and French revolutions to constructing two different ideal types of revolution, which had their own peculiar course of development. At a minimum, it made a case for the difficulty of addressing the social question in and through political revolutions; but she was far from convincing that all efforts of the state, in either senses of the term, to address the social question inevitably led to terror.

Coda: The (Second) American Revolution Revisited

Arendt's treatment of the social question in America in the late eighteenth century is limited to only seven pages. Like the Framers, ironically, she paid it remarkably little attention. Still, what she did write is far more complex than she is usually given credit for. Her first point was that there was a consensus among Americans and Europeans that "both the rich and poor, corruption and misery" as found in London and Paris went unmatched in America.[65] Taking off from John Adams, she proposed a kind of phenomenology of poverty: to be poor meant to suffer from "the crippling consequences of obscurity" and to be lost in "darkness." Indeed, she speculated that "darkness rather than want is the curse of poverty."[66] This theme of being seen in public is tied closely to Arendt's idea that the self, and being human, emerges when we appear with and before others. She also noted that when poor Americans later made their way up the social ladder, their goal was not political but economic and social prominence. That is why Thorstein Veblen's term "conspicuous consumption" fit the psychology of social advancement in the United States perfectly. People didn't just try to better themselves; they wanted to be seen to be better off. From this perspective, the dominant attitude toward politics was an instrumental one. Government was seen primarily as "the source of self-preservation" rather than as providing an opportunity for self-government.[67]

Yet Arendt also doubled back on her claim about want and misery when she noted that, in fact, "the absence of the social question from the American scene was, after all, quite deceptive, and that abject and degrading misery was present everywhere in the form of slavery and Negro labor." This powerful statement was followed closely by a telling judgment on the American Framers that "the passion of compassion has haunted and driven the best men of all revolutions, and the only revolution in which compassion played no role in the motivation of the actors was the American Revolution."[68] Contrary to what is sometimes claimed, these two passages show that Arendt was well aware of the moral implications of the Framers' failure to deal with serious deprivation, not to mention slavery. Her point about the compassion-driven morality of the leaders of the French—and the Russian—Revolution makes American Framers seem callow and callous. This is where Arendt becomes a tragic thinker rather than just a contradictory one, since she had condemned the role of compassion and pity in the French Revolution as politically destructive. Her way of reconciling these two positions was to say that, outside of politics, compassion and pity are admirable; within the political sphere where solidarity is so important, they are dangerous.

She did even things out a bit when she allows that Europeans as well as Americans overlooked the existence of chattel slavery in America: "Slavery was no more part of the social question for Europeans than it was for Americans."[69] But the evidence could also point in the other direction. One of the best known foreign observers, the Frenchman, Hector St. John de Crèvecoeur, included a chapter on slavery in his *Letters from an American Farmer* (1782). Arendt might also have remembered the urgency with which Alexis de Tocqueville described the immense threat slavery and racism posed to the new republic, while his traveling companion Gustave de Beaumont published a novel *Marie, ou l'esclavage aux Etats-Unis* (1835) that explored race and color prejudice in the New World. Nor were British travel accounts in America silent on the so-called peculiar institution. Whether all of these accounts linked slavery explicitly with the social question is doubtful. But European visitors to the new republic were often quite explicit about slavery's importance, even if out of *Schadenfreude*.

The final point to make here concerns Arendt's explicit description of slavery in the New World as racial. When she discussed slavery in *The Human Condition* and in the *Nachlass* to her published work, the references to slavery were to nonracial slavery in Greece and Rome. Arendt never hid the fact that slavery had been a central institution to the Greeks and that their understanding of political rule (*Herrschaft*) derived originally from the rule of master over slave. Slavery as an institution with important economic, social, and historical effects was not at all foreign to her thinking, something that makes her reluctance to deal with it in *On Revolution* all the more strange. But in *On Revolution*, the following two passages show the way she emphasized the importance of race for slavery and the social question in America: "The institution of slavery carries an obscurity even blacker than the obscurity of poverty; the slave, not the poor man, was 'wholly overlooked.'" This passage was preceded by a reminder of the inseparability of white satisfaction and black misery: "We are tempted to ask ourselves if the goodness of the poor white man's country did not depend to a considerable degree upon black labor and black misery."[70] Thus Arendt clearly saw slavery as a special (extreme) case of social invisibility and underscored the integral relationship between white power and black exclusion. From this perspective, slavery was not just a messy side issue. Arendt clearly, if briefly, acknowledged the long history and original flaw of racial slavery in America. She was well aware that America as a "people of plenty" was made possible by its refusal to confront slavery. The situation was a tragic one, since there would have been no beginning anew, no new republic, if the Northern states had tried to abolish slavery, as a few wished to do. That said, Arendt's treatment of the issue suggests that no sizable number of those whom Joseph Ellis calls "the founding brothers" was straining to grasp the wolf by the ears and do something about slavery.[71]

Still, Arendt's analyses leads on to three issues that needed further discussion by Arendt in *On Revolution* to do justice to her own analysis. First,
she never discussed to what extent the racial difference between slaves and
free people blocked the emergence of compassion and pity on the part of the
Framers. She does point to the way slavery excluded the slave/black population from social as well as political visibility. But if her Little Rock essay noted
the way that race made African Americans *more* visible, in *On Revolution* it
was slavery more often than race that was the determinant of social visibility. What was needed in any discussion of slavery in the postrevolutionary
United States was a sense of how race "worked" in antebellum America.

Second, Arendt never analyzed the way that slavery and race *became*
issues in the institutional politics of the antebellum years or the evolving
notion of American republicanism. Slavery went from being a *necessity* in
the founding years to being a *liability* by the 1850s. Originally, there was
no imagining a United States *without* slavery but seventy years later, it was
increasingly hard to imagine the United States *with* slavery outside the slave
states. In 1959, a disciple of Leo Strauss, Harry Jaffa published his massive
Crisis of the House Divided. It focused on the importance of natural law and
political morality in the Lincoln-Douglas debates and on the politicization
of the antislavery and abolitionist movement. In fact, there was, even in
Arendt's time, a vast literature on this topic. But Jaffa's book is important
because it was at least an attempt to rectify what Arendt bemoaned near
the end of *On Revolution*—the way American political (and constitutional)
thought had been forgotten after the Framers left the scene. [72]

Third, Arendt never raised the question of how slaves could have become political actors and agents in the way that the sansculottes had become
politicized in Paris in the early 1790s. At one level, this was a historical
question, but it had a more speculative dimension: how could slaves become
political beings, despite their experience in slavery? Even for those who
rejected Aristotle's idea of a natural slave or the mid-nineteenth-century
doctrines of black biological inferiority, the idea that a slave had ultimately
chosen to become a slave rather than perish in combat meant that there was
something suspect, even cowardly and corrupted, about the slave—and also
those who lived under political tyranny. [73] Fairly typical here was Rousseau's
pronouncement that "slaves lose everything in their chains, even the desire

of escaping them." Or as he wrote in his *Second Discourse*: "Once people are accustomed to masters, they are no longer able to do without them." People are "enervated or brutalized under tyranny," and the only cure for either is "severity of morals and [that] spirited courage."[74] If such realism seems to blame the victim, Rousseau also spoke scathingly of those who were skeptical of the value of freedom. He noted that when one sees even "entirely naked savages" risking everything for freedom, then "I feel that it does not behoove slaves to reason about freedom."[75] The ultimate corrupting effect of slavery was to make slaves question the value of freedom.

The tradition of thinking about slavery is full of similar expressions of such sentiments. Hegel's analysis of lordship and bondage built on this idea that the slave is the one who does not risk his or her life for freedom. His lapidary assertion "No man is a hero to his valet. Not because the hero is not a hero, but because the valet is a valet" captures some of the complex implications of the relationship between lordship and bondage. The slave or servant cannot recognize true excellence or courage even when faced with it but lives a life based on envy and resentment, that is, a slavish existence. Similarly, Tocqueville spoke in *Democracy in America* of how "oppression has with one blow taken from the descendants of the Africans almost all the privileges of humanity.... His intellect has been debased to the level of his soul."[76] And, as we have seen, he suggested that it was a slavish reaction even to ask what the use of freedom was. This whole line of reasoning leads to the self-contradictory conclusion that the people least willing or able to plan a slave revolt (or throw off tyranny) are the slaves themselves. In fact, this position was sometimes linked to the support for gradual emancipation, a process by which slaves could allegedly grow accustomed to freedom — and the economic system based on slavery would not be disrupted. At best, such a position was realistic, to the point of pessimism, about the possibility of successful slave revolts.[77]

Where does Arendt stand in relation to this tradition? Two passages in her *Denktagebuch* are relevant. An entry (of March 1953) concerns the Greek idea of slavery. For the Greeks, she writes, slavery was "the first and original form of rule and the presupposition of all political forms of life." The slave was closely associated with labor that had to do with the natural and the bodily: "the unfree character [*Zwangscharakter*] of a purely animal existence."[78] Later, in *The Human Condition*, Arendt would associate the biological sphere with labor and consumption. But the passage seems also to imply the unlikelihood that such a way of life can produce free agents. As we have already seen, Arendt also noted the "striking absence of serious slave revolts in ancient and modern times."[79] Yet, she also acknowledged that the main sources of political action in Europe in the post–French Revolution era were working-class movements, about which she notes that the "decisive point is that modern rebellions and revolutions always asked for freedom and justice for all."[80] Somehow modern working classes were able to counteract the unfree character of their work and organize not only for economic security but also for political goals, despite what her analysis of the social suggested.

Then, there is a 1965 entry in Arendt's *Denktagebuch*, volume 2, not long after *On Revolution* had appeared. Her entry in English is the one just quoted: "Rousseau: 'It is not for slaves to argue about liberty.'" To which she adds: "From which follows: No revolution made by slaves."[81] Is that what Rousseau's admonitory observation meant? I don't think so. Admittedly, an unnuanced reading would lead to the conclusion that Rousseau thought slaves could not, and hence should not, lead slave revolts. A more nuanced reading suggests that, first, Rousseau is not condemning all slaves but only those who question the value of freedom. The crucial ambiguity running throughout the discussion is whether legal and physical enslavement affects the slave to the point that he or she is incapacitated to lead a slave revolt. If Arendt agrees with this, then her follow-up comment clearly betokens a pessimism about slave revolts. There is not even a question mark to indicate a tentativeness about the conclusion. But, she may simply be drawing out the implications of the initial statement. Finally, in *On Revolution*, she maintains that the essence of rulership is "to emancipate himself from life's necessity." This suggests that it hasn't been "the rise of modern political ideas" but "the rise of technology" that has made the end of slavery possible.[82] With that she comes close to attributing causal efficacy to technology not human agency in ending slavery and the oppression of the wretched of the earth.

I have pursued this line of thought about Arendt's analysis of slavery because she never followed up her analysis of the political thought of the Framers with a study of what Charles Beard named the "Second American Revolution." But my larger point is to suggest, first, that, contrary to Arendt, the United States did have both a political and a social revolution of sorts.[83] As Charles and Mary Beard wrote, the Civil War was "a social war, ending in the unquestioned establishment of a new power in the government, making vast changes in the arrangement of classes, in the accumulation and distribution of wealth, in the course of industrial development, and in the Constitution inherited from the Fathers."[84] The second point is that the social upheaval, including of course the destruction of slavery, during the Civil War (1861–65) and Reconstruction (1965–77) followed Crane Brinton's developmental schema to a degree, but it did not give way to a Terror as that term was used in France or as Arendt suggested would happen when the state sought to solve the social question through political means. Third, it must be said that the difference between Beard's conception of a second American Revolution and the one I suggest here is that Beard paid little or no attention to the abolition of slavery as a—or the—main cause or goal of the war or the equal coexistence of the races as the goal of Reconstruction.[85]

There is another difference with France in reference to the first and second American Revolutions. Unlike France, where the deep divisions over the Revolution lasted past the end of World War II, in America there has always been a consensus on the justification for, and wisdom of, the War for Independence. Those Tories who objected strongly had already left, or had been driven out of, the colonies during the war (1776–83). But the divisions in France over the Revolution were more than matched in the United States by the lasting enmity over the Civil War, the deep material differences between regions and races confirmed and increased by it, and the significant differences in race relations between the regions as they become enshrined in law and custom.[86] There were also, of course, Northern and Southern understandings of the meaning of the Declaration of Independence and the Constitution, which were part of the enduring political-ideological divisions within the body politic after 1865.

All revolutions are also civil wars, but whether the converse is true is another matter. Can we compare the Civil War as a second American Revolution with the social and political upheaval brought about by the French Revolution? Historian James McPherson has suggested that the second American Revolution "changed the United States as thoroughly as the French Revolution changed that country." It freed four million slaves (33 percent of the

Southern population; 20 percent of the nation's population) and broke the stranglehold the South, geographically three times as large as France, had on the nation's politics since its founding. One decisive political result was that the "union" became a "nation," suggests McPherson.[87] But though there was no Terror perpetrated by the federal government or Union Army, or any change in the form of government or suspension of elections, much less of the Constitution, the cost of the war in terms of lives lost—600,000–750,000—far outstripped the numbers chargeable to the Terror in France. Moreover, more than 180,000 former slaves took up arms for the Union during the war, even before the abolition of slavery by the Thirteenth Amendment in early 1865. Thus Arendt's mistake in writing off the social dimension of the American Revolution was to confine her historical focus to the last quarter of the eighteenth century rather than looking further down the road to the 1860s for the social revolution to match the political revolution of the 1770s and 1780s.

Finally, there *was* a certain resemblance between the unfolding course of the Civil War and Reconstruction and Crane Brinton's schema in *Anatomy of Revolution*. Nothing much was done regarding slavery in the first year and a half of the War (1861–63), when the official war aims were confined largely to reuniting the Union. But from the Emancipation Proclamation (January 1863) to the end of the War in April 1865, the abolition of slavery joined reunion as a war aim. African Americans were enlisted in massive numbers as slavery not only crumbled at the edges but actually began collapsing within the Confederacy. In the spring of 1865, Lincoln even considered limited black suffrage in Louisiana after securing passage of the Thirteenth Amendment ending slavery. Ratification of the Thirteenth Amendment was mandatory for states wishing to return to the Union. On the legal front, three Constitutional amendments abolishing slavery (Thirteenth), making former slaves citizens (Fourteenth), and granting the right to vote to male freedmen (Fifteenth) were pushed through in 1865, 1868, and 1870, respectively. Together they rendered nugatory the infamous Dred Scott Supreme Court decision of 1857. Beyond that, basic social, economic, and educational assistance was given to former slaves by the Freedmen's Bureau, the first effort by the federal government to propose economic and social policy to aid the slaves' adjustment to freedom. There was even some confiscation of the land holdings of pro-Southern planters.

But the destruction of slavery was neither the product of the U.S. Army alone nor the result of a massive slave revolt à la Haiti. After all, slaves were a minority rather than a majority in the United States. Rather, it was a joint achievement of the federal government and the over 180,000 former slaves who fought for the United States against the Confederacy. The military victory of the North was only possible due to the participation of the former male slaves, which went a long way toward convincing Northern public opinion of their right to full legal and political rights. In contrast with the policy of the Jacobins or the Thermidorean reaction, in which state violence by no means disappeared, the defeated Confederate leadership from Jefferson Davis on down was not executed for treason. Relatively few Confederates went into exile, though a few ended up in Brazil. The early years of Reconstruction saw Union Clubs proliferating all over the South. In them, freed people came together for political discussion and education, prime examples of grassroots self-organization. Contrary to white Southern fears, where blacks held considerable power or a controlling majority in a state legislature (which happened only rarely), there were no mass executions or land confiscation. Nor were there *jacqueries*, marauding bands of former slaves on the lookout for whites to drive off their land or to terrorize. The important point here is that, contrary to Arendt's suggestions about the dire consequences of politicizing the social question, freed people did not institute their own Terror during Reconstruction, despite the alarmist panic of many Southern whites.

What did happen was this. From roughly 1867 on, something like a Thermidorean reaction set in. White Southerners in the various states organized themselves and ousted Republican and black-controlled state legislatures. By 1870, eleven Southern states had met the requirements for readmission to the United States imposed by Military Reconstruction. Federal troops were withdrawn when this happened. The U.S. Congress lost its radical edge, due to the aging of the Radical Republicans and an exhaustion of mood in the North. Much of the confiscated land in South Carolina, for example, was returned to former owners and the Freedmen's Bureau was allowed to expire. That is, a federally supported program of land reform was never passed and put into effect. There only example of grassroots violence against opponents was a white jacquerie in the form of secret terror organizations such as the Ku

Klux Klan. The Klan itself was only brought to heel in 1870–71 by means of unprecedented federal legislation. In most cases, white Southerners, often the same ones who had led the South during the war or men of the same background, returned to power in the Southern states. The prospects for significant grassroots change after the war came a cropper over the difficulty of cementing cross-racial alliances among farmers and farm laborers.

Overall, then, the war and Reconstruction were a kind of revolution insofar as they destroyed slavery and freed four million slaves. The relationship of the former slaves to the legal and political institutions of the country was radically recast by the constitutional amendments. Citizenship, including equality before the law, the right to own property, and the suffrage were extended to freedmen but not to freedwomen. In addition, the power of the federal government increased significantly because of the powers that had accrued to it during the war. But, for all the conservative fears that Lincoln and/or the Radical Republicans were following a "philosophy of democratic centralization," which might lead to a "Jacobin democracy," nothing approaching the ideology, much less the actuality, of a general will established itself. As W. R. Brock once observed, the "Jacobin model" couldn't work in America due to the separation of executive and legislative power and lack of internal discipline in American political parties. That is, the United States remained a federal republic bound to a written constitution; in the American context, this decisively limited social, economic, and political change in the country. What had happened was not a revolution against the existing forms of capitalism or against the social order in general, except for the abolition of slavery. Class inequalities persisted.[88]

Finally, contrary to Arendt's general pronouncement that "every attempt to solve the social question with political means leads into terror," the active state prosecution of the war and abolition of slavery did not lead to a state-sponsored Terror as such. Nonstate violence in the South during Reconstruction was not revolutionary but counterrevolutionary in nature. But the federal government's war against Southern secession led to a hugely costly war of four years duration. It also bears repeating that, however limited social and economic change was in the 1860s and 1870s, the number of lives lost to end slavery was greater than the numbers of people killed by the Terror in France.

CHAPTER 12

The Crises of Arendt's Republic

Mrs. Powel: Well Doctor, what have we got . . . ?
Ben Franklin: A republic, if you can keep it.

Hannah Arendt's thinking in the last decade of her life mirrored the state of the nation in that same period. Each was marked by a certain febrile quality that suggested instability as much as dynamism. During that period, the United States went from faith in the possibility of authentic political and cultural change to pervasive pessimism about the future of the country. A certain darkening mood was accentuated by the loss of two of the "bannisters" who had given her steady guidance over the years. First, Karl Jaspers died on February 26, 1969. A year and a half later, her husband Heinrich Blücher suffered a fatal heart attack. In several ways, her vision of participatory politics fit the idealistic, even utopian, political mood of the New Left in its pre-antiwar days quite well. Her political thought was also anchored in the work of the Framers. Yet what was she politically? At times she could sound as radically democratic as anyone, while, by the 1970s, the more accurate term of "republican" began to be used in connection with her thought. At other times, she defended states' rights, attacked Marxism and Marxists, and sounded like a cultural conservative. Certainly, the 1960s counterculture was foreign to everything she stood for, while sexual radicalism and ideas such as "the personal is the political" seemed to her to promise no good. What later would be called identity politics was also anathema to her. Thus, like the 1960s itself, she faced in several directions at the same time.

Never a public person, Arendt's life settled some when the Eichmann controversy subsided in mid-decade. But she by no means withdrew from her public commitments. If anything, her speaking appearances at universities seemed to increase. She served on boards of private and public organizations, traveled to Washington to consult on cultural and educational policy, and appeared at public meetings to discuss such topics as violence in politics and, above all, the Vietnam War. From the fall of 1963 through 1967, she taught regularly at the University of Chicago (in the autumn and then for another period each spring). She received a Chair at the New School for Social Research beginning in early 1968 and occupied it until her death. In her own way, Arendt had finally arrived. She had become a prominent figure in the intellectual landscape of the country.[1]

The middle years of the decade saw her without a specific book project for the first time in a long time. But it was not for long. By the end of the decade, she was working on what would become *The Life of the Mind*, which marked her return to philosophy from political thought. The only part of it to appear in Arendt's lifetime was "Thinking and Moral Considerations" in 1971, which grew out of further thinking about Eichmann.[2] A twelve-page piece on Rolf Hochhuth's play *The Deputy* appeared in 1964, a work subjected to the same sort of abuse that her Eichmann book had received, while she also wrote a thirty-page introduction to a memoir by Berndt Naumann about the Frankfurt Auschwitz trials, 1963–65. With that she was finished with Nazi Germany and totalitarianism.[3] *Men in Dark Times* (1968) contained profiles of writers, poets, philosophers, and one religious figure, Pope John XXIII (and only one American, writer-poet Randall Jarrell), while *Crises of the Republic* (1972), a collection of political essays and interviews, focused on contemporary America. In 1968, she added two more essays to *Between Past and Future* to bring its original six up to a total of eight.[4] She also gave four long interviews, each from thirty- to forty-pages long, between 1964 and 1973. Her last two pieces were a short tribute to W. H. Auden in 1974 and "Home to Roost," a jeremiad written to be delivered at a bicentennial event in 1975.[5] If all that were not enough, Arendt translated, that is, reworked, much of this work into German herself and also helped in getting Martin Heidegger's work translated into English for publication by Harper and Row.

Specifically, Arendt's work had three particular concerns that I want to examine in this chapter. The first was her analysis of the student movement, which she also linked with the Civil Rights Movement and the antiwar movement in general, not to mention black radicalism in the 1960s and early 1970s. Arendt had plenty of contact with students and faculty where she taught and she could get reports about what went on at Columbia and City University of New York. Her most interesting and provocative piece of political thinking in this period—"Civil Disobedience" (1970/71)—revived her concern with morality and politics from the 1940s and the concern with the nature of American political culture identified by Tocqueville in the 1950s. Finally, her nagging worry over the survival of the republic was expressed in several "decline of the Republic" jeremiads that dominated her darkening thinking at the time of her death.

The Movement Years

Arendt always assumed that the student movement was an international phenomenon. In particular, she kept up with what went on in Germany and had a particular interest in the "events" of May 1968 in Paris, since one of its student-leaders, Danny Cohn-Bendit, was the son of old friends of hers from France. At the same time, she had little interest in the Third World and would undoubtedly have found bewildering Fredric Jameson's claim that the political, social, and cultural movements of the 1960s had "Third World Beginnings."[6] She insisted that each national setting had its own peculiar qualities and thus generalizations across national and continental boundaries were extremely hazardous. Still, the Vietnam War, the emergence of independence movements and new nations in the Third World, the emphasis on race and ethnicity, and the felt urgency of university reform constituted a family of concerns that student movements on both sides of the Atlantic were engaged with. Yet, in certain respects, the American New Left was first among equals.

An interview in 1972 saw her pay tribute to the pioneering role that the Civil Rights Movement played in initiating the events that led to the New Left in a broad sense. At the same time, however, she seriously garbled the history of the Civil Rights Movement by highlighting the alleged centrality of "students from Harvard, who then attracted students from other famous universities. They went to the South, organized brilliantly." This succeeded in "changing the climate of opinion" about race and racism at least in "purely legal and political matters." The movement, however, "came to grief" in trying to organize the Northern urban ghettoes.[7]

But in her brief mininarrative, there was no mention of the students in historically black colleges in the South who had actually been responsible for the sit-ins and voter registration drives that constituted the backbone of the Southern movement. In fact, students (mostly white) from predominately northern and western universities only came South in any large number for Freedom Summer in 1964. She went on, more justifiably, to cite the importance of the Free Speech Movement at Berkeley in generating the emerging student movement. In fact, several of the leaders of the Free Speech Movement had spent time working for civil rights in the South. Her discussion then jumped to the antiwar movement but without mentioning the Students for a Democratic Society (SDS) or any specific antiwar organizations. She related this groundswell of public protest to the widespread assumption that "in America one can change things one doesn't like."[8] Overall, most of the ingredients of the narrative of the 1960s were there, but the way she arranged them and her attribution of importance were seriously flawed.

Arendt bemoaned the "the theoretical sterility and analytical dullness" that had characterized the student movements in both Germany and the United States: a more cogent analysis of the existing situation, she contended, was desperately needed.[9] Yet, she was being ungenerous here by ignoring the work of C. Wright Mills, Paul Goodman, Herbert Marcuse, and Noam Chomsky, along with recent work on race (Martin Luther King Jr., Harold Cruse) and the women's issues (Betty Friedan, Kate Millett). Though she doesn't really mention the SDS's *Port Huron Statement* of 1962, she was enthusiastic in her praise of the positive traits of the student movement, especially "the sheer courage, and astounding will to action."[10] All this naturally appealed to Arendt, the central category of whose political thought was action. Indeed she also linked this "appetite for action" with the eighteenth-century idea of public happiness, which played such a central role in the Framers' thinking.[11] With this, she underlined the continuity in the political tradition that she claimed Americans too easily forgot. At the time, Herbert Marcuse was usually identified as the main theoretician of the New Left, but Arendt herself exerted a good deal of influence on it in its early years, particularly in university settings such as Berkeley. Much later, Daniel Cohn-Bendit would look back and say of the French student movement in 1968 that "we read too much Marcuse, when instead we should have been reading Arendt."[12]

She was also attracted by the fact that the student movement was "almost exclusively inspired by moral considerations," something which was totally "totally unexpected." The student movement "has taught us a lesson" in the limits of "manipulation," even though it has been "trained like its predecessors in hardly anything but the various brands of the my-share-of-the-pie political and social theories."[13] Interestingly, her defense of a politics of morality jarred with her usual wariness of moral dogmatism and ideological absolutes in politics. (This was a standard theme in the work of postwar American thinkers such as David Riesman, Daniel Bell, and John Rawls, too.) But in her short book titled *On Violence* (1970), she looked more favorably on a politics that transcended the politics of self-interest and was a form of action oriented to the common good and undertaken to correct injustice.

Moreover, despite being unimpressed by the intellectual provenance of the student movement, she did point to "participatory democracy" as the "one positive political slogan" that the student movement had introduced into the political culture. It went well with her suspicion of parliamentary democracy and party politics. Arendt was by no means the only source of ideas of participatory politics in the 1960s, but she was an important one. When engaged in community organizing and voter registration drives, the organizers for the civil rights organizations stressed that ideas and leaders should emerge from the grass roots rather than having them imposed on the communities, while the SDS took the same approach in white communities in northern urban areas. Even the community action programs of the War on Poverty were charged with aiming for the "maximum feasible participation" in decisions by those whose communities were receiving aid.[14] In fact, James Miller stresses the varied sources of participatory democracy, ranging from the Old Left and the American labor movement to American religious movements such as the Quakers and African American religious institutions in the South. Arendt never used terms like "the system" or the "power elite," which probably sounded too conspiratorial for her taste. But she had read C. Wright Mills, and he was one of the New Left thinkers, along with Paul Goodman, who thought in terms of reviving the importance of "publics" and "community" in American radicalism. Her own preference, as we have seen, was "the best in the revolutionary tradition—the council system," which *On Revolution* established as central to her thought. Arendt also noted that the New Left's tendency in the late 1960s to relapse into a superannuated, hard-core Marxist posture was incompatible with the traditions of council democracy and a morally inflected politics.[15]

Arendt had a number of different experiences with campus protest, whether it concerned university governance, the penetration of the universities by Defense Department funding and corporate recruiting, or curriculum reform. She was particularly impressed by the students at the University of Chicago in 1966 when they occupied university offices to prevent the administration from reporting student grades and class rankings to the Selective Service, so that they could not be drafted. Michael Denneny remembered that, unlike most faculty members, Arendt "understood immediately what was at stake" and also recalls her "hopping up the stairs two at a time to talk to various students sitting in." Later that morning, when it was time for her to teach, most of the students left and went to her class, remembers Denneny.[16] However, during the Columbia student uprising in the spring of 1968, Arendt thought the SDS-led students had crossed the line from "legitimate protest against university support for defense research" to "an illegitimate attack upon the university itself." She also was put off by the "threat of armed revolt" from black students who were "allegedly supplied with arms from the Harlem community."[17] All this meant that she did not sign an appeal on behalf of the SDS urged on her by Dwight Macdonald, since, as she explained to him, she had "a little experience with some of their spokesmen" and that most of the SDS "are people whom it is difficult indeed to take seriously."[18]

Arendt could also be firmly practical and did not try to use the students to fulfill her own political dreams. In 1970 at the New School, Jerome Kohn remembers that the students sought Arendt's advice about whether "she thought the students ought to accept an offer to join forces with a labor union. Her response: 'Yes, like that you can use their mimeograph machine.'" Later at a meeting where the faculty was debating whether to call in the police to remove student protestors, Arendt "exclaimed, suddenly: 'For God's sake, they are our students, not criminals. So it is we who are responsible for them, not the police.' That was the end of the discussion, and the meeting broke up."[19] She had no problem with students' occupying buildings, sitting-in, and picketing on campus. She thought that Columbia and other universities had already "politicized" the university by inviting outside interests on to campus and thus didn't object strongly to student takeovers of offices and administration buildings. She was adamantly against calling in the police to remove protestors. But she also, like Herbert Marcuse, warned the students against provoking reactions that would undermine the university's relative immunity from outside control. The university was "the only place in society where power does not have the last word."[20]

In fact, she pinned most of the blame for the escalation toward violence on "the appearance of the Black Power movement on the campuses." Like many other academics, she was appalled by the armed black students who disrupted a public meeting at Cornell University in 1969. She seemed to believe that "the majority of [black students]" want to be "admitted without academic qualification." As "representatives of the black community," they had the community behind them and "their interest was to lower academic standards."[21] Not surprisingly, Arendt also opposed plans for the teaching of Swahili and the establishment of black studies programs, not to mention open admissions policies at the City University of New York in the late 1960s and early 1970s.[22] No one would deny that each of the proposals she mentioned had problems and needed more thought, but her failure to try to understand what might lie behind such proposals from black students meant that her opinions counted for little in these matters. Moreover, white radicals on campus and off also talked, planned, and carried out violence in these years as well. The Weather Underground faction of the SDS were involved in such actions, not to mention the August 24, 1970, bombing of Sterling Hall at the University of Wisconsin. But Arendt never pronounced on such events that I know of.

Finally, in her interview with Adelbert Reif, Arendt also expanded on a remark in *On Violence*: "The third world is not a reality but an ideology." As such, Arendt's claim was far from absurd, since what she (arguably) meant was that the non-European world was far from homogeneous ideologically or materially, as witness the differences between "a Chinese" and an "African Bantu tribesman." But then she went on to remark that it was "those who stand on the lowest step—that is, the Negroes in Africa" who were most keen on the Third World ideology.[23] Arendt expanded on her more general assertion by suggesting that the ideology of the Third World made no more sense than the earlier Marxist call for "workers of the world" to unite had made. Hers was an assertion that made a certain amount of sense. But her gratuitous comment about Africa's standing went unexplained.

It is difficult to recapture the bewildering claims and counterclaims, the alternating moods of hope and despair, of these years. Arendt's position was not reactionary or racist as such. Indeed, black leader Bayard Rustin was the source of her remarks about what she thought were the deeply unwise proposals, including calls for reparations, coming from black radicals such as James Forman.[24] Still Arendt always found it difficult to find the right register in speaking about race in America, whether it had to do with Little Rock or Harlem. Two private communications show the problematic nature of Arendt's views on race in America very clearly. One is a letter of November 21, 1962, to James Baldwin. In it Arendt spoke admiringly of his *New Yorker* article of November 17, 1962, "Letter from a Region of My Mind," which became part of the writer's widely read *The Fire Next Time* (1963). Clearly impressed by it as "an event in my understanding of what is involved in the Negro question," she nevertheless went on to "raise objections" to it. They had mainly to do with Baldwin's emphasis on the need for the "relatively conscious" members of both races, to, "like lovers, insist on, or create, the consciousness of the others." Arendt, however, thought it was dangerous to introduce love (and hate) into politics. It often produced hypocrisy, and love was best confined to the private realm. She also observed that the positive qualities Negroes (and all oppressed minorities) are known for will not "[survive] the hour of liberation by even five minutes." We don't have a response from Baldwin, but like most of Arendt's thoughts on racial matters, they mixed bewildering assumptions and lack of knowledge with insight and even good sense.[25]

Then, in a *Denktagebuch* entry of January 1968, she commented on the disparity between the group assimilation into American society of "all other minorities" and the assimilation by "individual Negroes" into American society without any group progress because "the group cannot be integrated" (*Die Gruppe unintegrierbar ist*). She went on to say that black power "could make sense" as a way of making Negroes "an integral part of the society" but in fact it was "an expression of helplessness or of secret despair over the impossibility of integration." Again, there was something to her reading of the situation, though why she thought some blacks could not be integrated is not clear—was it because of their own capacities and characteristics or because of those of white people?[26] It is also important to remember the distaste with which Arendt regarded the politicization of race after her own experience with Nazism and fascism. Only now it seemed to be coming from the left not the right.

Finally, if there was one idea of the New Left of the 1960s that was at odds with Arendt's thinking, it was "the personal is the political." At the time, this slogan could refer to the transformation of consciousness under the influence of drugs or it could also have to do with the importance of sexuality in reflecting the repressive realities or emancipatory possibilities of life in an advanced industrial society. But increasingly, the term became associated with the emergence of second wave feminism in the early 1960s and its articulation in well-known works such as Betty Friedan's *The Feminine Mystique* (1963) or Kate Millett's *Sexual Politics* (1969). The point behind the slogan was to dismantle the distinction between the personal and the political, since it was seen as one of the main obstacles to the emancipation of women.

One background explanation for Arendt's resistance to the idea was that she grew up after the early twentieth-century feminist movement and just before the emergence of second wave feminism. It was simply not the main issue of women of her background, particularly one who had been through what she had. Second, what Arendt found appealing in the classical conception of politics was a strong commitment to the public over the private realm and a normative conception of human beings as citizens of a polis or republic. For her, this, of course, included women, but the bias in the republican political tradition was traditionally against gender equality, and it was not obvious how to overcome this and other obstacles. An early attempt to make Arendt's emphasis on the public realm and citizenship compatible with a vision of feminist political equality was made by Jean Bethke-Elshtain in *Public Men, Private Women* (1981), but it would need a couple of decades before those interested in feminist political thought seriously explored the potentials as well as shortcomings of Arendt's political thought.[27] Finally, in cultural terms, Arendt's suspicion of deep subjectivity and her wariness about privileging private life, along with her exclusion of emotions such as love, intimacy, compassion, and pity from the public realm, also made it more difficult to see how issues traditionally linked with women's experience and feminist issues could be incorporated into her vision of politics. Proponents of abortion rights, for example, would find it hard to agree with her desire to keep public and private matters separate, but Arendt's defense of that distinction was a reminder of the dangers of making the private realm subject to public scrutiny, much less control.

The other large issue on the left in the 1960s was the question of political violence, in connection usually with the idea of revolution, a term that was all-pervasive in that decade. On December 17, 1967, there was a panel discussion cum debate at the Theatre for Ideas in Manhattan moderated by *New York Review* editor, Robert Silvers, with Noam Chomsky, Arendt, Susan Sontag, and Tom Hayden (from the audience) participating. The discussion was titled "The Legitimacy of Violence as a Political Act." In the discussion, Arendt was exceedingly wary about the uses of violence, certainly in domestic politics and in terror abroad, while Chomsky was willing to consider it in situations where it was understandable and, arguably, justifiable. The discussion of violence, as Chomsky rightly said, revolved around questions of context and possibilities of success rather than being a matter of absolutes. In fact, his most important point was that it was mainly at the level of tactics that moral distinctions arose. Calculations as to means and ends, possibilities versus probabilities of success were all-important rather than trivial matters.[28] Arendt's essay "Reflections on Violence," which first appeared in the *New York Review* on February 27, 1969, and then later was expanded into *On Violence*, grew out of the attempt to sort through the various issues that arose during that session. As she wrote to Mary McCarthy: "None of us was really good."[29]

Part 2 of *On Violence* was particularly important for revealing how Arendt engaged with the issue of political rulership and obedience. The basic dichotomy Arendt began with was between power and violence. She began by challenging the standard view of thinkers from Max Weber to C. Wright Mills (and conventional wisdom itself) that violence was a "manifestation of power" and/or that power was "a kind of mitigated violence."[30] Always the splitter, Arendt countered by maintaining that violence depended on "implements," while power depended on numbers. "It is," she insisted, "the people's support that lends power to institutions," thus making power a manifestation of the basic consent underlying political institutions in a representative democracy. This, she continued, was what Madison meant when he said "all government rests on opinion."[31] But power was not the same as democracy, since power as such did not entail democratic distribution and control, though it went without saying that a democratic government depended on the power of popular opinion. More novel, perhaps, was Arendt's insistence that there was an inverse relationship between violence and power. As a government loses power, which is also connected with the loss of "legitimacy," it tends to resort to violence: "the loss of power becomes a temptation to substitute violence for power." Though violence might be justifiable under the conditions of self-defense, it is never legitimate.[32]

But besides this basic distinction between power and violence, Arendt also rejected the "command-obedience" model of political power. Its extreme form was "terror," which is a "form of government" in which violence "remains in full control." In a political context of regime maintenance, the opposite of violence was not nonviolence but power and ultimately, as already mentioned, consent. One of the most fruitfully controversial aspects of her position was her claim that violence did not have anything to do with the political realm where speech and action ruled. At the same time, she also knew that frequently a legitimate political order had its origins in violence. This was a persisting tension in her political thought.

In the last chapter of the book, Arendt shifted her focus to a critique of the origins and uses of violence. As always, Arendt was deeply suspicious of explanations of human actions by reference to natural capacities or forces.

They explained too much and too little. If nature was a constant, then other factors were needed to explain why violence happened at this rather than that moment. But she also insisted that "violence is neither beastly nor irrational" as such. It "can remain rational only if it pursues short-term goals"— and/or is used to "dramatize" a situation.[33] She was also rather skeptical about the claims of Franz Fanon and Jean-Paul Sartre that violence could create anything positive. The solidarity of the battlefield or the unity experience by a group engaged in violence was, she thought, evanescent rather than permanent. Nor could such violence be easily controlled. Arendt was also suspicious of the links between violence and creativity, which often made use of "organic metaphors" and violence often generated ideologies of racism and extermination. Nor was there really any conclusive evidence supporting the therapeutic effects of violence.[34]

Most simply, Arendt's basic position in the debates about violence in the 1960s was that it had no chance of succeeding at home, and would also be impossible to control, and thus should be eschewed. Otherwise, it would certainly take on irrational forms and meet disproportionate responses. She was not opposed to the use of violence in independence struggles abroad or even by the Vietcong against U.S. forces in Southeast Asia. But she was skeptical about the uses of terror in wars of liberation. Again, her basic thought was that violence could destroy but rarely helped create and it failed the supreme test in her political thought—whether it could create lasting institutions of freedom. Except grudgingly for self-defense and, on occasion, to dramatize a larger wrong, violence had no role to play in public life. Of course, this ignored the creation of the American republic out of the American Revolution and the reconstitution of that republic as a result of the Civil War. As Chomsky pointed out, Arendt always sounded quite "absolutist" about violence, and yet she was no pacifist and could grant the necessity of violence in certain circumstances.[35]

Civil Disobedience

Hannah Arendt's essay "Civil Disobedience," published in the New Yorker in September 1970, was the only piece Arendt wrote about American political thought that really escaped the gravitational pull of the Framers. It originated as a paper at the New York University conference "Is the Law Dead?" on May 1 that same year and was criticized by a variety of figures, including Eugene Rostow from the pro-war center, Ronald Dworkin from the liberal left, and Robert Paul Wolff, an anarchist. Its central theme—the difference between moral and political thinking—was closely related to her essay "Thinking and Moral Considerations," to which I have already referred.[36]

It was also one of her most compelling pieces in a decade that saw the appearance of several approaches to civil disobedience across the political spectrum. For example, anarchist Paul Goodman treated civil disobedience less as a theoretical concept than as a seat-of-the-pants response to what he saw as a religious crisis, arising from "the social compact of the sovereign people." Civil disobedience was messier (and more vital) than academic conceptions of it allowed. In his essay finished just before Martin Luther King Jr.'s assassination in April 1968, Herbert Storing, a University of Chicago–based follower of Leo Strauss, attacked King's version of civil disobedience for wanting to undermine the legitimacy of existing political and legal institutions, yet King also failed, in contrast with Malcolm X, to be open about the need for revolutionary change. Harvard political philosopher John Rawls devoted nearly thirty pages of his landmark *Theory of Justice* (1970) to a liberal justification of civil disobedience as a "stabilizing device," that is, a safety valve. It "helps to maintain just institutions" because those who engage in it are "willing to go to jail for disobeying the law." Legal philosopher Ronald Dworkin's essay on civil disobedience, originally published in 1968, did not agree with Rawls (and many other liberals) that a civil disobedient was obliged to accept the punishment for violating the law, since the very constitutionality of most such laws was problematic. Overall, there was a surprising amount of disagreement about the exact scope and implications of civil disobedience, but also a surprising general acceptance of it, in one form or another, as legitimate.[37]

Not surprisingly Arendt's concept of civil disobedience did not fit altogether comfortably with any of these contributions, especially Storing's. Her essay harkened back to the pieces she and Dwight Macdonald had published in the first half of 1945, which I analyzed in chapter 1. But there were also several differences. That essay had focused on situations where disobedience and dissent were life threatening, as was the case under totalitarian regimes, while Dwight Macdonald's examined the willingness of citizens in relatively open societies such as Britain or America to accept their governments' morally dubious actions, including mass saturation bombing and the use of the atomic bomb. In fact, in her essay "Lying in Politics," Arendt referred to the use of the bomb as "the fateful war crime that ended the last world war."[38]

By the late 1960s, her focus had shifted to citizens in a liberal democracy who chose to disobey statutes that contradicted the "spirit of the laws" and/or threatened moral self-respect. These ranged from mass demonstrations by civil rights activists and average, generally black, citizens in the South against racial segregation to the unwillingness of young men to register for, or respond to, the draft in the midst of the Vietnam War. What linked these two moments in her thought, separated by a quarter century, was the similarity of the distinction she drew between guilt and responsibility near the end of her "Organized Guilt and Universal Responsibility" essay in 1945 to the distinction she made between acting morally and acting politically a quarter century later.

Arendt was not entirely alone in making a distinction such as this. Rawls distinguished "conscientious refusal" from civil disobedience in his writing on the topic, while Dworkin spoke of the contrast between "moral" and "legal" concerns in his treatment of the topic. Conscientious objection was linked, said Arendt, with "defense of individual conscience or individual acts" and was fundamentally concerned with the question of how I can live with myself if I continue to accept or do X or Y? From this perspective, Socrates, who thought that he "owed it to himself" to disregard his Athenian judges, and Henry David Thoreau, who occupied "the ground of individual conscience and conscience's moral obligation," were conscientious objectors not civil disobeyers.[39] In contrast, the person engaged in civil disobedience arrived at a decision to act through deliberation with others. In this sense she or he was being political. She or he was also being political in that the common good or the fate of the republic was more important for the person engaged in civil disobedience than keeping a clear conscience. Strictly speaking, Arendt's was not an individualist, rights-based theory of civil disobedience, since civil disobedience involved being "bound together by "common opinion."[40]

From this basic distinction, several other things followed. To draw the moral/political distinction, Arendt contended, revived the classical question, reintroduced by Machiavelli, of the relationship between "the good man" and "the good citizen." She also failed to see the sense in the "idea that paying the penalty justifies breaking the law," since that would allow a capital crime to be so justified.[41] In this she agreed with Goodman and Dworkin but disagreed with Rawls and Storing. Like Goodman, she doubted that civil disobedience was always accompanied by respect for existing legal and political institutions. Gandhi, she noted, hardly accepted the legitimacy of British rule in India; nor did the absolute distinction between the revolutionary and the civil disobeyer stand up to scrutiny.[42] Forgetting the example of Dr. King and the Civil Rights Movement, she also suggested that someone willing to go to jail voluntarily was likely to be averse to "rational discussion of the issues."[43] Not surprisingly, the conservative Storing feared the consequences of massive civil disobedience for the maintenance of law and order in the country.[44]

But the most interesting parts of the essay followed from her claim that civil disobedience was "primarily American in origins and substance" and in accordance with what Montesquieu called "the spirit of its laws." For her "the spirit of the [American] laws" arose from the idea of "consent . . . in the sense of active support and continuing participation in all matters of public interest."[45] It is important to note that she wrote "active support" rather than just (passive) "acceptance." She went on to distinguish among three forms of consent in the American political tradition. For once, she took into account the "Biblical covenant" between the people and God as exemplified by the New England Puritans and Pilgrims. The second form of consent was a "vertical version of the social contract" and involved the agreement to exchange certain rights and privileges for protection by secular authority à la Hobbes. Third, the "horizontal" type of contract established a society among a group of people, who in turn chose to form a government. In this two-stage, horizontal model, sovereignty rested with the people and the government could be dissolved without dissolving the people.[46]

Several things stand out as significant developments in Arendt's thinking here. First, she offered at least a rudimentary account of how the social can give rise to the political, thus remedying a weakness in her earlier thought.

Insofar as society is formed by a conscious intention, Arendt seems to suggest, it already has a proto-political nature. With that, the gap between the social and the political is significantly reduced. Second, her location of sovereignty in the people gave a fresh democratic feel to her thinking. Third, she explicitly underscored the importance of the Civil Rights Movement in "bringing into the open the 'American dilemma'" and underscoring the "enormity of the crime, not just of slavery, but of chattel slavery."[47] Civil disobedience played a role not only in gaining rights and privileges for African Americans but also in illuminating a particularly painful aspect of American history. With this in mind, Arendt called for a constitutional amendment to recognize that African Americans and Native Americans had "never been included in the original *consensus universalis*."[48] As already noted, Arendt clearly had difficulty dealing with post–civil rights, African American radicalism in the North, but she was in full agreement with the beneficial political and historical impact of the Southern movement.

From this, Arendt explored various ways that civil disobedience could be given stronger protection. Ironically, she introduced John C. Calhoun's idea of concurrent majority, which he had proposed to protect the minority rights of the South before the Civil War. Arendt was well aware of its "pro-slavery and racist" associations but speculated that Calhoun's idea of a bloc interest might be a way of providing protection for civil disobedience. Later in the essay, she wondered if the tradition of civil disobedience might be lent special status by something analogous to the "political question doctrine," which gives the Supreme Court leeway in "not raising issues or making decisions that cannot be enforced." Grasping for analogies, she also wondered if a group engaged in civil disobedience might not be seen as a "pressure group." Finally she speculated that the United States perhaps needed another constitutional amendment to "cover the right of association as it is actually practiced in the country," which, she claimed, the First Amendment failed to do.[49]

In reference to the American focus of her thought, Arendt's concluding claim that civil disobedience was the "latest form of [Tocqueville's] "voluntary associations" neatly tied together her early and late analyses of American political culture. She suggested, for instance, that civil disobedience was no more dangerous than the "right to free association," though this ignored the crucial matter of disobeying the law. Indeed, the final eight pages of "Civil Disobedience" represented the most sustained attention Arendt had actually paid to Tocqueville in her entire oeuvre. In the context of a decade full of public protest, she took heart at the reappearance, even in "mass demonstrations," of "the old traditions."[50] That "mass society" had failed so far to kill off or seriously weaken these traditions meant that the essay contained a definite note of hope.

A full evaluation of Arendt's position involves, of course, an assessment of her claim about the essential Americanness of civil disobedience. Though it sounds roughly correct, Arendt offers no further argument or evidence for this claim; nor does Lewis Perry's very recent study of that tradition try to prove it either. Perry, for instance, accepts Arendt's claim but also notes the importance of the ideas of Leo Tolstoy and especially Mahatma Gandhi in shaping the twentieth-century versions of civil disobedience, especially post World War II. Of course, he points out Thoreau's prior influence on Gandhi. One might also mention that the difference between constitutional and positive law and between federal and state law, not to mention the historical distinction between higher law and human-made law, contributed to a legal-constitutional culture within which one form of law could be played off against another. Nor could either citizens or officials of the United States easily dismiss the right to revolution as the basis for breaking the law. Overall, there is a prima facie case for American exceptionalism on this issue, though Arendt doesn't do much to make it.

Another problematic position taken by Arendt (along with Dworkin and Goodman) concerned the willingness of civil disobeyers to accept the legal consequences of their action. In rejecting this idea, Arendt et al. may have been right in the abstract. Laws were frequently unclear or clearly unconstitutional. Surprisingly, however, such a requirement did not come from Gandhi but from Holmes and the tradition of "legal realism."[51] But Arendt (and the others) was arguably being politically tone-deaf on this point. Breaking a law was only politically and morally compelling if it didn't seem disrespectful of the legal and political order. And as her friend Mary McCarthy observed, if you fail to punish the disobedience to the law or try to avoid the punishment, civil disobedience "would have no purpose."[52] Moreover, the example of Martin Luther King Jr. showed that acceptance of punishment for breaking the law was, contrary to what she suggested, not a sign of rigidity or of masochism. That said, acceptance of punishment was a necessary but by no means a sufficient justification for any action. On this Arendt was implicitly correct.

But Arendt's more historical point was an important one. Where can we find the foundations of good political faith in the vacuum left by loss of belief in higher law or God's will or history as the story of progress?[53] This same value pluralism led John Rawls to emphasize that, in a secular order, values, morality, and political beliefs should be treated as political not metaphysical entities, thus making it possible to compromise on them. It is also important to note that while nonparty political self-organization, often linked by her to the council system of government, has historically been an alternative to parliamentary and representative democracy, in "Civil Disobedience," she treated disobeying the law as a way of keeping representative democracy honest and responsive. From this perspective, it was a supplement to, not a replacement for, the existing system.

A third area of contention in the "Civil Disobedience" essay was Arendt's strict distinction between moral and political action. For one thing, her critics miss the point when they criticize her for neglecting the moral dimension of politics. For her, each form of political rule is superintended by one or a few principles, for example, the republic, by equality and virtue (public spiritedness) à la Montesquieu. Such a principle provides the standard of political morality in a republic. Another of her assumptions is also easy to overlook: if an individual or group follows its moral conscience alone in acting, then it is harder to prevent an escalation toward violence, since the apodictic and immediate claim of conscience brooks no argument. Of course, the place of personal or social morality in such a conception is left unexplored and would need considerable working out.

But Arendt's objections to moral absolutes in politics bear a certain resemblance to Max Weber's ethic of ultimate ends or conscience. The claims of absolute conscience, such as Henry David Thoreau and John Brown were acting on, led them away from nonviolent political action and toward morally propelled violence. Historically, Thoreau moved from nonviolence in his famous "Resistance to Civil Government" (1849) to active support for Captain John Brown as a "transcendentalist" insofar as he exemplified "action from principle."[54] Brown's purpose was to cleanse the nation of the moral taint of slavery without engaging in the tiring and futile process of political compromise and political coalition building. If anyone was not a political man (in Arendt's terms), it was Brown, though this is not to say that his actions did not have political effects. The only time Arendt ever referred to Abraham Lincoln was in the "Civil Disobedience" essay, where she notes that President Lincoln distinguished "official duty" from "personal wish" in the matter of slavery and abolition.[55] In contrasting Brown and Lincoln, Arendt assumed that political violence is by definition responsible to the body politic, while moral violence is primarily responsible to oneself.[56]

What then, finally, about Henry David Thoreau? Arendt does Thoreau the honor of grouping him with Socrates, thus making him the only American thinker after the Framers that she took seriously—but then she refuses to see either man as exemplars of civil disobedience. She is by no means the only analyst of Thoreau's writing to conclude that he was a deeply unpolitical man, constitutionally unfit for constitutional thinking, as it were.[57] It was nature rather than history or the public realm that provided Thoreau with the standards for judging himself and his society.

But there is an answer to such an Arendtian analysis from philosopher Stanley Cavell. In his *The Senses of Walden*, Cavell contended that "the completion of the act was the writing of the essay that completes it" and also calls *Walden* a "tract of political education, education for membership in the polis."[58] Cavell's point is that, in his own way, Thoreau did, in fact, speak and act publically in order to rid the republic of slavery not just to clear his conscience. Defenders may go on to call attention to Thoreau's essay "Slavery in Massachusetts" (1854), where Thoreau explicitly asks himself how he can remain entranced by nature while slavery expands and the nation falls apart. And there are also Thoreau's two powerful pieces on John Brown ("A Plea for Captain John Brown" and "The Last Days of John Brown") written after Brown's capture. Surely these are clear examples of political speech and not just an expression of private morality and a wish to keep one's conscience clean.

Mary McCarthy expressed her misgivings to Arendt when she wrote that the distinction between conscientious objection and civil disobedience was not "so cut-and-dried as you make it sound." In fact, there was, insisted

McCarthy, a "matter of conscience" even in civil disobedience.[59] I agree with the spirit of McCarthy's objections, on the condition that one first acknowledges Arendt's initial conceptual distinction as a kind of approximate starting point. For, however correct Cavell's response is, neither Thoreau nor Brown offers a very compelling model for what it means to be political in the explosive context of a United States headed for the conflagration of war, much less in normal times. We need not take President Lincoln as an alternative. William Lloyd Garrison, Wendell Phillips, or Frederick Douglass are much better exemplars of an abolitionist stance that ended by becoming political as well as moral.

Shine, Perishing Republic

The last decade of Hannah Arendt's life were marked by a series of crises in the republic of which she had been a citizen since 1951. Not only her European experience of flight and exile but the residual effects of the McCarthy period contributed to a certain pessimism, even paranoia, on her part about the state of American political institutions. This contrasted sharply with what she referred to in her last essay, "Home to Roost," as "the glorious beginnings two hundred years ago."[60] Where her account of the American founding in *On Revolution* stressed the politics of freedom that arose from "beginning anew," she now alluded to the need for a kind of civic humanist *ricorso*, a return to, via remembrance of, first principles. Enumeration of the shocks, even traumas, to the body politic between 1963 and 1968 makes the point. Four popular leaders—Malcolm X, John Kennedy, Martin Luther King Jr., and Robert Kennedy—had been assassinated, and there was an attempt on the life of Southern segregationist leader George Wallace in 1972 that left him wheelchair-bound. Nonviolent racial change in the South and the War on Poverty had given way to racial violence in many of the nation's cities and racial polarization within the American citizen body, which led to a white backlash most everywhere. Almost as traumatic was the ongoing American involvement in the Vietnam conflict, a war that had torn the country apart and undermined the consensus that held the country together.

Specifically, Arendt's own assessment of the crises of the republic was provoked by two startling events—the publication of the Pentagon Papers in

1971, followed not long thereafter by the Watergate crisis that led to Richard Nixon's resignation from the presidency. Her reflections on these crises are found in the essays "Lying in Politics" (1971) and "Home to Roost" (1975), as well as in her private correspondence with philosopher J. Glenn Gray.[61]

The correspondence with Gray, who taught philosophy at Colorado College from 1954 until his death in 1977, is of particular interest here. He and Arendt first met at the Humanities Institute at Wesleyan College in Connecticut as Arendt was finishing up *On Revolution* in late 1961. Aside from the shared interests in European thought and the work of Martin Heidegger, their relationship was undoubtedly helped along by her high opinion of Gray's meditative, book-length essay *The Warriors* (1959). Much of their correspondence concerned matters of translation, in this case the translation into English of Heidegger's work. Arendt was instrumental in Gray's becoming general editor at Harper and Row in charge of translating and publishing Heidegger there. She had kept up with Heidegger's thought over the years and knew her way around not only the subtleties of German but also English to a surprising degree. Arendt's letters on this topic were a kind of a master class conducted by her on how to translate Heidegger's notoriously difficult philosophical prose.

But translation matters were not the only topic taken up in the letters between the two figures. Together, they bemoaned the low standard of the teaching of continental philosophy in America and the "the low state of philosophic thinking in England and in the US." In commenting on *The Theory of Justice*, Gray contended that "Rawls' book, which I haven't finished, is hardly of first rank but is well ahead of anything English."[62] One of Gray's favorite topics, the philosophy of education, turns up periodically, as does their disagreement about the worth of psychoanalysis. Near the end of her life, Gray reported favorably on Michael Oakeshott's visit at Colorado College, noted the admiration the English philosopher had expressed for Arendt's work, and recommended that Arendt take a look at the work on Heidegger of a still obscure French philosopher, Jacques Derrida.[63] In addition, she and Gray often exchanged desultory political comments about Europe, America, and, for a time, Israel during the Eichmann controversy, not to mention the Vietnam War and the antiwar protests. (They shared the view that the war was a political and moral disaster.) But it was the

Watergate crisis that elicited the most extended political comment from Arendt, something to which I will return to shortly.

These epistolary exchanges about politics were not the grumblings of ivory-tower philosophers. Arendt had become a frequent commentator on public affairs in the *New Yorker* and the *New York Review of Books* since the mid-1960s. Her essay "Lying in Politics," in the *New York Review*, November 18, 1971, developed a lengthy analysis of what the publication of the Pentagon Papers revealed about American foreign policy and the factors in American society and politics that made it nearly impossible to extricate the country from Vietnam. Arendt was hardly a naive idealist in these matters. As she noted quite early in the essay, "Truthfulness has never been counted among the political virtues," the implication being that no one should be shocked that the American government (or any other government) had been caught lying and then covering up its lies. Moreover, she suggested that "facts" and "factuality" were far from being anchors of certainty either. They were easily manipulated, denied, or, for that matter, created, as it were. Still, she concluded, past a certain point, lying became politically "counterproductive."[64]

As she had observed much earlier in *Origins*, it was particularly ominous when a government began lying to its own citizens rather than to the enemy. The governmental lying revealed by the Pentagon Papers was intended "chiefly if not exclusively, for domestic consumption."[65] Beyond that, the effort to deceive the average citizen was closely linked to the self-deception of the policy makers themselves: "The deception started with self-deception" that perpetuated an "amazing and entirely honest ignorance."[66] Arendt also claimed that the main outlines of American foreign policy revealed in the Pentagon Papers did not point to "grandiose imperialist stratagems" but to a massive effort at image maintenance; not "the welfare of the nation" but "the reputation of the US and its President" seemed of prime concern. Overall, the object of the exercise seems to have been to "save face," though that was allegedly the cultural monopoly of Asian adversaries.[67]

Arendt's larger point was that public relations and image maintenance were the tails that wagged the dog of American foreign policy. Those who handled such matters came from two groups—image makers/manipulators and "problem solvers," the "public relations managers" at large in the "consumer society" and the technocrats brought into the government by people like Robert McNamara at the Defense Department. As a result, American policy from the dropping of the atomic bomb on Japan up to and including the war in Vietnam presupposed an "inability or unwillingness to consult experience and learn from reality" and the result was a "disregard for the actual consequences of action."[68] Supposedly pragmatic Americans had abandoned reality testing and succumbed to fantasies and images. Arendt concluded that only the newspapers and certain national traits such as the skepticism expressed in the antiwar movement had saved the country from a huge disaster. Though distressing, what the Pentagon Papers revealed was probably "not enough to destroy the Republic."[69]

In the analysis of the Watergate situation she sent to Gray in the late summer of 1973, Arendt was less nuanced and more suspicious than in her published analysis of the Pentagon Papers. On August 4, Gray wrote to Arendt in Switzerland (Tegna) that the "Watergate hearings are also a distraction," a letter to which Arendt replied eight days later in identical terms, that is, that she was "very much distracted by Watergate." (The use of "distraction" here should indicate the seriousness not the triviality of Watergate to both figures.) Arendt wrote at some length and with considerable passion about the situation arising from Watergate, especially in her letters of August 12 and 13, 1973. Read now, her comments are a kind of compendium of public reactions filtered through Arendt's own frame of reference. She was puzzled that most Americans thought Nixon guilty but didn't seem to want anything to be done about it. She allows that the source of Nixon's actions seems to have been "less moral depravity than sheer fear." But she then predicted that, if cornered, Nixon would "turn the tables," present himself as the savior in a crisis he had himself created, and arrange a "plebiscitary dictatorship." She also expressed doubts that the Republican Party "will pressure Nixon to resign to save the Party." If the Republicans try, she predicted, Nixon "will open a Pandora's box of shady deals." She concluded this line of thought by wondering "where should a viable opposition come from?" since the Democrats are a "shade more corrupt" than Nixon and the Republicans. Not from Teddy Kennedy, "as though he were any better"? Overall, she concurred with her friend Hans Morgenthau's article in the *New Republic* that Nixon "tried a veritable revolution."[70]

However, she also worked a republican reading of the Watergate crisis into her letter of August 12. Two-thirds the way down the first page, Arendt suddenly introduced Montesquieu into the discussion by noting that he had been "right" to identify the centrality of "virtue" to the life of a republic. From this she concluded that "when virtue has been completely lost—in consumerism on one side and image-making on the other—the republic simply dies an inglorious death."[71] Thus, Arendt's reading of the Watergate crisis focused on the way the American political republic had been corrupted by a society and economy dominated by consumption and the mass media. Clearly, her analysis fell quite squarely into the secular tradition of the republican jeremiad.

Looking back, it is too bad that Arendt never wrote at great length about republican virtue in America. But clearly, as we have seen, courage and public spiritedness, along with the pursuit of public happiness, were among the characteristics she associated with virtue. In the August 12 letter, she also echoed earlier claims when she noted that "consumerism" had undermined the republican spirit in America. Given the decline in public spirit and a rage for consumption, Watergate became, if not predictable, at least no surprise in Arendt's republican vision. She lacked much hope that the republic could correct itself and find a way to begin things anew. In the August 13 letter, she concluded by stating that "I am physically in good shpae [sic], only grief-stricken about the country." But Gray, the homegrown American, was more accurate in his reading of the politics of the Watergate crisis. By 1974, he didn't think that Nixon could ultimately refuse to step down once the momentum to remove him had gathered and still thought that Nixon would be impeached. In a letter of July 28, 1974, Gray wrote to her that many members of the House Judiciary Committee were "fairly impressive" in the Watergate hearings.[72]

Arendt's last published essay, "Home to Roost," appeared in the year of her death, 1975. Clearly anticipating the 1976 bicentennial, she returned to the factors she had explored in the "Lying" essay—the dominance of image making, the "wisdom of Madison Avenue," and self-deception—to indicate "swift decline in the political power" of the United States.[73] In fact, she suggested that the "glamorous trappings, more than power itself" seemed to be the object of gaining power. Again, she emphasized that what was at issue was not the expansion of the American empire but a cultural-psychological crisis of political memory. Here she cited the well-known dictum of one of her favorite American writers, William Faulkner: "The past is never dead, it's not even past." "The past *haunts* us," she observed.[74] If we do not explicitly remember what has happened, she was saying, the momentum of accumulated mistakes, that is, history, will simply overwhelm the United States. Finally, the crisis of the republic was a crisis of memory in which the past "comes home to roost." This theme of the return of the historical repressed was a constant one in Arendt's thinking about history. Still, as she wrote near the end, there was a glimmer of hope: "Let us not forget these years of aberration lest we become wholly unworthy of the glorious beginnings of two hundred years ago."[75] Once more she sounded the monumentalizing republican theme as a way of contrasting the republic as it had been with what it had become.

Even now, it is hard to say whether Arendt was overly pessimistic or not. She underestimated the degree to which the televised hearings—of the Joint Senate Select Committee on Watergate and of the House Judiciary Committee's impeachment proceedings—raised and addressed vital constitutional matters. As she noted, the "crimes" of Watergate seemed "so mild" to most non-Americans.[76] But she did note to her friend William Jovanovich that "I am developing a crush on Senator Ervin . . . long live old age." As her biographer notes, she, like a lot of Americans, thought that the effects of the hearings would be a kind of universal cynicism and feared that Americans would fall back on the old "all politicians are corrupt" line of analysis.[77] It certainly was a temptation to Arendt.

From our perspective, those hearings represented an "Arendtian" moment when key institutions of the republic sought to expose the corruption in the body politic and revive a commitment to first constitutional principles. During the Watergate crisis, there was a general, not just specialized, academic interest in constitutional matters, especially the question of impeachment. All this was less an exercise in "beginning anew," than it was an effort to bring back to life the principles that underlay the first new beginning. Thus the Watergate episode itself allows an Arendtian interpretation that works against the pessimistic tenor of Arendt's own analysis. It suggests that virtue had not totally departed the American republic and that republican institutions still worked. To be sure, Watergate was a crisis that resulted from the accumulation of other crises from the previous decade. It is possible that, ultimately, Arendt's analysis of the decline in republican political morality and of the watershed moment in America's role in the world will prove the more prescient. But, at the time, the Watergate hearings were, for many, a moment of hope not despair or cynicism, of generational reconciliation not festering generational division.

Finally, in a letter of April 9, 1975, Gray gently rebuked Arendt for saying she was now "ashamed" to carry a U.S. passport. That would have been a fair reaction a year or so earlier, he observed, but why now? In a July 6, 1975, letter, he suggests that the "Home to Roost" essay was too "Cassandra-like."[78] But by now, undoubtedly lonely after the deaths of Heinrich and of Jaspers, as well, exhausted from delivering the first installment of her Gifford lectures in Edinburgh, and facing another round of them in 1975, Arendt's reservoir of hope was just about empty.

Conclusion

Once More: The Film, Eichmann, and Evil

One startling index of Hannah Arendt's continuing importance in American intellectual life has been the response to Margarethe von Trotta's film *Hannah Arendt* (2012). The very idea that anyone would make a full-length, feature film about a political philosopher is pretty improbable; that it has been widely praised comes as even more a surprise. Ten years in the making, the film itself is rarely ponderous, surprisingly fast-paced, and full of energy; even Arendt's concluding seven-minute lecture on freedom of thought is compelling, even moving. The production faced difficulties in obtaining funding, tough decisions needed to be made on casting, and numerous aesthetic, historical, and philosophical issues had to be worked out. The most crucial single decision was to make the focus of the film the four-year period from the capture of Adolph Eichmann in 1960 through the trial in Jerusalem in 1961 to the publication of *Eichmann in Jerusalem* in 1963 and some of the ensuing controversy.[1]

Two observations about the film need stating immediately. First, it presents a distinctly European Arendt. Its director and coauthor of the screenplay, Margarethe von Trotta, is a highly respected German film director, whose previous subjects include a film on Rosa Luxemburg, one of the most respected and honored of German radicals. (In general, von Trotta's subjects have come from the history of the German left in the twentieth century.)

One of Arendt's most passionately felt essays, written during the 1960s, was on Luxemburg as an independent leftist who, Arendt contended, was as interested in republicanism as in the class struggle. The essay must have helped draw von Trotta to Arendt, though, because, as she tells it, she was only gradually convinced that Arendt would be a plausible, even attractive, topic.[2] The second thing is that the film operates with what was known and said about the Eichmann affair in the 1960–65 period. The only "new" material in the film, which would not have been generally available during the period depicted, has to do with three flashbacks to the affair Arendt carried on with philosopher Martin Heidegger in the mid-1920s and then their reunion in 1950. In general, though the film certainly is organized around the Eichmann controversy, it broadly assumes, rather than seriously questions, the validity of her banality of evil thesis.

What about the European versus American Arendt issue? The only American really integral to the making or production of the film was Pam Katz, a New Yorker, who cowrote the screenplay. Von Trotta gave ample tribute to the help given to her and the entire project by two of Arendt's former students, Jerome Kohn, director of Hannah Arendt Center at the New School for Social Research and editor of several volumes of her un-published work, and Elisabeth Young-Bruehl, author of the still definitive biography of Arendt, *For Love of the World* (1982). Ironically, the film was only completed because of the decision *not* to film it in America due to la-bor and production costs. Funding and filming involved a variety of places and sources — France, Germany, Israel, Canada, and Luxembourg. There was neither American nor British money in the film; nor are any of the major roles filled by American actors and actresses. Janet McTeer, who plays Arendt's good friend, Mary McCarthy, is a British actor, and Nick Wood-eson, who plays the *New Yorker* editor William Shawn, is the son of British parents and has acted and lived on both sides of the Atlantic. Indeed, even the Arendt-Blücher apartment overlooking the East River — a triumph of authenticity according to most — was reconstructed from scratch in a Lux-embourg studio.

Besides the scenes set in the Arendt-Blücher apartment, the ones set in the office of the *New Yorker*, a gathering in a hotel lobby before the contro-versial public meeting to discuss Arendt's *Eichmann in Jerusalem* in the fall of

1963, and a couple of outdoor shots at the New School for Social Research are relatively brief. What Americans there are have mostly minor roles in the film, except perhaps Harvey Friedman, an American-born actor who lives in Berlin and plays the egregious Thomas Miller. Miller is a fictional member of the New School faculty, who fawns over Arendt but then turns on her after the controversy breaks out. Shawn's female assistant at the *New Yorker* is a sourpuss, who sneers at Shawn's decision to send Arendt to Jerusalem and is skeptical that she will ever submit her manuscript. (It was, in fact, submitted late.) More seriously, von Trotta's film largely ignores Arendt the political thinker, an omission not unrelated to the neglect of America in the film. *On Revolution*, which explored the political origins of the United States as a modern republic, was, like *Eichmann in Jerusalem*, also published in 1963, but it gets no mention in the film.

The cocktail parties—an American institution particularly in the post-war years—are very nicely done. The one shown revolves generally around Hannah and Heinrich, with an ongoing argument between him and Hans Jonas taking center stage in one scene. There is a bit of political back and forth about Kennedy and Nixon at one point, but nothing really develops out of it, except Hannah's judgment that Kennedy should be the favorite in the upcoming election because he is good-looking. The American students in her New School seminar are earnest but naive and speak German with unmistakable American accents. (I've never seen evidence that she had her students speak German in class.) Institutionally, the New School gets all the blame for the hostile institutional reactions to Arendt after her book appears, but neither the New School, where she didn't begin teaching until early 1968, nor the University of Chicago, where Arendt began teaching in the fall of 1963, ever suggested she step down from teaching due to the controversy over her Eichmann book. The scene in which she is seen eating alone in the faculty cafeteria while the other faculty members gradually get up and leave does have a certain historical veracity. Young-Bruehl reports that, in the fall of 1963, Arendt frequently had to eat alone in the faculty club and was only joined by her old friend Hans Morgenthau and occasionally classicist-philosopher Richard McKeon.[3] Finally, her powerful, climactic, seven-minute speech does not correspond to any actual speech she made, though the ideas and some of the phrasing are either from her own writing and are faithful to it. None of this is fatal, but it is symptomatic of the way America is marginalized as a factor in Arendt's life and thought, and there is a certain lack of sureness of touch when dealing with America or American institutions. Though Arendt (Barbara Sukowa) remembers her first reaction to America—"Paradise!"—and jokes with Mary about the difference in European and American attitudes toward marital fidelity, nothing else in the film suggests anything very much about her attitude, positive or negative, toward her adopted country.

Von Trotta's decision to concentrate on the Eichmann affair is justified insofar as it was the "vehicle" by which Arendt became almost well-known. But the film does not do much to clarify how widespread awareness of the trial was in America or Europe or Israel. In fact, awareness was much greater in America than in Britain, though probably not greater than in Israel or Germany. In the film, the controversy's impact falls mostly on Arendt, her family and friends, and a narrow, but unidentified, segment of the New York academic and intellectual community. In fact, Arendt traveled a fair amount to defend her book. Aesthetically, there is also a lot to be said for von Trotta's decision not to try to do a life-and-times biopic of Arendt. If the film is anything, it is tightly focused.

This tight focus is reinforced by the fact that the film begins in almost total darkness. The first scene involves the capture of Eichmann on a dark road in Argentina and the second shows Arendt wandering through the darkened rooms of her New York apartment and then lying down to think, all the while smoking.[4] The natural world is all but excluded from the film, except when Arendt's walk in the woods is interrupted (absurdly) by a car of Mossad agents, the leader of whom warns her against publishing her book. There are also two scenes that show Arendt on a bus traveling through the Israeli countryside presumably toward Jerusalem.

Yet the closed-in, at times even claustrophobic, nature of the film is modulated by the time Arendt spends in Israel in the spring and early summer of 1961, socializing with her relatives and also discussing the impending trial with her old mentor, Kurt Blumenfeld. A fair amount of footage from the actual Eichmann trial is incorporated into von Trotta's film and represents a wise decision not to have someone "play" Eichmann. Shifting to Jerusalem in the lead-up to the trial also presents a more natural setting for arguments to take place about Eichmann and the actions of the Israeli government, not to mention Arendt's reunion with Blumenfeld. She later returns to Israel (from Europe) to visit him, and a moving deathbed scene shows him turning his back on Arendt when she tries to repair the breach between them due to her attitude toward the trial and Israel.

The Eichmann trial itself contributes a great deal to the dramatic and didactic power of von Trotta's film. From *To Kill a Mockingbird* to *Inherit the Wind*, from *Judgment at Nuremberg* to *The Reader*, there are many examples of films structured around historically and politically resonant trials. By definition, such films involve the public clash of ideas about momentous moral, political, and historical issues. Of course, von Trotta's film is not about one but two trials—Adolph Eichmann's and Hannah Arendt's. Her concluding apologia in New York echoes, though not too obviously, Socrates's defense before the jury in Athens. During and after her speech, she is confronted by hostile opposition from Miller and his two committee members and, more powerfully, from Hans Jonas as she leaves the lecture hall. Jonas breaks with her on the spot and assails her for acting like a "typical German intellectual, looking down on us Jews." But just as Kurt Blumenfeld channels Gershom Scholem's actual judgment on Arendt's failure to sufficiently love the Jewish people, so Jonas is given words that condemn Arendt for her typically German-Jewish arrogance. In fact, Jonas was also a German Jew and never completely broke with Arendt, though he did not speak to Arendt for two years after the book appeared.[5] Clearly, she failed to adhere to Kurt Blumenfeld's earlier plea that she "be patient with" the Israelis.

Is the movie *Hannah Arendt* a kind of hagiography? There is no doubt that the film is made from Arendt's point of view and that, from von Trotta on down, those involved with the film came to admire Arendt greatly. (Arendt's equation of Nazi Germany and Stalin's Soviet Union as totalitarian offended many on the left in Germany well past the 1960s.) Still, the film does underline her supreme self-confidence on intellectual matters and a general indifference to the opinions of others. Though the film is a thoroughly European production, Barbara Sukowa plays Arendt as an almost (American) "cocky" character. Though Arendt certainly could be full of herself, she wasn't a ponderous person. Von Trotta shows her with a good sense of humor and a nice ability to be playful, thus undermining

Arendt's reputation for humorlessness. The scene where she informs Kurt Blumenfeld and the other Israelis sitting with them how they should think about Eichmann conveys her tendency to play the "know-it-all". In fact, Blumenfeld's "this time you've gone too far" to Hannah indicates something about her history of challenging conventional opinion.

Interestingly, Sukowa, whom almost everyone wanted for the role of Arendt, offered some very sharp observations about the woman she was portraying. She urged von Trotta, as she wrote later, to "give Hannah Arendt strong opponents with strong arguments." Sukowa "admired her radical nature and refusal to compromise and her courage" but she was aware of how Arendt sometimes "adjusted the facts" and that "she could also be blind to the way she wounded others."[6] Sukowa is also successful in conveying Arendt's vulnerability on the question of whether she had needlessly hurt people and depicts being overcome by emotion when she remembers her father, who died when she was seven years old.

The film also skillfully works out a reasonably convincing way to show Arendt in the process of thinking. In fact, one critic of the film has suggested that von Trotta privileges thinking to the point that Arendt is implicitly associated with Heidegger's celebration of that capacity. But, as Daniel Nemenyi points out, it is not thinking per se but judgment that Arendt came to see as the crucial capacity involved in evaluating political and moral issues. Though in her "Thinking and Moral Considerations" essay (1971) she associated thinking—"the habit of examining and reflecting upon whatever happens to come to pass, regardless of specific content and quite independent of results"—with the working of conscience, she also saw it as "dangerous." She associated this sort of thinking with Heidegger. But it is judging that "realizes thinking," is worldly in its reach and its purposes, focuses on "particulars," and is associated with conscience.[7] It is difficult for a film to adjudicate the issue between judging and thinking, but this is an important critical point. As we shall see, Arendt associates this notion of thinking indirectly with "conscience," but the film achieves this quite differently from the way that Arendt described thinking in *Eichmann in Jerusalem*, where it is associated with universalizing moral thinking, that is, thinking in the place of the other.

In general, the film makes available the major arguments against Arendt's analysis of the banality of evil at various points in the film, often to great effect. But though the film has put such criticisms into play, the viewer doesn't get much in the way of direct debate or interchange about that idea. It is mentioned but not explored. Arendt never really gets to answer Jonas's charges of German-Jewish arrogance, and her standard response to criticism, in the film, is to deny that she wrote the book her critics say she did. Overall, what the film does most effectively is not persuade us that Arendt was right or wrong about Eichmann, the Jewish Councils, and related matters but, rather, it depicts her as standing for herself, and for anyone, who insists on asserting her right to express her opinions publicly. In that sense, it is the film that places the argument for the expression of ideas in public at its center. The strong defense of free thought with which the film concludes is practically the only representation in the film of being political in her sense—speaking and acting before others about matters having to do with the public realm.

Another important aesthetic-ideological issue in the film concerns the issue of gender and feminism. Von Trotta's films in general have been, it is claimed, "didactic feminist buddy movies," while Margaret Weigel has noted that von Trotta stressed private and feminine issues more than Arendt would have approved of.[8] No doubt the banter and gossip about men between McCarthy and Arendt shifts the center of gravity of the film at times toward the private and the domestic. McCarthy was herself a political intellectual (not just the tomboyish, pool-playing friend she appears as in the film) and used the Eichmann example in her book on the My Lai massacre.[9] In addition, though letters, memoirs, and Young-Bruehl's biography have gone a long way toward correcting the idea that Arendt was a "masculine" woman, von Trotta still made the right choice, I think, in giving her a private life and feminine persona. Her relationship with McCarthy and with her personal assistant Lotte Köhler, among others, also shows her capacity for friendship, whether with other women or with men such as Blumenfeld and Jonas. In fact, one of the film's most "realized" relationships is with her husband, Heinrich (Axel Milberg), whose depiction of Blücher is perhaps the most successful piece of acting in the film. Though he carried on several dalliances, Heinrich had a relationship with Hannah that was light and comical as well as serious, rarely dolorous or lugubrious. Yet the flashbacks to the young, eighteen-year-old Hannah's private meetings with the philosopher

Martin Heidegger, who was twice her age at the time their affair began in 1924, don't work very well. Though the young Arendt in the film looks remarkably like the young Arendt did in reality, the film lacks the time or inclination to develop how Heidegger's appeal, which she relates to what she calls "passionate thinking," actually worked, though a brief example of his lecture style is not without interest.

Two final considerations of the film *Hannah Arendt* take us back to von Trotta's choice of focus. While the trial was, in and of itself, momentous and the issues it raised of the highest order, it is how Arendt thought about the trial and what her reaction was to the uproar over it that are, in some ways, at the heart of the film. However, *Eichmann in Jerusalem* was hardly Arendt at her best in philosophical or historical terms. In calling her book a "report," she forswore extended philosophical or ethical reflection altogether. Thus the philosophical foundations for her judgments or the sources of her ruminations are often hard to pinpoint. Certainly, her book lacked the broad historical texture or philosophical depth of *The Origins of Totalitarianism*, *The Human Condition*, or, say, *Between Past and Future*. That she spent time later, even in the 1965 "Postscript" to the original text, exploring the relationship between thinking and acting, the problem of Eichmann's motives and his "thoughtlessness" (*Gedankenlosigkeit*), and, of course, the banality of evil indicates her own awareness of a job only partly finished. Overall, the film fails in somewhat the same way the book does on this issue: the idea (or the fact) of the banality of evil simply needed more exploration, to say the least.

A final problem with the focus is the difficulty in representing evil in film. For David Rieff, for instance, the central Arendtian concern in the film and afterward was the problem of "thinking."[10] But a more obvious choice would be the problem of evil. Von Trotta chose to show newsreel footage of Eichmann in order to convey something of the peculiar sort of evil that Arendt saw in him. Perhaps the viewers could have been granted more access to Arendt's ruminations, speculative though they might have been. There were other problems with using this footage as the sole representation of Eichmann. The way Eichmann looked and acted in Jerusalem was not, of course, how he was in Budapest in 1944. Should von Trotta have flash-backed to footage of Eichmann in full SS regalia, so as to hint at the radical nature of his evil and the presence of the demonic that Arendt associated with it? Or was the SS regalia itself a signifier of the banality, the lack of thought, and the missing moral dimension to Eichmann the man? Should von Trotta have staged a reprise of Heinrich Himmler's chilling speech to the SS officers in 1943 in Posen in which he praised them for the difficult job they were doing in carrying out the Final Solution, in the face of their inherited—and outmoded—ethical values. This was what Nietzsche called the "transvaluation of all values" with a vengeance. It is simply very difficult to *represent* evil so that it can match the effects conveyed by film footage of the manufacturing of corpses.[11]

Fifty Years On

Coming roughly fifty years after the trial of Eichmann and the publication of *Eichmann in Jerusalem*, the von Trotta film touched off a surprising amount of renewed interest in Arendt and her report. Not surprisingly, few of the reviews of the film confined themselves to film aesthetics. The summer of 2014 also saw the publication of Bettina Stangneth's monumental work of history, *Eichmann before Jerusalem*, in English, though it had been published in Germany in 2011. Of course, many books and articles exploring the Eichmann affair as a whole have also appeared over the last half-century, including David Cesarani's *Eichmann: His Life and Crimes* (2004) and Deborah E. Lipstadt's *The Eichmann Trial* (2011), both of which firmly rejected Arendt's banality of evil thesis as applied to Eichmann. All this made discussions of Arendt's book in relationship to Stangneth's study seem particularly urgent.[12]

Though there was genuinely new material in Stangneth's study, the arguments about Eichmann circa 2014 sounded, in many respects, like the ones of a half-century before. But Seyla Benhabib, Yale political theorist and author of a major study of Arendt, also noted that when Stangneth's book appeared in Germany, what excited most comment was her discovery of the pervasive presence of former Nazis in the postwar West German government (as the East German regime had always claimed). The Adenauer government had done remarkably little to bring Eichmann to justice, despite the fact that German intelligence agencies had all the necessary information in hand. The revelations about Eichmann in Argentina (from 1950 to 1960) were particularly important. There he was an active member of an extensive network of ex-Nazis, who sought to keep the flame of National Socialism alive and hoped, eventually, to return to Germany. He was a prize "catch" for this circle, dominated by Willem Sassen and Eberhard Fritsch, since he was thought to know more about what had happened during the war than any living ex-Nazi. But over a decade of discussions, formal interviews, and hundreds of written pages from Eichmann's pen steadily disabused his National Socialist colleagues in Argentina of the idea that the Final Solution was a Jewish lie intended to turn the world against Hitler and National Socialism. Rather, the Final Solution had been very real, and Eichmann was proud of having been a part of it.[13]

In contrast with the German reception, the early discussions of the Stangneth book in the United States focused on what it revealed about Hannah Arendt's analysis of Eichmann's motivation (or lack thereof) in *Eichmann in Jerusalem*. As Richard Wolin—an intellectual historian at City University of New York and author of *Heidegger's Children* (2001), a study of Heidegger and his students, including Arendt—insisted, the question about Eichmann's motivations went to the heart of Arendt's banality of evil thesis, since she had denied that any strong ideological or racist motivation was behind his actions. This is what might be called Arendt's "absence of motive" argument for Eichmann's banality.[14] As much as in the 1963–65 period, Arendt herself was the focus of recent attention. This led Benhabib to ask, rhetorically, or so the headline to her piece in the *New York Times* had it, "Who's on Trial, Eichmann or Arendt?"[15] Reviews of Stangneth's book appeared in several national dailies (including the *New York Times* and the *Wall Street Journal*), as well as in online journals (*Jewish Review of Books*) and blog sites (Corey Robin). Wolin's specific philosophical claim was that Arendt had been unduly influenced by Martin Heidegger, with the imputation that there was some sort of link between her views on Eichmann and her one-time relationship—personal and intellectual—with Heidegger. In fact, a big difference from the controversy in 1963–65 was this attempt to taint Arendt with her close association with Heidegger.

There were, put simply, two dimensions to the Heidegger connection. First, Arendt had had an affair with Heidegger when she was an undergraduate at Marburg in the mid-1920s, which did not become general knowledge until the publication of Elisabeth Young-Bruehl's biography of Arendt in 1982. Beyond that, many thought that Arendt had been insufficiently diligent in finding out what Heidegger had and had not done during the Nazi era and had taken his account of his thought and actions in those years as roughly the truth. This became clear in her "Martin Heidegger at Eighty," a piece that appeared in the *New York Review of Books* in October 1971. The effect of that article, particularly a long footnote, was to make it appear that she was exculpating Heidegger for a relatively minor error, rather than condemning him, or at least severely criticizing him, for his disgraceful ideological support of the Nazis as, for instance, in his public backing of them in his inaugural address as rector at Freiburg in 1933. Arendt was reconciled with Heidegger on her first trip back to Germany in 1950, then didn't see him for over the next ten years or so. Arendt was also instrumental in getting his works translated into English and helping him with various practical matters.[16]

The Heidegger issue aside, if anything, the range of issues covered in the most recent debate seems narrower than in the mid-1960s. There has been little or no further criticism of her attack on the *Judenräte*, aside from academic challenges over the years, though her views on this matter are as genuinely controversial and important as the banality of evil issue. One other persisting line of criticism is also still worth noting. It was first voiced by Gershom Scholem in 1963 when he warned against judging the Jewish Councils or European Jewry too harshly, since they had been faced with such a tragic and insuperable dilemma. In the 1960s, journalist Samuel Grafton also wondered if Arendt's banality argument and indictment of the Jewish Councils weren't premature. Much more recently, in 2014, the president of the American Historical Association, Jan Goldstein, described Arendt's *Eichmann in Jerusalem* as a "colossal rhetorical failure and maybe a moral failure as well. She has ignored her audience and its personal stake in her subject matter." Once again, Arendt was being charged with premature insensitivity. The lesson of the whole controversy, according to Goldstein, both in the 1960s and the 2010s, was that the "historian (or philosopher)" is a better source of historical judgment than the journalist or contemporary observer, since "subtle and complex issues . . . can be properly addressed in academic writing, which unfolds in slow time."[17] The problem with this sort of objection is that Arendt's critics never say how we will know when "enough time has passed" before certain historical judgments should be made. Just as importantly, to think academic historians are somehow immune to rash or unbalanced judgments is also quite strange.

Undoubtedly Wolin's critique of Arendt's thought represents the most formidable challenge to her reputation in recent years. In *Heidegger's Children* (2001), Wolin contended that "the lines between victims and perpetrators had been blurred" in *The Origins of Totalitarianism*, while *Eichmann in Jerusalem* showed a "tasteless equation of victims and executioners." This line of thought was repeated in his first *Jewish Review of Books* piece (Fall 2014) when he reiterated that Arendt "established an historical paradigm that managed simultaneously to downplay the executioners' criminal liability, which she viewed as 'banal' and bureaucratic, and to exaggerate the culpability of their Jewish victims." "One sees," wrote Wolin, "how readily Arendt blurred the line between victims and executioners."[18] This line of attack was, as we have seen in chapter 9, quite common in the 1963–65 period.

Moreover, his most recent attack on Arendt continued the strategy of never missing an opportunity to link Arendt's thought with Heidegger's. On one level, this is not a difficult task.[19] Wolin seemed to assume that influence of almost any sort meant that Arendt was "in Heidegger's thrall" for the rest of her life, a gross oversimplication at best. Not surprisingly, in his three 2014 articles on this topic, Wolin has continued to make every effort to establish the Heideggerian provenance of her notion of "thoughtlessness" (*Gedankenlosigkeit*), which she linked closely with what she identified as Eichmann's banality. However, Seyla Benhabib has effectively derailed this argument by arguing that, in regards to Eichmann, Arendt emphasized the obligation to "think consistently, but from the standpoint of everyone else." This was a far cry from Eichmann's firm commitment to thinking in "völkisch," that is, particularistic, racial terms, and distinct from Arendt's other characterization of thinking—"examining and reflecting upon whatever happens to come to pass."[20] For Arendt in her analysis of Eichmann, "thoughtlessness" had to do with a failure to universalize ("from the standpoint of everyone else") and, psychologically, with insensitivity to the other's position. In fact, thinking in the Eichmann book was closer to a form of conscience than to conventional ratiocination. As mentioned in chapter 9, failure to think, thoughtlessness, was linked to the lack of moral imagination. Overall, in her work from *Eichmann in Jerusalem* on, Arendt proposed two different kinds of links between thinking and conscience, one tracing back to Kant that emphasized the universalizing impulse and one back to Heidegger that emphasized the disruptive, unsettling effects of thinking.

There is also a matter of proportion here. Of course Heidegger's influence on Arendt was great, but it is puzzling why Wolin rarely mentions the great importance of Karl Jaspers on Arendt's life and thought, including during the Eichmann trial period. I mention this omission because it relates to another of Wolin's charges in *Heidegger's Children* that Arendt's theory of totalitarianism, for all its strengths, which Wolin grants, was also an attempt to exonerate German culture as having "no responsibility for the German catastrophe." Wolin also agrees with Scholem that Arendt showed insufficient "love of the Jewish people" and too much loyalty to the "European intellectual traditions that were more refined and sublime—the tradition of *Geist*" (spirit). It was this tradition that also included Heidegger as "one of its leading representatives." But Heidegger would have bridled at the thought of being a European before a German, while Arendt had no problem at all expanding her intellectual and cultural allegiances not only across the Rhine but across the Atlantic as well. All this amounts to a kind of influence mongering and guilt by insinuation on Wolin's part, topped off by a gossipy rhetorical question: "Could it have been those allegiances—uncanny and subterranean—that in some way led her to purvey such calumnies about the Jews in the Eichmann book? Could such remarks have been meant to absolve the Messkirch magician of his crimes on behalf of a regime that sought to wipe out the Jews, by insinuating that, in certain respects, they were no better than the Nazis?"[21] The only appropriate answer to this question is a simple *no*.

Finally, for Wolin, Arendt's *Eichmann in Jerusalem* was marked by a lack of empathy for her fellow Jews, who perished in the death camps and the "bloodlands" (Timothy Snyder's term) of eastern Europe. Indeed he underlined an orientalist disdain for *Ostjuden* in her reactions in a (private) letter to Karl Jaspers where she expressed a "breathtaking condescension" to chief prosecutor, Gideon Hausner. He was, she said, a "typical Galician Jew . . . Probably one of those people who don't know any languages." This *is* snobbery on Arendt's part, not to mention her remarks about Israel as a "half-Asiatic country."[22] I would add here is that such distasteful characterizations were common at the time, even among Europe's most enlightened and cosmopolitan types.[23] In addition, I would add that Arendt's opinions were expressed in a private letter. All this is distasteful snobbery but it is simply not the stuff of which genocide is made, nor does it indicate intellectual subservience to Heidegger. Wolin's larger purpose is to build the case for Arendt as a self-hating Jew who wants to feel superior to the masses of common Jews.

Here the contrast between Wolin's and Stangneth's treatment of Arendt is striking. Stangneth had no problem calling Arendt out on her mistaken judgment as to Eichmann's essential character/personality. No perfunctory bigot or time server among the Nazis, Eichmann's anti-Semitism was thoroughly thought through, marked by "vehemence," and, more importantly, he had proved himself an "agile, grandiloquent and ambitious image-maker," not a mere desk murderer during the war. But in contrast with Wolin's desire to catch Arendt out, Stangneth saw herself in "dialogue" with Arendt about the "fundamental ethical problems" the case raised. As she summed things up in an interview, "someone like Arendt does not need priests. We have to think with her, using the weapons she gave us and with the same aim she had: to understand."[24]

Stangneth's overall thesis, then, is that Eichmann was smart and determined enough to transform his personal style and social profile several times in the course of his life. He was a consummate role player, a man of Proteus-like capacities, a real shape-shifter: "Overall then, the renowned specialist on 'Jewish questions' . . . transformed himself into a helpless minute taker with no power of his own. . . . But now, in his cell in Israel, a bureaucrat sounded far more harmless than an SS man. . . . Again and again—even with experienced interpreters—Eichmann and his texts led people to false conclusions." She also challenges Arendt's judgment about Eichmann's "'inability to speak' and 'inability to *think*'" as "insupportable."[25] Thus, where Arendt went wrong was in underestimating Eichmann. But so did his minders and his interrogators, along with his defense attorneys, in Jerusalem. As Stangneth notes in an interview, the correspondent of "Germany's most important Jewish newspaper . . . described Eichmann as a 'pathetic weakling.'" Stangneth summed it up in another piece thus: "Hannah Arendt acted no differently than all the other serious researchers."[26]

Specifically, because what are known as "the Argentina Papers" weren't available to her in 1961, Arendt missed the overwhelming evidence of Eichmann's firm ideological convictions: "Hannah Arendt would not only have learned new things in the Argentina Papers, but also found the confirmation for much of what she suspected in 1961, even if it were strongly disputed: the Old Nazis in the Federal republic were more dangerous and organized than one wanted to believe."[27] In Jerusalem, it is clear to Stangneth, Eichmann was engaged in a calculated self-diminishment, a pursuit that can hardly have been easy, since he was exceedingly jealous of his self-image and reputation. In fact, he may have made a basic miscalculation—that if he came across as harmless and cooperated with the Israelis, he would be exonerated or receive a lesser sentence.[28] Eichmann, it turns out, was a master of "impression management," to borrow from Erving Goffman, and may have been acting to himself as well as to others. He also seems to have worked on his own to a surprising degree. He gave documents to his Israeli interrogators that his defense team knew nothing about. Still, there must have been considerable consultation among Eichmann and his defense team about how to present the former SS man as essentially a "cog" in the machine. But Stangneth doesn't have a lot of evidence to that effect, and I can't help wondering if she hasn't perhaps overdone the clear difference between the two Eichmanns. As Eichmann himself wrote in 1957: "I, the 'conscientious bureaucrat, that was me, . . . was attended by a fanatical warrior, fighting for the freedom of my blood.'"[29] Here we find Eichmann already reflecting, almost Walter Mitty–like, on his sense of doubleness, even to himself.

But though Stangneth challenged Arendt's "reading" of Eichmann, she also agreed with Arendt that Eichmann used language to distance himself from his own emotions. Eichmann had "no particular feel for words or language" and his expressions sometimes reached a level of "macabre humor." She praises Arendt's sensitive interpretation of documents and notes that Arendt was "one of the most thorough readers of the interrogation and trial transcripts." And she also notes Arendt's acute analysis of the function of the Theresienstadt camp in the Nazi extermination policy in some of her wartime pieces in *Aufbau*.[30] But she stopped short of dismissing Eichmann as anything like what Arendt called a "clown." In sum, she was critical of Arendt but treated her with respect.

Finally, then, the crucial question is how important was Nazi racial ideology in explaining what Eichmann thought and did? Here Wolin is right that the picture Stangneth presents of Eichmann before Jerusalem supplies him with a strong, credible motive, an ideological one at that. Clearly Nazi racial ideology played a—or perhaps the—major part in motivating Eichmann to act not only during the war when National Socialism was on the march but also after the war, in Argentina, and then, even, when he was brought back to Jerusalem to face trial. On the historical level, Eichmann contended that Germany had fought a war of self-defense against the Jews, who had themselves started the war. In this sense, his conscience was clear—he only did what the enemy itself had done and was only ready to be reconciled when they were. As Stangneth quotes him: "after all, the enemy wasn't confessing his guilt, either."[31] The basis of morality and conscience, in Eichmann's view, was not a shared universal standard (as with Kant) but a "völkisch" or "ethnic" one. In Darwinist terms, claims Stangneth, the National Socialists believed in "a nonvitalist philosophy of inescapable natural laws," which dictated a "racial-biological struggle." Intellectually and emotionally, this Nazi *Weltanschauung* or "ideology" was not just a "pastime or a theoretical superfluity." It was "the fundamental authorization for his actions."[32] Ironically, this comports well with the notion of ideology that Arendt proposed in *Origins* and with the central role she attributed to Darwinism in the Nazi ideology. Yet because Arendt also argued that modern racial ideology did not come from the mainstream or canonical figures of the Western tradition but from the gutter, she was not inclined to take racism that seriously as a motivating factor. Whether or not it would have helped, Stangneth also notes that Arendt was "unaware of Eichmann's lengthy essays," "the pieces he wrote in Israel" on Kant, and also a debate he had with a theologian while in Israel.[33] They were only released much later.

Once More, Banality and Evil

If Arendt's thesis is not "shattered" by Stangneth's research, as Deborah Lipstadt has insisted it has been, why not? One direct response came from

Benhabib when she asked in her piece of September 21, 2014: "Couldn't Eichmann have been a fanatical Nazi *and* banal?" Her answer was in the affirmative. In fact, it was precisely his "self-immunizing mixture of anti-Semitic clichés, his antiquated idiom of German patriotism and the craving for the warrior's honor and dignity" that indicated his inability to think. Along with Roger Berkowitz, Benhabib's one criticism of Stangneth is that she missed what Arendt meant by thinking. It was, as already mentioned, the ability to "think in the place of everybody else"—that is, with an "enlarged mentality."[34] Interestingly, in 2001, Ernst Vollrath noted that it was a mark of Eichmann's banality that in Budapest, for example, he "had to decorate himself with the insignias of power. . . . Banality of evil did not refer to a diminution or a trivialization of crimes and their perpetrators; rather just the opposite, an intensification of the insanity of the perpetrator and his crimes, for this banality is expressly marked as fearsome."[35] In other words, banality and the Nazi ideology, Vollrath maintained, could very well operate together. This may sound too much like a desperate attempt on the part of Arendt's defenders (and here I include myself) to save Arendt's fundamental concept of the banality of evil. It is plausible, though it comes at a price— the admission that Arendt's "absence of motive" claim about Eichmann is wrong and must be abandoned.

Along with that, those who adopt this position will have to emphasize that what Arendt settled on as Eichmann's "thoughtlessness" and lack of an "enlarged mentality" lies at the heart of his banality. It was this that Arendt emphasized near the end of *Eichmann in Jerusalem*. For those who accept this position, racial ideology—systematic anti-Semitism and not just garden variety bigotry—can be part of the package that blocks a person like Eichmann from thinking about what he is doing. But it also suggests that racism can always be, even perhaps always is, banal, a superficial and thoughtless way of characterizing other individuals or groups.

But there was another trait that Arendt increasingly associated with banality of evil: the concept of the demonic and its absence in Adolf Eichmann. What does "demonic" mean, except an exemplification or personification of evil, an aura that a particular human possesses that calls into question the existing structure of values? It was only really in the Eichmann book and thereafter that Arendt began mentioning the demonic as something that conflicted with banality. In *Origins*, radical evil referred to (1) deeds and effects that exceeded the possibility of adequate punishment; or (2) deeds and effects that confounded comprehensible explanation (motivation); and (3) the collective project to create a population of superfluous persons. This last characteristic meant the nullification of the humanity of a group, though not necessarily their lives. She sometimes referred to this as the attempt to change human nature. But it wasn't clear whether all three of these characteristics were necessary for radical evil to be at work. Nor is it clear whether radical evil is an internally coherent concept or more a cluster of associated characteristics bearing a family resemblance to one another. Clearly, Arendt never straightened all these matters out sufficiently.

Obviously there is a problem with ambiguity in terminology and the level at which the different senses of evil is pertinent. As clarified by Richard Bernstein, "radical evil" refers to the aims and effects of a collective project such as the Final Solution; but the "banality of evil" refers to a quality of thought and action of an individual or group involved in this larger project.[36] Indeed, some praise Arendt's idea of banality of evil because it is a way of avoiding mythologizing the great criminals of racism by attributing to them some great "psychological depth" that is fascinating in its implications. Thus, Eichmann's banality of evil is compatible with racist motivation in an individual, but all those involved in a collective project such as the Final Solution are not necessarily ideological racists. Moreover, the various concepts of evil can be used together. It is not an either-or matter, despite the fact that Arendt occasionally sounded like she meant it that way.[37]

What about racism? I have suggested that racism may be of a conformist sort, a state of mind and feeling that can come and go according to the situation a person finds him- or herself in. If racism is always banal, then the Benhabib position will always win the argument about the banality of evil, since radical racism/anti-Semitism by definition thwarts the possibility of an "enlarged mentality." But could there be a type of racism/anti-Semitism that is complex or even profound rather than simply banal? When Heidegger scholar Peter Trawny attributes to Martin Heidegger something Trawny calls "seinschichtlicher Antisemitismus" ("ontological-historical anti-Semitism," in Peter Gordon's translation) would we still call Heidegger's idea, however (ob)noxious, a banal mode of thought? What Trawny refers to is Heidegger's belief, as found in Heidegger's recently published *Schwarze Hefte* (*Black Notebooks*), that Jews were one of the groups who committed themselves to the technologization (i.e., Weberian rationalization) of the world as part of modernity. Trawny describes the process as one in which "well-known anti-Semitic stereotypes are given a philosophical treatment or dimension."[38] Werner Sombart's complex argument that European Jews were the main carriers of modern capitalism might also qualify as a nonbanal form of anti-Semitism.

To shift national contexts, there is also the complex and often compelling poetry of T. S. Eliot or Ezra Pound, both of whose verse was known to contain anti-Semitic opinions and stereotypes. Does great modernist poetry become banal the minute it articulates anti-Semitic positions or tropes? Is William Faulkner's work "great," even in those moments where it seems to fall victim to what it holds up for our examination and condemnation—the power of a culture founded on racism? Thomas Mann's Adrian Leverkühn in *Doktor Faustus* sells his soul to the devil, the premodern trope for access to extra dimensions of creativity and transgressive power that creates, in this case, music of new disturbing power. Here at least we can say that Arendt's refusal to call Eichmann demonic is a way of refusing to blame the German catastrophe on romanticism, since the demonic seems to be the opposite of the banal. Overall, then, the best we can say is that anti-Semitism/racism comes in various shapes and sizes and is a plural, not unitary, concept. On this view, Eichmann was committed to a radical anti-Semitism and was not just a perfunctory, conformist racist. At the same time, however, there was nothing of the demonic or radical about him or the way he expressed his beliefs. The notion of the banality of evil also has distinct limitations in its applicability.

Since the mid-1960s, another new position on the banality of evil has emerged. Christopher Browning describes it as follows: "Arendt grasped an important concept but not the right example."[39] Already in 1997, Yaacov Lozowick suggested that Eichmann had been too immersed in the ideological culture of the SS to have been innocent on the matter of racial politics. Drawing on Lozowick, I have also suggested that "administrative mass murder" can have worked without strong "ideological convictions" in all those who worked the machinery.[40] And we now know that that is the case. Yet the bureaucracy thesis needs to be handled with care. Lozowick has also suggested that the Nazi state and military bureaucracies were far from neutral in the matter of racial laws, since anti-Semitism was pervasive. And Stangneth reveals how compromised by Nazi associations much of the Federal Republic's governing institutions were after the war. This confirmed Arendt's claim in 1966 that the government of the Federal Republic government was "shot through with former Nazis."[41]

In contrast, Browning's *Ordinary Men* (1992) found relatively little hard-core, radical anti-Semitism among the German soldiers who participated in massacres of Jews. Rather, the familiar themes of group conformity to the existing power structure of a situation seemed to be more important. Ironically, this fits with Roger Berkowitz's suggestions that Eichmann's problem was that he was a joiner who wanted to be part of a cause larger than himself, even though Berkowitz does not otherwise accept the view that Eichmann failed to fit the banality of evil category.[42]

Arendt's analysis, for instance, of the Frankfurt Auschwitz trials in the mid-1960s was not entirely at odds with this split description of the workings of evil. She also scarcely mentioned either radical or banal evil in the essay. If Eichmann were a "desk murderer," then we need to differentiate between him and the "cogs" in the killing machine, what Arendt called "the small fry" in Auschwitz, the guards who kept order, inflicted casual violence, and frequently went over the line in injuring or killing prisoners.[43] Stangneth uses a better term for Eichmann when she refers to him as an "engineer" of, not a "cog" in, the Final Solution.[44] But the idea of being part of a larger structure or national-racial project still holds. All this, in turn, fits the macro-level generalizations about the workings of modern bureaucracy, which derive, as said, from Weber and even the Frankfurt School and with which Arendt is sometimes (wrongly) associated. This is what is sometimes called the functionalist analysis of the Holocaust. It would probably be possible to fit some version of the functionalist analysis with Arendt's all but forgotten mass society thesis, but no one has really tried it.

Whatever the case, in this functionalist model, those who kept it running need not, and often do not, have strong ideological convictions, as long as those setting policy and directing the machine determine the direction (racial extermination). They divide their normal private life from their work life. Then at work, they separate the making of policy from its execution, something like what Arendt once referred to as the distinction between "responsibility" and "guilt." This is what led Wolin to insist that Arendt's banality thesis best fits the functionalist interpretation of the Holocaust, which can seem deterministic and system driven. But Arendt doesn't quite fit in so neatly. Though she proposed something like a functionalist model for the Final Solution, her analytic focus nevertheless fell on a single individual: Adolf Eichmann. The question is then whether Eichmann is intended to be representative or exceptional in his apparent banality.

To conclude, I want to suggest two matters that might be fruitful approaches to consider. First, in all the discussions of evil, no one has really tried to construct a taxonomy of evil in or suggested by Arendt's work. There are examples of traditional evil (disobedience or selfishness); radical evil (in Kant's sense of a principled commitment to evil); radical evil (in the Arendtian sense); the banality of evil (Arendt); and, finally, whatever we might call what the cogs—the "small fry," the thugs, and the sadists among the guards on trial in the Frankfurt Auschwitz trials—were doing.

In writing about the Frankfurt trials, Arendt returned to her essay of 1945 "Organized Guilt and Universal Responsibility" where she emphasized that those who have the most power, for example, from Eichmann on up to Hitler, are guiltier than those who are commanded to actually pull the trigger or drop the pellets of gas. The Auschwitz guards denied or refused to admit what they had done, yet they also pled that they had been forced to follow orders. They had violated German criminal law in inflicting pain and death, yet they were also tried for their "complicity in mass murder," a different sort of charge.[45] Guards aren't there to kill prisoners; but this was Auschwitz. Echoing Paul Celan's "Death is a master in Germany," Arendt wrote "Death was the supreme ruler in Auschwitz, but side by side with death it was accident." There, "everything is possible."[46] In her essay on the Frankfurt trials, Arendt did not write as though the banality thesis could cover all the instances and types of evil. After all, making distinctions was her specialty.

The other curious thing in all the debate and dispute about evil and anti-Semitism/racism has been the total absence of any psychoanalytic or in-depth psychological probings into the complexities of motivation that are found in Eichmann's testimony and writings. What are we saying when we claim that Eichmann, for instance, was motivated primarily by racist ideas and opinions? Is this a claim about conscious intentions? Aren't there well-documented ways that unconscious patterns of thought are displaced onto "the other" and work themselves out through conscious intentions? Should we distinguish intentions (conscious) from motivations (unconscious) in all this? What seems obvious to me is the enormous amount of ambivalence that marked Eichmann's attitudes toward Jews. In Eichmann's view, Jews weren't inferior to Germans. Rather they were smarter than Germans were and therefore all the more dangerous. As we have seen, Eichmann already saw himself in two diametrically opposed ways—as "cautious bureaucrat" and as "crusading warrior." There are defense mechanisms such as "splitting" and "denial" that help explain how the psyche is working and might therefore help us figure out how Eichmann's worked, however banally he expresses himself. To claim he has an unconscious is not somehow to glorify him. Also, Arendt's emphasis on his lack of moral imagination, his inability to put himself in someone else's place, sounds something like the way narcissism is described as the inability to get the right balance between being absorbed by the other as the source of all wisdom (Hitler) and the failure to establish a connection with others at all. With this goes Lacan's mirror stage, with the self constructed as a defensive structure against external and internal threat. Here, I suspect Arendt's hostility to psychoanalysis has scared off those who have been shaped by her thought. Whatever the case with my two sugges-tions, the debate about the banality of evil has just about run out of steam.

ACKNOWLEDGMENTS

Far from isolating you from the world, working on a book like this is a way of meeting new people and making new friends. One problem with writing acknowledgments, however, is that the strong feelings of gratitude have often faded. Then, when written out as part of a list, the thank-yous look perfunctory. Still, there are at least three kinds of aid that are covered in my lists and comments. One sort has to do with tangible things like a tip about an article or a librarian's extra effort that turns up a letter or a file that contains something unexpected. Another kind has to do with intangible things—for instance, the sense of genuine involvement on the part of a reader of a chapter. Yet a third sort of help comes from those people for whom you write, who make the whole effort worthwhile. I won't be trying to make these distinctions public here, since it can too easily sound invidious. But they are on my mind as I write what follows.

Institutions: For heavy-duty research projects, libraries and archives are crucial. With intellectual history, they are not quite so central, perhaps. While it might once have required an extended trip to chase down a letter or the transcript of an interview, such material is now often published between hard covers fairly quickly. For this project on Hannah Arendt, I would like to thank Helen Tieger at Bard College's Stephenson Library for her help in looking at Hannah Arendt's personal library, which the Stephenson Library has on the premises. Though ultimately my time at the University of Chicago's Regenstein Library did not turn up what I thought it might, Leah Richardson and her colleagues were extremely helpful in chasing down possible leads in the John U. Nef Committee on Social Thought holdings. The Manuscripts and Archives division of Sterling Library at Yale University was very prompt in answering queries and supplying me with the correspondence between Dwight Macdonald and Hannah Arendt. Finally, a thank-you to whomever had the foresight to deposit the Hannah Arendt papers in the Library of Congress and to put them online. It is a great thing to be able to use them in the United Kingdom or in Australia or wherever else. I only wish the status of those items in the Arendt papers that are closed to off-site searches would be reassessed.

Presentations: Over several years, I participated in several lively sessions having to do with Hannah Arendt, particularly in Britain. In the last decade or so, interest in her work has taken off after indifferent to hostile treatment for many years. Overall, my experience has also been that if an audience isn't interested in Arendt's life or work, it is their—rather than her, or even my—fault. It is easy to find something in or about Arendt to disagree with; but it is difficult to remain indifferent to her lifelong project of trying to understand "the burden of our times."

Since retiring in 2008 from the University of Nottingham, I have done two presentations on Arendt at the nearby University of Leicester, one at an American studies conference organized by George Lewis and the other at the Holocaust Center there, having been invited by Martin Halliwell. Early on I spoke at University of Nottingham's Critical Theory Visiting Speaker series; discussed her work at a Politics Department staff seminar; and offered an early draft chapter to members of the Thought and Culture group in the American and Canadian Studies Department. I was also fortunate to participate in the conference "Crises of Our Republics: Hannah Arendt at One Hundred" at Yale University, September 29–30, 2006, and organized by Seyla Benhabib. Since then, I have participated in three day-long conferences on various aspects of Hannah Arendt's thought at Royal Holloway College of the University of London (organized by Dan Stone), Southampton University (organized by Stephen Morton), and Saint Mary's University (organized by Mark Donnelly) in Twickenham, London. Participants and audience—sometimes they were different and sometimes the same—have always been sharp and challenging, as they were at the American History Seminar at Cambridge University, presided over by Gary Gerstle as recently as November 10, 2014.

Further afield, I spent a month at the Liguria Study Center, Bogliasco, Italy, in the autumn of 2005, and got started in earnest on understanding the various stories of the German-Jewish intellectual émigrés to the United States. Alessandra Natale made the stay not only an intellectual but also a social pleasure, with very good company provided by the international group of fellows—and Italian lessons to boot. A three-month stint in mid-January to mid-April 2011 at the Humanities Research Centre at the Australian National University under the direction of Debjani Ganguly allowed me to present my research on Arendt to a public audience. While there, I also cotaught an afternoon seminar to those interested in Arendt with Ned Curthoys, who was a great unofficial host. I spoke on Arendt and the South at the University of North Carolina's Center for the Study of the American South, having been invited to do so by Bill Ferris, in May 2013, while Peter Kuryla at Belmont University in Nashville organized a day-long conference on philosophy and literature later the same month at which I spoke about Arendt and literature. More recently, on May 30, 2014, I had the chance to present a paper on the same topic at University College Dublin where Aine Mahon and her associates organized an extremely lively conference called "Philosophy, Literature and America." Finally, one organization that has been a constant source of intellectual stimulation and collegiality for nearly a decade and a half has been the Intellectual History Group organized by Michael O'Brien and myself. Our session on Hannah Arendt back in 2009 supplied plenty of fireworks. As one member of the group quipped: "It reminded me of what a typical editorial meeting of *Partisan Review* must have been like in the late 1940s."

People: Several of the people already mentioned have also read draft chapters of *Arendt and America*. But there were others who aided mightily in the book's completion. Jerome Kohn, the director of the Hannah Arendt Center at the New School for Social Research in New York and the editor of several volumes of Arendt's previously published and unpublished writings, not only provided quick responses but also interesting comments and invaluable advice when I directed questions to him. My editor at Chicago, Douglas Mitchell, went beyond the call of duty to put me in (e-mail) touch with a couple of former students of Arendt's, Michael Denneny and Marc Cogan. They provided a wealth of knowledge, experience, and anecdotes about the world Hannah Arendt inhabited and established for herself, both in New York and in Chicago. In fact, Arendt's academic and intellectual career could be named "a tale of two cities." (Except there is Berkeley, too.) Tom Hayden was quick to respond to my e-mails about his having participated in the roundtable on violence with Arendt, Noam Chomsky, Susan Sontag, and others that I write about in Chapter 12. Hanna Fenichel Pitkin helpfully responded to my questions early in the writing of the book, as did Leon Botstein at Bard when I asked him about Arendt's musical tastes. Both Susan Neiman and Richard Bernstein generously clarified aspects of their own thinking about Arendt and added their insights on her life and thought when I asked them.

From my friends in academia on both sides of the Atlantic (and in Asia), I have received nothing but valuable help. Jonathan Imber, editor of the always lively *Society* magazine, generously supplied information on the issues that included pieces by or about David Riesman. It was an enormous help. Robert Westbrook at the University of Rochester answered my e-mail questions about a piece he had written on Dwight Macdonald several years ago and then sent me a copy of his book that contained the piece. An old friend, Klaus Reitemeier, and a new one, Ulrich Rosenhagen, answered several questions about what this or that German word, phrase, or idiomatic expression meant as I struggled to translate Arendt's correspondence and also occasional articles from German. Dan Stone at Royal Holloway in London and Peter Baehr of Lingnan University in Hong Kong read the whole manuscript with care and provided two quite different, but valuable, perspectives on it.

There were several people who were always willing to give me their assessment of a chapter when I sprang it on them. Peter Kuryla enriched my analysis of Arendt's relationship to American thought, while Tony Hutchison at Nottingham added a literary perspective to his reading of several of my chapters. (He had also written his MA thesis on Arendt). Teaching at Trinity College in Dublin, Dan Geary had insights about post-1945 American social science and social thought that made him ideal to read several chapters, and Andrew Hartman at Illinois State University was generous with his knowledge of American intellectual history in the last half of the twentieth century. Similarly, Ned Curthoys at the University of Western Australia and Marije Altorf at Saint Mary's University, Twickenham, were particularly helpful with the now half-century long debate about the Eichmann case, while Martin Woessner helped me on various matters having to do with reception of Heidegger's work in America. Colin Jones set me straight on the historiography of the French Revolution, which I had to negotiate in chapter 11. Jennifer Ratner-Rosenhagen read several chapters with an impressive mixture of common sense (like insisting that the text be accessible) and a wide knowledge of modern American and European thought. Beyond that, her encouragement with the book was indispensable. In general, some of these people knew a lot about Hannah Arendt; others didn't. Some liked her; others didn't particularly. But all of them together provided me with invaluable help.

One of the pleasures involved in this project has been the chance to get to know Douglas Mitchell at University of Chicago Press and be on the receiving end of his considerable knowledge, experience, and insight. What he doesn't know about publishing isn't worth bothering with. He navigates around in the fields of history and the social sciences with impressive ease. He knows a lot about the history of jazz specifically and music in general. Besides that he plays drums in a jazz group. All of this made finishing up and discussing submission of my manuscript with him enjoyable rather than an onerous chore. New on the job at the University of Chicago Press, Kyle Adam Wagner handled early procedures and production matters with calmness and skillfully deflected my querulousness about any number of matters. It has been a pleasure and privilege to work with both. Yvonne Zipter was more tolerant than I deserved about my struggles with formatting and capitalization. I thank her for her eagle eye(s).

It seems like this time, even more than earlier, my wife Charlotte Fallenius has helped me hold things together as the deadline for submission loomed, not to mention months—oops: years—of patience and unfailing support while I slogged away at it. She also read and proofed some of the chapters. In the process, she caught various mistakes that made me blush when she found them. Through it all, she kept in touch with the crucial question: "how's it going?" For once, the cliché is true—I couldn't have done it without her.

I want to dedicate this book to two people who have read, criticized, and improved much of what I've written since my first book was published in 1972. I have known Steve Whitfield since 1964. If we had had saved our correspondence over the years, we could have filled several volumes by now. He's been a constant and always considerate friend, as good a reader of manuscripts and works in progress as can be imagined. I met Larry Friedman in Washington, DC, when I lived on Capitol Hill in the early 1970s and he was spending a year researching at the Library of Congress. Two more different reader-critics are hard to imagine, but Steve's close focus and exacting readings have always complemented Larry's wide-ranging questions, valuable hunches, and side observations that turn out to be right on the mark. Larry's capacity for archival research is so great that I didn't even try to match him (how's that for an excuse?), but I keep his example in mind. The only figure I can imagine matching Steve for argumentative power is Sidney Hook or Dwight Macdonald. All that aside, I do want to thank them for their generosity, their intelligence, and, above all, their friendship over the years.

NOTES

Introduction

1. Christian Wiese, *The Life and Thought of Hans Jonas: Jewish Dimensions* (Waltham, MA: Brandeis University Press, 2007), 179–80.

2. Hannah Arendt, "Ideology and Terror," in *The Origins of Totalitarianism*, 2nd ed. (Cleveland: Meridian Books, 1958), 478–79.

3. Harold Rosenberg, *The Tradition of the New* (1959; repr., New York: McGraw-Hill, 1965); J. G. A. Pocock, *The Machiavellian Moment: Florentine Political Thought and the Atlantic Republican Tradition* (Princeton, NJ: Princeton University Press, 1975); and James Ceaser, *Reconstructing America: The Symbol of America in Modern Thought* (New Haven, CT: Yale University Press, 1997).

4. Peter Baehr, *Hannah Arendt, Totalitarianism, and the Social Sciences* (Stanford, CA: Stanford University Press, 2010).

5. Marshall Berman, review of *Life History and the Historical Moment*, by Erik Erikson, *New York Times-on-the-Web*, March 30, 1975, 1, http://www.nytimes.com/books/99/08/22/specials/erikson-history.html.

6. Hannah Arendt to Karl Jaspers, letter of December 23, 1960, in *Hannah Arendt/ Karl Jaspers Briefwechsel, 1926–1969*, ed. Lotte Köhler and Hans Saner (Munich: Piper, 1985), 453. Arendt's words in German are: "angelsächsisch angesteckt."

7. Still the best source of biographical information on Arendt is Elisabeth Young-Bruehl, *Hannah Arendt: For Love of the World* (New Haven, CT: Yale University Press, 1982), 91. Four excellent recent works that deal with the transatlantic reception of ideas are Jennifer Ratner-Rosenhagen, *American Nietzsche: A History of an Icon and His Ideas*

(Chicago: University of Chicago Press, 2012); Martin Woessner, *Heidegger in America* (New York: Cambridge University Press, 2011), Joshua Derman, *Max Weber in Politics and Social Thought* (Cambridge: Cambridge University Press, 2012); and Lawrence A. Scaff, *Max Weber in America* (Princeton, NJ: Princeton University Press, 2011).

8. Susan J. Matt, *Homesickness: An American History* (New York: Oxford University Press, 2010), emphasizes that newcomers to the New World have often mourned a lost world of familiarity, stability, and warmth.

9. For Arendt as a refugee not a survivor, see Gabriel Motzkin, "Hannah Arendt: Von ethnischer Minderheit zu universeller Humanität," in *Hannah Arendt Revisited: "Eichmann in Jerusalem" und die Folgen,* ed. Gary Smith (Frankfurt am Main: Edition Suhrkamp, 2000), 188–89. For an exploration of the "contrapuntal" concepts of exile and nation (or "home"), see Edward W. Said, "Reflections on Exile," in *"Reflections on Exile" and Other Essays* (Cambridge, MA: Harvard University Press, 2000), 173–86; and James Wood "On Not Going Home," *London Review of Books,* vol. 36, no. 4 (February 20, 2014), 3–8. See Young-Bruehl, *Hannah Arendt,* 102–8, for Arendt's last weeks in Berlin, and 152–59, for the details of how she, Blücher, and her mother escaped from France. Crucial here was the work of Varian Frye (1907–67), who helped numerous European intellectuals and artists, particularly in France, escape the Nazis during the war. See Andy Marino, *American Pimpernel* (London: Arrow Books, 2000).

10. Arendt, "What Remains? The Language Remains": A Conversation with Günter Gaus," in *Essays in Understanding, 1930–1954* (New York: Harcourt Brace, 1994), 1–23.

11. Young-Bruehl, *Hannah Arendt,* xiv.

12. Stanley Cavell, *The Senses of Walden,* expanded and enlarged ed. (San Francisco: North Point Press, 1982), 33.

13. Arendt to Jaspers, letter of January 28, 1949, in *Briefwechsel,* 165.

14. Jochen Kölsch, "Denken und Leidenschaft—Hannah Arendt: Ein Portrait," 2006, 66 minutes, https://www.youtube.com/watch?v=HDKHevKaiR8, 11:06–11:42.

15. For Arendt on the South, see "Reflections on Little Rock," *Dissent* 6, no. 1 (Winter 1959): 46; Simone de Beauvoir, *America Day by Day,* trans. Carol Cosman (London: Victor Gollancz, 1998). Albert Camus spent three months in the spring of 1946 in New England, New York, and Washington, DC. See Camus, *American Journals* (London: Abacus, 1990).

16. See Scaff, *Max Weber in America,* chap. 9.

17. Seyla Benhabib, *The Reluctant Modernism of Hannah Arendt* (Thousand Oaks, CA: Sage, 1996). Of course there is a kind of modernist sensibility that is organized around ambivalence to modernity.

18. Catherine Zuckert and Michael Zuckert, *The Truth about Leo Strauss: Political Philosophy and American Democracy* (Chicago: University of Chicago Press, 2006), 58.

19. See Arendt, "The Crisis in Culture: Its Social and Its Political Significance," in *Between Past and Future: Eight Exercises in Political Thought,* introduction by Jerome Kohn (New York: Penguin, 2006), 196–204.

20. Arendt, "Reflections on Little Rock," 45–55.

21. See Barbara Hahn and Marie Luise Knott, *Von den Dichtern erwarten wir Wahrheit* (Berlin: Matthes & Seitz, 2006), 76. This valuable book of documents and commentary also contains letters to and from writers such as Robert Lowell, William Meredith, Richard Howard, Elizabeth Sewell, Elizabeth Bishop, and Theodore Weiss, among others.

22. George Kateb, "The Questionable Influences of Arendt (and Strauss)," in *Hannah Arendt and Leo Strauss: German Émigrés and American Political Thought after World War II*, ed. P. G. Kielmansegg, H. Mewes, and E. Glaser-Schmidt (Washington, DC: German Historical Institute; New York: Cambridge University Press, 1997), 29–58, and "Wildness and Conscience," in *Patriotism and Other Mistakes* (New Haven, CT: Yale University Press, 2006), 245–71. Robert D. Richardson, *Henry Thoreau: A Life of the Mind* (Berkeley: University of California Press, 1986), makes much of the theme of wildness in Thoreau's thought.

23. Kateb, "Wildness and Conscience," 247. It is manifested in what Garry Wills has called "anti-governmentalism" in *A Necessary Evil: A History of American Distrust of Government* (New York: Simon and Schuster, 1999).

24. See Kateb, "The Questionable Influence of Arendt," 32–34.

25. See George Kateb, "Arendt and Representative Democracy," *Salmagundi* 60 (Spring–Summer 1983): 20–59, for a thorough exploration of the participatory vs. representative democracy issue. See Arendt, "Civil Disobedience," in *Crises of the Republic* (New York: Harcourt Brace Jovanovich, 1972),49–102. The German version of Arendt's pronouncement is: "Keiner hat das Recht zu gehorchen."

26. Kateb, "The Questionable Influence of Arendt," 36.

27. Hannah Arendt to David Riesman, letters of June 13 and June 27, 1949, Hannah Arendt Papers, Library of Congress, Correspondence.

28. Arendt, *Denktagebuch*, ed. Ursula Ludz and Ingeborg Nordmann, 2 vols. (Munich: Piper, 2002), 2:734. In the entries in this period, Hegel, Heidegger, and Nietzsche are often cited and commented on.

29. See Arendt on solitude in "Ideology and Terror" (n. 2 above, this chap.). Arendt's exploration of these matters is found in "Thinking and Moral Considerations," *Social Research* 38, no. 3 (Fall 1971): 417–46, and as part of pt. 1 ("Thinking") of Arendt, *The Life of the Mind* (New York: Harcourt Brace Jovanovich, 1978).

30. Arendt, "Emerson Address," in *Reflections on Literature and Culture*, ed. and intro. by Susannah Young-Ah Gottlieb (Stanford, CA: Stanford University Press, 2007), 282–84. Arendt's library at Bard College contains one Emerson volume, *Selected Prose and Poetry*, ed. Reginald L. Cook (New York: Rinehart, 1958). Inside the back cover Arendt noted page numbers of interest. One refers to 473, which has Emerson praising Montaigne, September 29, 1838, and another entry on 479 also praises Montaigne, March 1843.

31. Young-Bruehl, *Hannah Arendt* (n. 7 above, this chap.), 538.

32. Ibid., 187–91.

33. Tony Kushner, *The Holocaust and the Liberal Imagination: A Social and Cultural History* (London: Wiley-Blackwell, 1994). See Peter Watson, *The German Mind: Europe's Third Renaissance, the Second Scientific Revolution and the Twentieth Century* (London: Simon and Schuster, 2010), 742; see, esp., 756, for the claim that German refugees were happier in the United Kingdom than the United States.

34. Irving Howe, *A Margin of Hope: An Intellectual Biography* (New York: Harcourt Brace Jovanovich, 1982), 344; Harold Rosenberg, "Death in the Wilderness," in *Tradition of the New* (n. 3 above, this chap.), 249; and Howe, "The New York Intellectuals: A Chronicle and a Critique," *Commentary* (October 1968).

35. William Barrett, *The Truants: Adventures among the Intellectuals* (Garden City, NY: Anchor Press, 1982), 102 — Schwartz is quoted at 103; Howe, *Margin of Hope*, 270; Alfred Kazin, *A Lifetime Burning in Every Moment: From the Journals of Alfred Kazin* (New York: Harper Collins, 1997), 105, and *New York Jew* (New York: Alfred Knopf, 1978), 196.

36. Hahn and Knott, *Von den Dichtern* (n. 21 above, this chap.),127.

37. David Laskin, *Partisans: Marriage, Politics, and Betrayal among the New York Intellectuals* (New York: Simon and Schuster, 2000), 147.

38. *Alfred Kazin's Journals*, edited and selected by Richard H. Cook (New Haven, CT: Yale University Press, 2011), 319 (entry dated 1/18/1964), 413 (entry dated 11/27/1970).

39. Kazin, *New York Jew*, 199; Saul Bellow, *Letters*, ed. by Benjamin Taylor (New York: Viking Press, 2010), 355.

40. Bellow, *Letters*, 391.

41. Kazin, *Lifetime Burning*, 109.

42. Arendt, "What Remains?" (n. 10 above, this chap.), 12.

43. Ibid., 15. See also Claudia Roth Pierpont, "Hearts and Minds/Hannah Arendt and Mary McCarthy," in *Passionate Minds: Women Rewriting the World* (New York: Vintage, 2001), 251–87; and Daryl Pinckney, "The Ethics of Admiration: Arendt, McCarthy, Hardwick, Sontag," *Threepenny Review* (Fall 2013), http://www.three penny review.com/samples/pinckney_f13.html.

44. This happened with Alfred Kazin and his wife, Ann Burstein, whom Arendt simply ignored at one public occasion and strode off with Kazin (Richard Cook, *Alfred Kazin: A Biography* [New Haven, CT: Yale University Press, 2007], 186–87). Randall Jarrell's wife Mary seems to have basically said to her husband, "me or her." Laskin, *Partisans*, 160.

45. See Norman Podhoretz, *Ex-Friends: Falling Out with Allen Ginsberg, Lionel and Diana Trilling, Lillian Hellman, Hannah Arendt and Norman Mailer* (New York: The Free Press, 1999), 139–77. Despite Podhoretz's efforts to be obnoxious about his talent for losing friends, his chapter on Arendt is actually quite moving—self-reflective on his part and observant about her.

46. Nathan Glazer, "Hannah Arendt's America," *Commentary* 60, no. 3 (September 1975): 61–67.

47. Stephen Salkever, "On Course: Bryn Mawr Courses and Their Reading Lists," 2, http://www.brynmawr.edu/alumnae/bulletin/crssu02.htm; Michael Hereth, cited in Peter Baehr, ed., "Debating Totalitarianism: An Exchange of Letters between Hannah Arendt and Eric Voegelin," *History and Theory* 51 (October 2012): 366.

48. Young-Bruehl, *Hannah Arendt* (n. 7 above, this chap.), 33, 36; Kazin, *New York Jew*, 195. Arendt also referred to the fact that she had her own "kind of melancholy" (Jochen Kölsch, "Hannah Arendt: Ein Portrait" [n. 14 above, this chap.], 8:46–8:48).

49. See Baehr, ed., "Debating Totalitarianism," 364–80.

50. Kazin, *Lifetime Burning*, 111, and *New York Jew*, 196. See Margareta von Trotta, "Hannah Arendt" (2012), http://zeitgeistfilms.com/hannaharendt/index.html. I will analyze von Trotta's film in the conclusion.

51. Richard Sennett, *The Conscience of the Eye: The Design and Social Life of Cities* (London: Faber and Faber, 1990), 136.

52. Arendt, *Denktagebuch*, 2:770–71. Besides the obligatory slap at psychoanalysis (she intends us to think of free association), Arendt also suggests that English philosophy finds the whole matter of "thinking a matter through . . . alien" and is more interested in establishing associations.

53. In philosophical terms, Seyla Benhabib refers to Arendt's propensity for making distinctions and thinking in terms of spheres or modes as her "phenomenological essentialism" (*Reluctant Modernism of Hannah Arendt* [n. 17 above, this chap.], 123–25).

Chapter 1

1. See Dwight Macdonald, "The Responsibility of Peoples," in *Memoirs of a Revolutionist* (Cleveland: Meridian Books, 1958), 33–72. The reference to Arendt is on page 60. The essay was originally published in *Politics* 2 (March 1945), 82–93. See *Politics: Vols. 1–6, 1944–1949*, introduction by Hannah Arendt, preface by Dwight Macdonald (New York: Greenwood Reprint Corporation, 1968). Arendt's "Organized Guilt and University Responsibility" (1945) is collected in *Essays in Understanding, 1930–1954*, ed. Jerome Kohn (New York: Harcourt Brace, 1994), 121–32, as is its companion piece "Approaches to the 'German Problem'" (1945), 106–21. The two pieces of early 1945 laid the basis of their friendship rather than being the result of it.

2. Stanley Milgram, *Obedience to Authority: An Experimental View* (1974; repr., New York: Harper Perennial Modern Classics, 2009) was strongly influenced by Arendt's *Eichmann in Jerusalem: A Report on the Banality of Evil*, 2nd ed. (New York: Viking Compass, 1965).

3. Macdonald, "Responsibility of Peoples," 61.

4. For the place of *Politics* and the "Responsibility" essay in Macdonald's career, see Richard King, *The Party of Eros: Radical Social Thought and the Realm of Freedom* (Chapel

Hill: University of North Carolina Press, 1972), 31–43; Stephen J. Whitfield, "The Responsibility of Peoples," in *A Critical American: The Politics of Dwight Macdonald* (Hamden, CT: Archon, 1984), 53–64; Robert B. Westbrook, "The Responsibility of Peoples: Dwight Macdonald and the Holocaust." *Why We Fought: Forging American Obligations in World War II* (Washington, DC: Smithsonian Books, 2004), 93–124. See Michael Wreszin, *A Rebel in Defense of Tradition: The Life and Politics of Dwight Macdonald* (New York: Basic Books, 1995); and Gregory D. Summer, *Dwight Macdonald and the "Politics" Circle: The Challenge of Cosmopolitan Democracy* (Ithaca, NY: Cornell University Press, 1996), for overviews of Macdonald's life and thought. Recently, Clive Bush, *The Century's Midnight: Dissenting European and American Writers in the Era of the Second World War* (Oxford: Peter Lang, 2010), 104–97, contains a long section devoted to Macdonald and the years of *Politics*.

5. For discussion of these ethical debates, see Christopher Phelps, *Young Sidney Hook: Marxist and Pragmatist* (Ithaca, NY: Cornell University Press, 1997); and Anthony Hutchison, *Writing the Republic: Liberalism and Morality in American Political Fiction* (New York: Columbia University Press, 2007), 72–75; see also Randolph Bourne, *War and the Intellectuals*, ed. Carl Resek (New York: Harper Torchbooks, 1964); Reinhold Niebuhr, *The Children of Light and the Children of Darkness: A Vindication of Democracy and a Critique of Its Traditional Defense* (New York: Charles Scribner's Sons, 1944); and Edward A. Purcell Jr., *The Crisis of Democratic Theory: Scientific Naturalism and the Problem of Value* (Lexington: University of Kentucky Press, 1973).

6. Thanks to Daniel Geary for this point and several other crucial ones in this chapter.

7. See Arendt, *The Jewish Writings*, ed. Jerome Kohn and Ron H. Feldman (New York: Schocken Books, 2007), 134–240. Her writings on this topic were published in *Aufbau*, a Jewish publication.

8. Max Weber, "Politics as a Vocation" (1919), in *From Max Weber: Essays in Sociology*, ed. Hans Gerth and C. Wright Mills (New York: Galaxy Books, 1958), 77–128. See Joshua Derman, *Max Weber in Politics and Social Thought: From Charisma to Canonization* (Cambridge: Cambridge University Press, 2012), esp. chaps. 2 and 3, for lucid discussions of these issues.

9. Peter Baehr, "The Grammar of Prudence: Arendt, Jaspers, and the Appraisal of Max Weber," in *Hannah Arendt in Jerusalem*, ed. Steven E. Aschheim (Berkeley: University of California Press, 2001), 306–24.

10. On "principles" vs. "rules," see Susan Neiman's *Moral Clarity: A Guide for Grown-Up Idealists* (London: Bodley Head, 2009), 214, for a stimulating discussion that emphasizes the flexibility in Kantian ethics. See Hannah Arendt, *Eichmann in Jerusalem*, and "Thinking and Moral Considerations" (1971), in *Responsibility and Judgment* (New York: Schocken, 2003), 159–89.

11. Arendt, "Some Questions . . . ," in *Responsibility and Judgment* (New York: Schocken, 2003), 49–147. See also Ronald Beiner, ed., *Hannah Arendt: Lectures on Kant's*

Political Philosophy (1982; repr., Chicago: University of Chicago Press, 1989). Though the unfinished third section of her *The Life of the Mind* was to be devoted to judging, the rudiments of the concept of judgment were in place by the mid-1960s.

12. Elisabeth Young-Bruehl, *Hannah Arendt: For Love of the World*, 2nd ed. (New Haven, CT: Yale University Press), xxxi.

13. Elisabeth Young-Bruehl and Jerome Kohn, "Truth, Lies, and Politics: A Conversation," *Social Research* 74, no. 4 (Winter 2007): 1046–48. More of the works she assigned are listed in Wolfgang Heuer, "'Imagination is the prerequisite of understanding' (Arendt): The Bridge between Thinking and Judging," in *Hannah Arendt: Filosofia e Totalitarismo*, ed. Francesco Fistetti and Francesca R. Recchia Luciani (Genoa: Il melangolo, 2007), esp. 1–4.

14. See Susan Neiman, *Evil in Modern Thought* (Princeton, NJ: Princeton University Press, 2002, and "Theodicy in Jerusalem," in *Hannah Arendt in Jerusalem*, ed. Steven E. Aschheim (Berkeley: University of California Press, 2001), 65–90.

15. I am, of course, alluding here to Raul Hilberg's *Perpetrators, Victims, Bystanders* (London: Lime Tree Press, 1993).

16. Macdonald, "Responsibility of Peoples" (n. 1 above, this chap.), 36–43. In a long 1953 footnote, he observes with typical candor that he had failed to distinguish explicitly between labor and extermination camps (42–43).

17. Ibid., 67.

18. Dwight Macdonald, "Two Footnotes to History," in *Memoirs* (n. 1 above, this chap.), 104; Arendt, *The Origins of Totalitarianism*, 2nd ed. (Cleveland: Meridian Books, 1958), 459; Young-Bruehl, *Hannah Arendt*, 329. For Arendt's inner division on this issue, see Alan W. Norrie, "Justice on the Slaughter Bench: The Problem of War Guilt in Hannah Arendt and Karl Jaspers," *New Criminal Law Review* 11, no. 2 (Spring 2008): 187–231.

19. Arendt, "Approaches to the 'German Problem,'" in *Essays in Understanding*, 107, 109, 110.

20. Ibid., 111.

21. Ibid., 116–20.

22. Whitfield, *Critical American* (n. 4 above, this chap.), 58.

23. Macdonald, "Responsibility of Peoples" (n. 1 above, this chap.), 42.

24. Ibid., 41.

25. Ibid., 37, 39.

26. Westbrook, "Responsibility of Peoples" (n. 4 above, this chap.), 116–23.

27. Ibid., 43.

28. Arendt, *Origins* (n. 18 above, this chap.), 456.

29. Dwight Macdonald, "Reply to Readers," *Politics* 2 (July 1945): 204. This issue of *Politics* included six pages of letters about his essay "Responsibility of Peoples," and Macdonald's response to them (203–9). The May 1945 issue of *Politics* (vol. 2, no. 5) had already included a long letter from Guenter Reimann and Macdonald's reply (154–56).

30. The following was first printed in the daily newspaper *New York PM*, Sunday, November 12, 1944, and reprinted in "Organized Guilt" (n. 1 above, this chap.), 127:

Q. Did you kill people in the camp? A. Yes.

Q. Did you poison them with gas? A. Yes.

Q. Did you bury them alive? A. It sometimes happened.

Q. Were the victims picked from all over Europe? A. I suppose so.

Q. Did you personally help kill people? A. Absolutely not. I was only paymaster in the camp.

Q. What did you think of what was going on? A. It was bad at first but we got used to it.

Q. Do you know the Russians will hang you? A. (Bursting into tears) Why should they? What have I done?

31. Arendt, "Organized Guilt," 121–24.

32. Macdonald, "Responsibility of Peoples,"59.

33. Arendt, "Organized Guilt,"124.

34. The initial response to "The Responsibility of Peoples" that Macdonald printed was from Guenter Reimann, who claimed that Macdonald had stressed German national character too much and the systemic and structural constraints too little in his analysis ("Letter from Guenter Reimann," *Politics* 2, no. 5[May 1945], 154–55).

35. Arendt, "Organized Guilt," 130.

36. Ibid., 129. I will return to this in the next chapter.

37. Ibid., 127. Arendt's strong sense of the ironic here should be kept in mind.

38. Ibid., 122–24.

39. Macdonald, "Responsibility of Peoples," 59; Arendt, "Organized Guilt," 126.

40. Arendt, "Organized Guilt," 125.

41. Ibid., 126.

42. Arendt, "Auschwitz on Trial," in *Responsibility and Judgment* (n. 10 above, this chap.), 248–49, and "Organized Guilt," 124.

43. "Organized Guilt," 126.

44. Ibid., 131–32. The only philosophical characterization of guilt by Arendt comes in her long piece on existentialism that appeared in 1946. In discussing Kierkegaard, she wrote of his idea of guilt "as the category of all human activity, which is doomed to failure not because of the world but by its own nature, in that I always take on responsibilities whose implications I cannot foresee, and in that, by the decisions I make, I am always obliged to neglect something else. Guilt thus becomes the mode by which I become real, by which I entangle myself in reality." This suggests that guilt arises from a lack, rather than from an active intention ("What Is Existential Philosophy?" in *Essays in Understanding* [n. 1 above, this chap.], 175).

45. Macdonald to Guenter Reimann, and Macdonald to Louis Clair (Lewis Coser)—both in *Politics* 2, no. 5 (May 1945): 155 and 206–7, respectively.

46. Macdonald, "Responsibility of Peoples," 45.

47. Karl Jaspers, *The Question of German Guilt* (1947; repr., New York: Capricorn Books, 1961), and "Die Schuldfrage" (1946), in *Lebensfragen der deutschen Politik* (Munich: Deutscher Taschenbuch Verlag, 1963), 36–114. Anson Rabinbach, "The German as Pariah: Karl Jaspers's *The Question of German Guilt*," in *In the Shadow of Catastrophe: German Intellectuals between Apocalypse and Enlightenment* (Berkeley: University of California Press, 1997), 129–65, is indispensable, while Alan W. Norrie, "Justice on the Slaughter Bench: The Problem of War Guilt in Arendt and Jaspers," *New Criminal Law Review* 11, no. 2 (2008): 187–231, is also valuable.

48. Jaspers, *Question of German Guilt*, 31–33.

49. Ibid., 60–61.

50. Macdonald, "Responsibility of Peoples" (n. 1 above, this chap.), 45–47.

51. Arendt, "Collective Responsibility," in *Responsibility and Judgment*, 149.

52. Ibid., 64–65.

53. Dwight Macdonald, "The Bomb," *Politics* 2, no. 9 (September 1945), 257–60.

54. Noam Chomsky, "The Responsibility of Intellectuals," in *American Power and the New Mandarins* (London: Penguin, 1969), 256, 284.

55. For a recent history of something like this tradition but not quite the same, see Lewis Perry, *Civil Disobedience: An American Tradition* (New Haven, CT: Yale University Press, 2013). The relationship of *Politics* to the New Left, including the examples of Chomsky and Lynd, is touched on in Whitfield, *Critical American*, 113–19. For histories of the New Left, see James Miller *"Democracy Is in the Streets": From Port Huron to the Siege of Chicago* (Cambridge, MA: Harvard University Press, 1994); and Maurice Isserman, *If I Had a Hammer: The Death of the Old Left and the Birth of the New Left* (New York: Basic Books, 1987).

56. Arendt, "Thoughts on Politics and Revolution" and "Civil Disobedience" in *Crises of the Republic* (New York: Harcourt Brace Jovanovich, 1972), 203.

57. See Arendt, "What Is Existential Philosophy?" (1946–48), "French Existentialism" (1946), and "Concern with Politics in Recent European Philosophical Thought" (1954) in *Essays in Understanding*, 163–87, 188–93, and 428–47, respectively. The last essay was not published during Arendt's lifetime. I will return to it in a future chapter.

58. George Cotkin, *Existential America* (Baltimore, MD: Johns Hopkins University Press, 2003); and William Barrett, *Irrational Man* (New York: Doubleday, 1958). See also Martin Woessner, *Heidegger in America* (New York: Cambridge University Press, 2011), for a discussion of how Heidegger's work, in particular, came to America.

59. Albert Camus, "Neither Victims nor Executioners," trans. D. Macdonald and intro. by Waldo Frank from *Liberation* (February 1960) first appeared in *Combat* in the fall of 1946 and was published in *Politics* in July–August 1947. The other two articles Macdonald named were Bruno Bettelheim's "Behavior in Extreme Situations" and Simone Weil's "Iliad: The Poem of Force." Arendt used the Bettelheim piece in *Origins* and may have first seen it in *Politics*, though she didn't cite from the *Politics* version. See Dwight

Macdonald, "Publisher's Preface," in *Politics: v. 1-6; 1944–1949*, ed. Dwight Macdonald (Westport, CT: Greenwood Press, 1968), 5–7.

60. Arendt, "French Existentialism," 188–93. George Cotkin rightly points out Arendt's neglect of *Being and Nothingness* in his *Existential America* (Baltimore, MD: Johns Hopkins University Press, 2003), 138.

61. Arendt, "What Is Existential Philosophy?" 179, 164, 187.

62. Arendt's essay was a direct response to the paper by Joel Feinberg at the American Political Science Association meeting in December 1967, which makes it difficult to follow with ease. See Joel Feinberg, "Collective Responsibility," *Journal of Philosophy* 65, no. 21 (1968): 674–88; and Arendt, "Collective Responsibility," 147–58. As she wrote to Mary McCarthy, Arendt was frustrated by the "irrelevancies" of such an academic paper (quoted in Jerome Kohn, "A Note on the Text," in Arendt, *Responsibility and Judgment*, xxxiv).

63. Arendt, "Collective Responsibility," 147, 149, 150.

64. Ibid., 151–53.

65. I am using here the suggestion made by Roy Schafer in *A New Language of Psycho-analysis* (New Haven, CT: Yale University Press, 1976), about de-reifying psychoanalytic concepts.

Chapter 2

1. The fiftieth anniversary of *The Origins of Totalitarianism* in 2001 called forth conferences and special issues of journals. Of particular interest is Alfons Soellner, "Hannah Arendt's *The Origins of Totalitarianism* in Its Original Context," *European Journal of Political Research* 3, no. 2 (2004): 219–38. See also "Hannah Arendt's *The Origins of Totalitarianism*: Fifty Years Later," ed. Arien Mack and Jerome Kohn, special issue of *Social Research* 69, no. 2 (Summer 2002). More recently, Timothy Snyder's *Bloodlands: Europe between Hitler and Stalin* (London: Vintage, 2011), 329, still felt compelled to go back to *Origins* as a starting point for his considerations some sixty year later and Slavoj Zizek, *Did Somebody Say Totalitarianism? Five Interventions in the (Mis)use of a Notion* (London: Verso, 2002), saw Arendt as the main architect of the concept to which he so objected.

2. Wolfgang Heuer, "Ein schwieriger Dialog: Die Hannah Arendt-Rezeption in deutschsprachigen Raum," in *Hannah Arendt: Nach den Totalitarianismus*, ed. Daniel Ganz-fried (Hamburg: Sebastian Hefti, 1997), 24. Though Heuer makes this point in connection with Germany, it holds true broadly for America. See also Les K. Adler and Thomas G. Patterson, "'Red Fascism': The Merger of Nazi Germany and Soviet Russia in the American Image of Totalitarianism, 1930s–1950s," *American Historical Review* 75, no. 4 (April 1970): 1046–64. Actually, Arendt was not extensively discussed in this particular article.

3. Jeffrey C. Isaac, "Critics of Totalitarianism," in *Cambridge History of Twentieth Century Political Thought*, Terence Bull and Richard Bellamy (Cambridge: Cambridge University Press, 2003), 196–201.

4. See Samuel Moyn, *The Last Utopia: Human Rights in History* (Cambridge, MA: Belknap Harvard University Press, 2010), 164–66, for the observation about the misleading nature of the dichotomy of morality and politics. See chaps. 1 and 12 for Arendt's discussion of the distinction between morality and politics.

5. The vast majority of the biographical data about Arendt comes from Elisabeth Young-Bruehl, *Hannah Arendt: For Love of the World* (New Haven, CT: Yale University Press, 1982), 187–89.

6. Ibid., 250.

7. Alfred Kazin, *A Lifetime Burning in Every Moment* (New York: Harper Perennial, 1997), 128.

8. Young-Bruehl, *Hannah Arendt*, 251. She delivered a first draft version as a lecture November 1951 at Notre Dame. See Roy Tsao, "Arendt and the Modern State: Variations on Hegel in *The Origins of Totalitarianism*," *Review of Politics* 66, no.1 (Winter 2004): 105–36, for the intellectual background to this essay, including Hegel's influence. Arendt tended to make changes when she translated her work into German from English. See Eberhard Kessel, *Historische Zeitschrift* 1, no. 1 (February 1962): 140–42. Some of the excised material from "Concluding Remarks" in the first edition was reinserted into the main text of the 1958 edition, especially into the "Totalitarian Domination" section of chaps. 12 and 9 ("The Decline of the Nation State and the End of the Rights of Man").

9. See Tsao, "Arendt and the Modern State," for this point.

10. Robert Burrowes, "Totalitarianism: The Revised Standard Version," *World Politics* 21, no. 2 (January 1969): 280; Steven E. Aschheim, "Nazism, Culture and *The Origins of Totalitarianism*: Hannah Arendt and the Discourse of Evil," *New German Critique* 70 (Winter 1997): 119.

11. Stephen J. Whitfield, *Voices of Jacob, Hands of Esau: Jews in American Life and Thought* (Hamden, CT: Archon Books, 1984), 31, 33. See also Robert Westbrook, "The Responsibility of Peoples: Dwight Macdonald and the Holocaust," in *Why We Fought: Forging American Obligations in World War II* (Washington, DC: Smithsonian Books, 2004), 95–102.

12. Stephen J. Whitfield, "The Theme of Indivisibility in the Postwar Struggle against Prejudice," *Patterns of Prejudice* 48, no. 3 (2014): 223–47.

13. Peter Novick, *The Holocaust in American Life* (New York: Houghton Mifflin, 1999).

14. Will Herberg, *Protestant-Catholic-Jew* (New York: Doubleday, 1951); Mark Silk, "Notes on the Judaeo-Christian Tradition in American," *American Quarterly* 36, no. 1 (Spring 1984): 65–85; Matthew Frye Jacobson, *Whiteness of a Different Color* (Cambridge, MA: Harvard University Press, 1998).

15. D. G. Myers, "Annotated Bibliography of Holocaust Writing in American Jewish Magazines, 1945–1952," accessed July 5, 2010, http://www.english.tamu/edu/pers/fac/myers/annotated_bib.htm (page no longer available).

16. Hannah Arendt, *The Origins of Totalitarianism*, 2nd ed. (Cleveland: Meridian Books, 1958), 158–61.

17. Dirk Rupnow, "Racialized Historiography: Anti-Jewish Scholarship in the Third Reich," *Patterns of Prejudice* 42, no. 1 (February 2008): 39, 53.

18. Peter Staudenmaier, "Hannah Arendt's Analysis of Antisemitism in *The Origins of Totalitarianism*: A Critical Appraisal," *Patterns of Prejudice* 46, no. 2 (2012): 157–64. Staudenmaier confirmed a claim that Arendt depended too much on the work of a leading Nazi racial scientist, Walter Frank, and also used the work of Heinrich Paulus, an opponent of Jewish emancipation and an anti-Semite in the first half of the nineteenth century, in her analysis of the German scene. In a short piece just after the war, Arendt noted that Frank's work "showed a strong anti-Semitic bias before Hitler" but also "managed to cling to some remnants of scholarship" (Arendt, "The Image of Hell," in *Essays in Understanding*, 201–2).

19. Ibid., 170, 177.

20. Ibid., 170.

21. Ibid., 173. Philip Rieff, "The Theology of Politics" (1952), in *The Feeling Intellect: Selected Writings*, ed. Jonathan Imber (Chicago: University of Chicago Press, 1990), also makes this criticism of Arendt.

22. David Nirenberg, *Anti-Judaism: The History of a Way of Thinking* (London: Head of Zeus Ltd, 2013), esp. 461–72.

23. David Riesman, "The Path to Total Terror," *Commentary* 11, no. 4 (1951): 394–96. For an assortment of articles on the boomerang thesis, see Richard H. King and Dan Stone, eds., *Hannah Arendt and the Uses of History: Imperialism, Nation, Race, and Genocide* (New York: Berghahn Books, 2007).

24. Perpetual war with Native Americans, counterinsurgency fighting in the Philippines after the Spanish American War, and periodic intervention in the Caribbean and Central America were consistent with some of the patterns that marked European intervention in Africa.

25. Moyn, *Last Utopia* (n. 4 above, this chap.), chap. 3.

26. Arendt, *Origins* (n. 16 above, this chap.), 250–51.

27. Ibid., 316.

28. Ibid., 297.

29. The quote can be found at ibid., 296, 298. The German is either *ein Recht, Rechte zu haben*, or *Recht auf Rechte*. See Arendt, *Elemente Totaler Herrschaft* (Frankfurt am Main: Europaische Verlagsanstalt, 1958), 48, 51. This German edition included chap. 9 plus pt. 3 of the full 1958 edition.

30. Stephen J. Whitfield, *Into the Dark: Hannah Arendt and Totalitarianism* (Philadelphia: Temple University Press, 1980), 111–12, 285nn47–48).

31. In *On Revolution* (New York: Viking Compass, 1965), Arendt footnoted Edward S. Corwin, *The "Higher Law" Background of American Constitutional Law* (Indianapolis: Liberty Fund, 1955. Corwin's long essay was originally published in the *Harvard Law*

Review 42 (1928–29): 149–85, 365–409. But it does not appear in footnotes in *Origins*. In a 1951 entry in her *Denktagebuch*, ed. Ursula Ludz and Ingeborg Nordmann, 2 vols. (Munich: Piper, 2002), Arendt wrote: "The fact of the Constitution, the establishing of the highest law, must be protected against all claims to domination—whether of the single, the few or the many. Only with the Constitution was a beginning fixed, for the first time without violence [*Gewalt*], without ruling and being ruled" (2:130–31).

32. Richard H. King, *Civil Rights and the Idea of Freedom* (New York: Oxford University Press, 1992), 103, 236n49. It is not clear whether Martin Luther King Jr. had read Arendt, but perhaps one of his speech writers, such as Harris Wofford, had picked up the phrase from the Pollak article or had read it in *Origins*. The Montgomery speech was of course the same year as Pollak's article in *Yale Law Review*.

33. Arendt, *Origins*, 269.

34. Arendt, *Origins*, 292, 293. Samuel Moyn has made clear in *The Last Utopia* that, until the late 1970s, human rights were understood as roughly equivalent to the group right to self-determination not the protection of individual rights by international treaties and authorities.

35. Christoph Menke, "The 'Aporias of Human Rights' and the 'One Human Right': Regarding the Coherence of Hannah Arendt's Argument," *Social Research* 74, no. 3 (Fall 2007): 752, 753, 755. For the point about the two functions of the state, see Tsao, "Arendt and the Modern State," 105–6. More recently, Seyla Benhabib has suggested that the "capacity for self-questioning is also the source of one's freedom," a distinctly Heideggerian reading of the passage. ("From the 'Right to Have Rights' to the 'Critique of Humanitarian Reason': Against the Cynical Turn in Human Rights Discourse," lecture, New School for Social Research, April 10, 2014, 7).

36. Arendt, *Origins*, 291. The German here is: "dass seine Meinungen Gewicht haben und seine Handlungen von Belang sind."

37. Moyn, *The Last Utopia*, 12–13.

38. Arendt, *Origins*, 465.

39. Rieff, "Theology of Politics" (n. 21 above, this chap.), 88; Arendt, *Origins*, 467.

40. For this and other points, Jan Klabbers, "Possible Islands of Predictability: The Legal Thought of Hannah Arendt," is invaluable (www.helsinki.fi/eci/Publications/Klabbers/JKHannah_Arendt.pdf).

41. Arendt, *Origins*, 463–64.

42. Kafka's "In the Penal Colony" (*Die Strafcolonie*) ends with the officer's crime and his sentence etched directly into his flesh with mechanized knives.

43. Arendt, *Origins*, 465. The English "iron band" echoes the translation of Max Weber's "iron cage," but the German versions—*das eiserne Band* and *stahlhartes Gehäuse*—don't quite.

44. See Abbott Gleason, *Totalitarianism: The Inner History of the Cold War* (New York: Oxford University Press, 1995). Arendt saw ideology as a "principle" analogous to

the way that Montesquieu thought each form of government was guided by a principle, e.g., "honor" is the principle of a monarchical regime.

45. The concern with ideology was, says Seymour Martin Lipset, expressed in the title of Edward Shils report on the September 1955 Congress of Cultural Freedom meeting in Milan. Neither Lipset's nor Bell's piece on ideology was presented at Milan. Basic to the debate are Arendt, "Ideology and Terror," in *The Origins of Totalitarianism* (1958), 460–79; and Daniel Bell, *The End of Ideology and the Exhaustion of Political Ideas in the 1950s* (Glencoe, IL: Free Press, 1960), 369–75 (a new edition of *The End of Ideology* [Cambridge, MA: Harvard University Press, 2000] includes a new introductory essay, "The Resumption of History in the New Century," xi–xxviii, and a new epilogue, "Afterword 1988: *The End of Ideology* Revisited," 409–47); Seymour M. Lipset, "The End of Ideology?" in *Political Man: The Social Bases of Politics* (1960; repr., Garden City, NY: Doubleday Anchor, 1963), 439–56; and George Lichtheim, *"The Concept of Ideology" and Other Essays* (New York: Vintage, 1967), 3–46.

46. Lichtheim, "The Concept of Ideology," in *"Concept of Ideology" and Other Essays*, 31. Bell and Arendt were generally on good terms, but Arendt and Lichtheim had a run-in over whether *Commentary* would print her "Reflections on Little Rock" in 1958. See chapter 8.

47. Bell, "The End of Ideology in the West," in *End of Ideology*, 370–71. The title of Richard Weaver's *Ideas Have Consequences* (Chicago: University of Chicago Press, 1948) reflects this general understanding of ideology. See also Louis Menand, *The Metaphysical Club* (New York: Farrar, Straus, Giroux, 2001), for this idea.

48. Arendt, *Origins*, 470.

49. See, e.g., H. Stuart Hughes, *The Sea Change: The Migration of Social Thought, 1930–1965* (New York: Harper and Row, 1975), 123, and, also, "Historical Sources of Totalitarianism," *Nation*, May 24, 1951, 281. Hughes's original review of *Origins* was much more favorable than his discussion of Arendt is in *The Sea Change*. See also Carl J. Friedrich, ed., *Totalitarianism* (1954; repr., New York: Universal Library, 1964), which is a collection of papers from a Harvard conference in 1953 plus question and answer sessions; Arendt attended and participated often in the discussions of the papers delivered at the conference.

50. Les K. Adler and Thomas G. Paterson, "Red Fascism" (n. 2 above, this chap.), 1046.

51. See, e.g., Niles Gilman, "Modernization Theory: The Highest Stage of American Intellectual History," in *Staging Growth: Modernization, Development, and the Global Cold War*, ed. David Engerman (Amherst: University of Massachusetts Press, 2003), 47–80.

52. Ibid., 57–60.

53. Thomas T. Cook, review of *Origins of Totalitarianism*, by Hannah Arendt, *Political Science Quarterly* 66, no. 2 (June 1951): 290.

54. Raymond Aron, "The Essence of Totalitarianism according to Hannah Arendt," *Partisan Review* 60, no. 3 (1993): 366–77. Aron's review originally appeared in the French journal *Critique* in 1954. Peter Baehr, *Hannah Arendt, Totalitarianism, and the Social Sciences* (Stanford, CA: Stanford University Press, 2010), 62–92, is particularly valuable as an analysis of Aron's position. Aron was something of an expert on the Soviet Union but not Nazi Germany, the reverse of the case with Arendt.

55. Herbert Marcuse, *Soviet Marxism: A Critical Analysis* (New York: Vintage 1961), xiv, 250.

56. Young-Bruehl, *Hannah Arendt*, 406–12,

57. Ibid., 411.

58. Hughes, *Sea Change*, 124. This is the case despite the fact that Aron had done much to bring German thought to French intellectual life in the interwar years. See Baehr, *Hannah Arendt*, 62–64.

59. Aron, "Essence of Totalitarianism," 373, 370.

60. Hughes, "Historical Sources of Totalitarianism," 281–82.

61. Hughes, *Sea Change*, 123–34.

62. Arendt was well enough acquainted with various Marxists to know that they came in a wide variety of shapes and sizes. Her second husband, Heinrich, was a Marxist until well into the 1930s and three of her best essays are on Bertolt Brecht, Walter Benjamin, and Rosa Luxemburg.

63. Burrowes, "Totalitarianism: The Revised Standard Version" (n. 10 above, this chap.), 289. This article was typical of the postwar emphasis in political science on comparative politics and empirical political theory.

64. Arendt, "Reply to Eric Voegelin," in *Essays in Understanding, 1930–1954* (New York: Harcourt, Brace and Company, 1994), 404.

65. Burrowes, "Totalitarianism: The Revised Standard Version," 279.

66. David Riesman, "Some Observations on the Limits of Totalitarianism," in *"Abundance for What?" and Other Essays* (Garden City, NY: Doubleday Anchor, 1965), 77, 84; and Peter Baehr, *Hannah Arendt*, 35–61.

67. Riesman, "Some Observations," 77.

68. Bettelheim's original piece was "Individual and Mass Behavior in Extreme Situations," *Journal of Abnormal and Social Psychology* 38, no. 4 (October 1943): 417–52, but it was later reshaped for inclusion in his *The Informed Heart: Autonomy in a Mass Age* (New York: Free Press,1960). Terence Des Pres, *The Survivor: An Anatomy of Life in the Death Camps* (New York: Oxford University Press, 1980) was a riposte to Bettelheim's pessimism about the possibilities of resistance and was quite similar to Riesman's discussions of resistance in the camps.

69. *Origins*, 437–59. See also Michel Foucault's idea of "bio-politics" as well as Giorgio Agamben's *Homo Sacer: Sovereign Power and Bare Life*, trans. Daniel Heller-Roazen (Stanford, CA: Stanford University Press, 1998).

70. Riesman, "Some Observations," 81.

71. Ibid., 86.

72. Besides the Eichmann book, see Arendt, "The Destruction of Six Million" (1964), in *The Jewish Writings*, ed. J. Kohn and R. H. Feldman (New York: Schocken Books, 2007), 494–95.

73. Arendt, *Origins*, 458.

74. Eric Voegelin, "The Origins of Totalitarianism" (1953), in *Published Essays, 1953–1965*, vol. 11 of *The Collected Works of Eric Voegelin*, ed. Ellis Sandoz (Columbia: University of Missouri Press, 2000), 21. More recently, see Peter Baehr, "Debating Totalitarianism: An Exchange of Letters between Eric Voegelin and Hannah Arendt," trans. Gordon C. Wells, *History and Theory* 51, no. 3 (2012): 364–80.

75. Voegelin, "Origins of Totalitarianism," 21.

76. Arendt, "A Reply to Eric Voegelin" (1953), in *Essays in Understanding*, 405.

77. Ibid. See Arendt, *Origins*, 158n3, for her mention of the "history of ideas" approach.

78. Arendt, "A Reply to Eric Voegelin," 408.

79. Rieff, "The Theology of Politics" (n. 21 above, this chap.), 87. Arendt actually distinguished between the idea that "everything is possible" and the idea that "everything is permitted." See *Origins*, 440.

80. Arendt, *Origins*, 459.

81. Herman Melville, *Billy Budd* (New York: Signet, 1961), 37.

82. Hannah Arendt to Karl Jaspers, letter of March 4, 1951, in *Briefwechsel, 1926–1969*, ed. Lotte Köhler and Hans Saner (Munich: Piper, 1987), 202–3. See also Richard J. Bernstein, *Radical Evil: A Philosophical Investigation* (Cambridge: Polity Press, 2002); and Susan Neiman, *Evil in Modern Thought: An Alternative History of Philosophy* (Princeton, NJ: Princeton University Press, 2002).

83. For the unpublished discussion of Kant and Montesquieu's part in her developing republicanism, see Arendt, "On the Nature of Totalitarianism: An Essay in Understanding," in *Essays in Understanding*, 329–38.

84. Söllner, "Hannah Arendt's *The Origins of Totalitarianism*" (n. 1 above, this chap.), 233–38. In "Nazism, Culture and The *Origins*"(n. 10 above, this chap.), 118, Steven Aschheim speaks of the original obscurity of the "philosophical baggage" informing *Origins*. See George Cotkin, *Existential America* (Baltimore, MD: Johns Hopkins University Press, 2003), for numerous references to Arendt.

85. Rieff, "The Theology of Politics," 87–89; Arendt, "Concern with Politics in Recent European Philosophical Thought," in *Essays in Understanding*, 428–45. Dana Villa, *Arendt and Heidegger: The Fate of the Political* (Princeton, NJ: Princeton University Press, 1996), has been particularly important in this respect.

86. Arendt, "What Remains? The Language Remains," in *Essays in Understanding*, 21.

87. See George Kateb, "Existential Values in Arendt's Treatment of Evil and Morality," in *Politics in Dark Times*, ed. Seyla Benhabib, Roy Thomas Tsao, and Peter J. Verovsek (New York: Cambridge University Press, 2010), 342–73.

88. Arendt, *Origins*, 474–75.

89. See Lawrence J. Friedman's *Love's Prophet: The Lives of Erich Fromm* (New York: Columbia University Press, 2013). Fromm was close to Riesman, but not particularly with Arendt, though they exchanged occasional letters.

90. Richard H. King, "Hannah Arendt and American Loneliness," *Society* 50, no. 1 (January–February 2013): 36–40.

91. Rieff, "The Theology of Politics," 93. This review was also one of the few early reviews that spent much time with Arendt on the status and psychology of Jews.

92. Ibid., 93, 88.

93. Ibid., 88. Robert Westbrook makes the interesting point that the abuse heaped on Arendt may have had something to do with its being the first time that the New York intellectuals had a chance to vent their complex reactions to the Holocaust (*Why We Fought*, 103–4).

94. Ibid., 89, 96.

95. See Hayden White, "The Politics of Historical Interpretation: Discipline and De-sublimation," in *The Content of the Form: Narrative Discourse and Historical Representation* (Baltimore, MD: Johns Hopkins University Press, 1987), 58–82.

Chapter 3

1. Sheldon S. Wolin, *Tocqueville between Two Worlds: The Making of a Political and Theoretical Life* (Princeton, NJ: Princeton University Press, 2001), 5. The single best piece Arendt wrote about these matters is "What Is Freedom?" in *Between Past and Future* (New York: Penguin, 2006), 142–69.

2. David L. Marshall, "The Polis and Its Analogues in the Thought of Hannah Arendt," *Modern Intellectual History* 7, no. 1 (2010): 128.

3. Hannah Arendt, "What Remains? The Language Remains," in *Essays in Understanding, 1930–1954*, ed. Jerome Kohn (New York: Harcourt Brace, 1994), 13–14. The interview was conducted by Günter Gaus.

4. Arendt, *Denktagebuch*, ed. Ursula Ludz and Ingeborg Nordmann, 2 vols. (Munich: Piper, 2002), 1:7. See Arendt, *The Origins of Totalitarianism*, 2nd ed. (Cleveland: Meridian Books, 1956), 454.

5. Arendt, *Denktagebuch*, 1:4.

6. Ibid., 315. At another level, this passage had relevance to Arendt's attempt to work out her attitude to Martin Heidegger.

7. Arendt to Karl Jaspers, letter of August 6, 1955, in *Hannah Arendt/Karl Jaspers Briefwechsel, 1926–1969*, ed. Lotte Köhler and Hans Saner (Munich: Piper, 1985), 301.

8. Arendt to Mary Underwood, letter, September 24, 1946, 1, Hannah Arendt Papers, Library of Congress, Correspondence; emphasis added to "against."

9. Besides Karl Popper, *The Poverty of Historicism* (New York: Harper Torchbooks, 1964); and Leo Strauss, *Natural Right and History* (Chicago: University of Chicago Press,

1953), see Walter Benjamin, "Theses on the Philosophy of History," in *Illuminations*, ed. Hannah Arendt (New York: Schocken, 1969), 253–69.

10. Arendt, "Understanding and Politics (The Difficulties of Understanding)," in *Essays in Understanding*, 311–12.

11. Albert Camus, *"The Myth of Sisyphus" and Other Essays* (New York: Vintage, 1955), 3. The philosophical—and existential—issue she was exploring reflected the thought with which Albert Camus opened *"The Myth of Sisyphus"*: "There is but one truly serious philosophical problem, and that is suicide."

12. Arendt, "Understanding and Politics," 308.

13. Arendt, *Denktagebuch*, 1:308. The Nietzschean "eternal return" is a morally self-centered choice, as Susan Neiman has pointed out. It affirms a willingness to live one's life again, even if that would mean the repetition of a massive historical evil such as the Holocaust. Susan Neiman, *Evil in Modern Thought* (Princeton, NJ: Princeton University Press, 2002), 202–24.

14. Arendt, "Concern with Politics in Recent European Philosophical Thought," in *Essays in Understanding*, 444.

15. Arendt, "Understanding and Politics," 307–8.

16. Arendt, *Denktagebuch*, 1:6–7.

17. Neiman, *Evil in Modern Thought*, 299–301; see also 250–58, 299–304.

18. Ibid., 301.

19. Arendt, "Epilogue," in *The Promise of Politics* (New York: Schocken, 2005), 204.

20. Arendt, *Denktagebuch*, 1:520. As she noted in her interview with Günter Gaus, she generally allowed herself to be verbally playful only when speaking or writing German.

21. In the *Odyssey*, the scene is set when Cyclops bellows in pain and demands to know who has put out his eye. The culprit, Odysseus, answers with the truth—"No man" or "No one," since he earlier told Polyphemus that his name was "No man." When Polyphemus repeats this to the other Cyclops, they refuse to come to his aid because they think he is joking with them.

22. Arendt, *Denktagebuch*, 1:523.

23. Martin Heidegger, *Being and Time*, trans. John Macquarrie and Edward Robinson (New York: Harper and Row, 1962), 32.

24. Arendt, "Understanding and Politics," 320–21.

25. Again, David Marshall's "The Polis and Its Analogues" (n. 2 above, this chap.) is important in determining the originary impulse behind political action.

26. Arendt, "What Is Freedom?" in *Between Past and Future* (New York: Penguin, 2006), 142–69, and *The Human Condition* (Chicago: University of Chicago Press, 1958). In the interview with Gaus, she identifies this tension between philosophy and politics as the reason that she does not, and cannot, call herself a philosopher.

27. Arendt, "The Tradition of Political Thought," in *Promise of Politics*, 60.

28. Arendt, "The Meaning of Politics," *Promise of Politics*, 135–41. See also Sheldon S. Wolin, *Politics and Vision*, expanded ed. (Princeton, NJ: Princeton University Press, 2004), 86–128, for a discussion of the politics of and within the Roman Church.

29. Arendt, "The Tradition of Political Thought," 40–62.

30. Ibid., 60–61.

31. In Michael Oakeshott's "The Voice of Poetry in the Conversation of Mankind" (1959), in *"Rationalism in Politics" and Other Essays* (London: Methuen, 1981), he writes that in "ancient Greece (particularly in Athens) 'politics' was understood as a 'poetic activity in which speaking (not merely to persuade but to compose memorable images) was pre-eminent and in which action for the achievement of 'glory and 'greatness'—a view of things which is reflected in the pages of Machiavelli" (202). Arendt's influence on Oakeshott here is quite clear.

32. Besides *On Revolution* (New York: Viking Compass, 1965), see Fred M. Dolan, *Allegories of America*: *Narratives, Metaphysics, Politics* (Ithaca, NY: Cornell University Press, 1994), chap. 5.

33. Arendt, *Human Condition*, 212–23.

34. Arendt, "Epilogue: Reflections on the Hungarian Revolution," in *Origins*, 480–510, and *On Revolution*. See Roy Tsao, "Arendt against Athens: Re-Reading *The Human Condition*," *Political Theory* 30, no. 1 (February 2002): 97–123; and Dean Hammer, "Hannah Arendt and Roman Political Thought: The Practice of Theory," *Political Theory* 30, no. 1 (February 2002): 124–49.

35. See Benjamin I. Schwartz, "The Religion of Politics," *Dissent* 17, no. 2 (March–April 1970): 144–61.

36. Arendt, "Concern with Politics in Recent European Political Thought" (1954), in *Essays in Understanding*, 428–47. The American Political Science Association held annual meetings.

37. Arendt, "What Is Existential Philosophy?" (1948), *Essays in Understanding*, 163–87.

38. Arendt, "Concern with Politics," 437.

39. Ibid., 439.

40. Ibid., 441–42.

41. See the interview with Gaus ("What Remains? [n. 3 above, this chap.]), where she first says it refers to "a space for politics" (17) and then later to a wider set of phenomena (20). Both politics and, say, mathematics can be "worlds," a usage something like Wittgenstein's "language game." In one formulation, Heidegger states it thus: "The stone (material object) is worldless [*weltlos*]; [2] the animal is poor in world [*weltarm*]; [3] man is world-forming [*welt-bildend*]" (Heidegger, *Fundamental Concepts of Metaphysics: World, Finitude, Solitude*, trans. William McNeill and Nicholas Walker (Bloomington: Indiana University Press, 2001), 177.

42. Arendt, *Men in Dark Times* (New York: Harcourt, Brace and World, 1968), 12.

43. Arendt, "Concern with Politics," 433.

44. Ibid.

45. Ibid.

46. Arendt to Jaspers, letter of September 28, 1951, in *Briefwechsel* (n. 7 above, this chap.), 213. Arendt's citizenship certificate is dated December 10, 1951.

47. Arendt, *Denktagebuch*, September 1951, 1:130-31.

48. "Prologue," in *Responsibility and Judgment*, ed. Jerome Kohn (New York; Schocken Press, 2003), 3-4.

49. For Arendt on Luxemburg's idea of revolution, see Elisabeth Young-Bruehl, *Hannah Arendt: For Love of the World* (New Haven, CT: Yale University Press, 1982), 293-94; Arendt, *Men in Dark Times*, 52, and *Origins*, 482.

50. Arendt, *Origins*, 298.

51. See Arendt, "Totalitarian Imperialism," *Journal of Politics* 20, no. 1 (February, 1955): 5-43.

52. Arendt, *Origins*, 482.

53. Ibid., 496.

54. Ibid., 499.

55. Ibid., 502.

56. Ibid. Cited in Young-Bruehl, *Hannah Arendt*, 201-2.

57. Arendt, *Human Condition*, 193, 195.

58. Ibid., 193. The classic history of this revolution is found in C. L. R. James, *The Black Jacobins*, 2nd ed. rev. (New York: Vintage, 1989). James was acquainted with Arendt's work and generally admired it.

59. Arendt, *Human Condition*, 356-57n51.

60. Ibid., 195-96.

61. Arendt, *Denktagebuch*,1:201. See Sheldon Wolin, "Democracy and the Political," *Salmagundi* 69 (Spring-Summer 1983):18.

62. Arendt, *Denktagebuch*, 1:202.

63. See her contribution to a 1954 symposium on totalitarianism in Carl J. Friedrich, ed., *Totalitarianism* (New York: Universal Library, 1964), 336-38.

64. Arendt, *Origins*, 509.

65. See Richard H. King, *Race, Culture and the Intellectuals, 1940-1970* (Washington, DC: Woodrow Wilson Press; Baltimore, MD: Johns Hopkins University Press, 2004), 225-26, on James's relationship to Arendt.

66. Young-Bruehl, *Hannah Arendt*, 294-96.

67. Ibid., 402. John Schaar and Hanna F. Pitkin joined the faculty in 1959 and 1962, respectively, while Wilson Carey McWilliams was a teaching assistant at Berkeley in the mid-1960s and later a well-known academic political theorist. See Emily Hauptmann, "A Local History of 'The Political,'" *Political Theory* 32, no. 1 (February 2004): 34-60. See also Jan Lundberg's interview with Brad Cleaveland in "What a Free Speech Movement

Instigator Teaches Us Today" *Culture Change*, Letter no. 183 (January 2008), http://www.culturechange.org/cms/content/view/146/1/.

68. Hauptmann, "A Local History," 44–45.

69. Young-Bruehl, *Hannah Arendt*, 294.

70. Arendt to Jaspers, letter of November 16, 1958, in *Briefwechsel*, 383.

71. Arendt to Jaspers, letter of January 31, 1959, in *Briefwechsel*, 235.

72. Heinrich Blücher to Hannah Arendt, letter of July 14, 1958, *Briefe, 1936–1968*, ed. Lotte Köhler(Munich: Piper, 1996), 488.

73. Arendt, "What Is Authority?" (1958), in *Between Past and Future*, ed. Jerome Kohn (New York: Penguin, 2006), 140.

74. Wolin, *Tocqueville between Two Worlds* (n. 1 above, this chap.), 5–6.

75. Jaspers to Arendt, letter of May 16, 1963, in *Briefwechsel*, 541.

76. Arendt to Jaspers, letter of December 30, 1961, in *Briefwechsel*, 504.

77. Young-Bruehl, *Hannah Arendt*, 403. Bernard Crick (1929–2008) was a political theorist who was one of Arendt's main champions in Britain against figures such as Isaiah Berlin and Stuart Hampshire. Young-Bruehl quotes from Crick's 1964 review of *On Revolution* in the *London Observer*, February 23, 1964 (*Hannah Arendt*, 529).

78. Arendt to Jasper, letter of April 14, 1963, in *Briefwechsel*, 537.

79. Jaspers to Arendt, letter of May 16, 1963, in *Briefwechsel*, 541.

Chapter 4

1. Arendt to Blücher, letter of July 8, 1946, in *Hannah Arendt/Heinrich Blücher Briefe,1936–1968*, ed. Lotte Köhler (Munich: Piper, 1996), 141.

2. Blücher to Arendt, letter of July 16, 1948, in *Briefe* 154.

3. Arendt to Blücher, letter of July 22, 1956, in *Briefe*, 156.

4. The obvious place to go for the relationship of Tocqueville to Arendt is Hanna F. Pitkin, *The Attack of the Blob: Hannah Arendt's Concept of the Social* (Chicago: University of Chicago, 1998), 115–44; Mark Reinhardt, *The Art of Being Free: Taking Liberties with Tocqueville, Marx, and Arendt* (Ithaca, NY: Cornell University Press, 1997), esp. chapter 5, 142–78; and Matthew Mancini, *Alexis de Tocqueville and American Intellectuals* (Lanham, MD.: Rowman and Littlefield, 2006), 228–37. For recent work on Tocqueville, see James T. Kloppenberg, "Life Everlasting: Tocqueville in America" (1995), in *The Virtues of Liberalism* (New York: Oxford University Press, 1998), 71–81, and "The Canvas and the Color: Tocqueville's 'Philosophical History' and Why It Matters Now," *Modern Intellectual History*, 3, no. 3 (November 2006): 495–521. Less celebratory are Judith Shklar, "An Education for America: Tocqueville, Hawthorne, Emerson," in *Redeeming American Political Thought* (Chicago: University of Chicago Press, 1998), 65–80; Sheldon S. Wolin, *Tocqueville between Two Worlds: The Making of a Political and Theoretical Life* (Princeton, NJ: Princeton University Press, 2001); and especially Garry Wills, "Did Tocqueville 'Get' America?" *New York Review of Books*, April 29, 2004, 1–14, http://www.nybooks.conv/articles/archives/2004/apri129/did-tocqueville.

5. Kloppenberg, "The Canvas and the Color," 504–7.

6. Alexis de Tocqueville, *Democracy in America*, 2 vols., ed. Phillips Bradley, trans. Henry Reeve, and rev. by Francis Bowen (New York: Alfred A. Knopf, 1945). See George W. Pierson, *Tocqueville and Beaumont in America* (New York: Oxford University Press, 1938); and James T. Schleifer, *The Making of Tocqueville's "Democracy in America"* (Chapel Hill: University of North Carolina Press, 1980). Not only sociologists but also analysts of American culture and politics, such as Marvin Meyers in his *The Jacksonian Persuasion: Politics and Belief* (Stanford, CA: Stanford University Press, 1957); and Louis Hartz in *The Liberal Tradition in America* (New York: Harcourt Brace, 1955) made heavy use of Tocqueville in their analyses of American political culture.

7. Tocqueville is taken up in vol. 1 of Raymond Aron's *Main Currents in Sociological Thought* (Harmondsworth, UK: Penguin, 1965), while Weber is analyzed in Aron's *Main Currents in Sociological Thought* (Garden City, NY: Anchor Edition, 1970), 2:219–317.

8. Hannah Arendt, *Denktagebuch*, ed. Ursula Ludz and Ingeborg Nordmann, 2 vols. (Munich: Piper, 2003),1:465.

9. See Larry Siedentop, "Two Liberal Traditions," in *The Idea of Freedom: Essays in Honour of Isaiah Berlin*, ed. Alan Ryan (Oxford: Oxford University Press, 1979), 153–74.

10. Alexis de Tocqueville, *Democracy in America*, trans. and ed. Harvey C. Mansfield and Delba Winthrop, 2 vols. (Chicago: University of Chicago Press, 2002), 2:673. I will be citing from this edition/translation of *Democracy in America*. See Arendt "What Is History?" in *Between Past and Future* (New York: Penguin, 1961), 77.

11. Shklar, *Redeeming American Political Thought*, 68.

12. Tocqueville, *Democracy*, 2:496–500; Pitkin, *Attack of the Blob*, 100–104. In her 1963 interview with Günter Gaus ("What Remains? The Language Remains," in *Essays in Understanding* [New York: Harcourt Brace and Company, 1994]), Arendt described civic associations as "the kind of association already described by Tocqueville" (22).

13. One way to distinguish the two volumes of *Democracy in America* would be to take vol. 1 to be a work of political science, with an admixture of political sociology, while vol. 2 is a primarily work of political and social theory. See Schleifer, *The Making of Tocqueville's "Democracy,"* 345, for Tocqueville's style of thinking.

14. Arendt, *The Human Condition* (Chicago: University of Chicago Press, 1958), 140.

15. Arendt, "What Remains?" 17, 22.

16. Thomas Bender makes this point concerning the difference between the social and political in Tocqueville in "Tocqueville," in *A Companion to American Thought*, ed. Richard Wightman Fox and James T. Kloppenberg (Oxford: Blackwell, 1995), 676–78. Thanks to James Kloppenberg for the Bender generalization. See Hanna F. Pitkin, "Membership, the Social, and the Political," in *Wittgenstein and Justice* (Berkeley: University of California Press, 1972), 193–218. In addition, her *Attack of the Blob* (n. 4 above, this chap.) explored Arendt's concept of the social at greater length and with

considerably more exasperation. Conceptually, Arendt confused the idea that the social was the realm of determinism with the claim that all forms of determinism were species of the social.

17. Pitkin, *Wittgenstein*, 199, 203. Pitkin suggests that Rousseau "confuse[d] political life with cultural education." In the later, acculturation or internalization happens "as if no enforcement were taking place. Conflict is disguised and denied."

18. Ibid., 201.

19. Arendt, "The Crisis in Education," in *Between Past and Future*, 178.

20. Tocqueville, *Democracy*, 1:245.

21. Ibid., 1:241.

22. Siedentop, "Two Liberal Traditions," 170, 172.

23. See Schleifer, *The Making of Tocqueville's "Democracy,"* 183–84.

24. Montesquieu, *The Spirit of the Laws*, ed. David Wallace Carrithers (Berkeley: University of California Press, 1977), 58–59, 132–33.

25. Arendt, "The Crisis of Education," 174–81.

26. I will return to this issue in the next chapter when I discuss Arendt's letter of March 1949 to sociologist David Riesman.

27. Cited in Arendt, *On Revolution* (New York: Viking Compass, 1965), 137. It is from Tocqueville's study of the ancien régime and is cited in Pitkin, *Attack of the Blob*, 124.

28. Tocqueville, *Democracy*, 2:497.

29. Ibid., 499.

30. Ibid., 482.

31. Ibid., 484.

32. Ibid., 502, 501.

33. Arendt, "Civil Disobedience" (1970), in *Crises of the Republic* (New York: Harcourt Brace Jovanovich, 1972), 94.

34. Arendt, "The Concept of History," 71, and "What Is Authority?" 130–33, both in *Between Past and Future*.

35. Arendt, "Religion and Politics," in *Essays in Understanding, 1930–1954* (New York: Harcourt Brace, 1994), 368–90.

36. See Robert Bellah, "Civil Religion in America" (1967), in *Beyond Belief: Essays on Religion in a Post-Traditional World* (New York: Harper & Row, 1970); Will Herberg, *Protestant, Catholic, Jew: An Essay in American Religious Sociology* (Garden City, NY: Doubleday Anchor, 1956).

37. Reinhardt, *The Art of Being Free* (n. 4 above, this chap.), chap. 5.

38. Tocqueville, *Democracy*, 2:406.

39. Ibid., 485.

40. Louis Hartz, *The Liberal Tradition in America* (New York: Harcourt Brace and World, 1955), 5–6.

41. Tocqueville, *Democracy*, 1;6.

42. Ibid. See also Arendt, *On Revolution*, 109, 259, for mentions of Tocqueville and necessity.

43. Reinhardt, *The Art of Being Free*, 65–66.

44. See Arendt to Karl Jaspers, letter of September 28, 1951, in *Hannah Arendt/Karl Jaspers Briefwechsel 1926–1969*, ed. Lotte Köhler and Hans Saner (Munich: Piper, 1985), 209; and Arendt, "Prologue," in *Responsibility and Judgment*, ed. Jerome Kohn (New York; Schocken Press, 2003), 4.

45. Elisabeth Young-Bruehl, *Hannah Arendt: For Love of the World* (New Haven, CT: Yale University Press, 1982), 403. Young-Bruehl here echoes a statement from Bernard Crick about *On Revolution*. See, chapter 3, n. 77.

46. Arendt, *The Origins of Totalitarianism*, 2nd ed. (Cleveland: Meridian Books, 1958), 296–97.

47. See Arendt, *Men in Dark Times* (New York: Harcourt Brace and World, 1968), for the essays on these three figures.

48. Arendt, "Rand School Lecture" (1948), in *Essays in Understanding*, 218.

49. Arendt, "The Eichmann Controversy" (1963), in *The Jewish Writings* ed. Jerome Kohn and Ronald H. Feldman (New York: Schocken Books, 2007), 465–66.

50. Young-Bruehl, *Hannah Arendt*, 288. What was proposed sounded like an updated version of Macdonald's *Politics*.

51. Ibid., 288.

52. Hannah Arendt and Karl Jaspers, letter of May 13, 1953, in *Briefwechsel*, 247, 251.

53. Arendt to Jaspers, letter of July 13, 1953, in *Briefwechsel*, 259.

54. Young-Bruehl, *Hannah Arendt*, 273–76.

55. All three pieces are collected in Arendt, *Essays in Understanding*.

56. Ibid., 226.

57. Ibid., 220–23.

58. Ibid., 225. American society was a "very complicated system of social interrelationships—determined by even more and more heterogeneous groups than one can find in a class system—that can underlie the surface of all the worst cultural elements of mass society."

59. Ibid.

60. Ibid.

61. Probably the best account of the arguments of the 1930s was Macdonald's mocking, half-affectionate account of the sectarian divisions plaguing the American left. See "Politics Past" (1957), in *Memoirs of a Revolutionist* (Cleveland: Meridian Books, 1958), 3–37.

62. Arendt, "The Ex-Communists" (1953), in *Essays in Understanding*, 395. In Tony Judt's essay "Hannah Arendt and Evil," in *Re-appraisals: Reflections on the Forgotten Twentieth Century* (New York: Vintage, 2008, 1984), he calls attention to these short pieces as particularly cogent (84). However, Peter Baehr concludes, in his "The Informers: Hannah

Arendt's Appraisal of Whittaker Chambers and Ex-Communists," *European Journal of Culture and Political Sociology* 45, no. 1 (2014): 84–102, that Arendt's distinction between ex- and former communists is empirically weak and that they don't work as ideal types.

63. Arendt, "The Ex-Communists," 394. See also George H. Nash, *The Conservative Intellectual Movement in America since 1945*, 3rd ed. (1976; repr., Wilmington, DE: ISI Books, 2006).

64. Arendt, "The Ex-Communists," 391–92.

65. Ibid., 393. See also Judith N. Shklar, *After Utopia: The Decline of Political Faith* (Princeton, NJ: Princeton University Press, 1957), for the idea of political ideology as ersatz religion.

66. Arendt, "The Eggs Speak Up" (1951), in *Essays in Understanding*, 280–81.

67. Arendt, "The Ex-Communists," 400.

68. Ibid.

69. Ibid., 396–97.

70. Michael Oakeshott, "Rationalism in Politics," in *"Rationalism in Politics" and Other Essays* (London: Methuen, 1981), 1–37.

71. Arendt, "The Ex-Communists," 396.

72. Indeed, American historian David Potter published an influential study of American national character: *People of Plenty: Economic Abundance and the American Character* (Chicago: University of Chicago Press, 1954).

73. Arendt, "Dream and Nightmare," in *Essays in Understanding*, 411.

74. Ibid., 412.

75. Ibid., 415–16.

76. See Martin Heidegger, "The Question concerning Technology (1953)," in *Basic Writings*, ed. David Krell, rev. and expanded (London: Routledge, 1993), 307–41.

77. Arendt, "Europe and the Atom Bomb," in *Essays in Understanding*, 419. See also James W. Ceaser, "*Katastrophenhaft*: Martin Heidegger's America," in *Reconstructing America: The Symbol of America in Modern Thought* (New Haven, CT: Yale University Press, 1997), 187–213.

78. Arendt, "Europe and the Atom Bomb," 420.

79. Arendt, "The Threat of Conformism," in *Essays in Understanding*, 423–24.

80. Ibid., 426.

81. Ibid., 424.

82. Ibid., 426–27.

83. Ibid.

84. Elisabeth Young-Bruehl, "New Preface," in *Hannah Arendt: For Love of the World*, 2nd ed. (New Haven, CT: Yale University Press, 2004), xxiii–iv.

85. Arendt to Jaspers, letter of October 6, 1954, in *Briefwechsel*, 285.

86. Arendt to Jaspers, letter of August 6,1955, in *Briefwechsel*, 300–301.

Chapter 5

1. Nathan Glazer, "Tocqueville and Riesman," *Society* 37, no. 4 (1999): 32. Glazer and Reuel Denney worked "in collaboration with" David Riesman on the project that led to *The Lonely Crowd: A Study of American National Character* (New Haven, CT: Yale University Press, 1967). Thanks to Jonathan Imber for supplying me with links to pieces in the archives of *Society* having to do with, or written by, Riesman.

2. Ibid., 27. For Riesman, I have used his "Foreword: Ten Years Later" (1960), in *The Lonely Crowd*, xi–xlviii, "Tocqueville as Ethnographer" (1961), in *Abundance for What?* (Garden City, NY: Anchor Books, 1964), 470–81, and "Innocence of *The Lonely Crowd*," *Society* 27, no. 2 (January–February, 1990), 76–79.

For interpretations of Riesman's work, I have drawn on Wilfred McClay, "The Strange Career of *The Lonely Crowd* or, the Antinomies of Autonomy," in *The Culture of the Market: Historical Essays*, ed. Thomas L. Haskell and Richard F. Teichgraeber III (New York: Cambridge University Press, 1993), 397–440, and "Fifty Years of *The Lonely Crowd*," *Wilson Quarterly* 22 (Summer 1998): 32–42; Neil McLaughlin, "Critical Theory Meets America: Riesman, Fromm and *The Lonely Crowd*," *American Sociologist* 32 (Spring 2001): 5–26; Daniel Horowitz, "From Law to Social Criticism," *Buffalo Law Review* 58 (2010): 1006–29, and "Reluctant Fascination," in *Consuming Pleasures: Intellectuals and Popular Culture in the Postwar World* (Philadelphia: University of Pennsylvania Press, 2012), 122–62.

There are two excellent treatments of Arendt and Riesman together. One is Wilfred McClay, *The Masterless: Self and Society in Modern America* (Chapel Hill: University of North Carolina Press, 1994), 223–61; and the other is Peter Baehr, "'Totalitarianism' in the Dialogue of David Riesman and Hannah Arendt," in *Hannah Arendt, Totalitarianism, and the Social Sciences* (Stanford, CA: Stanford University Press, 2010), 35–61.

3. David Riesman to Hannah Arendt, letter of February 27, 1947, Hannah Arendt Papers, Library of Congress, Correspondence File, 1938–1976.

4. See Peter Baehr, "Hannah Arendt's Indictment of Social Science," in *Hannah Arendt, Totalitarianism and the Social Sciences*, for a discussion of Arendt's suspicion of the social sciences. The following two essays by Arendt give a flavor of her attitude: "Social Science Techniques and the Study of Concentration Camps" (1950) and "Religion and Politics" (1953), both in *Essays in Understanding, 1930–1954* (New York: Harcourt Brace, 1994), 232–47, 368–90.

5. Riesman to Arendt, letter of November 11, 1948, Hannah Arendt Papers. Riesman had been in analysis with Erich Fromm and was a close friend of Erik H. Erikson. See Lawrence J. Friedman, *Identity's Architect: A Life of Erik H. Erikson* (New York: Scribner's, 1999), as well as Friedman with Anke M. Schreiber, *The Lives of Erich Fromm: Love's Prophet* (New York: Columbia University Press, 2013).

6. Arendt, preface (1956) to *Rahel Varnhagen: The Life of a Jewish Woman*, rev. ed. (New York: Harcourt Brace Jovanovich, 1974), xviii.

7. Arendt to Riesman, letter of June 13, 1949, Hannah Arendt Papers.

8. Riesman to Arendt, letter of August 26, 1949, Hannah Arendt Papers. The historian in question was Denis Brogan, author of *The American Character* (Gloucester, MA: Peter Smith, 1944).

9. Riesman to Arendt, letter of March 19, 1951, Hannah Arendt Papers. See David Riesman, "The Path to Total Terror," *Commentary* 11, no. 4 (1951): 392–98, and "Some Observations on the Limits of Totalitarian Power," in *Abundance for What?* 76–87.

10. Glazer, "Tocqueville and Riesman," 29; Baehr, *Arendt, Totalitarianism and the Social Sciences*, 50.

11. McClay, *The Masterless*, 223.

12. Carl J. Friedrich, ed., *Totalitarianism* (New York: Universal Library, 1964).

13. Arendt to Riesman, letter of June 13, 1949, 1, Hannah Arendt Papers.

14. Numerous entries on Hegel in vol. 2 of her *Denktagebuch* (ed. Ursula Ludz and Ingeborg Nordmann, 2 vols. [Munich: Piper, 2002]) indicate her surprising interest in the German philosopher, to whose work she was usually hostile in print. Her own idea of self-formation bore a certain resemblance to the interactive model based on the self-and-other relationship.

15. Arendt to Riesman, letter of June 13, 1949, Hannah Arendt Papers.

16. Riesman to Arendt, letter of June 27, 1949, Hannah Arendt Papers.

17. Riesman, "Foreword: Ten Years Later," xix–x.

18. Ibid., xx.

19. McClay, *The Masterless*, 256–57.

20. Riesman, *Lonely Crowd*, 20, 23n10, 173–74.

21. Ibid., 370.

22. Bell, "America as a Mass Society: A Critique" (1955), in *The End of Ideology in the West* (Glencoe, IL: Free Press, 1960), 33.

23. Hannah Arendt to Karl Jaspers, letter of January 29, 1946, in *Hannah Arendt/Karl Jaspers Briefwechsel, 1926–1969*, ed. Lotte Köhler and Hans Saner (Munich: Piper, 1985), 66–67.

24. Arendt to Riesman, letter of May 21, 1948, 1–2, Hannah Arendt Papers.

25. Arendt to Riesman, letter of March 9, 1949, 1–2, Hannah Arendt Papers.

26. Riesman, *Lonely Crowd*, 252.

27. See C. Wright Mills, *The Power Elite* (New York: Oxford University Press, 1956); and John Kenneth Galbraith, *American Capitalism: The Concept of Countervailing Powers* (New York: Houghton Mifflin, 1952).

28. Riesman, *Lonely Crowd*, 242–48.

29. Ibid., xxxviii.

30. Riesman to Arendt, letter of August 28, 1949, Hannah Arendt Papers. Arendt did not respond directly to Riesman's observations.

31. Bell, "America as a Mass Society," 21.

32. Even before *Origins*, she used the term "mass society" to describe American society. See, Arendt, "Rand School Lecture," in *Essays in Understanding*, 225. Leon Bramson, *The Political Context of Sociology* (Princeton, NJ: Princeton University Press, 1961), provides an intellectual history of this tradition and its problems.

33. Bell, "America as a Mass Society," 21; Bramson, *The Political Context of Sociology*, 122.

34. C. Wright Mills, "The Mass Society," in *The Power Elite* (New York: Oxford University Press, 1956), 298–324; and Daniel Geary, *Radical Ambition: C. Wright Mills, the Left, and American Social Thought* (Berkeley: University of California Press, 2009). In *The Masterless*, 213–25, McClay also places Arendt in the context of mass society analysis, but concentrates more on its European sources and relevance for totalitarianism than its postwar relevance.

35. See William Kornhauser, *The Politics of Mass Society* (Glencoe, IL: Free Press, 1959), 228.

36. Ibid., 15–16, 22. As Kornhauser put it: "Mass society is objectively the atomized society and subjectively the alienated population" (33).

37. H. Stuart Hughes, "The Critique of Mass Society," in *The Sea Change: The Migration of Social Thought, 1930–1965* (New York: Harper and Row, 1975), 134–35. As Hughes recognized, the Frankfurt theorists were really more interested in cultural criticism than social and economic analysis.

38. Bell, "America as a Mass Society," 22, 31.

39. Arendt to Riesman, letter of June 13, 1949, 2, Hannah Arendt Papers.

40. Arendt, *The Origins of Totalitarianism*, 2nd ed. (Cleveland: Meridian, 1958), 317.

41. Ibid., 311. The trope Emil Lederer used to describe this situation was of society as an "amorphous mass" in *State of the Masses* (New York: W. W. Norton, 1940), 18.

42. *Origins*, 317.

43. Ibid., 316.

44. Ibid., 338 (attributed to Konrad Heiden), 332.

45. Ibid., 331.

46. Ibid., 316. In her letter of June 13, Arendt seems to suggest that Americans had developed a mass psychology, while this passage suggests that they haven't.

47. Baehr, *Arendt, Totalitarianism and the Social Sciences*, 52.

48. Bramson, *The Political Context of Sociology*, 35–37.

49. Riesman to Arendt, letter(s) of August 26, 1949. In the archives, a thirteen-page handwritten letter and a one-page, single-spaced typed letter are both dated this same day.

50. Riesman to Arendt, letters of October 6, 1949, and August 28, 1949, Hannah Arendt Papers.

51. Riesman to Arendt, letter of September 22, 1949, Hannah Arendt Papers.

52. The definitive volume on this matter is Daniel Bell, ed., *The Radical Right* (Garden City, NY: Anchor, 1964). In addition to Bell, contributors included Richard

Hofstadter, David Riesman, and Nathan Glazer. Later, Michael Rogin's *The Intellectuals and McCarthy: The Radical Specter* (Cambridge, MA: MIT Press, 1967) challenged the social-psychological orientation of mass society analysis and linked McCarthy's support to normal conservatism rather than a new kind of populist right-wing culture.

53. Arendt, "Reflections on Little Rock," *Dissent* 6, no. 1 (Winter 1959): 51.

54. Arendt, "The Concept of History" (1958), in *Between Past and Future* (New York: Penguin, 2006), 90.

55. Arendt, *On Revolution* (New York: Viking Compass, 1965), 283; Irving Howe, *Steady Work: Essays in the Politics of Democratic Radicalism, 1953–1966* (New York: Harcourt, Brace and World, 1966), 24–28.

56. Raymond Williams, review of *Between Past and Future*, by Hannah Arendt, *Kenyon Review* 23, no. 4 (Autumn 1961): 698–702; Arendt to Williams, letter of April 11, 1962.

57. Riesman to Arendt, letter of August 26, 1949, 2, Hannah Arendt Papers.

58. Gershom Scholem to Arendt, letter of June 23, 1963, and Arendt to Scholem, letter of July 24, 1963, both in *The Jew as Pariah: Jewish Identity and Politics in the Modern Age*, ed. Ron H. Feldman (New York: Grove Press, 1978), 241 and 246, respectively.

Chapter 6

1. Details of Arendt's life and activities are drawn from Elisabeth Young-Bruehl's still definitive biography, *Hannah Arendt: For Love of the World* (New Haven, CT: Yale University Press, 1982). In 1952, Arendt's husband, Heinrich Blücher, accepted a teaching position at nearby Bard College. Eventually, she assumed a regular, part-time position at the University of Chicago (1963–67) and then a full-time position at the New School for Social Research from early 1968 until her death.

2. Hannah Arendt (with Günter Gaus), "What Remains? The Language Remains," in *Essays in Understanding, 1930–1954*, ed. Jerome Kohn (Harcourt Brace and World, 1994), 1–4.

3. Margaret Canovan, *Hannah Arendt: A Reinterpretation of Her Political Thought* (Cambridge: Cambridge University Press, 1992), 273.

4. Richard Rorty, "Philosophy in America Today," *American Scholar* 51, no. 2 (Spring 1982): 183–204. See also Martin Woessner, *Heidegger in America* (New York: Cambridge University Press, 2011), 95–99.

5. Sheldon S. Wolin, "Political Theory as a Vocation," *American Political Science Review* 64, no. 3 (December 1969): 1064. The standard works on this topic are John Gunnell, *The Descent of Political Theory: The Genealogy of an American Vocation* (Chicago: University of Chicago Press, 1993); and Richard J. Bernstein, *The Restructuring of Social and Political Theory* (London: Methuen, 1979), esp. pt. 1 on empirical theory, 1–54.

6. Background to this debate can be found in Emily Hauptmann, "A Local History of 'The Political,'" *Political Theory* 32 (February 2004): 34–60, "From Opposition to Accommodation: How Rockefeller Foundation Grants Redefined Relations between

Political and Social Science in the 1950s," *American Political Science Review* 100 (November 2006): 643–49, and "Defining 'Theory' in Postwar Political Science," in *The Politics of Method in the Human Sciences: Positivism and Epistemological Others,* ed. George Steinmetz (Durham, NC: Duke University press, 2005): 207–21. See also Fred R. Dallmayr, "Political Philosophy Today," in *Polis and Praxis: Exercises in Contemporary Political Theory* (Cambridge, MA: MIT Press, 1984), 15–46.

From around 1960, Sheldon Wolin became the spokesman for the theory side. Besides "Political Theory as a Vocation," see "Paradigms and Political Theories," in *Politics and Experience,* ed. Preston King and B. C. Parekh (Cambridge: Cambridge University Press, 1968), 125–53, and "Hannah Arendt and the Ordinance of Time," *Social Research* 44, no. 1 (Spring 1977): 90–105. For the younger theorists, see Michael Walzer, "The Art of Theory Interview," *The Art of Theory: Conversations in Political Philosophy* (2013), http://www.artoftheory.com/michael-walzer-the-art-of-theory-interview/?utim_source. More recently, Benjamin R. Barber, "The Politics of Political Science: 'Value-Free' Theory and the Wolin-Strauss Dust-Up of 1963," *American Political Science Review* 100, no. 4 (November 2006): 539–45; and Joel Isaac, "Tangled Loops: Theory, History, and the Human Sciences in Modern America," *Modern Intellectual History* 6, no. 2 (2009): 397–423, offer valuable perspectives on these earlier debates.

7. Morton White, *Social Thought in America: The Revolt against Formalism* (Boston: Beacon Press, 1957). Edward A. Purcell, *The Crisis of Democratic Theory: Scientific Naturalism and the Problem of Value* (Lexington: University Press of Kentucky, 1973), focuses on the prewar challenge to the liberal and progressive tradition, esp. to Dewey's naturalism, in the name of natural law theory. I ran across the reference to James T. Kloppenberg, "In Retrospect: Morton White's *Social Thought in America,*" *Reviews in American History* 15, no. 3 (September 1987): 507–19, after I had finished the first draft of this chapter.

8. White, *Social Thought in American,* 11–13.

9. Ibid., 101, 107.

10. Ibid., 248.

11. Ibid., 250. Richard Wightman Fox, *Reinhold Niebuhr: A Biography* (Ithaca, NY: Cornell University Press, 1985); John Patrick Diggins, *The Promise of Pragmatism: Modernism and the Crisis of Knowledge and Authority* (Chicago: University of Chicago Press, 1994); and Martin Halliwell, *The Constant Dialogue: Reinhold Niebuhr and American Intellectual Culture* (Lanham, MD: Rowman and Littlefield, 2005).

12. Sidney Hook, "The New Failure of Nerve," *Partisan Review* 10, no. 1 (1943): 2. David Riesman, "Some Observations on Community Plans and Utopia," in *Individualism Reconsidered (Selected Essays)* (Garden City, NY: Doubleday Anchor, 1964), 67.

13. White, *Social Thought in America,* 267. For an emphasis on pragmatism's commitment to the natural science model, see David Hollinger "The Problem of Pragmatism in American History," *Journal of American History* 67 (June 1980): 88–107.

14. Ibid., 274. In fact, Walter Lippmann made brief reference to Leo Strauss in *The Public Philosophy* (Boston: Little Brown, 1955), but White did not. A key distinction White made was between self-evidence in analytical statements such as 2 + 2 = 4 and in moral claims.

15. One of the few efforts to analyze Arendt as a conservative is Margaret Canovan's "Hannah Arendt as a Conservative Thinker," in *Hannah Arendt: Twenty Years Later*, ed. L. May and J. Kohn (Cambridge, MA: MIT Press, 1997), 11–33.

16. José Ortega y Gassett, *The Dehumanization of Art and Other Writings on Art and Culture* (Garden City, NY: Doubleday Anchor, 1956), 123–27.

17. Besides Martin Heidegger's well-known role in the history of existentialism, Arendt's other mentor, Karl Jaspers, made the "boundary situation" central to his analysis of human existence. William Barrett, *Irrational Man: A Study in Existential Philosophy* (Garden City, NY: Doubleday Anchor, 1962), was really the only work by a New York intellectual to address existentialism directly. He had also helped Arendt translate her writing into English in the mid-1940s. More recently, George Cotkin, *Existential America* (Baltimore, MD: Johns Hopkins University Press, 2003), discusses Arendt in the context of existentialist themes and mood in American popular culture.

18. Arendt, "On the Nature of Totalitarianism," in *Essays in Understanding*, 344.

19. See Gunnell, *Descent of Political Theory*, 35, for the three traditional constituent parts of German political thought: *Naturrecht* (natural law or right), *Staatslehre* (theory of the state), and *Politik* (political policy and practice). It is difficult to fit Arendt's thought into any of these categories.

20. Canovan, "Hannah Arendt as a Conservative Thinker," 14.

21. Arendt, *On Revolution* (New York: Viking, 1965), 94.

22. Gunnell, *Descent of Political Theory*, 161.

23. See Hanna Fenichel Pitkin, "Justice: On Relating Private and Public," *Political Theory* 9 (August 1981): 327–52.

24. Lizabeth Cohen, *A Consumer Republic: The Politics of Mass Consumption in Postwar America* (New York: Alfred A. Knopf, 2003).

25. See Jeremy Waldron, "Arendt and the Foundations of Equality," *Politics in Dark Times*, ed. Seyla Benhabib, Roy Thomas Tsao, and Peter J. Verovsek (New York: Cambridge University Press, 2010), 17–38, where he claims that Arendt not only insisted on formal equality among citizens but also assumed that human beings shared enough to make them substantively equal, despite very real differences among them.

26. Phillip Rieff, "The Theology of Politics," in *The Feeling Intellect: Selected Writings*, ed. Jonathan Imber (Chicago: University of Chicago Press, 1990), 86–97.

27. Arendt, "A Reply to Eric Voegelin," in *Essays in Understanding*, 406, 407.

28. Arendt, "Crisis in Education," in *Between Past and Future: Eight Exercises in Political Thought*, ed. Jerome Kohn (New York: Penguin, 2006), 189.

29. Arendt, "The Ivory Tower of Common Sense," in *Essays in Understanding*, 194–96. The book she reviewed was Dewey, *The Problems of Men*, a collection of his writings.

30. Arendt, "The Crisis in Education" (1958), in *Between Past and Future*, 175–77.

31. See, particularly, Purcell, *The Crisis of Democratic Theory*.

32. Robert Westbrook, *John Dewey and American Democracy* (Ithaca, NY: Cornell University Press, 1991), 508.

33. Arendt, "Crisis in Education," 188, 193. See also Richard Hofstadter, *Anti-intellectualism in American Life* (New York: Alfred A. Knopf, 1964), 299–390.

34. Arendt, "Crisis in Education," 177–78.

35. Ibid.,179.

36. Ibid., 179–80.

37. Diggins, *The Promise of Politics*, 401–402; Louis Menand, *The Metaphysical Club: A Story of Ideas in America* (New York: Farrar Straus Giroux, 2001), 439–40; Daniel Bell, *The End of Ideology* (Glencoe, IL.: Free Press, 1960), 44; Howard Brick, *Daniel Bell and the Decline of Intellectual Radicalism* (Madison: University of Wisconsin Press, 1986), 63.

38. Richard J. Bernstein, *The Abuse of Evil: The Corruption of Politics and Religion since 9/11* (Cambridge: Polity Press, 2005), chap. 2.

39. John Dewey, "Pragmatism and Democracy" (1927), in *The Political Writings*, ed. Debra Morris and Ian Shapiro (Indianapolis: Hackett Publishing, 1993), 33.

40. John Dewey, "Philosophy and Democracy" (1919), *The Political Writings*, 43–44.

41. Robert Westbrook, *John Dewey and American Democracy*, 452–55. See also Jeffrey Isaac, *Arendt, Camus and Modern Rebellion* (New Haven, CT: Yale University Press, 1992), 146.

42. Arendt, "Understanding and Politics," in *Essays in Understanding*, 317. See the footnote on this same page for a continuation of this line of thought.

43. Menand, *The Metaphysical Club*, 375.

44. Stanley Cavell, *The Senses of Walden*, expanded ed. (San Francisco: North Point Press, 1981), 33.

45. Arendt, "The Crisis in Culture: Its Social and Its Political Significance," in *Between Past and Future*, 195.

46. Thomas Wheatland, *The Frankfurt School in Exile* (Minneapolis: University of Minnesota, 2009).

47. See Wolfgang Heuer, "Ein Schwieriger Dialog: Die Hannah Arendt-Rezeption in Deutshsprachigen Raum," in *Hannah Arendt: Nach dem Totalitarianismus*, ed. D. Ganzfried (Hamburg: Sebastian Hefti, 1997), 21–28.

48. Hans Joas, "American Pragmatism and German Thought: A History of Misunderstanding," in *Pragmatism and Social Theory* (Chicago: University of Chicago Press, 1993), 94–121. As Arendt wrote to Karl Jaspers in 1949: "Sometimes I ask myself what is more difficult—to teach the Germans a sense of politics or to impart to the Americans a light dusting of philosophy. I'll wrack my brain some and then report what I have done" (Hannah Arendt to Karl Jaspers, letter of January 28, 1949, in *Hannah Arendt/Karl Jaspers Briefwechsel, 1926–1969*, ed. Lotte Köhler and Hans Saner [Munich: Piper, 1985], 165).

49. Martin Heidegger, "The Question concerning Technology" (1953), in *Basic Writings*, ed. David Krell (London: Routledge, 1993), 311–41. See Richard J. Bernstein, "Heidegger's Silence? Ethos and Technology," in *The New Constellation: The Ethical-Political Horizons of Modernity/Postmodernity* (Cambridge: Polity Press, 1991), 79–141.

50. Arendt, "Emerson Address" (1969), in *Reflections on Literature and Culture*, ed. Susannah Young-ah Gottlieb (Stanford, CA: Stanford University Press, 2007), 283.

51. One big exception to the German suspicion of people like Emerson was Friedrich Nietzsche. See Jennifer Ratner-Rosenhagen, *American Nietzsche: A History of an Icon and an Idea* (Chicago: University of Chicago Press, 2012).

52. Joas, "American Pragmatism and German Thought," 111. Joas was referring here to Eduard Baumgarten, Arnold Gehlen, and Helmut Schelsky among others.

53. Ibid., 111–14.

54. Joas, *Pragmatism and Social Theory*, 4, 19. For pragmatism as "creative redescription," see Morris Dickstein, ed., *The Revival of Pragmatism: New Essays on Social Thought, Law, and Culture* (Durham, NC: Duke University Press, 1998), 2–3.

55. Ibid., 25. Mitchell Aboulafia compares Arendt and Mead in *The Cosmopolitan Self: George Herbert Mead and Continental Philosophy* (Urbana: University of Illinois Press, 2001).

56. White, *Social Thought in America*, 147–56.

57. Richard J. Bernstein, *The Restructuring of Social and Political Theory*, 259n21. See Judith Friedländer, "A Philosopher from New York," in *Pragmatism, Critique and Judgment: Essays for Richard Bernstein*, ed. Seyla Benhabib and Nancy Fraser (Cambridge, MA: MIT Press, 2004), 344.

58. Richard J. Bernstein, "Judging—the Actor and the Spectator" and "Rethinking the Social and the Political," in *Philosophical Profiles* (Cambridge: Polity Press, 1986), 221–37, 238–41, 249.

59. Bernstein, "Heidegger's Silence?" 79–141.

60. Bernstein, *Hannah Arendt and the Jewish Question* (Cambridge: Polity Press, 1996), and *Radical Evil: A Philosophical Interrogation* (Cambridge: Polity Press, 2002). In the latter, only Levinas is a non-German-speaking thinker.

61. Bernstein, *Abuse of Evil* (n. 38 above, this chap.), 54.

62. Richard J. Bernstein, "The Normative Case of the Public Sphere," *Political Theory* 40, no. 6 (December 2012): 767–78.

Chapter 7

1. Hannah Arendt, *The Origins of Totalitarianism*, 2nd. ed. (Cleveland: Meridian Books, 1958). Emphases fell on pernicious political ideas such as "totalitarian democracy" (Talmon), the "closed society" (Popper), or "positive freedom" (Isaiah Berlin); spiritual-intellectual tendencies such as "gnosticism" (Eric Voegelin) and "historicism" (Strauss, Popper, Camus); sociocultural factors such as the "escape from freedom"

(Fromm), "the mass psychology of fascism" (Reich), and "mass culture" plus "the dialectic of Enlightenment" (Adorno and Horkheimer); and finally specifically German factors such as romanticism and national character generally (Viereck, Mann).

2. Arendt, "Organized Guilt and University Responsibility" (1945), in *Essays in Understanding, 1930–1954*, ed. Jerome Kohn (New York: Harcourt Brace and Company, 1994), 126.

3. For the postwar intellectual history of race, see Richard H. King, *Race, Culture and the Intellectuals, 1940–1970* (Baltimore, MD: Johns Hopkins University Press; Washington, DC: Woodrow Wilson Press, 2004); Nikhil Pal Singh, *Black Is a Country: Race and the Unfinished Struggle for Democracy* (Cambridge, MA: Harvard University Press, 2004); Michael Rothberg, *Multi-directional Memory: Remembering the Holocaust in the Age of Decolonization* (Stanford, CA: Stanford University Press, 2009); Jimmy Casas Klausen, "Hannah Arendt's Anti-primitivism," *Political Theory*, 38, no. 3 (June 2010): 394–423. See also Richard H. King and Dan Stone, eds., *Hannah Arendt and the Uses of History: Imperialism, Nation, Race, and Genocide* (New York: Berghahn Books, 2007).

4. See Ned Curthoys, "The Émigré Sensibility of 'World Literature': Historicizing Hannah Arendt and Karl Jaspers' Cosmopolitan Interest," *Theory and Event* 8, no. 3 (2005): 2.

5. Arendt, "Organized Guilt . . . ," *Essays*: 131.

6. Arendt, *Denktagebuch*, ed. Ursula Ludz and Ingeborg Nordmann, 2 vols. (Munich: Piper, 2002), 1:70. Translations are my own.

7. Arendt, "Organized Guilt," 131.

8. See King, *Race, Culture and the Intellectuals*, 209, for a brief discussion of this point. Wright was also disturbed by the resurgence of religious feelings and loyalties.

9. Arendt, "Organized Guilt," 131–32.

10. Arendt, *Origins*, chap. 9.

11. Ibid.

12. Seyla Benhabib, "International Law and Human Plurality in the Shadow of Totalitarianism: Hannah Arendt and Raphael Lemkin," in *Politics in Dark Times: Encounters with Hannah Arendt*, ed. Seyla Benhabib, Roy Thomas Tsao, and Peter J. Verovsek (Cambridge: Cambridge University Press, 2010), 221.

13. Arendt, *Origins*, 259.

14. According to Mark Mazower, by 1945 "human rights" referred to individual rights and the protections promised to them, while "minority rights" were linked with "national" or group rights and given little or no protection. Mazower, "The Strange Triumph of Human Rights, 1933–1950," *Historical Journal* 47, no. 2 (2004): 379–98. See also Samuel Moyn, *The Last Utopia* (Cambridge, MA: Harvard University Press, 2010), who pushes back the date to the 1970s.

15. Benhabib, "International Law."

16. Arendt, *Eichmann in Jerusalem: A Report on the Banality of Evil* (New York: Viking Compass, 1965), 7.

17. Arendt to Jaspers, letter of December 1, 1963, in *Hannah Arendt/Karl Jaspers Briefwechsel, 1926–1969*, ed. Lotte Köhler and Hans Saner (Munich: Piper, 1985), 575. Translations are my own, unless otherwise indicated. The English translation is *Hannah Arendt/Karl Jaspers Correspondence*, ed. Lotte Köhler and Hans Saner (San Diego, CA: Harcourt Brace "Harvest Books," 1992).

18. Arendt, *Responsibility and Judgment* (New York: Schocken, 2004), 4. Arendt spoke these words in accepting the Sonning Prize in Denmark.

19. Arendt to Jaspers, letter of September 28, 1951, in *Briefwechsel*, 209. The Benjamin Barber quote is from his "Hannah Arendt between Europe and America: Optimism in Dark Times," in *Politics in Dark Times*, ed. Benhabib, Tsao, and Verovsek, 261.

20. Ibid., 66.

21. Ibid., 67.

22. Arendt to Jaspers, letter of June 30, 1947, in *Briefwechsel*, 127.

23. Arendt to Jaspers, letter of January 29, 1946, in *Briefwechsel*, 67.

24. See Everett Helmut Akam, *Transnational America: Cultural Pluralist Thought in the Twentieth Century* (Lanham, MD: Rowman and Littlefield, 2002). More generally, see Gary Gerstle, *American Crucible: Race and Nation in the Twentieth Century* (Princeton, NJ: Princeton University Press, 2001), 349–57.

25. Arendt to Jaspers, letter of June 30, 1947, in *Briefwechsel*, 127.

26. John Murray Cuddihy, *The Ordeal of Civility: Freud, Marx, Levi-Strauss, and the Jewish Struggle with Modernity* (New York: Basic Books, 1974), 22.

27. Ron H. Friedman, "The Jew as Pariah: A Hidden Tradition," in *The Jew as Pariah* by Hannah Arendt, ed. Ron H. Friedman (New York: Grove Press, 1978), 67–90; Arendt, *Origins*, chap. 1, secs. 1–3. Edwin De Waal, *The Hare with the Amber Eyes* (London: Vintage, 2011), recounts the fascinating history of his Jewish family, the Ephrussi, whose fate resembled in many respects what Arendt was describing.

28. See Matthew Frye Jacobson, *Whiteness of a Different Color: European Immigrants and the Alchemy of Race* (Cambridge, MA: Harvard University Press, 1998); and Eric L. Goldstein, *The Price of Whiteness: Jews, Race, and American Identity* (Princeton, N.J. Princeton University Press, 2006).

29. This comes at the beginning of Arendt, "Reflections on Little Rock," *Dissent*, vol. 6, no. 1 (Winter 1959).

30. *Origins*, 297 301–2.

31. Arendt, "Reflections on Little Rock," 46–47.

32. Most of the discussion of the distinction between race thinking and racism comes from *Origins*, chap. 6, esp. 158–61. See Ivan Hannaford, *Race: The History of an Idea in the West* (Baltimore, MD: Johns Hopkins University Press; Washington, DC: Woodrow Wilson Press, 1996), 6–9.

33. Thomas Jefferson, *Notes on the State of Virginia* (New York: Harper Torchbooks, 1964). See Kathryn T. Gines, "Race Thinking and Racism in Hannah Arendt's *The Ori-*

gins of Totalitarianism," in *Hannah Arendt and the Uses of History* (n. 3 above, this chap.),
ed. King and Stone, 44–47, for an analysis of the relationship of Arendt's thesis on race
and racism to antebellum America. See also Stephen Jay Gould, *The Mismeasure of Man*
(New York: W. W. Norton, 1981) on the American school of anthropology.

On the history of modern race and racism in the United States, see Winthrop Jordan,
White over Black(Chapel Hill: University of North Carolina Press, 1968); George Fred-
rickson, *The Black Image in the White Mind: The Debate on Afro-American Character and
Destiny* (New York: Harper Torchbooks, 1971), and *Racism: A Short History* (Princeton,
NJ: Princeton University Press, 2002), particularly the appendix; Kwame Anthony
Appiah, *In My Father's House: Africa in the Philosophy of Culture* (New York: Oxford Uni-
versity Press, 1992), chaps. 2 and 3.

34. Arendt, "Reflections on Little Rock," 46.

35. See Arendt, *Origins*, chap. 7 ("Race and Bureaucracy"). King and Stone, eds.,
Hannah Arendt and the Uses of History, includes on overview of this controversy (1–17).
Otherwise, see King, *Race, Culture and the Intellectuals*; Singh, *Black Is a Country*; Rothberg, *Multi-directional Memory*; Klausen, "Hannah Arendt's Anti-primitivism" (all in n. 3
above, this chap.).

36. For a more extensive and detailed discussion of this issue, see Richard H. King,
"On Race and Culture: Hannah Arendt and Her Contemporaries," *Politics in Dark Times*
(n. 12 above, this chap.), ed. Benhabib, Tsao, and Verovsek, 113–36.

37. Ibid., 130.

38. *Origins*, 157. See Julia Hell, "Remnants of Totalitarianism: Hannah Arendt, Heiner
Müller, Slavoj Zizek, and the Re-invention of Politics," *Telos* 136 (Fall 2006): 89–90.

39. See King, "Conclusion: Arendt between Past and Future," in *Hannah Arendt and
the Uses of History*, ed. King and Stone, 251–55.

40. Contrast *Origins* with Karl Löwith's *From Hegel to Nietzsche* (1941; repr., Garden
City, NY: Doubleday Anchor, 1967), where the index includes no entry for race, racism,
or anti-Semitism and only four for Jews, though the book itself overlaps considerably with
Origins in the territory it covers.

41. See Stephen J. Whitfield, "The Theme of Indivisibility in the Post-War Struggle
against Prejudice in the United States," *Patterns of Prejudice* 48, no. 3 (2014): 223–47.
Elisabeth Young-Bruehl's *The Anatomy of Prejudice* (Cambridge, MA: Harvard University
Press, 1998) is a sophisticated attempt to differentiate among types of prejudice and is
largely successful in its effort.

42. Arendt, "Introduction *into* Politics," in *The Promise of Politics*, ed. Jerome Kohn
(New York: Schocken, 2007), 93–96, and *Denktagebuch*, 1:15–18.

43. Arendt, "Introduction *into* Politics," 94, and *Denktagebuch*, 1:16.

44. See Hanna F. Pitkin, *The Attack of the Blob: Hannah Arendt's Concept of the Social*
(Chicago: University of Chicago, 1998), 73–79.

45. *Origins*, 301.

46. Arendt, "Introduction *into* Politics," 95–96, and *Denktagebuch*, 1:15–18.

47. Arendt, *Eichmann in Jerusalem* (n. 16 above, this chap.), 7, 254–57.

48. *Origins*, 301.

49. *Origins*, 302.

50. Lotte Köhler, ed., *Within Four Walls: The Correspondence between Hannah Arendt and Heinrich Blücher, 1936–1968* (New York: Harcourt, Brace, 2000), 209–64. Lotte Köhler, ed. *Hannah Arendt/Heinrich Blücher: Briefe 1936–1968* (Munich: Piper, 1996), 331–90.

51. See Emily Hauptmann, "A Local History of 'The Political,'" *Political Theory* 32, no. 1 (February 2004): 34–60, for an overview of the Berkeley department.

52. Arendt to Blücher, letter of May 25, 1955, in *Within Four Walls*, 260, and, in the original German, in *Briefe*, 384.

53. Arendt to Blücher, letters of May 19, 1955, and June 15, 1955, both in *Within Four Walls*, 257 and 264, respectively, and, in German, in *Briefe*, 382, 390, respectively. See also Peter Stern and Jean Stein, "Hannah Arendt," *American Scholar* 47 (Summer 1978): 371–81, for an analysis of Arendt as a teacher.

54. Arendt to Blücher, letter of May 5, 1955, 254, in *Within Four Walls*, and, in German, in *Briefe*, 376.

55. Arendt to Blücher, letter of May 13, 1955, 356, in *Within Four Walls*, and, in German, in *Briefe*, 379.

56. Arendt to Blücher, letter of May 19, 1955, 258, in *Within Four Walls*, and, in German, in *Briefe*, 381.

57. Stanley Elkins, *Slavery: A Study in American Institutional Life* (Chicago: University of Chicago Press, 1959), 82–83. Elkins's book is the only study of American slavery in Arendt's personal library, and she refers to it in favorable terms in her essay "Civil Disobedience."

58. Thanks to Stephen J. Whitfield for this reference to James's comments about Booker T. Washington. See Henry James, ed., *The Letters of William James* (Boston: Atlantic Monthly Press, 1920), 2:60–61.

59. See Isaiah Berlin, *Enlightening: Letters 1946–1960*, ed. Henry Hardy and Jennifer Holmes (London: Pimlico, 2009), 33.

60. Hannah Arendt to J. Glenn Gray, letter of March 25, 1967, Hannah Arendt Papers, Library of Congress, Correspondence Files.

61. Susan Neiman, "Theodicy in Jerusalem," in *Hannah Arendt in Jerusalem*, ed. Steven E. Aschheim (Berkeley: University of California Press, 2001), 76.

62. Blücher to Arendt, letter of July 15, 1946, in *Briefe*, 146.

63. Ibid., 148, 149.

64. See Hannah Arendt, *Rahel Varnhagen: The Life of a Jewish Woman*, rev. ed. (New York: Harcourt Brace Jovanovich, 1974), for her characterization of psychoanalysis as a "modern form of indiscretion" (xviii).

65. Neiman, "Theodicy in Jerusalem," 78.

66. Ibid., 80, 82.

Chapter 8

1. Danielle S. Allen, *Talking to Strangers: Anxieties of Citizenship since Brown v. Board of Education* (Chicago: University of Chicago Press, 2004), 7; John D. Skrentny, *The Minority Rights Revolution* (Cambridge, MA: Belknap Press of Harvard University Press, 2002).

2. Norman Podhoretz, quoted in Thomas L. Jeffers, *Norman Podhoretz: A Biography* (New York: Cambridge University Press, 2014), 53. See also Elisabeth Young-Bruehl's account of the controversy in *Hannah Arendt: For Love of the World* (New Haven, CT: Yale University Press, 1982), 308–18; and Nathan Abrams, *Commentary Magazine: A Journal of Significant Thought and Opinion, 1945–59* (London: Valentine Mitchell, 2005), 160–63. Ralph Ellison, "The World and the Jug" (1963–64), in *Shadow and Act* (New York: Signet, 1966), 116.

In this chapter, I will use the original *Dissent* article, along with the two critical responses published with it, and her response in the issue that followed the article. See Hannah Arendt, "Reflections on Little Rock," *Dissent* 6, no. 1 (Winter 1959): 45–55; David Spitz, "Politics and the Realms of Being," *Dissent* 6, no. 1 (Winter 1959): 56–65; Melvin Tumin, "Pie in the Sky," *Dissent* 6, no. 1 (Winter 1959): 65–71; and Arendt "A Reply to Critics," *Dissent* 6, no. 2 (Spring 1960): 179–81. "Reflections" has been reprinted in *Responsibility and Judgment*, ed. Jerome Kohn (New York: Schocken, 2003), 192–213, but without the responses or Arendt's reply to them.

3. Arendt, "Reflections on Little Rock," 47.

4. Kathryn T. Gines, *Hannah Arendt and the Negro Question* (Bloomington: Indiana University Press, 2014), 15–20, has pointed out that the photo Arendt describes in "Reflections on Little Rock" (50) and "A Reply to Critics" (179) is not the one by Will Counts that shows Elizabeth Eckford apparently unaccompanied and surrounded by a white crowd with one particularly prominent white woman shouting vehemently. See Allen, *Talking to Strangers*, 4, for this photo of Elizabeth Eckford to which Arendt was reacting.

5. Arendt, "Reflections on Little Rock," 46.

6. Meili Steele, "Arendt versus Ellison on Little Rock: The Role of Language in Political Judgment," *Constellations* 3, no. 2 (1996): 200. See also Richard Kluger, *Simple Justice: The History of Brown v. Board of Education and Black America's Struggle for Equality* (New York: Random House, 1975). Arendt did not cite the very influential history of segregation by C. Vann Woodward, *The Strange Career of Jim Crow* (New York: Oxford University Press, 1955). Nor is it in her personal library.

7. Irving Howe, editorial note, *Dissent* VI, no. 1 (Winter 1959): 45. Howe worked for Arendt at Schocken Press after the war.

8. Carol Polsgrave's *Divided Minds: Intellectuals and the Civil Rights Movement* (New York: W. W. Norton, 2001) makes the point that timidity reigned among Northern intellectuals on matters having to do with civil rights. This hardly fits Arendt, who was certainly not timid in expressing her views—though they went against liberal orthodoxy. See also Daniel Matlin, *On the Corner: African American Intellectuals and the Urban Crisis* (Cambridge, MA: Harvard University Press, 2013).

9. Of particular interest here is George Lichtheim (1912–73). See Walter Laqueur's "George Lichtheim, 1912–1973," *Commentary* (August 1973), 46.

10. Lichtheim to Arendt, letter of November 20, 1957, Hannah Arendt Papers, The Library of Congress, Correspondence Files. Some of their notes and letters are in German.

11. Lichtheim to Arendt, letter of November 21, 1957, Hannah Arendt Papers. The remark about "biting irony" was made by Walter Laqueur in his obituary/profile "George Lichtheim, 1912–1973," 46.

12. Arendt to Lichtheim, letter of November 23, 1957, Hannah Arendt Papers.

13. See Abrams, *Commentary Magazine*; and also Young-Bruehl, *Hannah Arendt*, 313–18, for more context.

14. Lichtheim to Arendt, letter of February 10, 1958, Hannah Arendt Papers.

15. Ibid.

16. Ibid.

17. See Richard H. King, "The *Brown* Decades," *Patterns of Prejudice* 38, no. 4 (2004): 334–37, for a discussion of, and set of references for, the popularity of *Brown*. For an exhaustive study, see also Michael Klarman, *From Jim Crow to Civil Rights: The Supreme Court and the Struggle for Racial Equality* (New York: Oxford University Press, 2004); and Laura Kalman, *The Strange Career of Legal Liberalism* (New Haven, CT: Yale University Press, 1996), 234.

18. Kalman, *Strange Career of Legal Liberalism*, 13–59. The three doubters were Learned Hand, *The Bill of Rights* (Cambridge, MA: Harvard University Press, 1958); Herbert Wechsler, "Toward Neutral Principles of Constitutional Law," *Harvard Law Review* 73, no. 1 (1959): 1–35; and Alexander Bickel, "The Original Understanding and the Segregation Decision," *Harvard Law Review* 69, no. 1, (1955): 1–65. Kalman discusses the matters of constitutional interpretation, particularly Hand's and Wechsler's position, on pages 27–42.

19. Reinhold Niebuhr, "The Civil Rights Crisis," *New Leader*, 41, no. 34 (September 29, 1958): 6–7. Niebuhr also published numerous articles in *Christianity and Crisis* and the *Reporter* commenting on the unfolding racial crisis in the South. See Robert Penn Warren, *Segregation* (New York: Vintage, 1956), and *The Legacy of the Civil War: Meditations on the Centennial* (New York: Random House, 1961), along with David Blight's "'Gods and Devils Aplenty': Robert Penn Warren," in *American Oracle: The Civil War in the Civil Rights Era* (Cambridge, MA: Belknap Press of Harvard University Press, 2011), 31–80.

20. Arendt, "Reflections on Little Rock" (n. 2 above, this chap.), 51–52.

21. Ibid., 55.

22. Margaret Canovan, *Hannah Arendt: A Reinterpretation of Her Political Thought* (Cambridge: Cambridge University Press, 1992), 116–22. See also Jean L. Cohen and Andrew Arato, *Civil Society and Political Theory* (Cambridge, MA: MIT Press, 1992), 177–200.

23. Arendt, "Reflections on Little Rock," 53.

24. Hannah Arendt to Matthew Lipmann, letter of March 30, 1959, Hannah Arendt Papers, 1. Unfortunately the original of his letter no longer exists.

25. Arendt, "A Reply to Critics" (n. 2 above, this chap.), 179–80; See Jill Locke, "Little Rock's Social Question: Reading Arendt on School Desegregation and Social Climbing," *Political Theory* 41, no. 4 (August 2013): 536–61.

26. Howard Rabinowitz, "From Exclusion to Segregation: Southern Race Relations, 1865–1900," *Journal of American History* 63 (September 1976): 346. See also John Kirk, *Redefining the Color Line: Black Activism in Little Rock, Arkansas, 1940–1970* (Gainesville: University of Florida Press, 110–12.

27. Arendt, "Reply to Critics," 179.

28. In the version of this chapter originally published as "American Dilemmas, European Experiences," *Arkansas Historical Quarterly* 56, no. 3 (Autumn 1997): 314–33, I noted Arendt's problem with black parents trying to "force" their children on whites. But I didn't sufficiently emphasize that she saw their pressure as an American version of parvenu behavior that she had observed in reference to European, specifically German, Jews. See Locke, "Little Rock's Social Question"; and also Arendt's "Reply to Critics."

29. Arendt to Lipman, letter of March 30, 1959, 2, Hannah Arendt Papers.

30. Arendt, "Reflections on Little Rock" (n. 2 above, this chap.), 52.

31. James Bohman, "The Moral Costs of Political Pluralism: The Dilemmas of Difference and Equality in Arendt's 'Reflections on Little Rock,'" in *Hannah Arendt: Twenty Years Later* (Cambridge, MA: MIT Press, 1996), 53–80. This excellent article was the first full-length piece devoted to "Reflections."

32. Arendt, "Reflections on Little Rock," 46. And see Gunnar Myrdal's "Rank Order of Discrimination," in *An American Dilemma*, 2 vols. (New York: McGraw-Hill, 1964), 1:60–61.

33. Some variation on this dictum is attributed to Yale sociologist William Graham Sumner, whose massive study *Folkways: A Study of Mores, Manners, Customs and Morals* (New York: Cosimo Classics, 2007) was very influential in conservative Darwinist circles in the late nineteenth and early twentieth century.

34. Spitz, "Politics and the Realm of Being" (n. 2 above, this chap.), 58; Sidney Hook, "Democracy and Desegregation," *New Leader* (April 21, 1958), 11.

35. See Fred Hirsch, *Social Limits to Growth* (Cambridge, MA: Harvard University Press, 1978), for the notion of positional goods.

36. Arendt, "Reflections on Little Rock," 46.

37. Ibid., 55.

38. Arendt, "The Crisis in Education" (1958), in *Beyond Past and Future*, ed. Jerome Kohn (London: Penguin, 2006), 178–79.

39. Ibid., 189.

40. Arendt, "Reflections on Little Rock" (n. 2 above, this chap.), 50.

41. Kirk, *Redefining the Color Line* (n. 26 above, this chap.), 110–12. See also Kenneth Warren's "Ralph Ellison and the Problem of Cultural Authority," *Boundary 2* 30, no. 2 (Summer 2003): 160, for the serious doubts, even opposition, of black parents.

42. Daisy Bates, *The Long Shadow of Little Rock: A Memoir* (New York: David McKay, 1962), 63–67.

43. Arendt, "What Remains? The Language Remains: A Conversation with Günter Gaus" (1963), in *Essays in Understanding, 1930–1954*, ed. Jerome Kohn (New York: Harcourt, Brace, 1994), 8.

44. Young-Bruehl, *Hannah Arendt* (n. 2 above, this chap.), 316. Ellison referred briefly to Arendt in "The World and the Jug" (n. 2 above, this chap.), 116, and later in his interview with Robert Penn Warren in *Who Speaks for the Negro?* (New York: Random House, 1965), 342–44.

45. Ross Posnock, "Ralph Ellison, Hannah Arendt and the Meaning of Politics," in *The Cambridge Companion to Ralph Ellison*, ed. R. Posnock (Cambridge: Cambridge University Press, 2005), 201–16. Warren, "Ralph Ellison and the Problem of Cultural Authority," 165–66, also focuses on similar attitudes regarding tradition, and notes that there was a tradition in black thought of criticizing black leadership.

46. See *Talking to Strangers*, where Allen stresses the close link between "sacrifice" in a democracy and mutual "trust" among citizens and of their government.

47. Vicky Lebeau, "The Unwelcome Child: Elizabeth Eckford and Hannah Arendt," *Journal of Visual Culture* 3, no. 1 (2004): 51–62.

48. Cited in Young-Bruehl, *Hannah Arendt*, 316.

49. Werner Sollors, "Of Mules and Mares in a Land of Difference; or, Quadrupeds All?" *American Quarterly* 42, no. 2 (June 1990): 167–90. Peniel E. Joseph, "Rescuing Malcolm X from his Calculated Myths," *Chronicle of Higher Education* (May 1, 2011), notes that Malcolm recoiled at "King's use of children in demonstrations," e.g., at Birmingham. King and his staff, it should be said, were also divided on this issue.

50. Arendt to Lipman, letter of March 20, 1959, 1, Hannah Arendt Papers. Arendt, "Reply to Critics" (n. 2 above, this chap.), 179. If anything demonstrates that Arendt was not too arrogant or frightened to respond to stiff criticism, it is her reply to Lipman. Unfortunately the original of his letter no longer exists, but her reply is two single-spaced pages.

51. Walker Percy, "Mississippi: The Fallen Paradise" (1965), in *The South Today*, ed. Willie Morris (New York: Harpers, 1965). As discussed in the previous chapter, common descent is the factor that membership in a family shares with belonging to a race.

52. Hook, "Democracy and Desegregation" (n. 34 above, this chap.), 8.

53. Arendt, "Reflections on Little Rock" (n. 2 above, this chap.), 55.

54. Ibid., 54.

55. Ibid., 59.

56. Arendt, "Civil Rights" (lecture prepared for Emory University), 1, notes dated 5/1/1964, Hannah Arendt Papers, Library of Congress.

57. Arendt, "Reflections on Little Rock," 47.

58. Arendt, *The Origins of Totalitarianism*, 2nd ed. (Cleveland: 1958), 301.

59. For a discursive statement about invisibility, see the prologue and epilogue to Ellison, *Invisible Man*, 2nd ed. (1952; repr., New York: Vintage International, 1995), 3–14, 572–81. Thanks to Peter Kuryla, esp., and also Dave Murray and Steve Whitfield for sharing their thoughts on Ellison's concept of invisibility.

60. Arendt, "Reflections on Little Rock," 48.

61. Canovan, *Hannah Arendt* (n. 22 above, this chap.), 242.

62. Arendt, "Reflections on Little Rock," 48.

Chapter 9

1. Peter Novick, *The Holocaust in American Life* (Boston: Houghton Mifflin, 1999); Hasia Diner, *We Remember with Affection and Love and the Myth of Silence after the Holocaust, 1945–1962* (New York: New York University Press, 2009).

2. Novick, *The Holocaust in American Life*, 133, 144.

3. Ibid., 129. Novick covers the Eichmann affair in chap. 7 (127–45) of *The Holocaust in American Life*.

4. Hannah Arendt, "The Destruction of Six Million: A *Jewish World* Symposium" (September 1964), in *The Jewish Writings*, ed. Jerome Kohn and Ron H. Feldman (New York: Schocken Books, 2007), 490–95. This was the basis of the remarks she made at College Park. Dwight Macdonald, one of the main defenders of the Eichmann book, and Norman Podhoretz, who had written bitingly of Arendt's "perversity of brilliance," were commentators.

5. Ibid., 493.

6. Peter Viereck, *Meta-Politics: From the Romantics to Hitler* (New York: Alfred Knopf, 1942); and Thomas Mann, "German and the Germans," *Yale Review* 35, no. 2 (1945): 223–41. Adorno's claim that "to write poetry after Auschwitz is barbaric" has been the subject of much discussion. For Steiner's thesis, see "The Hollow Miracle," in *Language and Silence* (New York: Atheneum, 1967), 96–97. With Arendt's stress on Eichmann's language, her approach bore a certain resemblance to George Orwell's "Politics and the English Language" (1950), http://www.npr.org/blogs/ombudsman/Politics_and_the_English_Language-1.pdf, though this linguistic approach to politics was also developed by Victor Klemperer in Germany.

7. Novick, *The Holocaust in American Life*, 128.

8. Kirsten Fermaglich, *American Dreams and Nazi Nightmares: Early Holocaust Conscious-ness and Liberal America, 1957–1965* (Waltham, MA: Brandeis University Press, 2006).

9. Norman Fruchter, "Arendt's Eichmann and Jewish Identity," in *For a New America: Essays in History and Politics from Studies on the Left, 1959–1967*, ed. J. Weinstein and W. Eakins (New York: Vintage, 1970), 323–54.

10. Hannah Arendt, *Eichmann in Jerusalem: A Report on the Banality of Evil*, rev. and enlarged (New York: Viking Press, 1965), 7. Surprisingly, Arendt had already used this distinction in "The Image of Hell" (1946), in *Essays in Understanding, 1930–1954*, ed. Jerome Kohn (New York: Harcourt Brace, 1994), 200.

11. See Elisabeth Young-Bruehl, *Hannah Arendt: For Love of the World* (New Haven, CT: Yale University Press, 1982), 328–30. Hannah Arendt to Karl Jaspers, letter of December 23, 1960, in *Hannah Arendt/Karl Jaspers Briefwechsel, 1926–1969*, ed. Lotte Köhler and Hans Saner Munich: Piper, 1985), 453–54.

12. Arendt to Jaspers, letter of December 23, 1960, in *Briefwechsel*, 453–54.

13. Arendt, *Eichmann in Jerusalem*, 289. Arendt with Joachim Fest, "Eichmann Was Outrageously Stupid" (November 1964), in *The Last Interview and Other Conversations* (Brooklyn, NY: Melville House, 2013), 59.

14. Arendt, *Eichmann in Jerusalem*, 246–47. The italics are Arendt's.

15. Ibid., 52–53.

16. Arendt to Mary McCarthy, letter of September 20, 1963, in *Between Friends: The Correspondence of Hannah Arendt and Mary McCarthy, 1949–1975*, ed. Carol Brightman (London: Secker and Warburg, 1995), 147–48, emphasis in original; Arendt, *Eichmann in Jerusalem*, 232–33, emphasis in original.

17. As an indication of Arendt's high opinion of *Billy Budd*, she wrote in a letter of July 21, 1972, to Martin Heidegger that "I have tracked down Melville, *Billy Budd*, and will receive it here, probably tomorrow, I will then have it sent directly from the book-store to you" (*Letters 1925–1975: Hannah Arendt and Martin Heidegger*, ed. Ursula Ludz (Orlando, FL: Harcourt, 2004), 148.

18. Arendt, *Eichmann in Jerusalem*, 230.

19. In her 1975 essay "Remembering Wystan H. Auden, Who Died in the Night of the Twenty-eighth of September 1973," Arendt doesn't mention Auden's poem on Mel-ville. Nor does she do so anywhere else that I can find. Peter E. Firchow, *W. H. Auden: Contexts for Poetry* (Newark: University of Delaware Press, 2002), 189, mentions the similarities but doesn't explore them. The same goes for Edward Mendelsohn's piece on Auden: "The Secret Auden," *New York Review of Books*, March 20, 2014, http://www.nybooks.com/articles/archives/2014/mar/20/secret-auden/, part of which has been reproduced by the Hannah Arendt Center and is found at http://www.hannah arendt center.org/?tag=w-h-auden, under the heading Amor Mundi, 3/2/14. Most surprisingly, Susannah Young-ah Gottlieb's excellent *Regions of Sorrow: Anxiety and Messianism in Hannah Arendt and W. H. Auden* (Stanford, CA: Stanford University

Press,2003 neither analyzes nor even refers to a possible link between the two on this matter.

20. Steven E. Aschheim, "Introduction: Hannah Arendt in Jerusalem," in *Hannah Arendt in Jerusalem* (Berkeley: University of California Press, 2001), 12. See Fredric Jameson, *The Antinomies of Realism* (London: Verso, 2013), for a discussion of the modern denunciation of the "ethical binary" (120). This revival of religious and moral concern was an alternative of sorts to the therapeutic culture of postwar American thought and culture.

21. Arendt, *Eichmann in Jerusalem* (n. 10 above, this chap.), 85. Language "regulations" not "rules" might have been a better translation of this term.

22. Flannery O'Connor, letter to "A," January 25, 1957, in *The Habit of Being: The Letters of Flannery O'Connor*, ed. Sally Fitzgerald (New York: Farrar, Straus and Giroux, 1988), 198–99. Though O'Connor was writing well before *Eichmann* appeared, she was an admirer of Arendt's Eichmann book: "My what a book. I admire that old Lady [*sic*] extremely" (letter to Cecil Dawson, September 16, 1963, *The Habit of Being*, 540).

23. Arendt to McCarthy, letter of September 20, 1963, in *Between Friends*, 147.

24. Arendt, *Eichmann in Jerusalem*, 26, 33.

25. Ibid., 146.

26. Arendt to McCarthy, letter of October 10, 1963, in *Between Friends*, 152.

27. Arendt, *Eichmann in Jerusalem*, 287.

28. Arendt with Fest, *The Last Interview* (n. 13 above, this chap.), 48, 45–46.

29. Susan Sontag, "Fascinating Fascism" (1975), in *Under the Sign of Saturn* (New York: Farrar, Straus, Giroux,1980).

30. Arendt, "A Letter to Gershom Scholem," in *The Jewish Writings*, 470–71.

31. Arendt, *Eichmann in Jerusalem*, 289, and "Auschwitz on Trial (1966)," in *Responsibility and Judgment*, ed. J. Kohn (New York: Schocken Books, 2003), 250. See also Devin O. Pendas's excellent *The Frankfurt Auschwitz Trial, 1963–1965: Genocide, History, and the Limits of the Law* (Cambridge: Cambridge University Press, 2006).

32. Seyla Benhabib, "Hannah Arendt and the Redemptive Power of Narrative," *Social Research* 57, no. 1 (Spring 1990): 185.

33. Harry Mulisch, *Criminal Case 40/61, The Trial of Adolf Eichmann: An Eye Witness Account*, trans. Robert Naborn (Philadelphia: University of Pennsylvania Press, 2005/1961), 111–12.

34. See Robert Zaretsky, *A Life Worth Living: Albert Camus and the Quest for Meaning* (Cambridge, MA: Belknap Press of Harvard University Press, 20013), 139. Camus was, of course, one of Arendt's favorites.

35. Arendt, *Eichmann in Jerusalem* (n. 10 above, this chap.), 287.

36. Arendt, "Thinking and Moral Considerations" *Social Research* 38, no. 3 (Autumn 1971): 417. This blithe kind of tone-deafness is illustrated in the following example. In the early 1950s, Senator Joseph McCarthy allegedly met one of his journalistic adver-

saries, Drew Pearson, in an elevator by chance. Despite having smeared Pearson publicly McCarthy stuck out his hand and said, "No hard feelings, Drew."

37. Marie Syrkin, "Miss Arendt Surveys the Holocaust," *Jewish Frontier* (May 1963), 12.

38. Ibid., 11, 12.

39. Arendt, *Eichmann in Jerusalem*, 125.

40. Susan Neiman, *Evil in Modern Thought* (Princeton, NJ: Princeton University Press, 2002), 276–81, and "Theodicy in Jerusalem," in *Hannah Arendt in Jerusalem*, ed. Steven E. Aschheim (Berkeley: University of California Press, 2001), 65–90.

41. Arendt, "For the Honor and the Glory of the Jewish People," in *The Jewish Writings*, 199 (originally printed in *Aufbau*, April 21, 1944).

42. See Young-Bruehl, *Hannah Arendt*, 522n56. The full review of Poliakov's book is reprinted as "The History of the Great Crime," in *The Jewish Writings*, 453–61.

43. Rainer Schimpf, "Das dunkelste Kapitel—Hannah Arendt and the Jewish Councils," in *Hannah Arendt: Ihr Denken Veränderte die Welt*, ed. Martin Wiebel (Munich: Piper, 2013), 230. The relationship between Arendt and Raul Hilberg was a troubled and troubling one. See Nathaniel Popper, "A Conscious Pariah: On Raul Hilberg," *Nation*, April 19, 2010, http://www.thenation.com/article/conscious-pariah, for discussion, particularly of Hilberg's feeling that Arendt had used too much of his book without attribution. Arendt, for her part, thought Hilberg's book, *The Destruction of the European Jewry* (New York: Quadrangle Books, 1961), was "really outstanding, but only because he just reports." The more general historical and speculative parts, she thought, were "drivel" and worse. Arendt to Jaspers, letter of April 20, 1964, in *Briefwechsel*, 586.

44. Arendt, *Eichmann in Jerusalem*, 119, and "The Eichmann Controversy: A Letter to Gershom Scholem," in *The Jewish Writings*, 468.

45. Arendt, "The Destruction of Six Million," in *The Jewish Writings*, 494.

46. Ibid., 494–95.

47. Arendt with Fest, *The Last Interview* (n. 13 above, this chap.), 63.

48. Justine Lacroix, "Arendt, Human Rights, and French Philosophy," paper delivered at the annual meeting of American Political Science Association, August 29–September 1, 2013, Chicago. Available at the Social Science Research Network, http://ssrn.com/abstract=2300419.

49. Wolfgang Heuer, "Ein schwieriger Dialog: Die Hannah Arendt-Rezeption in Deutschsprachigen Raum," in *Hannah Arendt: Nach dem Totalitarianismus*, ed. D. Ganzfried (Hamburg: Sebastian Hefti, 1997), 23–24; Hans Mommsen, "Hannah Arendt's Interpretation of the Holocaust as a Challenge to Human Existence: The Intellectual Background," in *Arendt in Jerusalem*, ed. Aschheim, 224–31; Richard I. Cohen, "A Generation's Response to Eichmann in Jerusalem," in *Arendt in Jerusalem*, ed. Aschheim, 274–75.

50. David Caute, "The Banality of Evil," in *Isaac and Isaiah: The Covert Punishment of a Cold War Heretic* (New Haven, CT: Yale University Press), 262–71.

51. Alfred Kazin, October 19, 1963, entry, in *Journals*, ed. Richard M. Cook (New Haven, CT: Yale University Press, 2011), 311; Irving Howe, quoted in Michael Ezra, "The Eichmann Polemics: Hannah Arendt and Her Critics," *Dissent* 9 (Summer 2007): 142–43. It is not clear whether the meeting was held at Hotel Woodstock (Kazin) or Hotel Diplomat (Howe, quoted in Ezra).

52. Dagmar Barnouw, *Visible Spaces: Hannah Arendt and the German-Jewish Experience* (Baltimore, MD: Johns Hopkins University, 1990), 181–83.

53. Arendt to Jaspers, letter of November 24, 1963, *Briefwechsel* (n. 11 above, this chap.), 535.

54. Ibid., 535.

55. Ezra, "The Eichmann Polemics," 144; Barnouw, *Visible Spaces*, 355.

56. Jennifer Ring, *The Political Consequences of Thinking: Gender and Judaism in the Work of Hannah Arendt* (Albany, NY: SUNY Press, 1998), 91–92.

57. Ibid., 99.

58. Alfred Kazin, "'In Every Voice, in Every Ban,'" *New Republic* (January 10, 1944), 46.

59. Hannah Arendt to Leni Yahil, letter of May 8, 1961, http://www.eurozine.com/articles/2010-09-24-arendtyahil-en.html.

60. Arendt, "The Eichmann Controversy" (n. 44 above, this chap.), 467.

61. Yahil to Arendt, letter of May 18, 1961.

62. Yahil to Arendt, letter of March 7, 1963.

63. Arendt to Yahil, letter of April 10, 1963.

64. Yahil to Arendt, letter of April 30, 1963.

65. Ring, *The Political Consequences of Thinking*, 110.

66. Ibid., 39.

67. Syrkin, "Miss Arendt" (n. 38 above, this chap.), 7, 8, 10, 12.

68. Barbara Tuchman, "The Final Solution" (1966), in *Practicing History: Selected Essays* (New York: Alfred Knopf, 1981), 121. The remarks on Arendt are found in a review of Gideon Hausner's *Justice in Jerusalem*, which appeared originally in the *New York Times Book Review*, May 29, 1966, 3, 12.

69. Gertrude Ezorsky, "Hannah Arendt's View of Totalitarianism and the Holocaust," *Philosophical Forum* 36, nos. 1–2 (Fall–Winter 1984–85): 63–81.

70. Judith Shklar, "Hannah Arendt as Pariah," in *Political Thought and Thinkers*, ed. Stanley Hoffman (Chicago: University of Chicago Press, 1998), 366, 374.

71. Ibid., 372–75.

72. Kazin, January 18, 1964, and April 27, 1982, entries in *Journals*, 319 and 489, respectively.

73. Norman Podhoretz, *Ex-Friends: Falling Out with Allen Ginsberg, Lionel and Diana Trilling, Lillian Hellman, Hannah Arendt and Norman Mailer* (New York: Free Press, 1999), 139–77.

74. Anthony Grafton, "Arendt and Eichmann at the Dinner Table," *American Scholar* 68, no. 1 (Winter 1991): 10–19; and Arendt, "Answers to Questions Submitted by Samuel Grafton," in *The Jewish Writings*, 472–89.

75. Ron H. Feldman, ed., *The Jew as Pariah* (New York: Grove Press, 1978), 241; Arendt, "Letter to Gershom Scholem," in *The Jewish Writings*, 467.

76. Richard Sennett, *The Conscience of the Eye: The Design and Social Life of Cities* (London: Faber and Faber, 1990), 132–41.

77. See Michael Ignatieff, "Arendt's Example," Hannah Arendt Prize Ceremony, Bremen, November 28, 2003 (http://www.hks.harvard.edu/cchrp/pdf/arendt.24.11.03 .pdf). Arendt never commented on Berlin's work but claimed to Jaspers (privately) that he had an "intimate connection with the Israeli government" during the Eichmann controversy (Arendt to Jaspers, letter of November 24, 1963, in *Briefwechsel*, 571).

Chapter 10

1. Hannah Arendt, *On Revolution* (New York: Viking Compass, 1965). For example, Hannah F. Pitkin came close to thinking the book "profoundly incoherent." See *The Attack of the Blob: Hannah Arendt's Concept of the Social* (Chicago.: University of Chicago, 1998), 217–25.

2. I will subsume these various traditions under the concept of "republicanism." The radical Whig tradition was more exclusively political and English, while the republican and, esp., civic humanism labels widen the scope to French and Italian sources as well.

Richard Hofstadter, *The American Political Tradition* (New York: Alfred Knopf, 1948), and *The Progressive Historians: Turner, Beard and Parrington* (New York: Alfred Knopf, 1968), chaps. 5–7; Louis Hartz, *The Liberal Tradition in America* (New York: Harvest Books, 1955); and Jesse Lemisch, "The American Revolution Seen from the Bottom Up," and Staughton Lynd, "Beyond Beard" — both in *Towards a New Past*, ed. Barton J. Bernstein (New York: Random House, 1968), 3–45, and 46–64, respectively. For the republican turn, see Bernard Bailyn, assisted by Jane N. Garrett, ed., *Pamphlets of the American Revolution, 1750–1776* (Cambridge, MA: Belknap Press of Harvard University Press, 1965), and *The Ideological Origins of the American Revolution* (Cambridge, MA: Belknap Press of Harvard University Press, 1967); Gordon S. Wood, *The Creation of the American Republic, 1776–1787* (Chapel Hill: University of North Carolina Press, 1969); and J. G. A. Pocock, *The Machiavellian Moment: Florentine Political Thought and the Atlantic Republican Tradition* (Princeton, NJ: Princeton University Press, 1975), esp. 506–52. See also Pocock's "Civic Humanism and Its Role in Anglo-American Thought" (1968), and "Machiavelli, Harrington and English Political Ideologies in the Eighteenth Century" (1965), both in *Politics, Language and Time: Essays on Political Thought and History* (New York: Atheneum, 1973),80–103 and 103–47, respectively. Pocock's "*The Machiavellian Moment* Revisited: A Study in History and Ideology," *Journal of Modern History* 53 (March 1981): 49–72, reviews some of the crucial issues raised by the reception of his book.

The historiographical assessments of the republican synthesis are many, but the ones I have learned most from are Daniel Rodgers, "Republicanism: The Career of a Concept," *Journal of American History* 79 (1992): 11–38; Joyce Appleby, *Liberalism and Republicanism in the Historical Imagination* (Cambridge, MA.: Harvard University Press, 1992); James T. Kloppenberg, "The Virtues of Liberalism: Christianity, Republicanism and Ethics in Early American Political Discourse," and "Premature Requiem: Republicanism in American History," both in *The Virtues of Liberalism* (Oxford: Oxford University Press, 1998),21–37 and 59–70, respectively; Jeffrey C. Isaac, "Republicanism vs. Liberalism? A Reconsideration," *History of Political Thought* 9 (1988): 349–77; and, most recently, Mira L. Siegelberg, "Things Fall Apart: JGA Pocock, Hannah Arendt, and the Politics of Time," *Modern Intellectual History* 10, no. 1 (April 2013): 109–34.

3. One history of the New Left that acknowledges Arendt's influence is Wini Breines's *Community and Organization in the New Left, 1962–68* (Boston: Beacon Press, 1982). Martin Jay has also noted Arendt's considerable influence on the Free Speech Movement at Berkeley ("The Political Existentialism of Hannah Arendt," in *Permanent Exiles: Essays on the Intellectual Migration from Germany to America* (New York: Columbia University Press, 1986), 238. For an account that stresses the Arendtian dimensions of the Civil Rights Movement, see Richard H. King, *Civil Rights and the Idea of Freedom* (New York: Oxford University Press, 1992).

4. Harvey Mansfield, contribution to panel discussion, in *Hannah Arendt and Leo Strauss: German Émigrés and American Political Thought after World War*, ed. P. G. Kielmansegg, H. Mewes, and E. Glaser-Schmidt (Washington, DC: German Historical Institute; New York: Cambridge University Press, 1997), 170.

5. Pocock, *The Machiavellian Moment*, 516n16, 550n83. If there is a single source for Arendt's republican historiography, it is Zera S. Fink's *The Classical Republicans* (1945; repr., Evanston, IL: Northwestern University Press, 1962). But Arendt's anticipation of the civic humanist/republican historiography has been noted by few until recently. Christopher M. Duncan focuses on the idea of "public happiness" among the Anti-Federalists in "Men of Different Faith: The Anti-Federalist Ideal in Early American Political Thought," *Polity* 26, no. 3 (Spring 1994): 387–415; and Joseph R. Stromberg's profiles an Arendt-influenced anarchist: "Walter Karp: Jeffersonian Republican," *First Principles: ISI Web Journal*, December 10, 2009, http://www.firstprinciplesjournal.com/articles .aspx?article=1354&loc=fs.

6. Arendt, "Walter Benjamin: 1892–1940," in *Men in Dark Times* (New York: Harcourt, Brace and World, 1968), 204. Of course, Arendt had explored the Greek (Athenian) experience of politics in *The Human Condition* (Chicago: University of Chicago Press, 1958).

7. Arendt, "Walter Benjamin," 205, 206. Nietzsche's idea of "monumental" as opposed to "antiquarian" and "critical" historical consciousness is developed in *The Use and Abuse of History* (New York: Cosimo, 2006).

8. Arendt, *On Revolution*, 156. See also David L. Marshall, "The Polis and Its Analogues in the Thought of Hannah Arendt," *Modern Intellectual History* 7, no. 1 (2010): 123–49.

9. Arendt, *On Revolution*, 151–52.

10. Judith N. Shklar, "Montesquieu and the New Republicanism," in *Political Thought and Political Thinkers*, ed. Stanley Hoffmann (Chicago: University of Chicago Press, 1998), 244–61.

11. Contrary to George Kateb and Pocock, I am struck by the relative paucity of "virtue talk" in *On Revolution*, though I take Kateb's point about the various virtues or qualities needed for citizenship. See Kateb, "Political Action: Its Nature and Advantage," in *The Cambridge Companion to Hannah Arendt*, ed. Dana Villa (Cambridge: Cambridge University Press, 2000), 136–38.

12. Arendt, *On Revolution* (n. 1 above, this chap.), 115, 124, 117.

13. Ibid., 115.

14. George A. Peek, ed., *The Political Writings of John Adams* (Indianapolis: Liberal Arts Press, 1954), 176–77. Arendt later wrote of "the urge to appear-shows a claim for recognition and praise. All that appears wants to be seen and recognized and praised." In her *Denktagebuch*, ed. Ursula Ludz and Ingeborg Nordmann, 2 vols. (Munich: Piper, 2002), 2:748.

15. Arendt, *On Revolution*, 258.

16. See, of course, Madison's *Federalist* Paper, #10. The most powerful critique of Arendt's preference for participatory over representative democracy is George Kateb, *Hannah Arendt: Politics, Conscience, Evil* (Oxford: Martin Robertson, 1983), chap. 4 ("Modern Democracy").

17. Kateb, *Hannah Arendt*, 196, 205.

18. Frederick M. Dolan, *Allegories of America: Narratives Metaphysics Politics* (Ithaca, NY: Cornell University Press, 1994), 186.

19. Arendt, *On Revolution*, 40–45; see Pocock, "Civic Humanism" (n. 2 above, this chap.); and Siegelberg, "Things Fall Apart" (n. 2 above, this chap.), where expansion becomes another way of renewing the republic and forestalling the workings of time.

20. Arendt, *On Revolution*, 264–66.

21. Fink, *Classical Republicans* (n. 5 above, this chap.), 186.

22. Dean Hammer, "Hannah Arendt and Roman Political Thought: The Practice of Theory," *Political Theory* 10, no. 1 (February 2002): 125.

23. See Arendt, *On Revolution*, 29–30 and, more generally, 28–34, 225–26. As Dean Hammer emphasizes, the Romans located the stories of their founding as actions and deeds "within the realm of human affairs" and without a transcendent "source" (128). See Leo Strauss, *Natural Right and History* (Chicago: University of Chicago Press, 1953), 177.

24. Arendt, *On Revolution*, 148, 226, 148.

25. Wood, *Creation of the American Republic* (n. 2 above, this chap.), 29.

26. Bailyn, "Sources and Traditions," in *Pamphlets of the American Revolution* (n. 2 above, this chap.), 23–28.

27. Ibid., 29.

28. Arendt, *On Revolution*, 23, 109, 55–56.

29. Pocock, *Machiavellian Moment*, 523; Wood, *Creation of the American Republic*, 607. Though Wood and Arendt are in broad agreement on much, Wood thinks that John Adams totally missed the point of the new Constitution in which sovereignty was lodged in the people as a collection of individuals not as a collection of ranks, orders, and classes.

30. Arendt, *On Revolution*, 133, italics mine.

31. Pocock spends a fair amount of time in the concluding chapter of *The Machiavellian Moment* sparring with Wood over whether "classical politics" had come to an end with the Constitution. See also Siegelberg, "Things Fall Apart," for further discussion of this theme.

32. Arendt, *On Revolution*, 213.

33. For Hartz's use of the term "American general will," see *The Liberal Tradition* (n. 2 above, this chap.), 10–11; James Kloppenberg, "In Retrospect: Louis Hartz's *The Liberal Tradition in America*," *Reviews in American History* 29, no. 3 (September 2001): 472–73.

34. See, of course, Arendt's critiques of Sartre and Fanon in *On Violence* (New York: Harvest Books, 1970).

35. George Lichtheim, "Two Revolutions," in *"The Concept of Ideology" and Other Essays* (New York: Vintage, 1967), 119–121. See my chap. 8 here for Lichtheim's role in *Commentary*'s nonpublication of Arendt's Little Rock essay.

36. Eric Hobsbawm, "Hannah Arendt on Revolution," in *Revolutionaries* (London: Weidenfeld and Nicholson, 1973), 202. Ironically, David Scott has recently criticized Arendt for neglecting the Haitian Revolution and thus assuming its potentially great relevance for an understanding of this non-European revolution. See *Conscripts of Modernity* (Durham, NC: Duke University Press, 2004), 211–21, 202.

37. Arendt, *On Revolution*, 265; Hobsbawm, *Revolutionaries*, 202, 207.

38. Hobsbawm, *Revolutionaries*, 205; Lichtheim, *The Concept of Ideology*, 117.

39. Hobsbawm, *Revolutionaries*, 204.

40. Sheldon Wolin, "Democracy and the Political," *Salmagundi* 60 (Spring–Summer 1983), 3–19. An article by Wolin's one-time colleague at Berkeley, Hanna Fenichel Pitkin, "Justice: On Relating Private and Public," *Political Theory* 9, no. 3 (August 1981): 327–52, focuses special attention on the absence of social justice from Arendt's work. See also Thomas Pangle, *The Spirit of Modern Republicanism: The Moral Vision of the American Founders and the Philosophy of Locke* (Chicago: University of Chicago Press, 1988), 294n7.

41. Jeffrey Isaac, *Arendt, Camus, and Modern Rebellion* (New Haven, CT: Yale University Press, 1992), 145–48. Isaac also suggests Arendt's affinities with the French liberal tradition of Montesquieu, Tocqueville, and Constant, along with Rosa Luxemburg's lib-

ertarian Marxism and Max Weber's position in "Politics as a Vocation," *From Max Weber: Essays in Sociology*, ed. H. H. Gerth and C. Wright Mills (New York: Oxford University Press, 1958), 77–128.

42. See Dick Howard, "Keeping the Republic: Reading Arendt's *On Revolution* after the Fall of the Wall," *Democratiya* 9 (Summer 2007): 122–40.

43. Hofstadter, *American Political Tradition* (n. 2 above, this chap.), viii.

44. Ibid., 5, 356, 8.

45. Ibid., 15.

46. Wood, *Creation of the American Republic* (n. 2 above, this chap.), 475.

47. Ironically, Richard Hofstadter, "The Paranoid Style in American Politics" (1963), in *"The Paranoid Style in American Politics" and Other Essays* (New York: Alfred A. Knopf, 1965), 3–40, echoed the paranoia theme that Bernard Bailyn, *The Origins of American Politics* (New York: Vintage, 1968), chap. 1, noted as one of the salient traits of the radical Whig position.

48. Hartz, *Liberal Tradition*, 50. As one source of this idea, Hartz cites a passage by Gunnar Myrdal.

49. Ibid., 46–47.

50. Ibid., 23, 45.

51. Ibid., 61.

52. Kloppenburg, "In Retrospect," 465.

53. More than anyone else at the time, Hartz recognized the important differences between American liberalism and antebellum Southern conservatism. Southern conservatism was not simply the ideology of large-scale agrarian capitalists but neither was it merely a form of republicanism.

54. Robert Nisbet, "Hannah Arendt and the American Revolution," *Social Research* 44, no. 1 (Spring 1977): 63–79; Peter Baehr, "Totalitarianism in America? Robert Nisbet on the 'Wilson War State' and Beyond," *American Sociologist* 1, no. 1 (2014): 35–66.

55. Leo Strauss, *Natural Right and History* (Chicago: University of Chicago Press, 1953). 202–51. For the discussion here, I have drawn upon Harry T. Jaffa, "Crisis of the Strauss Divided: The Legacy Reconsidered," *Social Research* 54, no. 3 (Autumn 1987): 579–604; Gordon S. Wood, "The Fundamentalists and the Constitution," *New York Review of Books* 35, no. 2 (February 18, 1988): 33–40; Pangle, *Spirit of Modern Republicanism*; T. G. West, "Leo Strauss and the American Founding," *Review of Politics* 53, no. 1 (1991): 157–92; Christopher Bruell, "A Return to Classical Political Philosophy and the Understanding of the American Founding," *Review of Politics* 53, no. 1 (1991): 76–86; David Lewis Schaefer, "Leo Strauss and American Democracy: A Response to Wood and Holmes," *Review of Politics* 53, no. 1 (1991): 187–99; Catherine Zuckert and Michael Zuckert, *The Truth about Leo Strauss: Political Philosophy and American Democracy* (Chicago: University of Chicago Press, 2006); Richard H. King, "Rights and Slavery, Race and Racism: Leo Strauss, the Straussians, and the American Dilemma," *Modern Intellectual*

History 5, no. 1 (2008): 55–82; and Jonathan O'Neill, "Straussian Constitutional History and the Straussian Political Project," *Rethinking History* 13, no. 4 (2009): 459–78.

56. See Pangle, "The Classical Analysis of Civic Virtue," in *Spirit of Modern Republicanism*, 48–61. See 291–92n5 for his observation regarding the republican neglect of the Declaration of Independence.

57. Arendt makes this point in *The Origins of Totalitarianism* (Cleveland: Meridian Books, 1958), 158, but doesn't mention Strauss.

58. Pangle, *Spirit of Modern Republicanism*, 286n7, 33, 35. See also Herbert J. Storing, introduction to *Anti-Federalist: An Abridgement of the Complete Anti-Federalist* (Chicago: University of Chicago Press, 2006), 1–4, for a similar view of the Anti-Federalists.

59. Pangle, *Spirit of Modern Republicanism*, 49.

60. Ibid., 53.

61. Arendt, *The Human Condition* (Garden City, NY: Doubleday Anchor, 1959), 12–13.

62. Ibid., 59.

63. Ibid., 52.

64. Pangle, *Spirit of Modern Republicanism*, 24. Thus he, too, fails to come to terms with the Protestant/Calvinist origins of American liberalism as proposed by John P. Diggins in *The Lost Soul of American Politics: Virtue, Self-Interest, and the Foundations of Liberalism* (New York: Basic Books, 1984).

65. Pangle, *Spirit of Modern Republicanism*, 50.

66. Ibid., 51–52.

67. O'Neill, "Straussian Constitutional History," 459–78; Jaffa, "Crisis of the Strauss Divided," 590.

68. Harry T. Jaffa, *A New Birth of Freedom: Abraham Lincoln and the Coming of the Civil War* (Lanham, MD: Rowman and Littlefield, 2000), 263–64, 395–97, for discussions of consent and particularly the election of 1800.

69. Richard A. Primus, "Rights after World War II," in *The American Language of Rights* (1999; repr., Cambridge: Cambridge University Press, 2004), 130. For treatments of the reluctance of American political elites to confront slavery, see Garry Wills, *Lincoln at Gettysburg* (New York: Simon and Schuster, 1992); Joseph J. Ellis, "The Silence," in *The Founding Brothers* (New York: Vintage, 2002), 81–119; Eric Foner, *The Fiery Trial: Abraham Lincoln and American Slavery* (New York: W. W. Norton, 2012).

70. Gordon S. Wood once wrote of the Straussians that they showed "no feel for history and what history does" in their analysis of the Framers' work. Wood, "The Fundamentalist and the Constitution" (n. 55 above, this chap.), 39.

71. See Michael Zuckert, *The Natural Rights Republic* (South Bend, IN: University of Notre Dame Press, 1996).

72. Arendt, *On Revolution*, 191. The notion of law as a command requiring obedience came from the Hebrews. See also Hammer, "Hannah Arendt and Roman Political Thought," 128.

73. Arendt, *On Revolution*, 196; John Adams, "A Defense of the American Constitu-tion," in *The Political Writings of John Adams: Representative Selections*, ed. George A Peek (Indianapolis: Bobbs-Merrill, 1954), 117.

74. Lisa Disch "How Could Hannah Arendt Glorify the American Revolution and Re-vile the French? Placing *On Revolution* in the Historiography of the French and American Revolutions," *European Journal of Political Theory* 10, no. 3 (2011): 351; for "layered au-thority," see 353. Duncan, "Men of Different Faiths" (n. 5 above, this chap.), 387–415, also places Arendt near to the Anti-Federalists. Wood, *Creation of the American Republic*, sees the Anti-Federalists as old-style republicans, spokesmen for citizen participation, and commit-ted to republican virtue, not advocates of centralized representative democracy (516).

75. George Kateb, "Death and Politics: Hannah Arendt's Reflections on the Ameri-can Constitution," *Social Research* 54, no. 3 (Autumn 1987): 607.

76. Arendt, *On Revolution*, 123–24.

77. Jeremy Waldron, "Arendt's Constitutional Politics," in *The Cambridge Compan-ion to Hannah Arendt*, ed. Dana Villa (Cambridge: Cambridge University Press, 2000), 212–13.

78. Melville, *"Billy Budd" and Other Tales* (New York: Signet, 1961), 26.

79. Arendt, *On Revolution*, 221–23.

80. Hartz, *The Liberal Tradition*, 10.

81. Judith Shklar, "Redeeming American Political Theory" (1991), in *Redeeming American Political Thought*, ed. Stanley Hoffmann and Dennis F. Thompson (Chicago: University of Chicago Press, 1998), 92.

82. Kloppenberg, "In Retrospect," 472, 473.

83. Arendt, *On Revolution*, 222–23.

84. See, most recently, Lewis Perry, *Civil Disobedience: An American Tradition* (New Haven, CT: Yale University Press, 2013), who also neglects the rights tradition.

85. See Ronald Dworkin, *Taking Rights Seriously* (Cambridge, MA: Harvard Univer-sity Press, 1977); and John Rawls, *Political Liberalism* (New York: Columbia University Press, 1993).

86. For discussions of how liberalism and republicanism fit together historically and conceptually, see Edward S. Corwin, *The "Higher Law" Background of American Consti-tutional Law* (1928–29; repr., Indianapolis: Liberty Fund, 1955); J. G. A. Pocock, "The Machiavellian Moment Revisited," *Journal of Modern History* 53, no. 1 (March 1981): 49–72; Jeffrey C. Isaac, "Republicanism vs. Liberalism? A Reconsideration," *Journal of Political Thought* 9 (1988): 349–77; Celeste M. Condit and John L. Lucaites, *Crafting Equality: American's Anglo-African Word* (Chicago: University of Chicago Press, 1993); and James T. Kloppenberg, "The Virtues of Liberalism: Christianity, Republicanism and Ethics in Early American Political Discourse," in *The Virtues of Liberalism* (n. 2 above, this chap.), 21–37.

87. Primus, "Rights after World War II."

88. Carl Becker, *The Declaration of Independence* (1922; repr., New York: Vintage 1962); Morton White, "The Nature of Rights," in *The Philosophy of the American Revolution* (New York: Oxford University Press, 1978); Primus, "Rights of the Founding," in *The American Language of Rights*; Eric Slauter, "Slavery and the Language of Rights," in *The Cultural Origins of the Constitution* (Chicago: University of Chicago Press, 2009). And yet, such comprehensive works as John P. Diggins, *The Lost Soul of American Politics* (n. 64 above, this chap.); and James T. Kloppenberg, "The Virtues of Liberalism," scarcely mention rights in discussing the essence of liberalism.

89. Arendt, *On Revolution*, 169, 215.

90. Duncan, "Men of Different Faith" (n. 5 above, this chap.), 409.

91. Arendt, *On Revolution*, 219–20.

92. Ibid., 256.

Chapter 11

1. In the 1960s, the two best known works on theories of revolution when *On Revolution* (New York: Viking Compass, 1965) was published were Crane Brinton, *The Anatomy of Revolution* (1938; repr., New York: Vintage, 1965); and Barrington Moore Jr., *The Social Origins of Dictatorship and Democracy: Lord and Peasant in the Making of the Modern World* (Boston: Beacon, 1966).

For the French Revolution, I have consulted Alexis de Tocqueville, *The Old Regime and the French Revolution* (New York: Doubleday Anchor, 1955); R. R. Palmer, *Twelve Who Ruled: The Year of the Terror in the French Revolution* (1941; repr., Princeton University Press, 1989), and *The Challenge* and *The Struggle*, vols. 1 and 2, respectively, of *The Age of the Democratic Revolution: A Political History of Europe and America, 1760–1800* (Princeton, NJ: Princeton University Press, 1959–64); François Furet, *Interpreting the French Revolution*, trans. Elborg Forster (Cambridge University Press: 1981); Patrice Higonnet, *Goodness beyond Virtue: Jacobins during the French Revolution* (Cambridge, MA: Harvard University Press, 1998), and "Terror, Trauma and the 'Young Marx': Explanation of Jacobin Politics," *Past and Present* 191, no. 1 (May 2006): 121–64 (doi: 10.1093/pastj/gtj010); and Lynn Hunt, "The World We Have Gained: The Future of the French Revolution," *American Historical Review* 108, no. 1 (February 2003): 1–19. More general recent histories are Simon Schama, *Citizens: A Chronicle of the French Revolution* (New York: Vintage, 1990); William Doyle, *The Oxford History of the French Revolution*, 2nd ed. (Oxford: Oxford University Press, 2002); Dan Edelstein, *The Terror of Natural Right: Republicanism, the Cult of Nature, and the French Revolution* (Chicago: University of Chicago Press, 2009).

2. Hunt, "The World We have Gained," 17. Higonnet, "Terror, Trauma and the 'Young Marx,'" 8.

3. Tocqueville, *The Old Regime and the French Revolution*, 13. See also Hunt, "The World We Have Gained"; and Keith Michael Baker, "Political Languages of the French

Revolution," in *The Cambridge History of Eighteenth Century Political Thought*, ed. Mark Goldie and Robert Wokler (Cambridge: Cambridge University Press, 2006), 628–59.

4. Very few historians of the French revolution factor in the great historical significance of the Haitian Revolution. Besides the classic, C. L. R. James, *The Black Jacobins*, 2nd ed. rev. (1963; repr., New York: Vintage, 1989), see David Scott, *Conscripts of Modernity: The Tragedy of Colonial Enlightenment* (Durham, NC: Duke University Press, 2004); and Robin Blackburn, *The American Crucible: Slavery, Emancipation and Human Rights* (London: Verso, 2011).

5. Arendt, *On Revolution*, 63.

6. Ibid., 54.

7. Ibid., 58.

8. Ibid.

9. Ibid., 108.

10. For discussions of Brinton's classic study, see Theda Skocpol, *States and Social Revolutions* (Cambridge: Cambridge University Press, 1979), 33–40; and Torbjørn L. Knutsen and Jennifer L. Bailey, "Over the Hill? *The Anatomy of Revolution* at Fifty," *Journal of Peace Research* 26, no. 4 (1989): 1421–31.

11. Brinton, *Anatomy* (n. 1 above, this chap.), 235; Skocpol, *States and Social Revolutions*, 35–36.

12. Brinton, *Anatomy*, 262. Brinton was aware of this awkward aspect of his framework.

13. Ibid., 31.

14. Ibid., 49. Lawrence Stone, "Theories of Revolution," *World Politics* 18 (1966): 159–76.

15. Brinton, *Anatomy*, 24.

16. Brinton, "Reigns of Terror and Virtue," in ibid.; Victor Serge, *Memoirs of a Revolutionary* (1951; repr., New York: New York Review Books, 2012).

17. Palmer, *The Age of the Democratic Revolution* 1:11.

18. Brinton, *Anatomy*, 291.

19. Tocqueville, *The Old Regime and the French Revolution*, 169; and Hunt, "The World We Have Gained"; Gemma Betros, "François Furet: Finding 'Revolution' within the French Revolution," *Access: History* 2, no. 2 (1999): 53–63; Doyle, *The Oxford History of the French Revolution* (n. 1 above, this, chap.), app. 3, 446–60; and Higonnet, "Terror, Trauma and the 'Young Marx'" (n. 1 above, this chap.), 14–15.

20. Neither Tocqueville nor Arendt was a liberal in the nineteenth- or twentieth-century Anglosphere sense.

21. Furet, *Interpreting the French Revolution* (n. 1 above, this chap.), 13. Thanks to Colin Jones for explaining some of these complicated matters.

22. Ibid., 12; Lisa Disch, "How Could Hannah Arendt Glorify the American Revolution and Revile the French? Placing *On Revolution* in the Historiography of the French

and American Revolutions," *European Journal of Political Theory* 10, no. 3 (July 2011): 359. Though Arendt didn't "revile" the French Revolution but instead treated it as a tragic failure, Disch's article is a very important rereading of *On Revolution* (n. 1 above, this chap.).

23. Palmer, *The Age of the Democratic Revolution*, 1:446; Schama, *Citizens* (n.1 above, this chap.), 859, 861.

24. Moore, *Social Origins of Dictatorship and Democracy* (n. 1 above, this chap.), 102–3, 104.

25. Higonnet, *Goodness beyond Virtue* (n. 1 above, this chap.), 70–73, stresses the atavistic, backward-looking rather than modern utopian sources of Jacobin-directed violence.

26. Edmund Burke, *Reflections on the Revolution in France* (Indianapolis: Library of Liberal Arts, 1955), 36.

27. Jean Hyppolite, "The Significance of the French Revolution in Hegel's *Phenomenology*," in *Studies on Marx and Hegel*, ed. and trans. John O'Neill (1955; repr., New York: Harper Torchbooks, 1973), 59. See also Alan Ryan, "Hegel: The Modern State as the World Spirit," in *On Politics* (London: Penguin, 2012), 652–94.

28. Jean Hyppolite, "Absolute Freedom and the Terror: The Second Type of Spiritual Self," in *Genesis and Structure of Hegel's "Phenomenology of Spirit"* (Evanston, IL: Northwestern University Press, 1974), 453. See also Robert Wokler, "Contextualizing Hegel's Phenomenology of the French Revolution and the Terror," *Political Theory* 26, no. 1 (February 1998): 33–55; and Roy Tsao, "Arendt and the Modern State: Variations on Hegel in *The Origins of Totalitarianism*," *Review of Politics* 66, no. 1 (Winter 2004): 105–36.

29. Albert Camus, *The Rebel* (New York, Vintage, 1956), 133–34.

30. See Hunt, "The World We Have Gained" (n. 1 above, this chap.), 4–5.

31. Arendt, *On Revolution*, 116.

32. See Edward S. Corwin, *The "Higher Law" Background of American Constitutional Law* (Indianapolis: Liberty Fund), a text that Arendt used in *On Revolution*. See also Arendt, "Civil Disobedience," in *Crises of the Republic* (New York: Harcourt Brace Jovanovich, 1972).

33. Arendt, *On Revolution*, 105.

34. I echo John Rawls's late distinction between "political" and "metaphysical" liberalism. See his introduction to *Political Liberalism* (New York: Columbia University Press, 1993), xiii–xxxiv; Arendt, *On Revolution* (n. 1 above, this chap.), 79. She neglects to say that the French document referred to the rights of "Man and Citizens," thus taking into account human beings as civil as well as natural beings.

35. Arendt, *On Revolution*, 79. Edelstein, *Terror of Natural Right* (n. 1 above, this chap.), explained the differences in the way the appeal to right(s) worked in the two countries. He, too, fails to make the natural right/rights distinction.

36. The quoted material is from Edelstein, *Terror of Natural Right*.

37. Palmer, *Twelve Who Ruled* (n. 1 above, this chap.), 277.

38. Arendt, *On Revolution*, 70–71.

39. Palmer, *Twelve Who Ruled*, 277.

40. Gordon S. Wood, "The American Revolution," in *The Cambridge History of Eighteenth Century Political Thought*, ed. Goldie and Wokler (n. 3 above, this chap.), 601–25, is an invaluable summary/analysis of American constitutionalism. Baker, "Political Languages of the French Revolution" (n. 3 above, this chap.), 628–59, analyzes some of these same issues in the French Revolution, while Edelstein's *The Terror of Natural Right* stresses the similarity between natural right and the general will.

41. See Disch, "How Could Hannah Arendt Glorify" (n. 22 above, this chap.), 350–58.

42. Arendt, *On Revolution*, 104. See, more generally, Arendt's discussion of hypocrisy (94–104). Baker notes that "virtue, corruption, conspiracy: the lexicon was to permeate Robespierre's language" ("Political Languages of the French Revolution," 644).

43. Ironically, Richard Hofstadter's later study of the origins of the American party system located the emergence of the idea of a "loyal opposition" in the 1790s, with the acceptance of faction as a way station on the road to the idea of non-treasonous political opposition. See Hofstadter, *The Idea of the Party System* (Berkeley: University of California Press, 1970); and Bernard Bailyn, *The Origins of American Politics* (New York: Vintage, 1968), 33–39.

44. Palmer, *The Age of the Democratic Revolution* (n. 1 above, this chap.), 1:215.

45. Arendt, *On Revolution*, 88.

46. Palmer, *Twelve Who Ruled*, 264–65. Patrice Higonnet notes that constitutionalism "never acquired durable specificity for the Jacobins" in *Goodness beyond Virtue*, 153, while Dan Edelstein also suggests that there was a weak tradition of constitutionalism in France (*The Terror of Natural Right*, 258).

47. François Furet characterized the classic view as one that stressed the political revolution but grounded it in class conflict that foreshadowed the coming class struggle and Enlightenment values in *Interpreting the French Revolution* (n. 1 above, this chap.), 18–19, 118.

48. Palmer, *Twelve Who Ruled* (n. 1 above, this chap.), 225–26; 371–72, 395.

49. Palmer, *The Age of the Democratic Revolution*, 2:106, 108–9.

50. Disch, "How Could Hannah Arendt Glorify," 358.

51. Moore, *Social Origins*, 102.

52. Higonnet, *Goodness beyond Virtue*, 54, 55, 118.

53. Ibid., 123; Doyle, *The Oxford History of the French Revolution*, 294–66.

54. Palmer, *The Age of the Democratic Revolution*, 2:124.

55. The expansion of the meaning of the Terror is traced in ibid., 2:124–29.

56. Colin Jones, "The Overthrow of Maximilien Robespierre and the 'Indifference' of the People," *American Historical Review* 119, no. 3 (June 2014): 689–713.

57. Arendt, *On Revolution*, 85.

58. Ibid., 86.

59. Ibid., 84. For political "friendship," see Arendt, *The Human Condition* (Chicago: University of Chicago Press, 1958), 218.

60. Arendt, *On Violence* (New York: Harcourt Brace Jovanovich, 1970).

61. Arendt. *On Revolution*, 242–44. See also Disch "How Could Hannah Arendt Glorify," esp. her discussion of the Girondin societies.

62. Arendt. *On Revolution*, 247.

63. Ibid., 248–249. Arendt's discussions of the clubs and societies is found on 241–51.

64. At least I read this distinction in that manner. See Furet, *Interpreting the French Revolution* (n. 1 above, this chap.), 18.

65. Arendt, *On Revolution*, 62. See 62–68 for her discussion of poverty.

66. Ibid., 64. See Michael Harrington, *The Other America* (New York: Macmillan, 1962), for the claim that America's poor were invisible in part because they had become a minority of the population and dress style had been homogenized.

67. Arendt, *On Revolution*, 64.

68. Ibid., 65.

69. Ibid., 66.

70. Ibid., 66, 65.

71. Joseph J. Ellis, "The Silence," in *Founding Brothers: The Revolutionary Generation* (New York: Vintage, 2002), 81–119, is a telling account of the variety of ways the Framers avoided the whole issue of slavery.

72. Harry V. Jaffa, *Crisis of the House Divided: An Interpretation of the Issues in the Lincoln-Douglas Debates* (Chicago: University of Chicago Press, 1959); and John Burt, *Lincoln's Tragic Pragmatism: Lincoln, Douglas, and Moral Conflict* (Cambridge, MA: Belknap Press of Harvard University Press, 2013) has much more recently renewed this analysis of the crisis of the union from the standpoint of political philosophy.

73. Orlando Patterson, *Slavery and Social Death* (Cambridge, MA: Harvard University Press, 1982), explores the way that being a slave and having been a slave entailed a negative image as well as status in the eye of free society.

74. Jean-Jacques Rousseau, *The Social Contract*, ed. Lester G. Crocker (New York: Washington Square Press, 1967), bk. 1, and "Discourse on the Origin and Foundations of Inequality," in *The First and Second Discourses*, ed. Roger D. Masters (New York: Saint Martin's Press, 1964), 80.

75. Rousseau, "Origin and Foundations of Inequality," in *The First and Second Discourses*, 165.

76. Alexis de Tocqueville, *Democracy in America*, ed. Harvey C Mansfield and Delba Winthrop (Chicago: University of Chicago, 2000), 1:304.

77. Nick Nesbit, "On the Political Efficacy of Idealism: Tocqueville, Schoelcher, and the Abolition of Slavery," in *America through European Eyes: British and French Reflections*

on the New World from the Eighteenth Century to the Present, ed. Aurelian Craiutu and Jeffrey C. Isaac (University Park: Pennsylvania State University Press, 2009): 91–114.

78. Arendt, *Denktagebuch*, ed. Ursula Ludz and Ingeborg Nordmann, 2 vols. (Munich: Piper, 2002),1:329.

79. Arendt, *The Human Condition* (n. 58 above, this chap.), 193.

80. Ibid., 356–67n51.

81. Arendt, *Denktagebuch*, 2:639. See Richard H. King, "Hannah Arendt and the Concept of Revolution in the 1960s," in "Hannah Arendt 'After Modernity,'" ed. Jeremy Gilbert, special issue, *New Formations*, no. 71 (Spring 2011), 30–45.

82. Arendt, *On Revolution*, 110.

83. Seyla Benhabib is one of the few analysts of Arendt's thought who have pointed out that the United States did have a social revolution, one that came to a head with the Civil War in April 1861. See Seyla Benhabib, *The Reluctant Modernism of Hannah Arendt* (Thousand Oaks, CA: Sage Publications, 1996), 160.

84. Charles A. Beard and Mary R. Beard, "The Second American Revolution," in *The Rise of American Civilization* (New York: Macmillan, 1930).

85. James M. Macpherson, *Abraham Lincoln and the Second American Revolution* (New York: Oxford University Press, 1991); Harry S. Stout, *Upon the Altar of the Nation: A Moral History of the Civil War* (New York: Viking Penguin, 2006); and Eric Foner, *The Fiery Trial: Abraham Lincoln and American Slavery* (New York: W. W. Norton, 2011).

86. See, e.g., David W. Blight, *Race and Reunion: The Civil War in American Memory* (Cambridge, MA: Belknap, Harvard University Press, 2001) and *American Oracle: The Civil War in the Civil Rights Era* (Cambridge, MA: Belknap Press of Harvard University Press, 2011).

87. Macpherson, *Abraham Lincoln*, vii.

88. George M. Fredrickson, *The Inner Civil War: Northern Intellectuals and the Crises of the Union* (New York: Harper Torchbooks, 1968), 190–91. It was Orestes Brownson who referred to "Jacobin democracy." Though the historiography of the Reconstruction is vast and complex, Eric Foner's *Reconstruction: America's Unfinished Revolution* (New York, Harper Collins, 1988) remains the best single synthesis of the period and the process.

Chapter 12

1. See Elisabeth Young-Bruehl, *Hannah Arendt: For Love of the World* (New Haven, CT: Yale University Press, 1982), chaps. 8 and 9, for the range and quantity of Arendt's public engagement in these years.

2. Hannah Arendt, "Thinking and Moral Considerations," *Social Research* 38, no. 3 (Autumn 1971): 417–46. Parts of this essay found their way into *The Life of the Mind* (New York: Harcourt Brace Jovanovich, 1978).

3. Both pieces were only reprinted in her posthumously published *Responsibility and Judgment*, ed. Jerome Kohn (New York: Schocken Press, 2003).

4. Arendt, *Men in Dark Times* (New York: Harcourt, Brace and World, 1968), *Crises of the Republic* (New York: Harcourt Brace Jovanovich, 1972), and *Between Past and Future: Eight Exercises in Political Thought*, ed. Jerome Kohn (New York: New York: Penguin, 2006).

5. Hannah Arendt, "Remembering Wystan H. Auden, Who Died in the Night of the Twenty-eighth of September, 1973," in *Reflections on Literature and Culture*, ed. Susannah Young-Ah Gottlieb (Stanford, CA: Stanford University Press, 2007), 294–304. "Home to Roost" is collected in *Responsibility and Judgment*. The interviews have been collected in Arendt, *The Last Interview and Other Conversations* (Brooklyn, Melville House, 2013).

6. Fredric Jameson, "Periodizing the 1960s" (1984), in *The Syntax of History*, vol. 2 of *The Ideologies of Theory: Essays 1971–1986* (London: Routledge, 1988), 178–208.

7. Arendt, interview by Adelbert Reif, "Thoughts on Politics and Revolution," in *The Last Interview*, 70–71.

8. Ibid., 71.

9. Ibid., 74–75.

10. Arendt, *On Violence* (New York: Harcourt, Brace and World, 1970), 16.

11. Ibid., 16; Arendt, "Thoughts on Politics and Revolution," 71.

12. Cited in Stephen J. Whitfield, "Refusing Marcuse: Fifty Years after *One-Dimensional Man*," *Dissent* 61, no. 4 (Fall 2014): 104, http://www.dissentmagazine.org/article/refusing-marcuse-fifty-years-after-one-dimensional-man.

13. Arendt, *On Violence*, 28.

14. The best single account of the American student movement remains James Miller, *"Democracy Is in the Streets": From Port Huron to the Siege of Chicago* (Cambridge, MA: Harvard University Press, 1994). A well-known critique of participatory politics is Daniel Patrick Moynihan's *Maximum Feasible Misunderstanding: Community Action in the War on Poverty* (New York: Free Press, 1969).

15. Arendt, *On Violence*, 22–23.

16. Michael Denneny, e-mail to author, June 17, 2013; Young-Bruehl, *Hannah Arendt*, 416.

17. Young-Bruehl, *Hannah Arendt*, 417.

18. Arendt to Macdonald, letter of May 25, 1968, Dwight Macdonald Papers, Sterling Library, Yale University.

19. Jerome Kohn, e-mail to author, February 24, 2014.

20. Arendt, *On Violence*, 93–94. Pages 89–102 contain paragraph-length elaborations on the issues involved in university reform at the time.

21. Ibid., 18–19.

22. Young-Bruehl, *Hannah Arendt*, 417–18; Arendt, *On Violence*, 18–19, 94–97. Mary McCarthy to Hannah Arendt, letter of February 9, 1968, in *Between Friends: The Correspondence of Hannah Arendt and Mary McCarthy, 1949–1975*, ed. Carol Brightman (London: Secker and Warburg, 1995), 229–30. See Fabio Rojas, *From Black Power to*

Black Studies: How a Radical Social Movement Became an Academic Discipline (Baltimore, MD: Johns Hopkins University Press, 2007). The subsequent story of black studies has by no means been as dismal as Arendt predicted. Overall, it has worked best at elite universities, with plenty of funding and where scholarly research—not community activism—has been emphasized.

23. Arendt, "Thoughts on Politics and Revolution," 78–79.

24. Ibid., 94–97.

25. "The Meaning of Love in Politics: A Letter by Hannah Arendt to James Baldwin," letter of November 21, 1962, *Journal of Political Thinking* 1, no. 2, (September 2006), http://www.hannaharendt.net/index.php/han/article/view/95/156.

26. Arendt, *Denktagebuch*, ed. Ursula Ludz and Ingeborg Nordmann, 2 vols. (Munich: Piper, 2002), 2:678. Thanks to Klaus Reitemeier for help with the translation.

27. Jean Bethke-Elshtain, *Public Men, Private Women: Women in Social and Political Thought* (Princeton, NJ: Princeton University Press, 1981). See also Carole Pateman, *The Disorder of Women: Democracy, Feminism and Political Theory* (Cambridge: Polity Press, 1990); and Bonnie Honig, ed., *Feminist Interpretations of Hannah Arendt* (University Park: Pennsylvania State University Press, 1995).

28. Noam Chomsky et al., "The Legitimacy of Violence as a Political Act? Noam Chomsky Debates with Hannah Arendt, Susan Sontag, et al.," December 15, 1967, http:www.chomsky.info/debates/19671215.htm. The meeting at which this debate took place was sponsored by the *New York Review of Books*.

29. Hannah Arendt to Mary McCarthy, letter of February 9, 1968, in *Between Friends*, 212. See Young-Bruehl, *Hannah Arendt*, 412–22, for coverage of this meeting and the context.

30. Arendt, *On Violence*, 35–38.

31. Ibid., 3–4, 40–41.

32. Ibid., 54, 52.

33. Ibid., 63, 79. Alexander Keller Hirsch, "The Promise of the Unforgiven: Violence, Power and Paradox in Arendt," *Philosophy and Social Criticism* 39, no. 1 (January 2013): 45–61, http://psc.sagepub.com/content/39/1/45.full.pdf+html, is a particularly astute exploration of the paradoxes generated by the power/violence and promise/forgiveness oppositions in Arendt's thought.

34. Arendt, *On Violence*, 75–76.

35. Chomsky et al., "The Legitimacy of Violence," 4.

36. Young-Bruehl, *Hannah Arendt*, 427–30.

37. Lewis Perry, *Civil Disobedience: An American Tradition* (New Haven, CT: Yale University Press, 2013), 273–83, covers this convergence on civil disobedience. For the others, see Paul Goodman, *New Reformation: Notes of a Neolithic Conservative* (New York: Random House, 1970), 130; Herbert Storing discussed in Perry, 274–76; John Rawls, *A Theory of Justice* (Cambridge, MA: Belknap Press of Harvard University Press, 1971), 383; Ronald Dworkin, "Civil Disobedience," in *Taking Rights Seriously* (London: Duck-

worth, 1977), 206–23; and Abe Fortas, *Concerning Dissent and Civil Disobedience* (New York: A Signet Broadside, 1968).

38. Arendt, "Lying in Politics," in *Crises of the Republic* (n. 4 above, this chap.), 43.

39. Arendt, "Civil Disobedience," in *Crises of the Republic,* 56, 58–60.

40. Ibid., 56.

41. Ibid., 65–66.

42. Ibid., 76–77.

43. Ibid., 66–67 (citing Marshall Cohen).

44. But Arendt, like Goodman and Dworkin, sharply distinguished the meaning and impact of civil disobedience from that of "criminal disobedience."

45. Arendt, "Civil Disobedience," 85.

46. Ibid., 86–88.

47. Ibid., 81.

48. Ibid., 90.

49. Ibid., 76, 100–101. She also suggested that some version of the "scrutiny" doctrine might be applied to cases involving civil disobedience in ways similar to the way it had been applied to cases involving group discrimination.

50. Ibid., 94, 97, 95.

51. Ibid., 66.

52. McCarthy to Arendt, letter of October 14, 1970, in *Between Friends* (n. 22 above), 264.

53. Arendt "Civil Disobedience," 66–68.

54. Thoreau calls Brown a transcendentalist in "A Plea for Captain John Brown" and makes the idea of "action from principle" central to his "Civil Disobedience" essay. All the essays by Thoreau in the text are also collected in Henry David Thoreau, *Collected Essays and Poems,* ed. Elizabeth Hall Witherell, Library of America Series (New York: Literary Classics of the United States, distributed by Penguin Putnam, 2001), 703.

55. Arendt "Civil Disobedience," 61.

56. See Max Weber, "Politics as a Vocation," in *From Max Weber* (New York: Oxford Galaxy, 1958), 128.

57. See the essays in Jack Turner, ed., *A Political Companion to Henry David Thoreau* (Lexington: University Press of Kentucky, 2009).

58. Stanley Cavell, *The Senses of Walden* (San Francisco: North Point Press, 1981), 85.

59. Mary McCarthy to Hannah Arendt, letter of October 14, 1970, in *Between Friends,* 263.

60. Arendt, "Home to Roost" (n. 5 above, this chap.), 275.

61. Ibid., 257–75; "Lying in Politics" (n. 38 above, this chap.), 1–47; and Correspondence between J. Glenn Gray and Hannah Arendt, Hannah Arendt Papers, Library of Congress, Correspondence,1962–67 and 1971–73. For an introduction to Gray's life

and thought, see Martin Woessner, "An Officer and a Philosopher: J. Glenn Gray and the Postwar Introduction of Heidegger into American Thought," in *Heidegger in America* (New York: Cambridge University Press, 2011), chap. 4, 132–59.

62. Gray to Arendt, letter January 2, 1973, Hannah Arendt Papers. In general, I have not paginated either Gray's or Arendt's letters. None of Gray's letters that I have quoted from are longer than one page and only one Arendt letter (actually partly written on one day and then on the next) is two pages long.

63. Gray to Arendt, letters of October 21, 1974, and October 6, 1973, Hannah Arendt Papers.

64. Arendt, "Lying in Politics," 5–7.

65. Ibid., 14.

66. Ibid., 35, 31.

67. Ibid., 28, 15, 18.

68. Ibid., 42–43.

69. Ibid., 46–47.

70. Arendt to Gray, letters of August 12–13, 1973, Hannah Arendt Papers, from Tegna, Switzerland, cover two typed, single-spaced pages of a blue airmail letter. Her discussion of Hans Morgenthau's article is on page 2 of the letter and written August 13.

71. Arendt to Gray, letter of August 12, 1973, Hannah Arendt Papers.

72. Arendt to Gray, letter of August 13, 1973, Gray to Arendt, letter of July 28, 1974, both in Hannah Arendt Papers.

73. Arendt, "Home to Roost" (n. 5 above, this chap.), 261, 259.

74. Ibid., 270.

75. Ibid., 275.

76. Ibid., 266.

77. Young-Bruehl, *Hannah Arendt*, 446, 453.

78. Gray to Arendt, letters of April 9 and July 6, 1975, Hannah Arendt Papers.

Conclusion

1. Margarethe Von Trotta's film was first shown in September 2012 at the Toronto Film Festival and released in Germany the following January. There are also numerous reviews listed on Google. Though not (yet) translated into English, Martin Wiebel, ed., *Hannah Arendt: Ihr Denken Veränderte die Welt* (Munich: Piper, 2012), contains useful interviews with the director, producer, script writer, and cast, along with historical background on Arendt and Eichmann.

2. See the interview with and notebook entries of von Trotta in *Hannah Arendt*, ed. Wiebel; plus Hannah Arendt, "Rosa Luxemburg: 1871–1919" (1966), in *Men in Dark Times* (New York: Harcourt, Brace and World, Inc., 1968), 33–56.

3. Elisabeth Young-Bruehl, *Hannah Arendt: For Love of the World* (New Haven, CT: Yale University Press, 1982), 355–56. Richard Bernstein confirms the confusion between

the University of Chicago and the New School for Social Research in New York. Arendt wasn't even teaching at the New School in 1963 but did start at Chicago that fall ("Richard Bernstein on the Film 'Hannah Arendt,'" New School for Social Research (September 27, 2013), https://www.youtube.com/watch?v=EbFOD0oLnps.

4. Roger Berkowitz, "Lonely Thinking: Hannah Arendt on Film," *The Daily* (blog), *Paris Review*, May 30, 2013, http://www.theparisreview.org/blog/2013/05/30/lonely -thinking-hannah-arendt-on-film//.

5. Information from "Richard Bernstein on the Film 'Hannah Arendt.'"

6. Barbara Sukowa, "Wie Hannah Arendt im Film lebendig wird," in *Hannah Arendt*, ed. Wiebel, 179.

7. Daniel Nemenyi, "Rose-Tinted Lens," *Radical Philosophy* 186 (July–August 2014); 60–63. See Arendt, "Thinking and Moral Considerations," *Social Research* 38, no. 3 (Autumn 1971): 418, 435, 444–46

8. Mark Lilla, "Arendt and Eichmann: The New Truth," *New York Review of Books* 60, no. 18 (November 21–December 4, 2013): 36; Moira Weigel, "Heritage Girl Crush: On 'Hannah Arendt,'" *Los Angeles Review of Books*, July 16, 2013 (http://lareviewofbooks .org/essay/heritage-girl-crush-on-hannah-arendt/?print=1&fulit); Comment: Adam Kelly, response to Weigel, "Heritage Girl Crush."

9. Mary McCarthy, *Medina* (New York: Harcourt Brace Jovanovich, 1972).

10. Along with Richard Bernstein's discussion of the film, David Rieff's "Hannah and Her Admirers," *Nation*, November 19, 2013 (http://www.thenation.com/print/ article/177277/Hannah-and-her-admirers), is probably the best single piece on the film and its context combined.

11. "Himmler's October 4, 1943, Posen Speech: 'Extermination,'" Nizkor Project, http://www.nizkor.org/hweb/people/h/himmler-heinrich/posen/oct-04-43/ ausrottung-transl-nizkor.html.

12. Bettina Stangneth, *Eichmann before Jerusalem: The Unexamined Life of a Mass Murderer*, trans. Ruth Martin (New York: Alfred A. Knopf, 2014). Stangneth also provided a seven-page overview of her book in German in *Hannah Arendt*, ed. Wiebel, 234–41. It is very interesting for what it reveals about Stangneth's sympathy for Arendt.

13. See Stangneth, "Eichmann in Argentine," in *Eichmann before Jerusalem*, 105–82.

14. Richard Wolin, *Heidegger's Children: Hannah Arendt, Karl Löwith, Hans Jonas, and Herbert Marcuse* (Princeton, NJ: Princeton University Press, 2001); Wolin, "The Banality of Evil: The Demise of a Legend," *Jewish Review of Books* (Fall 2014), 1, http://jewish reviewofbooks.com/articles/1106/the-banality-of-evil-the-demise-of-a-legend/.

Wolin published three pieces in the *Jewish Review of Books* in the autumn of 2014, the first reviewing Stangneth's book, the second and third involving exchanges with Seyla Benhabib: "The Banality of Evil," "Thoughtlessness Revisited: A Response to Seyla Benhabib," *Jewish Review of Books* (September 30, 2014), http://jewishreviewofbooks.com/ articles/1287/in-still-not-banal-a-response-to-seyla-benhabib/, and "Arendt, Banality,

and Benhabib: A Final Rejoinder" *Jewish Review of Books* (October 14, 2014), http://
jewishreviewofbooks.com/articles/1315/arendt-banality-and-benhabib-a-final
-rejoinder/.

15. Seyla Benhabib, "Who's on Trial, Eichmann or Arendt?" *The Stone* (blog), *New
York Times*, September 21, 2014, http://opinionator.blogs.nytimes.com/2014/09/21/
whos-on-trial-eichmann-or-anrendt/?_r=0.

16. "Martin Heidegger at Eighty," *New York Review of Books* (October 21, 1971),
50–54.

17. Jan Goldstein, "Hannah Arendt Turns Public Historian," *Perspectives on History*
52, no. 2 (February 2014): 6.

18. Wolin, *Heidegger's Children*, 33, 52, and "The Banality of Evil," 1.

19. Here is an example of a generalization that gets the main thing wrong about
Arendt's relationship with Heidegger: "Heidegger's intellect was immensely seductive, as a young Jewish student named Hannah Arendt discovered in spite of all
the National Socialist cant" (Ingrid Rowland, "A Banker, a Scholar, and the Invention
of Art History," review of *Dreamland of Humanists: Warburg, Cassirer, Panofsky, and
the Hamburg School*, by Emily J. Levine, *New Republic*, July 5, 2014 (http://www
.newrepublic.com/article/118330/dreamland-humanists-emily-j-levine-reviewed
-ingrid-rowland). But no one before 1933, certainly not Arendt in the mid-1920s, had
heard anything from Heidegger about being a supporter of the Nazis or as holding
anti-Semitic views. For a recent, careful examination of Heidegger's anti-Semitism, see
Peter Trawny, *Heidegger und der Mythos der Jüdischen Weltverschwörung* (Frankfurt-on-
Main: Klosterman, 2014).

20. Wolin, *Heidegger's Children*, 38; Seyla Benhabib, "Richard Wolin on Arendt's
'Banality of Evil' Thesis," *Jewish Review of Books*, October 14, 2014, 1–2, http://jewish-
reviewofbooks.com/articles/1313/richard-wolin-on-arendts-banality-of-evil-thesis/.
Hannah Arendt, *Eichmann in Jerusalem: A Report on the Banality of Evil*, rev. and enlarged
(New York: Viking Press, 1965), 287–88.

21. Wolin, *Heidegger's Children*, 51, 56–57.

22. These are cited in Wolin, "The Banality of Evil," 1.

23. See King, "On Race and Culture: Hannah Arendt and Her Contemporaries," in
Politics in Dark Times: Encounters with Hannah Arendt, ed. Seyla Benhabib (New York:
Cambridge University Press, 2010), 113–34. Unless a white American intellectual has
never used the term "redneck" in private life, he or she should not come on too self-
righteous in these matters.

24. Stangneth, *Eichmann before Jerusalem*, 101; Gal Beckerman "Taking the Banality
Out of Evil" (an interview with Bettina Stangneth), *Jewish Daily Forward*, September 19,
2014, 1.

25. Stangneth, *Eichmann before Jerusalem*, 364, 268. Here Stangneth is ignoring both
of Arendt's concepts of thinking.

26. Beckerman, "Taking the Banality," 2; Stangneth, "Eichmann nach Jerusalem," in *Hannah Arendt*, ed. Wiebel, 238.

27. Stangneth, *Eichmann before Jerusalem*, 239.

28. Susan Neiman, "Philosophy Not History: Reading *Eichmann in Jerusalem*," Philip B. Hallie Keynote Lecture, delivered at the international conference "Exercising Judgment in Ethics, Politics, and the Law: Hannah Arendt's *Eichmann in Jerusalem*," Wesleyan University, September 26–28, 2013; available at http://sacw.net/free/SusanNeiman PhilosophynotHistory.pdf.

29. Stangneth, *Eichmann before Jerusalem*, 303.

30. Ibid., 268, 529–30, 37.

31. Ibid., 202.

32. Ibid., 221–22.

33. Ibid., 219–20

34. Benhabib, "Richard Wolin on Arendt's 'Banality of Evil' Thesis," 1.

35. Ernst Vollrath, "Vom 'radikal Bösen' zur 'Banalität des Bösen,'" in *Hannah Arendt*, ed. Wiebel, 135.

36. Richard J. Bernstein, *Radical Evil: A Philosophical Interrogation* (Cambridge: Polity Press, 2002), 232.

37. See, e.g., Slavoj Zizek, *Did Somebody Say Totalitarianism? Five Interventions in the (Mis)Use of Notion* (London: Verso Books, 2011), 70–71.

38. Peter Trawny, "Eine neue Dimension," *Die Zeit*, December 27, 2013, http://www .zeit.de/2014/01/heidegger-schwarze-hefte-herausgeber-peter-trawny; Peter Gordon, "Heidegger in Black," *New York Review of Book* 61, no. 15 (October 9–22, 2014), 28.

39. Christopher Browning, "How Ordinary Germans Did It," *New York Review of Books* 60, no. 11 (June 20–July 10, 2013), 31. See also Roger Berkowitz, "Misreading 'Eichmann in Jerusalem,'" *The Stone* (blog), *New York Times*, July 7, 2013, 3 (http:// opinionator.blogs.nytimes.com/2013/07/07/misreading-hannah-arendts-eichmann-in -jerusalem/).

40. Yaacov Lozowick, "Malicious Clerks," in *Hannah Arendt in Jerusalem*, ed. Steven E. Aschheim (Berkeley: University of California Press, 2001), 214–23; Richard H. King, "Culture, Accommodation, and Resistance II: The Eichmann Trial and Jewish Tradition," in *Race, Culture and the Intellectuals, 1940–70* (Baltimore, MD: Johns Hopkins University Press; Washington, DC: Woodrow Wilson Press, 2004), 191.

41. Hannah Arendt, "Auschwitz on Trial" (1966), in *Responsibility and Judgment* (New York: Schocken, 2003), 236.

42. Christopher Browning, *Ordinary Men: Reserve Police Battalion 11 and the Final Solution in Poland*, new ed. (London: Penguin, 2001); Roger Berkowitz, "Misreading 'Eichmann in Jerusalem.'" Much of this debate about Eichmann and his racist motivation is a preliminary to, and a continuation of, the dispute of the mid-1990s over Daniel Goldhagen's claim that Germans in general were disposed toward "eliminationist" anti-

Semitism. See Daniel Jonah Goldhagen, *Hitler's Willing Executioners: Ordinary Germans and the Holocaust* (New York: Alfred A. Knopf, 1996).

43. Arendt, "Auschwitz on Trial," 237.

44. Beckerman, "Taking the Banality" (interview with Bettina Stangneth [n. 24 above, this chap.]), 1, 2.

45. Arendt, "Auschwitz on Trial," 242.

46. Ibid., 254.

INDEX